The Geopolitics of Energy

The Geopolitics of Energy

Jean-Pierre Favennec

GYAN

First Published, 2017

Published by

Gyan Publishing House
5, Ansari Road
Daryaganj, New Delhi-110002
Phone: 9811692060
E-mail: books@gyanbooks.com

Printed at: G. Print Process, Delhi.

Cataloging in Publication Data—DK
Courtesy: D.K. Agencies (P) Ltd. <docinfo@dkagencies.com>

Favennec, Jean-Pierre, author.
The geopolitics of energy / Jean-Pierre Favennec.
pages cm
ISBN 9788121214100

1. Energy policy. 2. Energy industries—Political aspects. 3. Power resources—Political aspects. I. Title.

LCC HD9502.A2F38 2017 | DDC 333.79 23

Contents

Preface

The timing for this book could not be better: for many years now, energy has made front-page news. Headlines have covered the huge variations in oil price ($10/b in 1999, $148 in 2008, $100 from 2010 to 2014, $50 now); the strong growth in energy demand; threats to supplies (tensions and bombings in some producing countries, accidents, etc.); controversies regarding reserves; the threat of climate change; and now the production of shale gas and shale oil.

There are many different forms of energy (oil, natural gas, coal, nuclear, hydroelectricity, wind and solar), but they are often interchangeable and we need all energies to be developed. Many books have been written in particular about oil and its geopolitics. This book is dedicated to the geopolitical aspects of energy, and oil of course plays a major role[1].

The book provides a clear overview of the various challenges of the energy sector: how are the various energies produced, what is their future, which stakeholders are involved on the energy stage, what are the supply constraints, and what are the major characteristics of the various regions throughout the world?

The book is divided into two sections: the first section specifies the major characteristics of the energy sector; the second section provides a region-by-region analysis of the challenges, and details the geopolitical aspects.

Four chapters make up the **first section.**

The first chapter describes the major sources of energy, lays out the production and processing techniques and sets out some economic aspects.

The second chapter includes an analysis of prices, demand and resources: although many geopolitical and financial factors (e.g. the role of pension fund investments) influence prices, supply and demand remain fundamental elements. This chapter ends with an analysis of the constraints associated with protection of the environment at a local, regional or global level: climate

1. It has been estimated that 70 per cent of the geopolitics of energy relate to oil, 20 per cent to natural gas and the remaining 10 per cent to other energies.

change will have a significant impact on global energy consumption and on the structure of the future “energy mix”.

The third chapter is dedicated to the structures of companies and organisations that manage the energy sector. There have been numerous and spectacular changes in this area. A small group of large, private companies – the *Majors* – were responsible for the development of oil up until roughly 1960. This situation was transformed by the formation of OPEC, followed by the nationalisations of the 1970s. The major state-owned companies of producing countries - who often have near (or indeed actual) monopolies over exploitation on their territory - attained sizes that were equivalent to or even greater than those of major international companies. At the end of the 1990s, the return of non-national companies next to – or in partnership with – the state-owned companies seemed a foregone conclusion. For several years up to 2008, very high oil prices once again provided significant financial resources to state-owned companies, and reduced the need for them to turn to outside companies. The debate is still alive regarding the respective roles of state-owned and international companies, but it seems more and more that the producing countries and their national oil companies are seeking to increase their control over the oil sector. That makes the future role of international oil companies more difficult to predict.

There have been many changes in the structures of companies operating in the gas and electricity sector. Following World War II, small private companies operating over a small territory were replaced by powerful state-owned companies operating over vast areas in order to benefit from the advantages of a natural monopoly. For more than 30 years now, Americans and Europeans, followed by many developing countries, have instituted policies designed to promote active competition, resulting in the end of monopolies, the appearance of new stakeholders and a determination to impose a policy of deregulation (which is in fact a new form of regulation made all the more necessary – although not necessarily more efficient – as more and more stakeholders become involved).

The fourth chapter covers the security of supplies and the means to ensure it. While the best means of ensuring stable energy supplies during the 1990s seemed to involve improving the operation of markets, current tensions favor active intervention on the part of States. The Americans and Chinese, for example, are using diplomacy intensely to advance their oil interests and Moscow makes no secret of its desire to use energy as a weapon in relations with its European and Asian neighbors.

The second section of the book covers the current situation in every major area of the planet, continent or region (such as the CIS/Russia or the Middle East) that plays a particularly important role on the world energy stage.

North America is distinguished by very high energy consumption, high oil consumption, gas consumption that is also significant, high consumption of coal for electricity production, and significant needs for replacing production facilities in the power sector. Due to its needs and its power, North America is a key zone.

The energy sector in South America is dominated by a few countries. With oil prices at more than $100 a barrel, Venezuela rediscovered its increased power, but at $50 the situation is a disaster. Brazil - an economic and geographical giant - is a critical player in the oil and gas game despite the present poor situation. The nationalisations of 2006 in Bolivia did not create a significant backlash since the trend that brought leftist leaders (albeit of highly differing views) to power in the various countries militates against conflicts becoming too violent. But latent tensions exist between the ambitions of Venezuela - which wants to impose itself as the leader of South America, at least in the energy sector - and the other countries.

Europe consumes and imports a large amount of energy and its dependency on imports will continue to grow. Over the long term, the Middle East will once again become a major supplier of oil and European foreign policy must take this into account. Governments are preoccupied by Russia's very significant role in European gas imports. Europe, the main partner in the Kyoto protocol, must confront its increasing energy needs while also limiting its CO_2 emissions, with the added difficulty that some countries have decided to reduce their nuclear production.

The Commonwealth of Independent States (CIS) – where Russia plays a critical role – has once again become a major player on the energy stage. Blessed with extremely abundant reserves of oil, gas and coal, Russia is a giant oil and gas exporter, supplying America, Europe and Asia, and able to use the threat of a change in the destination of its exports against any of them. Relations with Europeans - the main purchasers of gas - are particularly critical. Europeans would like the Gazprom monopoly to be broken – which the Russians refuse to do – while Gazprom would like to have equity stakes in certain European companies, a proposal opposed by European governments. Coal is still widely used in Russia to allow them to export as much oil and gas - which are more profitable - as possible.

Africa accounts for little with regard to energy consumption. Only South Africa - and the countries of North Africa to a lesser extent - are significant consumers. But the vast majority of countries in Sub-Saharan Africa have very low energy consumption, with the possible exception of Nigeria due to its enormous population. On the other hand, North Africa and West and South-Central Africa are significant hydrocarbon producers. West and South-Central Africa, the zone most open to foreign companies, is coveted by all: Americans and Chinese play a vast game of poker here and nearly all companies are present in the zone.

Asia, which includes more than half the world's population, is the region where the increase in energy demand is strongest due to the extraordinary economic growth in China, and to a lesser extent that in India and in neighboring countries. This increase is at the heart of energy-related issues: Asia's needs weigh on demand and production capacities, and consequently on prices. But it would be absurd to hold this region responsible for current difficulties, since per-capita consumption there remains low. It is consumption by the West which is incompatible with current production and reserves. Nonetheless, this leads to significant tension between the major consumers to ensure their future supplies.

The Middle East remains the key region for oil supply and thus for meeting the fuel needs of many countries, particularly in Asia. There are many geopolitical tensions in the region. The Israeli-Palestinian conflict is at the heart of these tensions: The tensions between Iran and Saudi Arabia and now the conflict between Qatar and the other Gulf Counties Council members is worrying. Over the short and medium term, Middle East hydrocarbons will become increasingly important since this is the only region that can meet the increased needs of the world.

The conclusion of this book is that energy will remain in the headlines. Although for several decades now there have been few major changes in this sector; revolutionary changes - or even total breaks with the past - will be necessary, particularly to respond to the needs of emerging countries and the constraints of climate change.

Jean-Marie Chevalier

Director of the Center for
Geopolitics of Energy
and Raw Materials

Introduction

Energy: A New Environment

At the end of the 20th century energy seemed to be abundant. It was therefore cheap. Reserves of oil, gas and coal appeared to be large. The price of oil collapsed to $10 a barrel at the end of 1998. It climbed to $147 in 2008, and was close to $100 before the collapse (price is now about $50). The energy industry is confronted with demand increase and climate change.

Why Energy?

Energy is mainly used for heating and transport. Energy can be oil, natural gas, coal, nuclear, hydroelectricity, biomass, and the new renewable energies (particularly wind and solar). Total energy consumption throughout the world (including firewood) is of the order of 14.5 billion metric tons of oil equivalent p.a. Generally speaking, nearly 20 per cent of energy is used for transport, and roughly 80 per cent (in one form or another) is used to produce heat (for residential uses like heating, cooking and air conditioning, as well as industrial uses and electricity production).

About 95 per cent of transport sector needs are met by petroleum products. Other energy sources (gas, electricity or even coal) could replace them. But petroleum products have two advantages: they are liquid and therefore easy to access, and they are concentrated forms of energy. By spending a couple of minutes at a service station filling up your tank with gasoline or diesel, you obtain several hundred miles of autonomy. Charging the batteries of an electric car or filling tanks with compressed gas requires far more time. Alternatives to petroleum products will be found. But for now gasoline, diesel and jet fuel remain the most widely used fuels.

For the production of heat, all energies compete with each other. In some cases, constraints on pollutant emissions will guide the choice to a less-polluting fuel like gas or a light petroleum product. In many cases, the choice will be based on practicality and financial aspects (e.g. coal has been abandoned for domestic heating since domestic heating oil and natural gas are much easier to use).

Using Resources Wisely

We mainly consume fossil fuels (oil, gas and coal) whose reserves - although not precisely known - are by definition finite. The problem of peak oil, i.e. oil production reaching its maximum level, is real. What is important is not the volume of energy reserves, but the way in which these reserves are used. If tomorrow every inhabitant of the planet wanted to consume as much oil as an American, oil reserves would be exhausted in less than 10 years. If by a miracle, tomorrow we all became very thrifty and consumed no more oil than an African, the reserves would last several hundred years.

What does the future hold?

The link between economic growth and increased energy demand has been established. For a long time, particularly during the post-war boom years of 1945-1975, energy consumption grew at the same pace as wealth (measured by GDP). Currently, energy consumption is increasing more slowly than GDP. At the start of the 1980s, after the price of oil increased by a factor of 10, we even observed a significant decrease in oil demand and lower overall energy demand. The price increase at the start of the 2000s was linked to strong worldwide growth. Energy demand only fell with the start of the economic crisis.

A larger world population (which is expected to grow from 7.3 to 9 billion between now and 2050), and the increase in average living standards (recently spectacular in Asia), should result in increased energy demand. The most conservative scenarios, which are based on the assumption of reduced economic growth to limit pollutant emissions, predict an increase of roughly 30 per cent between now and 2050. Other scenarios, based on maintaining current trends, predict that requirements will double. Two recognised organisations, the IEA (International Energy Agency) and the DOE (US Department of Energy) predict a strong increase in energy demand between now and 2030. The reason is simple: economic growth is needed to reduce under-employment in developed countries, and poverty in emerging countries. And economic growth means growth in energy demand.

The increase in needs seems to be enormous. Currently, the Chinese "only" have 100 cars per 1,000 inhabitants, while Europeans have 600 and Americans 800. How could we want to prevent the Chinese (and soon the Indians, followed by the rest of Asia) from having as many cars as Westerners? And why not SUVs, since we love them and find them comfortable and indispensable - for safety reasons - to drive our kids to school in the morning.

Two constraints will lead us to change our policies:

- By 2050, inevitable shortages of gas and oil
- The necessity of confronting climate change

Profound changes will be needed. Some countries have studied ways to reduce greenhouse gas emissions drastically, e.g. by a factor of 4 or 5. In order to succeed, consumption must be substantially reduced in all sectors. In the transport sector, "mileage consumption" must be reduced. The era of cheap fuel favored energy-consuming practices which are well-illustrated by the example of yogurt manufacture, where the components have been transported thousands of miles before being used. Private transport cannot be spared: "To put China on four wheels, we would need five planets". Thus it is not possible - thankfully (or not) - for every inhabitant of the planet to consume as much gasoline or diesel as an American (or even European) citizen. In the residential sector, savings must be sought through better home insulation. Increasing numbers of "smart home" prototypes are being produced: these houses produce (via solar, geothermal, etc.) enough energy to cover their heating and electricity needs, and over the longer term we can envisage houses producing electricity to supply electric vehicles. The European Commission recommends that by 2020 new buildings should be "energy positive".

The objective must therefore be to reduce our consumption to the extent possible and make best use of all types of energies while respecting environmental constraints (in particular while taking climate change into account, the consequences of which remain to be determined). The objective is ambitious. Since 1945, energy consumption has multiplied by a factor of 10 and our needs have been met by increasing production, particularly of oil and gas. Our future will likely be very different. The measures proposed here (and previously proposed in detail by many specialists) are technically feasible, but politically difficult to accept. An enormous educational effort needs to take place in order to increase awareness. Let us hope that the education is sufficient and allows us to avoid recourse to coercive measures.

Acknowledgements

I would like to thank for their support and help Julien Bassaler, Thibault Servan and Yann Balay who prepared the documentation. For this last version of the book I was helped by Amit Rao Singh.

Chapter - 1

Different Forms of Energy

WHAT IS ENERGY?

• Energy at the Heart of the Development of Civilisation

The term "energy" is taken from the Greek *energon*, which means "force in action". Energy is the capacity to perform work, impart movement or raise temperature (heat a building, cook food, etc.). It is produced via the use of natural forces like wind or solar energy, from the combustion of fuels or combustible materials (oil, gasoline, diesel fuel, fuel oil, natural gas, coal, wood, etc.), or from electricity.

Energy has always been vital for mankind. Living organisms use a large quantity of energy, for which the main natural source is the sun. Human beings obtain their energy from food, which is transformed in the cells of their bodies during a multitude of biochemical reactions, allowing them to maintain their body temperature, grow, multiply and move about.

Although the rest of the animal kingdom has always been content with what nature provides for it, mankind has been able to free itself from the weather variations and random food resources that threatened the demographic growth of its species. Through the discovery of fire, man was able to cook food—leading to the development of agriculture and breeding—and produce heat, thereby promoting his longevity. In addition, this allowed him to forge tools and weapons to ensure his survival.

Much later, various energy innovations helped to shape society as we know it today.

Energy is present at every moment of our lives. We continuously use motors: in industry, for transport and at home. These motors operate with petroleum products, gas or electricity.

In the same fashion, light has become indispensable to us. Light that once came from a candle, then from oil lamps and street lamps powered by town gas, today is mainly produced by electricity.

Thus, energy, now essential to our well-being (reduction of physical effort, heating and lighting of premises, etc.) and economic development, has become a key element of progress.

But energy needs continue to increase, although today nearly two billion people still do not benefit from even the simplest of modern energy resources. Access to abundant and inexpensive energy sources and an increasing worldwide population are leading to an explosion in the demand for energy at the same time as mankind is becoming aware of the impact of its lifestyle on the environment.

The survival of the human species now depends on its intelligence and creativity.

- **Energy: Major Stages and Innovations in its History**

In antiquity, the only resources available were manpower (it is estimated that one-third of the population of Rome was composed of slaves), animal traction (for transport) and biomass, in particular wood for cooking and heating. In Europe, during the Middle Ages, the use of windmills was imported from the Orient, providing efficient energy, particularly for the industries of food (nuts and olives) and textiles (fabric milling). More powerful watermills allowed for the development of paper mills and iron mills.

Modern forms of energy did not make their appearance until just over 200 years ago, starting with coal. In the eighteenth century, England had exhausted its forestry resources and started to use its coal resources to develop the use of the steam engine, thereby paving the way for the advent of the industrial age.

One of the major stages in this energy evolution was the discovery of electrical energy, created by the expansion of steam produced by the combustion of coal.

Next, the use of oil—with the invention of the internal combustion engine powered by petroleum products (gasoline or diesel fuel)—made individual transport convenient and comfortable.

Finally, during the last century, the use of electricity produced by nuclear energy and by combined cycle power plants powered with natural gas resulted in the massive deployment of energy.

- **Main Forms of Energy**

  The main forms of energy are:

  – ***Mechanical:*** the cause or result of a change in potential energy (e.g. waterfall) or kinetic energy (moving body).
  – ***Thermal:*** expressed in the form of heat.
  – ***Chemical:*** liberated via a chemical reaction that can be explosive.
  – ***Electrical:*** produced by a difference in electrical charge between two points; can result in a direct electrical current.
  – ***Nuclear:*** can be created by fission (splitting atomic nuclei) according to the principle of nuclear reactors currently in use, or by the fusion of atomic nuclei (two nuclei combine to form a new, single nucleus with the release of energy). Nuclear fission has been widely used since the Second World War. First there was the development of the atomic bomb and then the start of the use of nuclear energy for electricity generation in the United States in the 1950s. But although, after the atom bomb, the hydrogen bomb was successfully developed, electricity generation by nuclear fusion is still in the research phase and it is not thought that a commercial plant will be commissioned for several decades yet.

- **Other Forms of Energy**

  – ***Biomass:*** a versatile source of energy which can provide heat and electricity. It consists of gas and liquid fuels produced from all organic matter derived from living organisms.
  – ***Hydraulic:*** produced by the movement of water.
  – ***Wind:*** as the name implies, produced by wind.

Units

In the International System (SI), the unit of energy is the joule, which represents the work done by a force of one newton (N) traveling through a distance of one meter. Another definition comes from energy's use to heat water. Thus, a calorie is the quantity of energy required to raise the temperature of one gram of water by one degree Celsius. Physicists have shown that this energy, referred to as calorific or thermal, is equivalent to mechanical energy (or work). Another important type of energy is electrical energy: the joule is also the energy produced by a direct current of one ampere at a voltage of one volt for one second.

Another important concept is power, which is measured in watts (W), and is the energy consumed or generated per unit of time, i.e. one second:

(Cont'd...)

1 Watt is equivalent to 1 joule/second. For large facilities, power is expressed in kilowatts (1 kW = 1,000 W) or megawatts (1 MW = 1,000 kW), and energy in kWh, i.e. 1 kW (produced by a generator or consumed by a machine) for one hour.

Oil companies use the metric ton of oil equivalent (toe), which is the energy that can be produced by one metric ton of oil, or the barrel of oil equivalent (boe), which is the energy that can be produced by one barrel of oil. Gas can be measured in cubic feet or cubic meters, and its calorific value in kWh or British Thermal Units (BTUs).

One fundamental property of energy is that it can be converted from one form to another, with the following equivalents:

1 calorie = 4.18 J, 1 toe = 42 billion J (approximately), 1 toe = 42 million BTU (approximately), 1 kWh = 3.6 million J.

Prefix	*Symbol*	*Value*	*Example*
Kilo	K	10^3 (thousand)	kilowatt (kW)
Mega	M	10^6 (million)	megawatt (MW)
Giga	G	10^9 (billion)	gigawatt (GW)
Tera	T	10^{12} (trillion)	terawatt (TW)

- **Solar:** produced by solar radiation. There are several forms of solar energy:
  - Solar thermal energy used to produce hot water in a dwelling.
  - Concentrated solar power, which uses a parabolic system to concentrate solar rays onto a heat transfer fluid, often water, in a pipe or another vessel, thereby generating steam and ultimately producing electricity.
  - Solar photovoltaic energy, which directly transforms some of the sun's rays into electricity via panels made up of cells.
- **Tidal:** produced by tides.
- **Marine** energy from swells and waves used to produce electricity from undersea turbines.
- **Geothermal:** heat generated in the Earth's core.

ENERGY IN ITS DIFFERENT FORMS

Different forms of energy change continuously from one to another: light energy to thermal energy, chemical energy (from fuels or food) to mechanical energy, nuclear energy to heat, mechanical energy to electrical energy, etc. Yet these conversions are subject to two principles of thermodynamics:

1. **The principle of the conservation of energy:** The quantity of energy subjected to a transformation process is equal to the energy output in other forms once the process is finished.
2. **The principle of degradation of energy:** In a closed system, the quantity of energy that is available for use must diminish. Thus, an electric motor transforms electrical energy into mechanical energy and operates by releasing heat (the motor heats up).

Nonetheless there are limits to the energy conversions possible: a car's brakes slow it by transforming kinetic energy into heat, but we cannot move a car forward by heating the brakes.

Different energy sources may be used for the same purpose. For example, heat can be produced by burning wood, coal, gas or petroleum products, or by using nuclear energy. In the same way, electricity can be generated from many forms of primary energy (e.g. natural gas, oil or coal in a thermal power plant). Conversely, about 95 per cent of today's transport needs depend on petroleum-based products: gasoline, diesel fuel, heavy fuel oil (for ships) and jet fuel.

In addition, there is a distinction between energy from fossil fuels and renewable energies. The former is a limited resource, and the time needed to replenish it is on the planetary—not human —scale. Its sources are mainly oil, natural gas and coal, but the same principle also applies to uranium. Conversely, renewable energy sources are continuously created by nature, but the available resources depend on natural conditions: solar energy (day/night), wind energy (strong wind/dead calm) or hydraulic energy (large river/absence of precipitation).

There is a further distinction between three types of energy sources: energy sources such as fossil fuels, which can be stored; flux energies, which are characterised by random availability and cannot be stored (wind and solar energy); and semi-renewable energies like biomass (depends on replacement planting) or hydroelectricity (depends on precipitation).

Primary and Secondary Energy

Primary energy is energy directly resulting from the exploitation of a resource available in nature: wood, coal, oil, natural gas, wind, solar radiation, hydraulic or geothermal energy. But these energies cannot always be used directly; they must first be converted (e.g. oil refining to obtain gasoline).

(Cont'd...)

Secondary energy results from the transformation of a primary energy by the use of a conversion system: for example, electricity (secondary energy) is produced via the use of coal (primary energy) or gas (primary energy) in a thermal power plant, or uranium (primary energy) in a nuclear power plant.

Changing primary energy into secondary energy involves transformation or conversion losses.

In order to analyze global energy consumption, we must add up—and therefore compare—the consumption of oil, coal, gas, etc. A common unit is used for these comparisons: the metric ton of oil equivalent (toe). This is the quantity of energy contained in a metric ton of crude oil. Why do we refer particularly to the "oil equivalent"? Simply because oil is the most widely used energy source. Fifty years ago, the metric ton of coal equivalent was used. To generate the same quantity of heat as that contained in one metric ton of oil; we must burn roughly 1.5 metric tons of high-quality coal (anthracite); for lignite, a larger quantity, 3 tons, is required. 1,100 cubic meters of "gaseous" natural gas are needed to obtain one metric ton of oil equivalent. The energy content of liquefied natural gas (LNG) is greater than that of oil: one metric ton of LNG is equivalent to 1.23 toe.

The case of electricity, which is a secondary energy, is more complex.

The quantity of heat provided by 1 kWh is equivalent to that provided by 0.083 kg of oil.

Therefore, 1,000 kWh = 0.083 toe.

But the average efficiency of a power plant is of the order of 38 per cent. So roughly 0.083/0.38, i.e. 0.22 kg of oil equivalent is needed to generate 1 kWh. Using this input assumption, 1,000 kWh = 0.22 toe. This is the equivalence that is generally used to convert kWh into toe, particularly for nuclear energy.

1,000 m^3 of natural gas	0.9 toe
1 metric ton of LNG	1.23 toe
1 metric ton of coal (anthracite)	0.67 toe
1 metric ton of brown coal (lignite)	0.33 toe
1 megawatt-hour (MWh)	0.22 toe (production) or 0.083 toe (consumption)

From Secondary Energy to Final Energy and Useful Energy

Final energy is the energy actually delivered to consumers to be converted by them into useful energy: electricity, gasoline, etc. Between the secondary energy (output of the transformation process) and the final energy (received by the consumer), losses resulting from transport are incurred.

Useful energy is the energy available to the consumer after losses in the equipment that is being used. Between the final energy and this quantity of energy actually consumed, there are use losses.

Considering all energies together, energy losses between primary energy and useful energy can be broken down as follows:

- 25 per cent during conversion,
- 5 per cent during transport,
- 35 per cent during end use.

The result is that useful energy only represents one-third of the primary energy used in the process.

OIL – THE REFERENCE ENERGY

• The Characteristics of Oil

Oil remains the reference energy because it presents several essential characteristics.

– *It is a Strategic Raw Material*

Much of our civilisation is based on the transport of individuals or goods. In addition, passenger cars operate mainly with gasoline or diesel fuel, trucks with diesel fuel, and planes with jet fuel. Other fuels exist: gas, fuels produced from biomass, or even hydrogen; but currently, none of these products are economically competitive when compared with petroleum products. Petroleum products supply 95 per cent of fuel requirements. Oil is therefore indispensable in the transport sector, and without it no economic activity is possible.

Oil is a major source of fuel in a war. The importance of oil became apparent before and during World War I. In 1914, Winston Churchill, British First Lord of the Admiralty, committed the Royal Navy to the use of heavy fuel oil rather than continuing with coal as its fuel. While, at the start of World War I, the horse was still the most important draft force, tanks and motor vehicles were soon to take the leading role. Fighter planes made their appearance in the final months of the conflict.

– *"Oil is Liquid"*

This famous sentence spoken by the economist Paul Frankel may seem trivial, but this characteristic makes oil an energy that is easy to produce, transport and use. In addition, oil is a concentrated energy source: gas is much more costly to transport and distribute, coal is a solid which is more difficult to handle, and electricity is also an energy that is costly to produce and very difficult to store. This ease of production means that oil trading dominates world trade in terms of both volume and value: depending on the price of crude oil, oil transactions can represent 2 to 4 trillion dollars per year. The oil market is global since oil can be easily transported from one part of the world to another.

– *Oil is a Raw Material Whose Price Can Be Much Higher than the Cost of Production*

Oil only costs a few dollars per barrel to produce in the Middle East, and a few tens of dollars at most in more difficult conditions, but the price of oil at the start of the twenty-first century often exceeded the highest cost of its production. Is this a consequence of its strategic nature? The effect of actual or planned scarcity? Whatever the case, oil is what is referred to as a rent industry: the rent is the difference between the price (which is supposed to represent a fair value for the consumer) and the cost of production. In Saudi Arabia, where the cost of production (excluding capital) is roughly $5 per barrel, for a selling price around $50— on average —in 2017, the rent for this year is roughly $45. This rent goes to the State, which returns a portion of it to the national company, Saudi Aramco, which holds the monopoly on exploitation of the kingdom's hydrocarbon resources, to finance exploration, production and processing operations. Except in the US, in countries where private international companies (International Oil Companies or IOC: ExxonMobil, BP, Shell, Total, Chevron, etc.) operate alone or in association with a state-owned company (as is the case for Nigeria, Angola, and even on a more limited scale in Venezuela or Iran), the rent is shared between the State and the oil company. In principle, when prices vary widely, the portion of the rent retained by the oil company increases more moderately, with the implicit rule being: the State is the owner of the deposits; thus, it is generally accepted that most of the value generated by exploitation returns to the State, and therefore the people.

Economics: Profit Margins and Costs

Oil can sell for a price much higher than its cost of production. Economists refer to the difference between the selling price and the cost of production as the rent, and often distinguish between differential and absolute rent.

(Cont'd...)

Consider wheat as an example. If producing one ton of wheat costs efficient producers \$100 and inefficient producers \$300, and if the wheat that costs \$300 to produce is necessary to meet the needs of consumers, the price should reach \$300. A producer who is able to produce at a cost of \$100 will benefit from a differential rent of \$200 (\$300-\$100). If, for reasons linked to pressure in the markets, the price reaches \$400, all producers will benefit from an additional absolute rent of \$100 (\$400-\$300).

In the case of oil in August 2017, the cost of production (depending on the zones) was roughly between \$5 (Saudi Arabia) and \$40 per barrel (in some cases it could be more) for a selling price of \$50. The absolute rent for all producers was therefore \$10 (\$50-\$40) and Saudi Arabia received an additional differential of \$35 (\$40- \$5).

- **The Origins of Oil**

According to the most widely recognised theory, "rock oil" (petroleum or petrol) is formed from microorganisms. Tens of millions of years ago, these microorganisms accumulated in sediments and were then gradually buried in the soil. Under the effect of temperature and pressure, they were transformed into kerogen—immature crude oil—composed of a mixture of large hydrocarbon molecules.

These petroleum precursors were then expelled from the source rock. The "oil" rose towards the surface. There were then two possibilities. In the first stage, the "oil" rose to the surface without encountering an obstacle. The light fractions then either evaporated or were destroyed by bacteria and a residue remained, natural bitumen, whose traces and uses have been recorded in many periods of history (caulking for Noah's Ark and Moses' cradle, bitumen found by Marco Polo in today's Iraq, sources of pitch from the Massif Central in France, and the oil sands deposits of Canada). Alternatively, the oil encountered a reservoir rock—carbonates, sandstone, compacted sand and corals—and crept into the pores and interstitial spaces of these rocks. Provided the reservoir had an impermeable overburden or cap rock, the oil remained trapped in this rock until the bit from a drilling device allowed it to escape.

Quite often, above the layer which contains the crude oil there is a sedimentary layer whose pores are filled with gas, natural gas mainly composed of methane, which is called associated gas (associated with the crude oil). Other deposits—similar in many points—will only contain what is known as "dry" gas, i.e. there are no liquid hydrocarbons in the reservoir. This results from different conditions than those giving rise to the formation of heavier hydrocarbons, e.g. a higher temperature. Under the sedimentary layer(s) containing the crude oil and/or gas, there is another sedimentary layer that is water-saturated.

– Hydrocarbons in Crude Oil

Crude oil and natural gas are mixtures of hydrocarbon molecules. As the word hydrocarbon implies, each molecule is composed of atoms of carbon and hydrogen. Crude oil includes molecules that range from the simplest, methane, with just one carbon atom—to very heavy molecules that contain twenty to thirty or more carbon atoms. Natural gas—whether associated or dry—mainly consists of methane, but also contains variable proportions of heavier molecules.

To simplify, there are three types of hydrocarbon deposits: oil deposits covered by associated gas, oil deposits without associated gas, and "dry" gas deposits with no liquid in the reservoir.

Crude oil must be processed to separate the liquid fractions—which make up most of the flow—from the gaseous fractions. This separation, also referred to as stabilisation, is necessary to avoid the risk of explosion during transport.

When natural gas exits the subsoil, the reduction of temperature and pressure causes condensation of the heaviest molecules present in a gaseous state in the deposit. These heavy fractions are called condensates or Natural Gas Liquids (NGL). A condensate is therefore a very light oil which, via distillation, will provide a high proportion of gasoline and diesel fuel.

Various Categories of Oil

The following categories of oil can be distinguished:

(1) Conventional oil: Each deposit or field contains a different crude oil, meaning that there are in fact 4 to 500 different qualities of crude oil, whose density varies from roughly 0.8 to 1. A conventional crude oil can be produced with traditional processes. When they are refined, the lightest, i.e. those with a density close to 0.8, mainly provide gasoline and diesel fuel (the highest value products) while the others will mainly provide heavy fuel oil. The condensates (light liquids associated with natural gas production) correspond to a very light conventional oil which provides a large proportion of gasoline and diesel fuel.

(2) Unconventional oils:

– Very heavy or extra-heavy oils and oil sands, which are mainly concentrated in Canada and Venezuela. They require specific production and transformation processes in order to be transformed into synthetic crude oils that can be used in refineries.

(Cont'd...)

- Oil shale, i.e. rocks that contain organic matter whose conversion into hydrocarbons is not complete.
- Liquids obtained *via* the chemical transformation of coal, gas or (perhaps shortly) biomass (GTL-Gas to Liquids, CTL-Coal to Liquids, BTL-Biomass to Liquids).
- Biofuels.
- Shale oil (Light Tight Oil – LTO) extracted by fracking is also unconventional oil.

The nomenclature has not been fully established, but for users—who are above all interested in the gasoline and diesel they buy at the pump—these distinctions are not very important. All of these "liquids" can be transformed into fuel or combustible material.

FROM OIL EXPLORATION TO OIL MARKETING

- **Oil Exploration**

Initially, geologists search for clues that might indicate the presence of hydrocarbons. Next, geophysicists proceed with seismic projects that send sound waves from the surface to the depths of the soil. These waves will be reflected by the interface between ground layers which, after processing of the raw data, enables maps and cross-sections of the subsoil to be prepared. These diagrams, previously in two dimensions, can now be produced in three dimensions (seismic 3D). Seismic 4D has even been proposed, by adding in the time dimension (e.g. seismic projects done on exactly the same zone but at six month intervals).

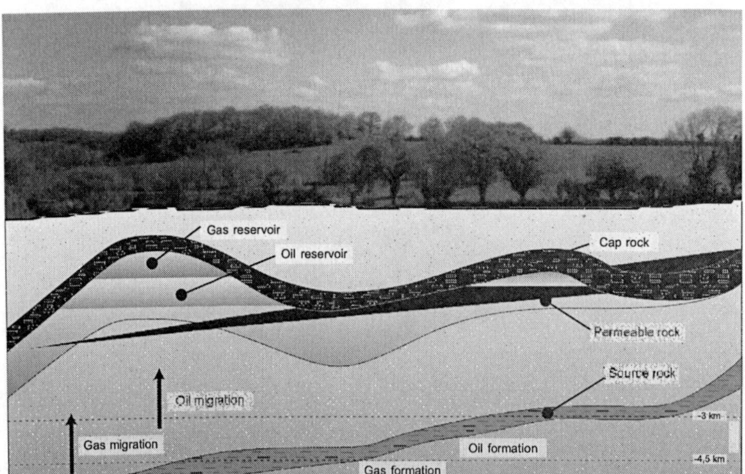

Figure 1: Oil Formation.

Once the possibility of the presence of hydrocarbons has been assessed with reasonable certainty, exploration drilling takes place. This drilling will be referred to as "dry" if it does not uncover a deposit of hydrocarbons (gas or oil). In case of success, where indications of oil or gas are found, in many cases more extensive drilling must take place to assess the volume of reserves and whether the deposit has commercial potential.

- **Oil Production**

Production from oil (or gas) deposits is developed by drilling several producer wells (Fig. 2). The flows from the various wells are collected by a

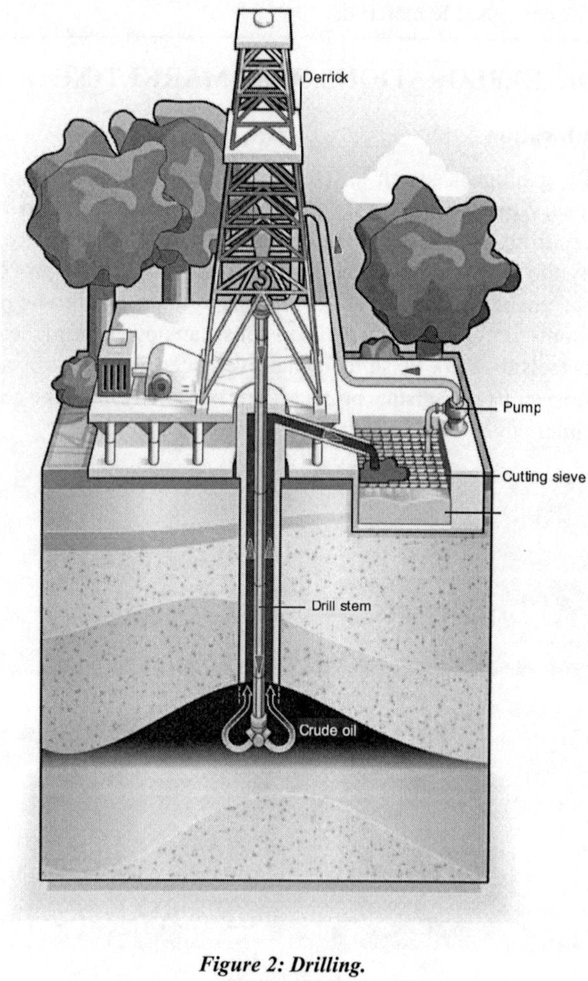

Figure 2: Drilling.

network of pipes and directed to processing facilities where the crude oil is "stabilised". Stabilisation means separating the gaseous and liquid fractions to permit transport of the oil safely. If the crude oil were not degassed, it would give rise to a high risk of explosion.

If production is onshore, the liquid crude oil will then be routed either directly to a refinery that may be either close or some distance from the oil field[1], or to a marine terminal where it will be loaded onto tankers to be shipped to consuming regions.

If production is offshore the crude oil may be processed above the oil field on platforms carrying separation facilities, then sent to the coast via pipelines (in the North Sea, this is the case for Brent crude oil which is stored and loaded on ships at Sullom Voe, the Shetland Islands port). It can also be stored on a platform which includes production, storage and shipping facilities. This type of platform is referred to as FPSO (Floating Production, Storage and Offloading). This is an extremely large barge (usually made of steel, but sometimes made of concrete) connected to pipes that bring up the crude oil from undersea deposits. This is where the oil is stored, and where the ship will dock to take delivery of the crude oil (Fig. 3).

- **Oil Transport**

Crude oil may be transported entirely via pipelines (this may be necessary if imposed by the location of the production fields and the refinery) or by ships. Over long distances— greater than several thousand miles—transport by large ships is generally more economical.

The size of ships used to transport crude oil varies from several thousands to several hundreds of thousands of tons. The capacity of oil tankers has significantly increased over time. It especially increased between 1945—when it did not exceed 15–20,000 tons—and the start of the 1970s, when several tankers of more than 500,000 deadweight tons (dwt) were built. This increase was made possible by progress in construction techniques, which resulted in economies of scale and met the needs of a significant increase in consumption in the 1950s and 1960s.

Different Methods for Transporting Hydrocarbons

Oil and gas pipelines have been particularly developed in North America and Europe but traverse all continents and, on a worldwide scale, total roughly 1.2 million miles in length. Although sometimes located offshore, pipelines are mainly ground-based, built either on the ground or buried at a depth of several yards for safety reasons. Depending on the zones crossed, they will include varying degrees of insulation, protection or even heating.

(*Cont'd...*)

Highly capital intensive, it is essential for pipelines that the zones they cross be secure, as has been illustrated negatively in countries such as Nigeria, Colombia, Iraq, etc. They create relationships of economic dependence between countries, as reflected by throughput tariffs that may equate to several percentage points of the value of the oil transported. Where geopolitics prevent them, or there are no sea outlets or transported hydrocarbon volumes are low, other alternatives exist. Thus, between China and Russia, several hundred thousand barrels are transported daily by rail. In Iraq, although most crude oil is exported via pipelines, recent years have seen the transport of nearly 200,000 barrels daily by road tank wagons heading for Turkey, Syria or Jordan. Although pipelines and tankers are therefore the mainstay for transporting oil and gas, rail tank cars and road tank wagons provide other options and are a major means of distribution for refined products. As an indication, the following figures were recorded for the Indian market in 2007: 45 per cent of oil was transported by pipeline, 20 per cent by road and 35 per cent by rail. In terms of average cost, transporting one ton of oil over 1,000 kilometers (620 miles) in India costs $17 using a newly built pipeline, $13 if the pipeline is fully depreciated, $37 by road tank wagon and $30 by rail tank car.

By decreasing the demand for oil and favouring production in zones close to consuming countries, the oil shocks reduced the advantages of very large tankers, which also required special and costly facilities to accommodate them. Currently, the main types of tankers used are as follows:

- ULCCs (*Ultra Large Crude Carriers*), which are larger than 320,000 dwt (deadweight tons); 1 dwt is roughly 1 ton of cargo.
- VLCCs (*Very Large Crude Carriers*), which are tankers from 200,000 to 320,000 dwt, used to transport large quantities of crude oil over long distances, particularly from the Middle East to the United States, Europe and the major consumers of Asia.
- Suezmax tankers for transport via the Suez Canal, which are 120,000 to 200,000 dwt.
- Aframax (80,000 to 120,000 dwt), and Panamax (60,000 to 80,000 dwt), etc.

Petroleum products are generally transported in smaller ships, simply because the quantities to be transported are lower. Their size varies from several hundred to some twenty-five thousand tons. Typically, the barges that ship end-products manufactured in Rotterdam down the Rhine to Germany, Switzerland or France have a capacity of 1,000 to 3,000 tons. The tankers that carry gasoline from Europe to the US have capacities of the order of 10,000 tons.

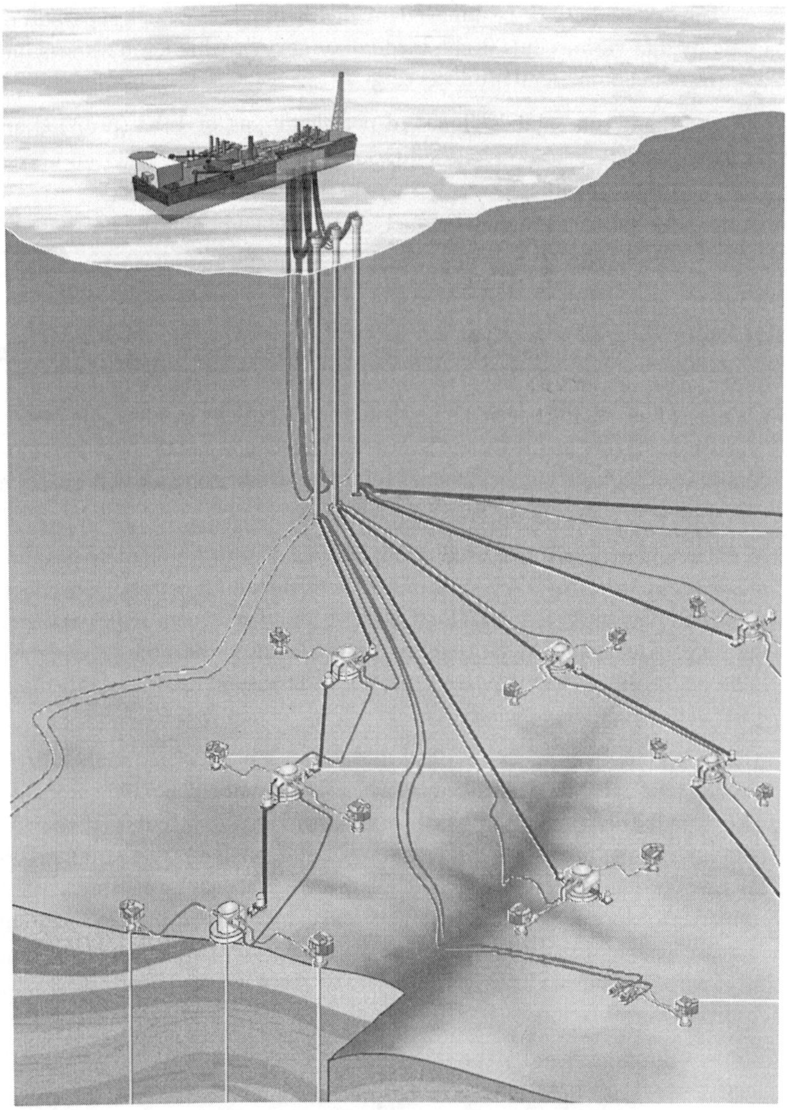

Figure 3: Example of Offshore Crude Oil Production.

- **Oil Processing: Refining Principles and End Uses for Products**

It is better to speak of the consumption of petroleum products rather than oil, since all oil is consumed in the form of gasolines, diesel fuels, heavy fuel oils, etc. Crude oil is transformed into these end products in refineries, made up of groups of processing units.

The first of these is the atmospheric distillation unit, which separates the crude oil into various cuts (light, medium or heavy), which, after upgrading, will result in commercial products (Fig. 4):

- Light cuts include liquefied petroleum gas or LPG (propane and butane), automotive gasolines and naphtha, a raw material needed for the manufacture of basic petrochemical products.
- Medium cuts include jet fuel, diesel fuel and domestic heating oil.
- Heavy cuts include heavy fuel oil, bitumens and lubricating oils.
- *Automotive Fuels: Gasoline and Diesel Fuel*

The internal combustion engines that power most automobiles are either spark ignition engines (which use gasoline) or diesel engines (which use diesel fuel). In Europe and many countries, all trucks and still a number of cars use diesel fuel. In the United States, the situation is just the opposite: most cars and a significant number of small transport vehicles operate with gasoline.

With five per cent of the population, the US consumes nearly 50 per cent of the automotive gasoline used throughout the world. Automotive gasoline also represents nearly 50 per cent of the total demand for petroleum products in the US. Why such a demand? First, because the development of the petroleum industry started in the US. Next, this is also the country where the development of the automobile industry has been greatest, and transport needs are particularly great in this very large country.

As a consequence, the US had to develop a particularly sophisticated refining tool, capable of transforming a heavy raw material into light products, which are the components of gasoline. But there are limits to this strategy. In 2000, the strong increase in oil prices was accompanied by very high prices for gasoline and diesel fuel. In 2005, Hurricane Katrina, by causing several refineries to close and resulting in significant damage to them, led to an abrupt increase in motor gasoline prices (more than 30 per cent) even though, overall, the price of oil showed little increase. This increase in gasoline prices was the result of several factors:

- Strong demand in the US.
- Lack of light crudes to be processed. The crude oils for which production could be increased were mostly heavy crudes, giving low yields of gasoline.
- Stagnation of refining capacities in the US and the need to import the deficits from the Caribbean and Europe.
- *Jet Fuel*

An intermediate product (by density) between gasoline and diesel fuel, jet fuel is definitely the product for which consumption is increasing the fastest,

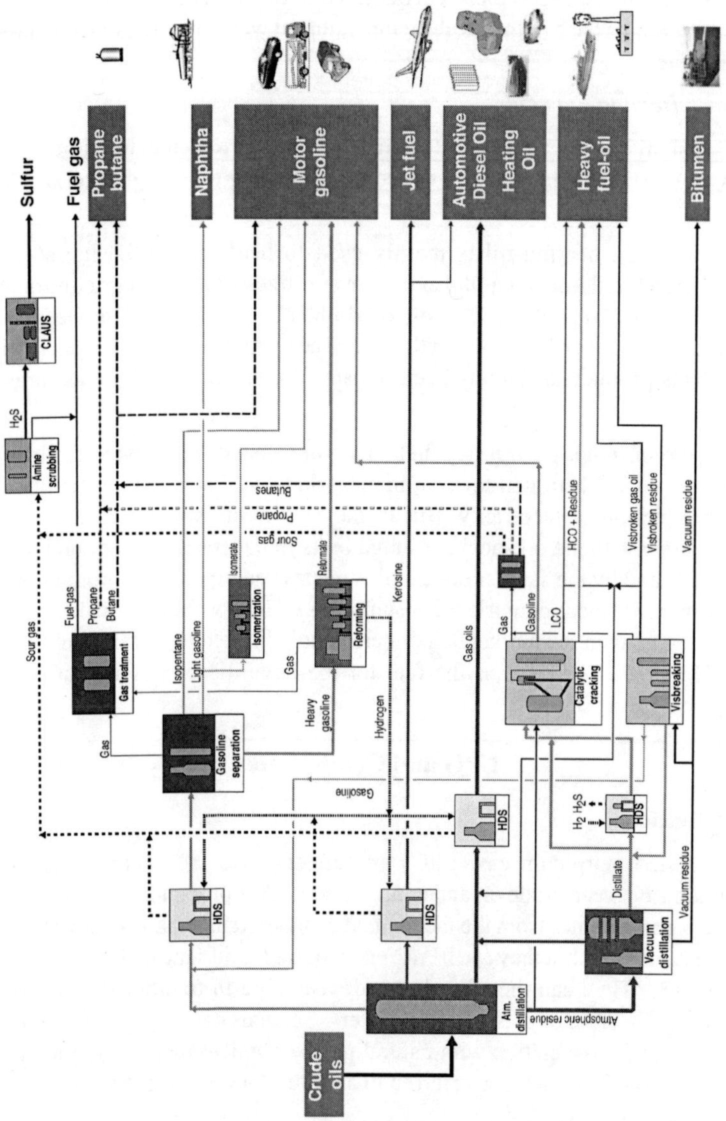

Figure 4: Refinery Flow Diagram.

due to the strong growth in air transport. The main constraint in manufacturing this product is the combination of the need to control its cold temperature behaviour: jet fuel must of course remain liquid at temperatures of the order of -50° Celsius, close to those encountered in the upper atmosphere; and the need to limit its flash point, i.e. the temperature at which it will ignite if exposed to a flame.

– *Heating Fuel Oils*

A significant quantity of oil continues to be consumed in the form of fuel oils: domestic heating oil (also called home heating oil or light fuel oil) and heavy fuel oil.

Domestic heating oil is mainly used to heat residential homes and commercial buildings, but it also has several trade outlets in agriculture and fishing. The large consumption of domestic heating oil in the major industrialised countries significantly decreased after the oil shocks, and remains low. This product has largely been replaced by natural gas in industrialised countries.

The consumption of heavy fuel oil has developed similarly: in the 1960s, it was rapidly substituted for coal in many industrial applications, including the production of electricity. But in the 1980s, the strong increase in its price along with the oil shocks resulted in its replacement by gas and coal in industry, and by the same products plus nuclear energy for the production of electricity. In most countries, consumption of heavy fuel oil is decreasing relentlessly, with the market being increasingly limited to that of bunker fuel oil. Heavy fuel oil remains the fuel for the large diesel motors that power major transport ships.

LPG and Condensates

Definitions

Liquefied petroleum gas (LPG) and condensates are intermediate oil streams between crude oil and natural gas. LPG is propane and/or butane. Their name comes from the fact that, at ordinary temperatures, they are in a gaseous state, but they can be maintained in a liquid state under moderate pressure. They can therefore be made available in traditional forms of packaging: tanks or pressurised canisters. Condensates are liquid fractions produced in association with natural gas by condensation at the time of production. They are also referred to as natural gas liquids (NGL).

Liquefied Petroleum Gas

There are two sources of LPG: the propane and butane recovered during the production of crude oil or natural gas and the propane and butane

(*Cont'd...*)

recovered at the refinery. All together, roughly 60 per cent of LPG available in the world comes from the production sector, and 40 per cent from refining.

World production of LPG is roughly 250 million tons p.a. With similar characteristics, natural gas and liquefied petroleum gas also have similar markets. LPG is mainly used for cooking and heating, either alone or as a complement to natural gas. It is also used as an industrial fuel in sectors that require a very clean type of fuel. LPG is also used in transport as a replacement for gasoline, thereby reducing pollutant emissions. But its distribution and storage are costly, which is why its use is largely limited to vehicles drawing fuel from a central depot, particularly in natural gas producing countries which have an attractive source of LPG (e.g. in Europe, Italy and the Netherlands).

Condensates

The production of condensates is increasing strongly with the rapid development of natural gas production. Light condensates can be directly used as feedstock in the petrochemical industry, but heavy condensates must be treated in refineries in order to extract gasoline, diesel fuel and other products. Due to its characteristics, a condensate cannot be processed in a traditional refinery. Several specialised refineries have been or will be constructed, but the majority of production is mixed with other crude oils for transport and subsequent processing.

– Naphtha and Petrochemicals

Petrochemicals are omnipresent in our lives. They are used to produce plastic materials, synthetic fibers, drugs, solvents, perfumes, fertiliser, insecticides, etc.

The petrochemical industry is based on two basic processes. Steam cracking brings naphtha (or in some cases LPG or middle distillates) to temperatures that are far higher than those used in other refining methods, of the order of 900°C. Steam cracking produces mainly olefins, particularly ethylene and propylene, but also heavier streams (e.g. steam cracked gasoline) which contain aromatics including benzene. Another process—catalytic reforming—provides aromatics, which are other base molecules that along with ethylene and propylene undergo polymerisation (the molecules become linked) to produce plastics, synthetic fibers and synthetic rubbers, which we are all familiar with.

The proportion of oil used as a raw material for petrochemicals represents around ten per cent of world oil production. But the added-value is high.

- **Marketing and Distribution of Petroleum Products**[2]

Depending on the type of products and the users, delivery and storage will vary significantly. Large users (industry, airports, etc.) are often directly supplied by refineries using pipelines, inland waterways or rail. Road transport fuels sold in service stations follow a more complex route. They are transported as above from the refinery to a storage depot and from there by road tank wagon to the service stations. The latter requires very good logistics, and has proven to be costly (two-thirds of jobs in the oil sector are created by this last stage). However, it is fundamental since it allows for direct contact with the user. For the past 30 years in developed countries companies have been streamlining their distribution network by reducing the number of their service stations, concentrating them on major traffic routes and expanding the services they offer, to fight competition from new entrants, particularly the hypermarkets, which have won a large market share in many countries. In emerging countries, with the development of product consumption, the tendency is reversed and new, modern service stations are built.

NATURAL GAS

Natural gas, like oil, consists of hydrocarbons, but contains molecules with a higher proportion of hydrogen and a lower proportion of carbon. Thus, for the same amount of energy, natural gas releases less CO_2 than oil. It has far lower CO_2 emissions and an energy efficiency of nearly 60 per cent in combined cycle gas turbines (CCGT), versus barely 40 per cent for other thermal fuels such as coal, heavy fuel oil, etc. This means that, in competition with other sources of primary energy, it has significant advantages for the production of electricity. The production of electricity from natural gas was therefore preferred in many countries recently.

The geography of gas production is very different from the geography of oil production. Although the cost of transporting oil represents only a small part of its price, the cost of gas transport and distribution is very high. Natural gas can be transported by gas pipeline, or by ship following liquefaction (LNG chain: Liquefied Natural Gas). The vessels are called methane tankers or LNG carriers. In the case of a gas pipeline, the same pipeline can transport five to ten times more energy in liquid form (oil) than in the form of gas. Trade is therefore subject to the constraint of proximity and it is harder to speak of a worldwide price for this product. Furthermore, the nature of the supply, *via* gas pipeline or LNG, greatly affects prices. This is why, for example, Japan pays more for its gas, since it must be imported in methane tankers.

Thus, for a long period the gas market remained mainly regional, and several trade zones developed relatively independently from one another (North America, Europe with North Africa and Russia, Asia with the Middle East, Malaysia, Indonesia and Australia). The main gas producers are therefore either consumers (United States and Russia), or countries that are close to major consumers (Canada, Norway, Algeria and Indonesia).

However, this situation is rapidly evolving. Increased demand has led to greater interest in solutions involving transport *via* LNG. Thus, Europe, which previously was mainly supplied by Algeria, Libya and Russia, now imports LNG from Nigeria. In the Middle East, Qatar is a major player on the gas scene and exports to the entire world. Higher gas prices and decreased transport costs are gradually leading to a more unified market.

- **Natural Gas: Exploration and Production**

The formation of natural gas is analogous to that of oil. The evolution of microorganisms into either liquid (crude oil) or gas (natural gas) mainly depends on temperature and pressure conditions.

The cost of producing gas is generally lower than that of oil: once wells have been drilled, gas rises spontaneously from the reservoir. Furthermore, when it is "associated" with oil production, its production cost may be considered to be zero—or nearly so—since both the capital and operating costs are primarily incurred to produce the oil.

- **Natural Gas Processing**

Natural gas processing is also simpler. Raw gas from the reservoir is processed to remove the major impurities and heavy fractions. Natural gas is mainly composed of methane, but it also contains varying proportions of ethane, propane, butane, etc. Processing consists of recovering most of the propane and butane, as well as the heavier fractions.

- **Natural Gas Transport**

Natural gas may be transported by pipeline, or in liquid form on ships specialised in the transport of liquefied natural gas (LNG), or in methane tankers.

Transport by pipeline remains the preferred method, particularly over short distances. It is more economical than the LNG chain, which only becomes competitive beyond several thousand miles. Used to transport gas over long distances, a gas pipeline must be resistant to the high pressure (exceeding 150 bars) provided by compressor plants located throughout the route (every 30 to 120 miles), permitting the gas to be transported at speeds of tens of miles per hour (mph). The number of compressor plants and their power depends on the resistance of the gas pipeline, and that depends on its diameter, which may reach 120 cm (50 inches).

Transport by ship requires that the natural gas be liquefied. To do this, the temperature of the gas must be lowered to -162°C, the liquefaction temperature of methane. This operation is extremely expensive. A liquefaction plant generally includes several parallel units (trains), and each train can process up to several billion cubic meters of gas per year. Thus, Qatar now has LNG trains with a unit capacity of 8 Mt/yr.

The liquid gas is then loaded onto a specialised ship, called a methane tanker. In 2005, the capacity of a methane tanker was of the order of 100 to 150,000 cubic meters, but today it may reach 260,000 cubic meters. Of course, the liquid gas must be regasified upon arrival in the consuming country, to be introduced into the mass transport network (Fig. 5).

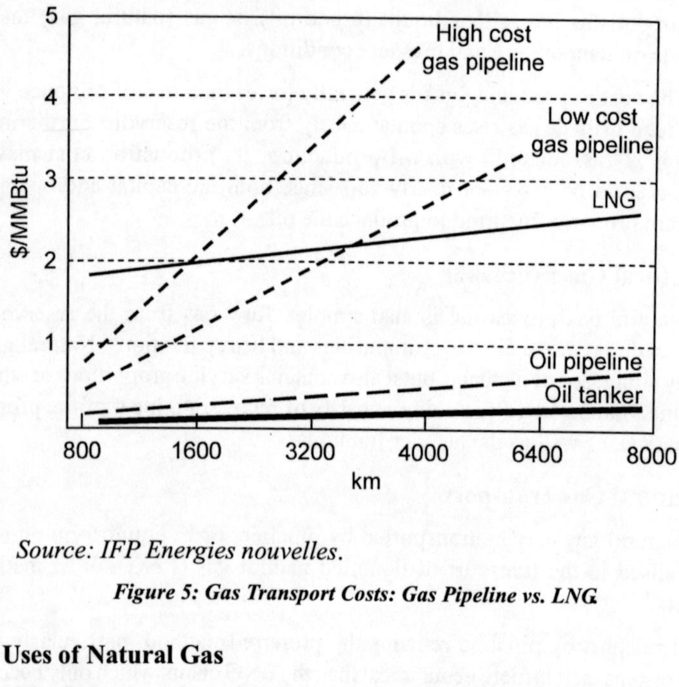

Source: IFP Energies nouvelles.

Figure 5: Gas Transport Costs: Gas Pipeline vs. LNG

- **Uses of Natural Gas**

The first gas used on a large scale was town gas, simultaneously discovered at the end of the eighteenth century by the Frenchman Philippe Lebon and the Englishman William Murdoch. This gas is produced by pyrolysis of hard coal or wood, i.e. heating it to a high temperature in the absence of air. Up to the mid nineteenth century, it was mainly used to light streets and buildings; then other uses, such as heating, were developed.

After 1880, the development of electricity slowed growth in the use of town gas, which came to a halt around 1929 with the Great Depression.

LNG Development

Trade in LNG has doubled in the past ten years. It represents 28 per cent of the international trade in gas, or eight per cent of worldwide gas consumption. About 30 export or liquefaction terminals are operating in 18 countries, and connected to nearly 60 import terminals via 300 methane tankers in operation (versus barely 100 in 1998). In view of the many projects under construction or appraisal, these figures should continue to increase.

By 2030, LNG is therefore expected to account for more than half of the international gas trade.

Natural gas then took over from town gas, principally in the US, from the start of the century. Its use would remain marginal in the rest of the world until World War II. In France, town gas manufacturing plants still existed in the 1960s (the last one at Belfort closed in 1971). But the discovery of the natural gas deposit in Lacq in 1951 would encourage rapid development of natural gas. The same situation occurred in Italy with the reserves of the Po Plain and, in the Netherlands, with the Groningen deposit (discovered in 1960, it would allow the Netherlands to export natural gas throughout Europe).

Natural gas is a fuel that can be used in most sectors where the production of heat is needed, the residential and commercial sector for cooking and the heating of buildings, the industrial sector, and the electricity generating sector.

Finally, natural gas can be used to produce methanol, a basic raw material used in the manufacture of many chemical compounds and fertilisers. Currently, its main use nevertheless remains the generation of electricity.

GTL: Gas to Liquids

GTL is a process used in the chemical conversion of natural gas, for the production of high quality liquid petroleum products (naphtha, diesel and lubricants). It is based on the same principle as CTL (*Coal to Liquids*), which starts by gasifying coal. Then—in both cases—the gas is partially burned, resulting in a mixture of carbon monoxide and hydrogen, which are used to synthesise heavy molecules, leading finally to the production of fuels.

For a long time there was only one CTL plant in the world, Secunda, operated by SASOL in South Africa, and also only one large GTL plant in the world (the PetroSA Mossel Bay plant also in South Africa). However, a few new plants have recently started operations or are under construction in major gas-producing countries (Qatar, Nigeria, etc.).

COAL

Coal is a mixture of mineral elements, sulfur and nearly pure carbon. Its combustion therefore releases large amounts of CO_2 (and also SO_2 and NOx). Major efforts are currently underway to make coal "cleaner", both for old and new power plants.

The steam engine was the key factor in the Industrial Revolution and its use depended on coal. This use of coal marked a dual break: first, the switch from renewable energies to fossil energies; second, the switch to a system in which energy distribution became a structured industry. It was only by roughly 1800 that it replaced wood as the main source of energy, and it was in turn replaced by oil as the main source of energy at the start of the 1950s.

Clean Coal

A clean coal plant has the following characteristics:

- It eliminates sulfur oxides (SO_2) and nitrogen oxides (NOx) upstream via a circulating fluidised bed and downstream via the processing of exhaust gases.
- It shows improved efficiency: the average efficiency of coal-fired power plants is only 38 per cent. The switch to supercritical cycles can achieve 40 to 45 per cent, while ultra-supercritical cycles (700°C) can achieve 50 per cent.
- It can operate using co-combustion with biomass.

In summary, the majority of traditional pollution is eliminated and CO_2 emissions are reduced.

Coal is available throughout the world. The main consumers of coal are also major producers (China, United States, India, etc.), since transport costs are relatively high. More than 85 per cent of coal extracted throughout the world is currently consumed in the country of production.

Coal production is increasingly concentrated in countries where exploitation is possible at a low cost: open-cast mines or those of shallow depth, with significant reserves. European production—located in deep mines and therefore costly—is strongly declining.

The use of coal is being gradually reduced to the production of electricity and steel. However, it remains the main source of energy for the production of electricity and its consumption continues to grow in this sector (in recent years, coal consumption significantly benefitted from increased oil prices). Nonetheless, there are large differences between geographical zones. The large volume of coal reserves, prices that are lower and less volatile than those of competing energies, and "clean coal" technologies have recently made coal a very interesting energy source. But the problem of CO_2 emissions remains unsolved.

- **Origin of Coal**

The formation of coal results from the accumulation of plant debris in sediments and its gradual burying under successive layers of material. This process of overlaying deposits gives birth to solid and combustible substances of high carbon content. Depending on how old the formation is, there may be three major categories of fuel: bituminous, lignite or peat.

- *Bituminous coal* was formed 200 to 300 million years ago, during the so-called Carboniferous period at the end of the Paleozoic era. At that time, the Earth resembled a vast greenhouse, covered with marshes and luxurious vegetation favoured by a warm, humid climate. Bituminous coal is the best solid fuel. Compact and black, it has undergone in-depth transformation and no trace of plant life is visible to the naked eye.
- *Lignite*, also known as brown coal, is of more recent formation (Mesozoic and Tertiary eras). It is a fuel of limited calorific value and more polluting.
- *Peat* is found in recent sedimentary formations, is still forming today in peat bogs, and is a very mediocre fuel[3].

- **Coal Production**

Coal is extracted either in open-cast mines or underground tunnels. Choice of the exploitation method depends on the deposit's geological configuration and its environment. If the overburden which covers the layers of coal is not very thick, the deposit is exploited by open-cast mining. If the coal layer is deep, it is mined by digging a network of underground tunnels. This process is complex and costly, and may be spread out over ten years.

Thanks to increasingly complex modern equipment, open-cast mining may be used for deposits under overburden as thick as 400 meters (1,300 feet). In this way, yields and results are much better than those obtained using tunnels. First, a large surface area must be cleared; the overburden is removed in successive "terraces" and extracted from the cut. It will be used for backfill during site reclamation. The coal layers appear gradually.

This method has many advantages: working conditions that are less harsh, far greater productivity than that of underground mines, and reduced timeframes for entry into production (2–5 years). Furthermore, since they offer great management flexibility, open-cast mines can adapt better to market demand. This type of extraction more closely resembles an earthworks and transport business than an underground mine. Because of this fact, it is easier to implement and less costly.

- **Transport**

Over limited distances, coal is mainly transported by rail and inland waterways. A slurry pipeline may also be used, which is a pipe that carries a suspension of coal in water.

More than 75 per cent of international coal commerce is carried by sea. Most major coal ports have been modernised due to this increasing trade. Coal is carried either by bulk carriers, or by mixed cargo vessels that can also transport oil. The larger the capacity of the transporter, the greater the reduction in the cost of sea freight. However, although large cargo loads have increased, there are ships that can cross the Panama or Suez canals and small cargo loads for cabotage operations between European countries.

- **End Use**

In contrast to oil or gas, coal is a physically stable material. It carries no risk of leakage and thus its transport today involves no major risk of damage to the environment.

The name coal is sometimes reserved for bituminous coal alone. But there are several qualities of bituminous coal:

– *Anthracite* is highly sought after but its reserves are limited. It is most widely used for individual home heating.
– *Coking coal* is used for the manufacture of steel. In the blast furnace, iron ore is mixed with coke, which provides the heating and chemical energy needed to transform the ore into molten cast iron, which will then be used to produce steel. The production of a ton of steel requires roughly 600 kg of coke.
– *"Steam"* coal is the main coal used in industrial boilers.

Lignite and peat are used only in electrical power plants and such plants pose serious environmental problems. Like its neighbours, the former Czechoslovakia and Poland, the former East Germany used enormous quantities of lignite—which has low calorific value but is very rich in sulfur—for the production of electricity. The neighbouring forests suffered significant damage because of this. Following German reunification, the use of lignite ceased.

But the use of coal is strongly defended in the major coal producing countries (China, India and North America), and its future is linked to the possibility of generating "cleaner" coal, as well as the possibility of CO_2 sequestration.

ELECTRICITY

Units

Voltage (V): analogous to pressure.

Current (I): analogous to flow – measured in amperes.

Power (P) = V x I measured in Watts. A Watt is 1 joule per second.

Impedance (Z) = V/I measured in Ohms.

Electrical energy = Power x time, is measured in watt hours (Wh) or multiples of that such as kilowatt hours (kWh, 10^3 Wh), megawatt hours (MWh = 10^6 Wh), gigawatt hours (GWh = 10^9 Wh), terawatt hours (TWh = 10^{12} Wh) etc.

Frequency of alternating current is measured in hertz.

Worldwide electricity production reached some 24,816 TWh in 2016. Had this electricity been entirely of thermal origin, it would have required the use of five billion tons of oil equivalent, i.e. about the total world oil production for that year. Electricity use is growing more quickly than that of any other form of energy: its production was less than 1,000 TWh in 1950. But a third of the planet's inhabitants still do not have access to it, and one of the major challenges in the years to come will be to reduce this number. Those without electricity are mainly concentrated in Africa and Asia.

Projects to increase electricity supplies have met with variable rates of success, but China's achievement in this domain has been spectacular: 90 per cent of Chinese households now have electricity although only 30 years ago the proportion was very low.

Electricity has several particular characteristics:

- It is very difficult and costly to store. Of course, dams can be considered as stores of electricity, since surplus electricity produced during off-peak hours (times of low demand) can be used in mountainous regions to pump water from one dam to another at a higher location. This water can be released during times of high electricity demand and can help to smooth out differences between supply and demand. Although batteries are valuable, they do not allow for major storage. Production must therefore be in real time; it must continuously adapt to demand.
- It is the consumer who controls demand, and this demand fluctuates continuously. Electricity is supplied from the producer to the consumer instantaneously, and so users never have to wait for their supplies.

- Electricity can travel through all links in the network, so according to the law of physics, it is difficult for the producer to determine the supply route the energy will take.

A distinction must be made between production during off-peak hours and production during peak hours. The former is base-load production. Base-load generating plants operate continuously to meet that portion of electricity demand that is constant, i.e. the level below which demand does not fall. In contrast, plants used for peak-load generation are only used as needed to respond to peaks in consumption, the timing of which is not always predictable. But it is essential that production capacity is adequate for peak demand.

These physical characteristics result in the following specific characteristics of the electricity market:

- No storage is possible, making it continuously necessary to balance supply and demand.
- No substitution is possible over the short term.
- Demand is highly dependent on time and very sensitive to temperature variations.
- Significant losses occur during distribution (e.g. average losses in Europe are on the order of five per cent throughout the high-voltage network). The location of generating plants is therefore determined by two considerations. The first is the advantage of proximity to areas of consumption. The second is the benefit of optimising the site's position with regard to the fuel supply (coal-fired power plants close to coal mines or ports), or in consideration of technical and environmental constraints (nuclear power plants close to a source of cold water such as river lakes or seawater).

But despite the above, it is possible to transport electricity over large distances — 1,200 km (720 miles) between Canadian hydroelectric power plants and major centres of consumption via very high-voltage lines (735 kilovolts)—and to trade electricity between neighbouring countries when production costs are far lower in a given country. Thus, Canada and Norway are very large producers of hydraulic energy, and this energy is exported (in the case of Canada, to the US; in the case of Norway, to countries of Northern Europe through interconnected lines).

- **Electricity Generation**

The sources of electricity supply vary considerably (Fig. 6):

- Thermal processes operate by producing steam from water or hot gases by combustion and passing them into a turbine to make it rotate. This rotation drives an alternator that generates electricity.

The steam is produced by the combustion of wood, coal, gas, oil or petroleum products (diesel, heavy fuel oil or even crude oil), or by splitting atoms, or even by concentrating sunrays on a heat transfer fluid.

- Electricity can also be generated hydraulically by water flowing through turbines or by wind driven turbines.
- Finally, electricity can be produced by photovoltaic cells that transform solar radiation into electricity without the use of turbines.

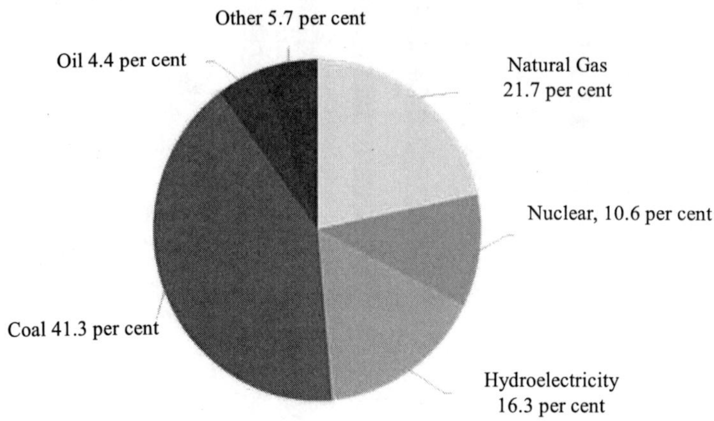

Source: IEA.

Figure 6: Worldwide Electricity Generation by Source in 2016.

Most electricity produced throughout the world comes from fossil fuels. The main source remains coal (40 per cent of electricity is produced from coal, and roughly 75 per cent of coal is used to produce electricity), particularly in major coal-producing countries like the US, China, South Africa, and even Germany in Europe. The use of oil is decreasing because of competition from both coal, which is cheaper, and natural gas which is not only cheaper but also less polluting).

Conversely, natural gas has been increasingly used recently due to the higher efficiency of natural gas powered CCGT plants, low cost of plant construction and significantly decreased emissions of pollutants (no dust or sulfur oxides and lower CO_2 emissions than coal or oil). However, increased gas prices raised doubts regarding the competitiveness of natural gas as a fuel a few years ago but the recent (2015-2016) decline in natural gas prices has made this fuel competitive again.

Nuclear energy went through a strong development phase in the US during the 1950s, then in France, Japan and several European countries during the oil shocks of the 1970s. However, its development was halted by incidents such as that of Three Mile Island in the US in 1979 and particularly by the accident at Chernobyl in 1986. In many countries, large proportions of the population are opposed to nuclear energy because of the risk of accidents and fears associated with nuclear waste storage, and this opposition has been strengthened by the damage at Fukushima in March 2011.

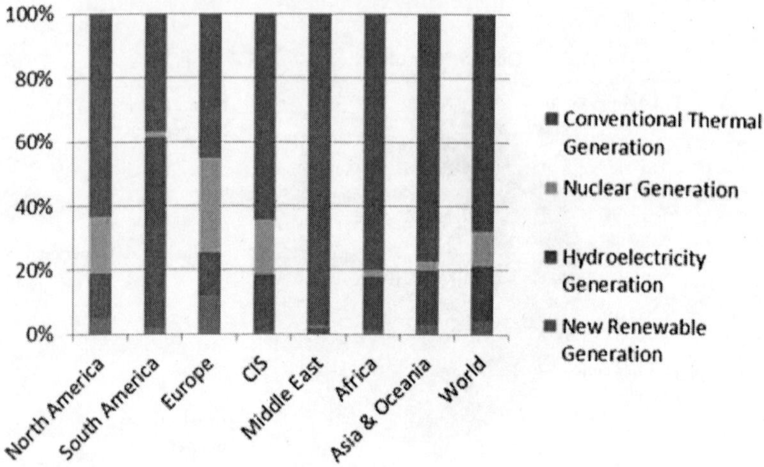

Source: doe/eia.

Figure 7: Electricity Production by Zone 2016 (percentage).

The development of hydraulic energy, which was significant in Latin America and Europe following the war, seems to have reached a saturation level with the construction of the Three Gorges dam in China. That was inaugurated in May 2006, and has a capacity of roughly 22 GW, twenty times that of the typical nuclear plants built in the 1980s and fulfills 10 per cent of the Chinese energy demand.

Electricity is generally produced in large plants to permit production at a low average cost to benefit from the economy of scale. In regions where consumption is low, production based on coal, nuclear energy, or even natural gas is more costly because of high unit capital costs. Some countries (Fig. 7) still rely on diesel power plants operating with heavy fuel oil, or even diesel fuel, but this route has become prohibitively expensive with oil prices of more than $100 per barrel a few years ago.

Nuclear Energy Today

Electronuclear energy is based on the use of uranium as a fuel to produce electricity. Uranium is a highly concentrated source of energy, and is available throughout the world in what are considered to be sufficient quantities. In most reactors operating today one ton of uranium can produce roughly as much electricity as 15,000 to 20,000 tons of coal (this excludes the yield from recycling material from reprocessed irradiated fuel).

When an additional neutron is added to the nucleus of a uranium atom, it splits and releases thermal energy. When the nucleus splits, several neutrons are released, which will in turn collide with other nuclei and result in new fission reactions in other uranium atoms. This leads to a chain reaction. The heat produced during fission transforms a heat transfer fluid (often water) into vapour, which then powers a turbine and produces electricity.

There are various types of nuclear power plants (Fig. 8), based on different types of heat transfer fluids and coolants (the term "moderator" is preferred for the element that slows—or cools —the neutrons): graphite-gas, ordinary water (or light water reactor-LWR), heavy water, boiling water, fast neutron (breeder reactor), etc. Ordinary water (or LWR) nuclear plants are most widely used throughout the world, particularly those which use pressurised water (abbreviated to PWR: pressurised water reactors, which represent 60 per cent of worldwide nuclear power plants).

During the primary combustion of uranium, plutonium is released as a byproduct. This plutonium can be partially reprocessed and then used as a new fuel source. Pure plutonium is only used in fast reactors, often for research purposes (Japan, United States, and Phoenix in France), but the Superphoenix reactor was intended for the commercial production of energy. Most of the time, the plutonium is mixed with uranium: the fuel produced in this manner is called MOX (Mixed Oxide) and can be used either in adapted LWRs, or in fast neutron reactors. In France, 20 of the 58 PWRs are equipped to operate with this type of fuel. Its use is also authorised in Japan, Germany, Belgium and Switzerland.

Currently, the first generation III reactors are being built, such as the EPR (European Pressurised Reactor or Evolutionary Power Reactor). These reactors have higher capacity and a longer operating life. But research is now underway into generation IV reactors, which will have far higher efficiencies and so be able to produce up to 50 times more electricity from uranium than today's plants. However, it is thought that their deployment is still several decades away.

The advantage of nuclear energy is that it does not produce greenhouse gases. However, it does give rise to radioactive waste and the storage and

(Cont'd...)

disposal of this must be managed with care to minimise the risk to people and to the environment. Although its radioactivity decreases over time, the handling of this waste remains a very important concern over the long term as their radiation can continue for many decades.

- **The Atom: Will It Lead to the Third Energy Revolution?**

Known uranium resources, accessible at a cost of less than $130/kg, are sufficient for existing nuclear power plants to operate for at least 100 years. But higher uranium production costs would have a relatively small impact on the overall cost of the electricity produced, since the cost of natural uranium represents only a small percentage of this. There has so far been little exploration of uranium deposits, which are relatively abundant. So taking into account a higher potential price, there is potential for uranium reserves to be significantly increased.

The price of uranium increased significantly at the beginning of the 2000s because a major proportion of the resources come from the recycling of military material, and these resources have decreased. In the longer term, with waste fuel recycling and new power plant technologies, there is less concern regarding reserve levels: fast neutron reactors (so-called Generation IV or fast breeder reactors) may use 50 times less fuel for the production of electricity than today's plants.

Despite the problem of waste, prior to the accident at Fukushima in March 2011, nuclear energy had been expected to be a high-growth and profitable industry. From North America to the Middle East and including Southeast Asia, the vast majority of nations were seen as ready to start or to return to this exciting development. While there was the risk that, in a climate of major economic crisis and financing difficulties, any fall in the prices of hydrocarbons and coal could halt certain power plant projects such as those in South Africa, world demand was nevertheless expected to remain strong.

After the Fukushima accident which has resulted in the shut down of nearly all nuclear plants in Japan, there can now be no question of the "third energy revolution" being mainly based on nuclear energy, at least in the medium term. The challenges faced by the nuclear industry; the complexity of political processes and environmental studies to build new power plants, replacement of power plants at the end of their operating life, the low number of players with the know how, the extremely high barriers to entry and, above all, public fear of catastrophes however irrational some of it may be, have become even more difficult to overcome. So while the position of the nuclear industry in the world energy balance may eventually still grow, that growth will now be delayed. The nuclear industry is unlikely to gain significant market share from other energy sources in the medium, and perhaps even into the long term.

Figure 8: Nuclear Power Plant.

Nuclear Fusion Outlook: the ITER Project (International Thermonuclear Experimental Reactor)

Studies are underway to try to reproduce the atomic fusion reactions that take place within the sun's core. Proposed in the mid-1990s, the ITER project has at last been launched: the experimental reactor is being built in France, at the Cadarache site. The money involved amounts to more than $10 billion.

The production of helium from the fusion of heavy isotopes of hydrogen (deuterium and tritium) has still only been achieved on an experimental scale because the conditions for fusion are extremely difficult to produce. A temperature of 100 million degrees Celsius is needed for the fusion reaction to take place. Although deuterium is available naturally in large quantities from the oceans (but requires a very complex extraction process), tritium must be prepared artificially, since it is only found in very small quantities in the natural world.

Nuclear fusion is interesting because it can potentially produce far more energy than fission for an equal mass of fuel. However, even if the results are conclusive, they cannot be exploited industrially before the second half of the twenty-first century.

- **Electricity: Distribution and Commercialisation**

Although electricity is often produced near the area of consumption, an efficient distribution system must be set up in order to serve each consumer. In towns and other areas where overhead lines would present a risk and technical difficulties, electric cables are laid underground; that also protects the environment.

At production site outlets, transformers change the voltage of alternating current—generally used in modern electrical networks—into high, medium or low voltage. The electrical distribution network consists of five main elements: the outlet station of the power plant with the transformers that increase the electrical voltage for transport over high-voltage lines to minimise the loss of power; the high-voltage lines themselves; substations in which the voltage is lowered for medium-voltage transmission; the medium-voltage distribution lines; transformers, which then decrease the voltage to the level used by the consumers' equipment. Thus, each phase of the network can operate at the appropriate voltage.

Alternating Current and Direct Current

Alternating current is easier to use for:	*Direct current is necessary for:*
Electricity generation, even in high capacity plant.	Undersea transmission over long distances (about 30 km at 400 kV).
Changing voltage in transformers.	Transmission over very long distances (beyond 600-800 km for power of 1,000 MW) to limit the losses from transmitting alternating current.
Preventing short circuits.	Asynchronous links between networks of different frequencies (e.g. the interconnection between Great Britain and France where, although both countries operate at 50 Hz, the networks are not synchronised).
	Limiting the number of conductors (two wires instead of three).

To transport electrical current over long distances, high-voltage lines are used to limit losses. Power is the product of voltage and intensity (P=U*I) so the higher the voltage, the lower the intensity needed for the same power. Losses are reduced because they are proportional to the square of the intensity (power dissipation = $R*I^2$). This also means that fewer lines have to be used and, since the size of the network is smaller, its environmental footprint is reduced.

In an electricity distribution network, the lines used have the following voltages:

- The domestic power network is supplied at low voltage 230 V.
- At the neighbourhood level, the network is supplied at 20 kV. Small and medium industries, shopping centres, commercial superstores, major local authorities, hospitals and schools are connected to the medium voltage network. These institutions and businesses have access to power of several hundreds or thousands of kW and account for nearly one-third of national consumption.
- Regional transport is powered by lines whose voltage varies from 63 to 90 kV.
- Finally, transport at the national level is powered by lines of 225 or 400 kV. The major industrial consumers, e.g. chemical industries, steel-making and metallurgical plants, railways and the RATP (Paris Transport Authority), which account for nearly one-third of the country's electricity consumption, are connected to this network.

The 400 kV lines that connect the distribution networks of different countries are known as international interconnection lines. They serve a dual function: providing mutual backup between countries and providing a means for international trade in electricity which favours the operation of power plants with the lowest cost at the expense of those with the highest cost.

The interconnected networks are complex and large: they include parts controlled by different operators and enable significant savings to be made. To protect against electricity blackouts, hospitals, public buildings and other facilities for which continuous electricity supply is crucial, all have backup generators (blackouts are most often caused by distribution networks, or even regional transport networks).

- **Electricity: End Use**

Electricity serves a very wide range of needs. At present only non-rail transport is still a captive customer for petroleum products (90 per cent of rail transport is now powered by electricity).

However, hybrid cars (combining internal combustion engines and electric motors) are coming into use, which suggest further encouraging developments could emerge in the future. Current hybrid cars produce their electricity from their internal combustion engine; they are not recharged from the electricity distribution network. However, development is now underway of rechargeable hybrid vehicles, which will give a further reduction in the vehicle's hydrocarbon consumption.

Electricity consumers can be classified according to the type of energy that results from the different uses of electricity:

- *Mechanical use:* motors and machines.
- *Thermal use:* heating buildings or water.
- *Household appliance use:* alarm clocks, vacuum cleaners, computers, refrigeration and air conditioning.
- *Radiant use:* lighting (residential, industrial or public spaces), lasers, radar, and radio-frequency emissions like radio, television, telephone, etc.

A single device may use several forms of electrical energy simultaneously: a computer uses mechanical energy to operate the hard disc and cooling fan, as well as radiant energy for the monitor.

End uses of electricity can also be classified by categories of consumers: i.e. the industrial, commercial and institutional, residential and transport sectors.

Cogeneration

Thermal electricity generating plants have low efficiencies: roughly 40 per cent for coal-fired or fuel oil power plants, and 60 per cent at best for gas-fired combined cycle power plants. The rest of the energy is lost in the form of heat. This has led to the idea of so-called cogeneration power plants, which simultaneously produce heat and electricity. The heat must of course be used nearby.

Combined heat and power or Cogeneration Unit allows for optimal management of natural resources, since it can result in efficiency of the order of 80–90 per cent. A gas turbine equipped with a recovery boiler can produce roughly 35 megajoules (MJ) of electricity and 50 MJ of heat from 100 MJ of fuel. If the same quantities of heat and electricity were produced separately, consumption would be roughly 90 MJ of fuel for the generator set and 55 MJ for the boiler, or a total of 145 MJ. In this simplified example, cogeneration results in a fuel savings of more than 30 per cent.

RENEWABLE ENERGY

Renewable energy is derived from the major forces that operate on our planet, i.e. sun, water, wind, etc. It also includes wood. Such energy is inexhaustible, at least over a very long timescale. Historically, renewable energy was the first energy source used by mankind; until the end of the seventeenth century wood was the most widely used energy source.

Because of recent technical developments that have decreased their costs and reduced some of the problems in their use (they are often intermittent and of low intensity), their use is now increasing. The main application is for electricity generation, but they are also used in thermal applications and to produce fuels. On a worldwide scale, renewable energy (biomass, hydroelectricity, and new renewable energies like solar, wind, geothermal, etc.) represent roughly 20 per cent of total energy production. However, it should be noted that traditional biomass (firewood) represents about half of this production, while hydraulic energy represents one third. New renewable energies meet barely three per cent of the world's energy needs.

- **Water-Hydroelectricity**

On Earth, water is neither created nor destroyed, but it is constantly moved around. This is known as the water cycle: runoff, evaporation, precipitation, etc. Water runoff provides energy that can be transformed into electricity and the process has a high efficiency (of the order of 95 per cent). It is thus a good source of electricity, and is often coupled with irrigation. Many dams were built in the 1950s, and today it is thought that, in zones such as Europe, most of the best sites are already being exploited. The construction of a dam has significant consequences, such as the flooding of extended areas and population displacement, which are increasingly unacceptable. The Three Gorges dam in China required the displacement of more than one million people.

Tidal energy produces electricity using the same principle as hydroelectricity, but its production is intermittent. The Rance Estuary in France is an example of a successful tidal power plant. However, it is of moderate capacity. Sihwa Lake Tidal Power Station (South Korea) completed in 2011 is the world's largest tidal power installation, with a total power output capacity of 254 MW which surpassed the 240 MW Rance Tidal Power Station which was the world's largest for 45 years. Such plants can only be built in locations where the tidal range is significant, and there are very few of these. Moreover, there is a problem of corrosion for the equipment functioning in the sea water. A station with 1320 MW power is under construction in Korea.

Ocean wave energy is a combination of wind and hydraulic energy. The wind applies a force which is concentrated on the ocean surface and this energy can be recovered by floats equipped with pumps by Pelamis technology. Like tidal power plants, offshore wave power plants are just completing their experimental phase (Japan, India, Portugal, Great Britain and Norway). Examples are operating in the Azores, in Scotland (0.5 MW capacity per unit), and recently in Agucadoura, Portugal (target installed capacity of 21 MW for an electricity cost that is lower than the cost of solar).

Finally, differences between the temperatures of sea water at different depths can be used to produce electricity.

- **Biomass**

Biomass occurs in highly varied forms: wood, charcoal, plant debris, crop residues, animal debris, agricultural and urban waste. It is considered a renewable energy source since the energy it contains comes from the sun. In contrast to other renewable energies, during its use (by combustion), biomass releases CO_2 into the atmosphere. However, this combustion only releases into the atmosphere the CO_2 the plant absorbed from it by photosynthesis; while the use of fossil fuels involves the atmospheric release of carbon dioxide that has been buried in the Earth's crust for millions of years.

Traditional biomass —wood, charcoal and manure —contributes at least 10 to 15 per cent of the planet's energy needs. However, the efficiency of its use is generally very low and its use is harmful to the environment. Total biomass could represent world energy potential of 2.2 G toe p.a., broken down as follows: 900 Mtoe p.a. for crops, 850 Mtoe p.a. for forests and 450 Mtoe p.a. for organic wastes. Between half and two-thirds of this potential is apparently effectively used.

– *Biofuels* (Fig. 9)

Known as first generation biofuels or agrofuels, ethanol and biodiesel are two fuels obtained from raw plant material. Biodiesel results from the processing of vegetable oils (palm, sunflower, canola (a variety of rapeseed), soybean, karanga, coconut, jatropha, etc.), while ethanol is obtained by the fermentation of sugarcane (in tropical countries like Brazil), beets (France) or cereals (United States). Biofuels incorporate oxygen molecules that promote combustion and decrease pollutant emissions such as carbon monoxide and unburned hydrocarbons. In addition, the plants used for the manufacture of biofuels absorb CO_2 during their growth.

Like crude oils, the quality and production cost of biofuels are highly variable, depending on agricultural yields as well as the cost of harvesting, transport and processing. It was estimated that a liter of Brazilian bioethanol cost US 60 cents, one liter of US ethanol amounted to $0.5 to $1.1 and one liter of Ivory Coast biodiesel—produced from palm oil—was roughly $1. With variable costs that are significant and also volatile, many biofuels depend on tax subsidies for their viability and these depend on political decisions. World biofuel production is significant and represents nearly 1.5 per cent of world oil production. Ethanol is mainly produced in the US and Brazil; it represents 65 per cent of more than 74.8 Mtoe of biofuels produced in 2015.

Water: At the Crossroads of Challenges in Energy, Climate and Development

Although water covers 70 per cent of the Earth's surface, only 2.5 per cent of it is fresh water, and less than 1 per cent of that is in liquid form (the majority being present in the form of glaciers). The fact that just nine countries hold 60 per cent of the world's fresh water illustrates the uneven distribution and vulnerability of water resources. Fresh water consumption has increased by a factor of five since 1940—largely due to agriculture, which consumes nearly 70 per cent— one-third of the world's population is already facing water shortages and low quality supply, and 3 to 5 million people die every year throughout the world from water-borne illnesses.

Crucial for the very survival of populations and fundamental for agriculture, water also has a strategic role in the transport and production of energy. With regard to energy, water is crucial in the production of both electricity and heat (hydraulic dams, marine turbines, geothermal energy, nuclear power plants etc.). Energy production based on geothermal technology, tidal power facilities or marine turbines has little effect on the state of water resources, but the construction of dams and control of river flows have a major impact on water management. In the US, the massive reservoir system used on the Colorado River to supply the Great American West adversely effects water supplies in Mexico.

Other energy industries also have an impact on water quality: for example, two to six barrels of water are needed to produce one barrel of synthetic crude oil from Canadian oil sands, and this process also carries the risk of pollution.

In the future, even if the quantity of rainfall is not likely to change, its distribution between different areas and its frequency will be altered, often to the disadvantage of countries already facing a deficit in water supplies.

A final example of the close relationship between energy and water is the desalination of seawater. With freshwater production at nearly 50 million cubic meters per day, desalination plays a key role in a number of countries, most of them (led by Saudi Arabia and the United Arab Emirates) oil producing states. The volume of fresh water produced is about one per cent of worldwide fresh water consumption.

Thermal desalination processes consume massive amounts of energy; recently this resulted in a price of more than 1 $\$/m^3$ fresh water from such plants. Filtration and particularly reverse osmosis, which represent nearly 50 per cent of world capacity, can provide water for half that cost and limit energy consumption to some 5 kWh/m^3 of water produced.

The production of ethanol fuel was started in Brazil at the beginning of the 1980s, at a time when the price of crude oil was very high. But the decrease in crude oil prices made ethanol two to three times more expensive than fuels made from oil in the 1990s. The subsequent rise in crude oil prices made ethanol competitive once again. Lower taxes were also levied to compensate for the price difference between traditional fuels and ethanol when the price of oil was low.

A subsequent development is second generation ethanol produced from lignocellulosic biomass, i.e. agricultural and forest residues, and plantings such as copse. Another method, the production of biofuels via the gasification of biomass followed by synthesis (BTL: *Biomass to Liquids*), seems promising but is not yet in commercial exploitation.

Biofuels may also be produced from algae in the future.

Agrofuels: Forbidden Fruit or Means of Development?

With biofuels alternately described as an "environmental protection focused on a country's sustainable development" or "crime against humanity", opinions on them are far from unanimous. After several years of development supported by a chorus of praise, a number of worries are now apparent.

Biofuels have profited from the awareness of global warming. Of renewable origins and utilisable as an alternative to petroleum products—which are the cause of 60 per cent of additional CO_2 emissions for zones like the European Union—biofuels were quickly perceived as a green energy source: the World Bank reported that Brazilian sugarcane would decrease emissions by 80 to 90 per cent, US corn by 20 to 30 per cent and Malaysian oil palm by roughly 40 per cent. However, such optimistic projections are theoretical: the Nobel Prize winning chemist Paul Crutzen estimates that, in some cases, the production of one liter of agrofuel can create twice the amount of greenhouse gases compared with "traditional" fuels. In fact, beyond the emissions released during the production and processing of biomass, everything depends on the land used to produce it. Depending on whether fallow land is used to plant oil palm or an equatorial forest is razed, the balance may be very positive or catastrophic. In Southeast Asia, nearly 48 per cent of oil palm surface area was taken from virgin or secondary forests, and in Malaysia, nearly 87 per cent of deforestation is attributable to oil palm cultivation. In Brazil, although sugarcane cultivation is displacing land used for pasture and does not directly threaten the Amazon basin (the climate is ill-suited to its cultivation), the livestock displaced

(*Cont'd...*)

may be moved into the forest and so lead to land clearing. Beyond greenhouse gases, the production of biofuels may cause other environmental damage: over-fertilisation, soil acidification, etc.

So there is conflict between the need to feed a growing population and the ecological necessity of conserving the "green lungs" which emit oxygen. Available land is becoming scarce while "to substitute 10 per cent of gasoline and diesel fuel consumption in Europe and the US will require roughly 20 per cent and 25 per cent, respectively, of the arable land in these regions". At a time when the Intergovernmental Panel on Climate Change (IPCC) predicts worsening weather phenomena including droughts and floods, which may cause shortages of water and food supplies and a 50 per cent decrease in agricultural production for some countries, there are legitimate concerns that such plans will provide "full tanks" at the cost of "empty stomachs". In that context it is interesting to recall that the opportunity cost of producing five liters of biofuel, enough to fuel a car for 30 miles (50 kms), is 485 lbs (220 kg) of corn, which can feed a child for one year or be used to produce 250 eggs, 44 lbs of chicken, 15 lbs of duck or 30 lbs of pork. Moreover, the importance of the water needed should also be emphasised. While 118 US gallons (450 l) of water are needed for 2.2 lb (1 kg) of maize fodder, the UN anticipates 2.3 billion people will lack access to water between now and 2025.

Beyond the economic self-interest of the various energy stakeholders, which logically guides their views on the impact of biofuels, beyond the determination shown by Brazil with its vested interest in developing the market or the alarmist speeches emanating from oil producing states or oil companies, biofuels can serve as either political scapegoat or flagship. In this respect the strength with which President Bush defended biofuels should be noted, as he did so in a Latin America torn between "Bolivarian" governments largely dependent on hydrocarbons (Venezuela, Bolivia, etc.), and liberal socialist governments often based on major agricultural power (Brazil, Argentina, Chile, etc.). Nevertheless, the virulence of the alarms raised on biofuel developments from Latin America to Southeast Asia and Africa goes beyond ideological differences and is requiring decision takers to face up to the need for prudence and the necessity for in-depth studies on the impact of biofuels.

- **New Renewable Energies**
  - *Wind Energy*

Air moves around the Earth due to differences in temperature and atmospheric pressure. This air movement has been used to move sailboats or operate windmills for a long time.

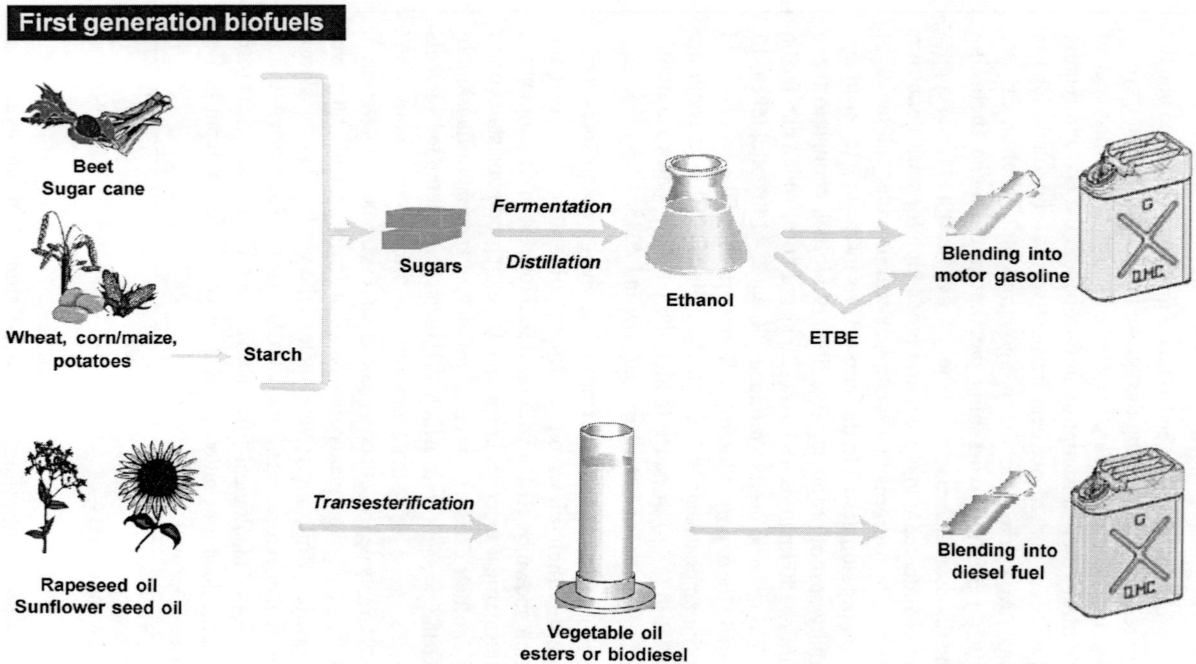

Source: IFP Energies nouvelles.

Figure 9: Traditional Biofuel Supply Chains.

For several decades now, wind turbines—propellers connected to a generator—have used the movement of air to produce electricity, without emitting pollution. They are sometimes criticised for being noisy. In any case, they are all subject to the inconsistency of wind: on an average, wind turbines can only be used 30 per cent of the time (Fig. 10).

Wind power potential worldwide is 12 TW. This energy source is being increasingly used. Installed capacity was 432 GW in 2015, compared with 14 GW fifteen years earlier: this may be considered both significant and insufficient. Nearly half of this capacity is installed in Europe. Denmark obtains almost 40 per cent of its electricity from wind power; estimated global generation from wind power in 2015 was 717 terawatt hours, i.e. some three per cent of the world's total electricity production.

At the start of the twenty-first century, offshore wind farms are the fastest growing source of electricity generation: they have a better capacity factor and do not give rise to the problems of the impact on those living nearby faced by ground-based wind turbines.

– *Solar Energy*

The Earth's surface receives a quantity of solar energy equivalent to 10,000 times worldwide energy demand. So this gives a potential, albeit highly theoretical, of 1 to 4 MWh/m^2/yr.

The sun's energy can be used in different ways. For example, "passive solar" involves designing buildings that use direct sunlight for heating, thereby reducing the need for electricity. These buildings must be extremely well insulated; hence the importance of technical innovations in the domain of thermal insulation and that of materials, glazing, etc.

Solar thermal energy can mean:

– either the use of solar panels to capture heat and transfer it to a heat-transfer fluid,
– or the use of parabolic mirrors to concentrate the heating power of solar radiation on a vessel containing water. The water is boiled and the steam drives a turbine (Concentrated Solar Power or CSP).

These facilities can only operate during daylight and their use is subject to variations in the weather. However CSP allows the production of electricity a few hours after sunset because the heat can be stored.

Finally there are solar photovoltaic systems which convert solar radiation directly into electricity using cells made of silicon or any other material capable of light-to-electricity conversion (Fig. 11). Although its efficiency is average, this system is easy to implement and very light. It is practically the only real technological innovation being used for renewable energy. There is considerable research in this area; prices are continuously decreasing and the efficiencies of commercially available systems have increased from five per cent to more than 20 per cent in the past 20 years. Japan, Germany and the US represent 75 per cent of the world market.

– *Geothermal Energy*

The Earth is composed of a crust overlying a mantle of molten rock. The quantity of heat contained beneath the Earth's surface and down to a depth of 10,000 meters (33,000 feet) represents 50,000 times more energy than total worldwide hydrocarbon reserves. Hot springs and geysers are manifestations of this intense underground activity. In Iceland and the Philippines, this energy—which is easy to put into operation—is widely used. Worldwide electricity production from geothermal energy will soon reach 100 TWh (0.5 per cent of total worldwide production). The great advantages of this form of energy are its wide availability – 70 per cent on average – and its environmental benefits (CO_2 emissions amount to 10 per cent of those from a gas-fired power plant).

Figure 10: Wind Turbine.

However, drilling depths vary considerably from one location to another, and there is a risk of failing to find a geothermal source. It is therefore important to establish the precise characteristics of the area to be drilled before starting this type of operation. Twenty countries in the world, mostly in Asia and North America, produce "geothermal" electricity. Apart from the traditional players who are largely responsible for the relaunch of geothermal projects, other areas such as the East African Rift and Australia are being chosen for new developments. It is thought that the number of countries using geothermal energy could more than double over the next five years. Seven to eight years are typically needed to develop a geothermal project; its subsequent life largely depends on the acidity of the water and the extent of the resulting corrosion of the pipes.

As well as traditional geothermal energy, Hot Dry Rock (HDR) projects are currently being developed. These involve the injection of heat-transfer fluids at great depth, often in former oil reservoirs (which means that a detailed knowledge of the reservoir is available at a lower cost), and their recovery at the surface after they have been heated underground.

Hydrogen

Hydrogen has often been presented as a miracle solution to the world's energy needs. One well-known book—*The Hydrogen Economy* by Jeremy Rifkin— played a major role in developing this image.

The reality is more complex. Hydrogen is not a source of energy: it does not exist in a natural state. But as part of the energy supply chain it has one major advantage: its combustion is clean and the only combustion product is very pure water. Publicity for vehicles operating on hydrogen-powered fuel cells is generally limited to showing the rear of the vehicle and the exhaust pipe, which, rather than releasing the usual pollutant gases, emits pure water which is being drunk by a small, brightly-coloured bird. The problem is at the front of the vehicle: the "engine" is large and expensive.

There is also the problem of producing the hydrogen. There are two possibilities. The first is by electrolysis of water and its decomposition into hydrogen and oxygen, by passing an electrical current through an aqueous solution. The pollution from the vehicle exhaust gas is replaced by the pollution resulting from the electricity generation. If this electricity comes from a nuclear power station there will be no greenhouse gas emissions, but there are other risks. If the electricity generation is thermal (e.g. from coal), the pollution will be displaced rather than reduced. Hydrogen can also be produced by the "reforming" of natural gas or petroleum products. These products are composed of hydrogen and carbon

(*Cont'd...*)

atoms which can be separated in a chemical reaction. But this reaction releases carbon in the form of CO_2, thereby adding to the greenhouse gas effect. Hydrogen is not easy to use. It is even more difficult to liquefy than natural gas and its energy density is very low: the calorific value of hydrogen is only 3 kWh/m^3, compared with 16 kWh/m^3 for methanol and 40 kWh/m^3 for natural gas. As we have seen, its production is complex. Pollution is not avoided; merely one type of pollution—the emission of greenhouse gases by vehicles—is replaced by another, which it is hoped will be less dangerous and thus more acceptable.

Hydrogen transport and distribution are also very complicated. Finally, storing hydrogen in a vehicle is difficult. This has led to projects for hydrogen production onboard the vehicle via the reforming of petroleum products, with the hydrogen produced used to power a fuel cell. But where are the gains with regard to pollution?

The risks associated with the use of hydrogen must also be emphasised. It is a highly explosive gas, as was shown by the Zeppelin accidents before World War II. On May 6, 1937, the German hydrogen filled Zeppelin LZ-129 Hindenburg, having left Frankfurt with 97 passengers, burst into flames upon arrival at the Lakehurst airport near New York. The accident claimed the lives of 35 victims and was the end of passenger transport in dirigible balloons.

Figure 11: Solar Panel in Africa.

- **Challenges, Advances and Constraints**

Increasing environmental concerns (see Chapter 2) and issues regarding supply security (see Chapter 4) have resulted in considerable interest in renewable energies. In particular, there is much hope for wind energy and photovoltaic technology. Their contribution to the world energy balance remains limited, but there is strong political will in some countries—particularly in Europe—to develop them. The European Union has set an objective of generating 20 per cent of electricity from renewable resources by 2020. It is clear that hydraulic energy will maintain a major role, but wind energy will develop rapidly too.

Renewable energy has a low impact on the environment and can be used to meet all requirements for heat and electricity and to a certain extent for fuels. The technologies are available, even though considerable progress must still be made to improve efficiencies, decrease manufacturing costs and make the energy available on a continuous basis. Resistance to their development is both economic and political: profitability is often low; there is resistance in principal to change and insufficient motivation on the part of decision-makers and consumers. An example is the support in principle given to wind turbines but the opposition often encountered from those living near the proposed plant because of fear of visual and noise pollution: i.e. the NIMBY syndrome (Not In My Back Yard[4]).

Renewable energy is also a means of supplying energy to regions that are remote and not connected to traditional energy distribution networks. In many parts of Africa, solar or wind energy may provide electricity supply for populations, particularly rural populations that are currently denied access to it.

$1700 billion per year is currently invested in energy projects. Of this, more than 300 billion is dedicated to alternative energies, with wind energy leading the way. The United States and the European Union (EU) have contributed, equally, more than 70 per cent of these investments.

ENERGY AND SOCIOLOGY

The problems of pollution associated with the massive use of fossil fuels may lead to changes that will transform the energy landscape. In the absence of any significant constraint, the transport sector will continue to use petroleum products for many years, since oil provides the concentrated energy it requires. The industrial sector also requires large quantities of energy for which fossil fuels are best suited—for the time being. But, in the residential and commercial sector, there could be rapid developments in energy supply over the next few years.

International Oil Companies: "Beyond Petroleum"?

According to the American Petroleum Institute, between 2000 and 2005 ExxonMobil, Shell, BP, Chevron and ConocoPhillips invested $110 billion in alternative energies and emerging technologies, or nearly 25 per cent of their profits. However, only $1.2 billion was invested over the five years in solar, wind, geothermal and biogas, compared with the $11 billion spent on application technologies (energy savings, batteries, etc.) and $98 billion on unconventional crude oils. Despite their need for profitability over the medium term and their business relationships with oil producing states, IOCs are nonetheless increasing investments in renewable energy, often giving preference to sectors in which they are already present, even if only symbolically.

By rebranding itself "Beyond Petroleum" in 2000, BP was the first to cross the symbolic beyond-petroleum threshold. Already benefitting from its subsidiary BP Solar's (target turnover of $1 billion in 2008) 30 years of experience in solar energy, in 2005, BP announced the formation of BP Alternative Energy to manage an investment programme of $8 billion over 10 years. They have invested $2.9 billion on wind, solar, carbon capture and storage and biofuels since 2005, including a commitment of 1$ billion in Brazilian ethanol in the summer of 2008.

The world's largest non-government-owned international company, great advocate of profitability and financial pragmatism, ExxonMobil, was late in turning to alternative energies and showed only minor interest, preferring to focus on energy savings and pollution risks, as well as providing subsidies to research organisations such as Stanford's Global Climate and Energy Project of $100 million over 10 years.

In 2016, the Oil and Gas climate initiate was launched which is a CEO led initiative of top ten oil companies to reduce greenhouse gas emissions with a fund of $1 billion to be invested over a decade.

Significant savings can be made through better building design and insulation. Solar or even wind equipment could make such buildings autonomous in terms of heating, electricity and air conditioning. It is even possible that the electricity generated could exceed the building's needs and be sold to the local producers via a connection to the grid.

The sociological aspect of this problem is significant. A centralised system of electricity production, in which each citizen is a passive consumer, may be replaced by a structure in which citizens have become autonomous producers. This autonomy may extend to transport, with individuals producing electricity which they use to recharge their automobiles.

Utopia? Absolutely. But climate change may make this utopia necessary.

References

1. The crude oil produced in some inland American states is routed over several miles via pipes (or by truck in the case of stripper wells or marginal wells) to nearby refineries where it will be processed. In Russia, crude oil from Western Siberia can be routed over thousands of miles to refineries in the region of Moscow or the Ukraine. Within the framework of the "socialist sharing of work" and to avoid concentrating production and processing activities in the same region—which would give it major strategic power—Stalin ordered the construction of very large refineries in regions lacking in crude oil.
2. *Source: Le pétrole – Au-delà du mythe*, Xavier Boy de la Tour, Ed. Technip, 2004.
3. Peat is nevertheless used for electricity generation in the Republic of Ireland, where two peat burning stations were commissioned in 2004/2005.
4. Another variant is BANANA: Build Absolutely Nothing Anywhere Near Anything.

Chapter - 2

Energy Markets: Outlook and Challenges

ENERGY DEMAND

After World War II and throughout the second half of the twenty-first century, world consumption of commercial primary energy boomed, going from two Gtoe in 1945 to more than 13 Gtoe in 2017. This increase was the consequence of unprecedented economic growth (except in 2009), combined with the discovery of apparently unlimited deposits of oil, natural gas and coal.

> **Commercial and Non-Commercial Energy**
>
> Commercial energy refers to forms of energy sold on different markets. This includes oil, natural gas, coal, electricity of nuclear and hydraulic origin, and new renewable energies.
>
> Non-commercial energy refers to traditional biomass (wood and charcoal) which, particularly in developing countries, is directly harvested and used by the consumer.

To illustrate commercial energy consumption today, imagine a cube a little more than three times the height of the Burj Khalifa tower in Dubai (about 2.4 kilometers or 1.5 miles) on each side, filled with oil: this is equivalent to the total quantity of energy consumed throughout the world every year. In fact, oil per se only accounts for 32 per cent of this, a consumption of 150 m^3 per second, which is exactly the flow rate of the river Seine in France. The rest is consumed in the form of natural gas (24 per cent), coal (29 per cent), nuclear electricity (four per cent) and hydraulic electricity (seven per cent) and hydraulic electricity (seven per cent). New renewable energies represent only some 0.4 Gtoe or a little more than three per cent of worldwide demand (Fig. 12).

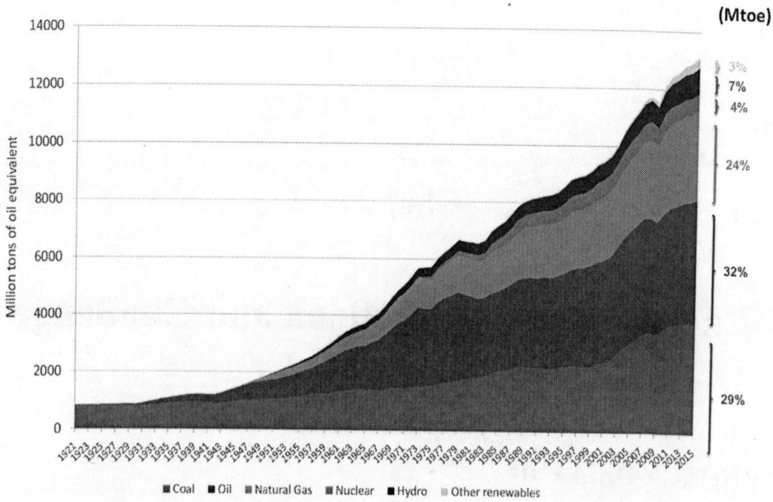

***Figure 12: Worldwide Commercial Energy Consumption by Energy Source. Source:* BP Statistical Review, 2016.**

In addition to so-called commercial energy consumption, we must add non-commercial energy consumption—mainly biomass—which represents roughly 1.5 Gtoe.

The world can be divided into three groups, with each mainly using one of the three energy systems that have succeeded each other throughout history: wood and manpower in much of Sub-Saharan Africa and the Amazon; coal and steam in China and India; and oil in the OECD countries (Organisation for Economic Cooperation and Development) and producer countries.

After a period of moderate growth in the 1990s, energy consumption grew much more strongly from 2000 to 2007. Growth in 2004 was the highest in 20 years and it lasted from 2005 to 2008. Strong worldwide economic expansion, the runaway growth of China and to a lesser extent India, plus sustained demand in the US (until 2008), were all responsible for this increase. Most of the additional energy demand was met by coal. China commissioned a new coal-fired power plant every week. Total electricity production in China was 6143 Twh in 2016 compared with 3287 Twh in 2007, an increase in 9 years of 9 times the total electricity production in the UK. The increase in the demand for coal is spectacular, but total demand for energy, including oil and gas, is increasing.

The economic crisis of 2008 led to a significant reduction in the rate growth in world energy demand in 2008 and to a decrease in consumption in 2009. Since 2010 energy consumption worldwide is increasing by

1-2 per cent per year. There is an increase in the demand for oil, gas and renewable. The demand for coal and nuclear is stagnant.

DETERMINANTS OF ENERGY DEMAND

- **Wealth**

Wealth is the determining factor for energy consumption. On an average, each citizen of the United States has an annual income of \$55,000 (per capita GDP). This income is 40 times higher than that for a citizen of Senegal (roughly \$1,000 per year). An American's annual energy consumption (more than 7 tons of oil equivalent) is about 40 times greater than that of a Senegalese citizen (slightly more than 200 kilos of oil equivalent, not including biomass) (Fig. 13).

Energy consumption increases very quickly with income when the latter is low or moderate for as long as industrialisation in the country is growing. Then, when services play a greater role in the economy, energy consumption increases more slowly than income. Thus, in developed countries, the ratio between growth in electricity demand and economic growth is roughly 0.6, while this ratio is greater than one for developing countries.

For high income levels, energy consumption increases very slowly since household use of appliances is close to saturation. Thus, the number of

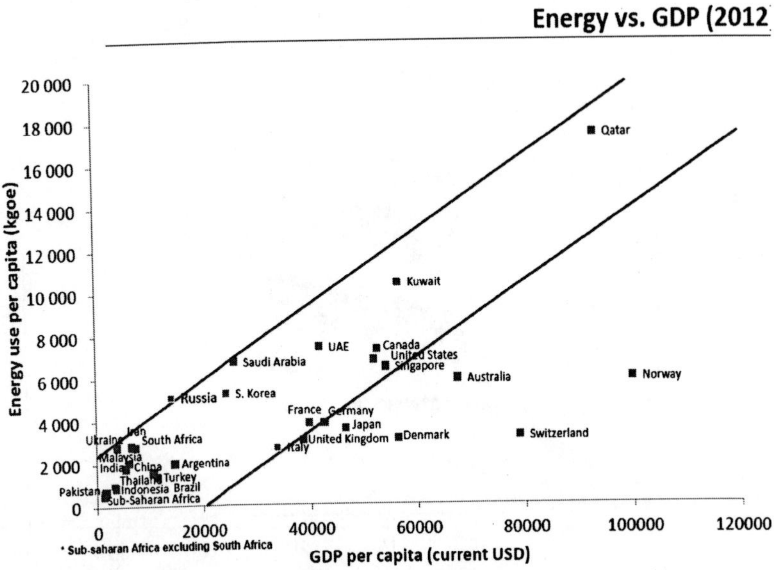

Source: *World Bank and IFP Training.*

Figure 13: Commercial Energy Consumption and Income – 2012.

automobiles stabilises at one or two cars for every two inhabitants, and the number of heating devices and home appliances per household no longer increases in the wealthiest countries. Finally, growth in energy consumption simply follows the very slow rate of population growth (Fig. 14).

Nevertheless energy is indispensible for economic development. If the relationship between energy consumption and wealth is analysed, several groups of countries can be identified. First there are major non-OECD oil producing countries (the Middle East and Russia), whose energy consumption is very high in relation to their level of income; they consume large quantities because energy is cheap. Secondly, energy-rich OECD countries (US, Canada, Norway, Australia and Finland) whose per capita income is much higher than that of the previous group and whose per capita consumption is relatively high; their consumption grew in part because their oil, gas, coal or hydroelectricity resources were abundant and made it unnecessary for them to try to optimise their energy consumption. The third group comprises the major European countries and Japan, mostly lacking in energy reserves and who, despite high per capita income, limit their energy consumption in order to reduce imports. Finally there are, as already mentioned, the world's poorest countries, where per capita commercial energy consumption (excluding wood) is extremely low, which slows the country's economic development.

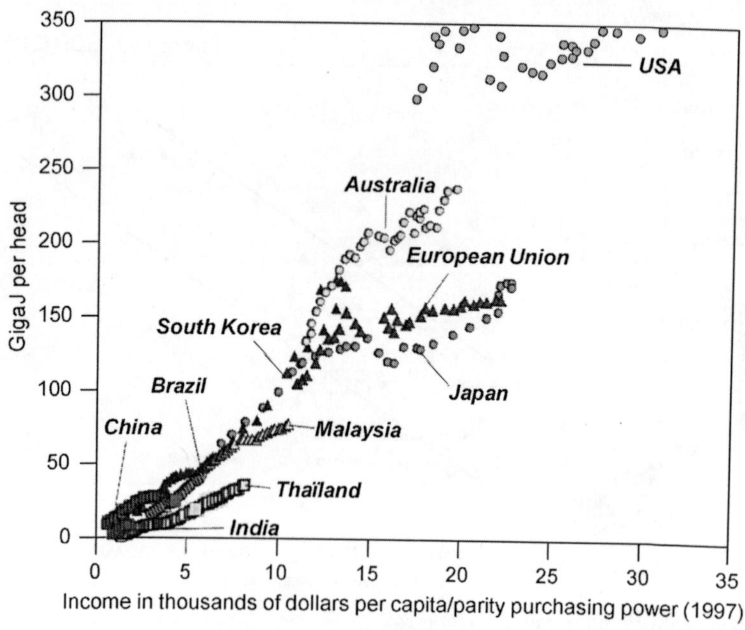

Figure 14: Per Capita Energy Consumption Levels as a Function of Wealth.

In addition to the factors listed above, there are other issues that influence countries' energy consumption:

- Climate has a direct effect on the use of lighting, heating and air conditioning.
- Geography and land use planning affect both the transport network and energy-consuming facilities such as water desalination plants.
- Industrial and energy production, e.g. the production of unconventional crude oil, mining or shipbuilding consume large amounts of energy.
- Cultural factors affect energy consumption, as can be seen from the differences in consumption between Northern Europe and the US or Australia (Fig. 15).

- **Price**

The analysis is simple: the higher the price, the less the user consumes (all other things being equal). Rapid price increases have the effect of slowing consumption. Between 2003 and 2008, oil price increases seemed to have no major effect on consumption. However, consumption did finally decrease—strongly in industrialised countries and more modestly in emerging countries—which led to the fall in prices during the second half of 2008.

ENERGY PRICING

Energy includes oil, natural gas, coal, nuclear, hydroelectricity, wood, etc. So can there really be such a thing as the price of energy? Yes, because all types of energy are needed to meet world demand and one form can often be substituted for another: to produce electricity, we can use coal, oil, gas or of course nuclear or hydraulic energy or wind turbines. And where there is competition between energies, their prices are linked.

A characteristic of most parts of the energy industry is its high capital intensity, very large investments are needed for production: millions or even billions of dollars are required to put an oil or natural gas field into production, develop a coal mine, and build a nuclear power plant or a dam. Once the investment is made, the capital invested must be remunerated so production needs to be at maximum capacity. Otherwise the unit average costs will increase. However, in a highly competitive situation with surplus capacity and low marginal production costs, there is a risk that unit revenue will decrease because operators will tend to sell at low prices, almost down to their marginal costs.

The petroleum industry presents particular characteristics. The size and the location of deposits in the Middle East are such that the production costs are only a few dollars per barrel. In addition, because oil is liquid it can be

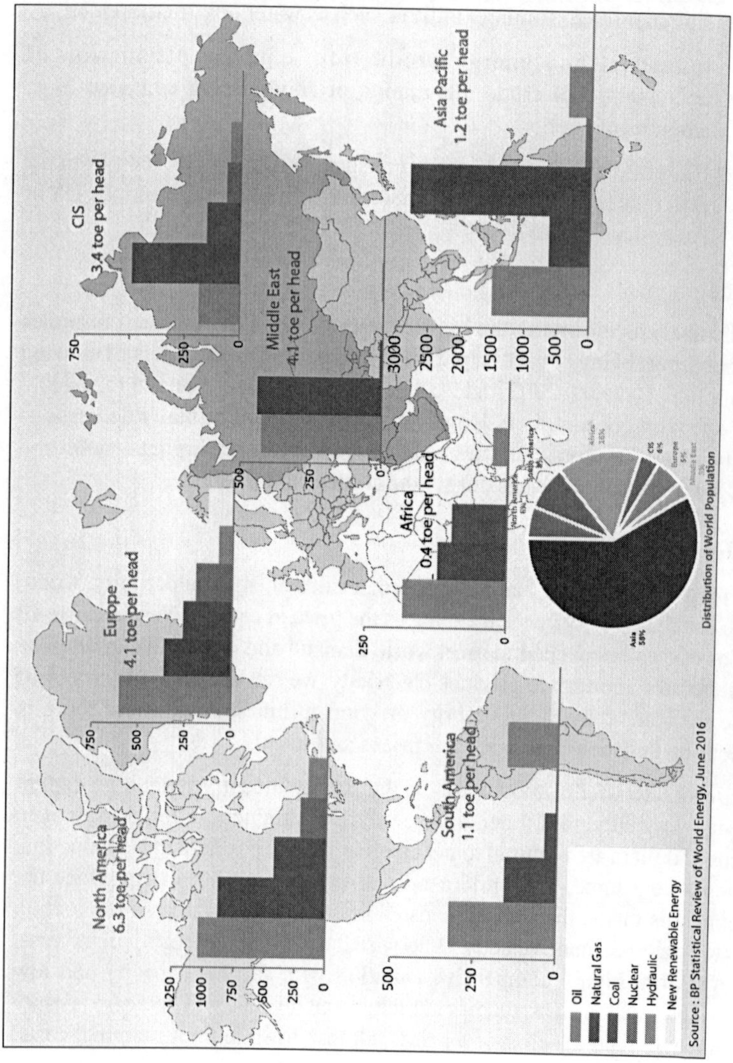

Figure 15: World Primary Energy Consumption in 2015 (Mtoe).

transported inexpensively, even over long distances. Consequently, Middle East oil is undoubtedly the world's least expensive energy source, even though—paradoxically—it is currently not the most intensively used, mainly for geopolitical reasons (see note 7).

This means that there are two distinct components of world energy supply:

- The supply of energy other than oil, and petroleum production outside of OPEC. This component has high production costs.
- OPEC oil supply, and particularly Middle East oil supply, which is characterised by far lower costs.

The situation of the oil industry has been changed for several years by the development of the Light Tight Oil (shale oil) production. The LTO production increased from a few hundred thousand barrels per day in 2010 to more than five Mb/d at the beginning of 2015. The market was then oversupplied and the price of oil collapsed. This will be discussed in the next pages.

Capital costs are an important element of the cost of non-OPEC energy. Once such energy sources have been developed, it is better to use the production facilities at maximum capacity, since capital remuneration represents most of the cost. The adjustment of supply to demand is consequently undertaken by the OPEC countries, which means that they are the price setters, i.e. they determine the price of oil and therefore of other energy sources too[1] (Fig. 16).

This is why the price of oil is dominant in the energy market and why it has always fluctuated.

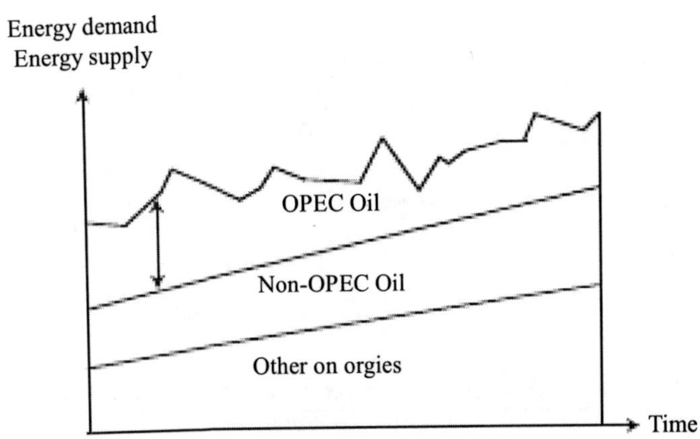

Figure 16: OPEC in Overall Energy Supply.

- **The Historical Development of Oil Prices up to 2000**

Between 1859, the date Colonel Drake drilled the first oil well, and 1960, the year that OPEC was formed, the price of oil was controlled by the major oil companies. There was, initially, a certain level of anarchy since there were numerous producers and the price moved according to supply and demand. When major discoveries had been made, prices collapsed and they climbed again when demand rose. In 1928, the main companies agreed to limit competition and stabilise prices (the Achnacarry Agreement) and, until 1960, it was the majors—or the "Seven Sisters"[2]—who controlled the oil market.

After 1950, the oil industry changed its nature and its scale, following the major discoveries made in the Middle East between 1930 and 1950. These deposits were controlled by the majors, who took advantage of this abundant and low cost resource to establish a dominant position in the major markets of America, Europe and Asia. This massive penetration into new markets was achieved at the same time that the price of crude oil fell from $3 to $2 per barrel.

From 1960 to 1985, the oil-producing countries played a dominant role. On September 14, 1960 in Bagdad, five producing countries—Venezuela, Saudi Arabia, Iran, Iraq and Kuwait—created the Organisation of Petroleum Exporting Countries–OPEC, to fight against the decrease in prices and the reduction in their revenues per barrel[3]. OPEC's objective was to stabilise the price of crude oil; this objective was achieved and the price remained stable from 1960 to 1970, (the price of Arab Light crude, which was used as

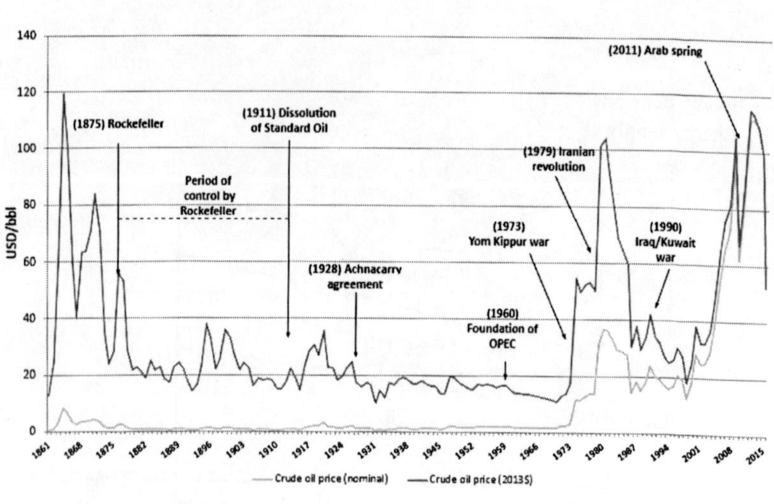

Source: BP Statistical Review

Figure 17: Crude Oil Prices (Annual Average) from 1861 to 2016.

the price reference within OPEC, was $1.80 per barrel[4] ($/bbl)–equivalent to $20 in 2010 prices (Fig. 17 and 18)).

From 1970, both the political and the economic situation changed. The political change was the growing strength of third-world countries, including the oil-exporting states. The economic change was the world's fear of a shortage of crude oil. Reserves were seen as limited because of the high growth in consumption, which had more than doubled between 1960 and 1970, bringing proved reserves down to roughly 30 years of annual consumption. There was a general fear among experts that the strong growth of the post-war boom years could result in the exhaustion of raw materials. The Club of Rome report, "Limits to Growth", published in 1972, recommended an economic slowdown to conserve natural resources. This was the start of the environmental and the "sustainable development" movements.

Then two political crises resulted in substantial increases in the oil price. In 1973, during the Yom Kippur war between Israel and the Arab nations, the posted price rose from $3 to $5 in October (this was the first time that the producing states had unilaterally changed the posted price), then to $11.65 per barrel on January 1st 1974, although the actual selling price was then $7 or $8. A few years later, in 1979–1981, the Iranian crisis, with the departure of the Shah of Iran and the arrival of Ayatollah Khomeini in power, led to an even higher increase in the oil price, which reached $35 per barrel. The other fundamental event of the 1970s was that most major producing countries (particularly the Gulf countries) nationalised their oil fields.

But the ten-fold increase in the price of oil resulted in a fall in consumption of nearly 15 per cent between the end of the 1970s and the mid–1980s. At the same time, new production encouraged by the increase in prices was being developed in the North Sea and Alaska. Lower prices quickly became inevitable.

OPEC initially reacted to the lower prices by instituting production quotas. Each country was allocated a production ceiling, which was gradually reduced to prevent the market collapsing. In 1985, the official price remained at $25 per barrel. But this level was only maintained thanks to a decrease in OPEC production of nearly 50 per cent between 1979 (30 million barrels per day – Mb/d) and 1985 (15 Mb/d). The situation was particularly serious for Saudi Arabia, which acted as the swing producer and whose production decreased by nearly 70 per cent. To regain market share, Saudi Arabia effectively started a price war by introducing netback contracts[5]. Their sales started to climb, but the price of oil collapsed from $25 per barrel in January 1986 to less than $10 six months later.

From 1986, new players (new producing countries, independent companies, traders and financial institutions) captured much of the oil market

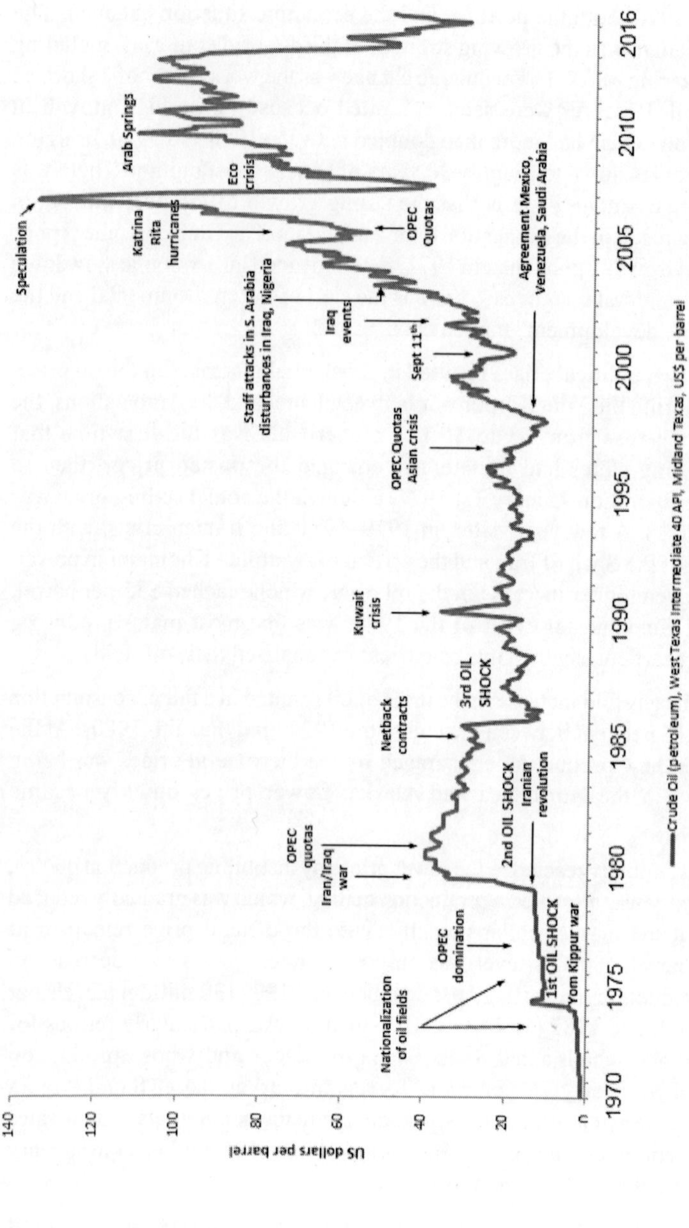

Figure 18: Crude Oil Prices 1970-2016.

Source: IMF.

from both the majors and OPEC. The oil price that resulted was relatively low (about $18 per barrel) but increasingly volatile. In general between 1986 and 1999 the price of oil stayed at a moderate level, but there were important exceptions. These included the price hikes that resulted from Iraq's invasion of Kuwait in 1990 and the very cold winter of 1997, so the price of oil swung from scarcely $10 per barrel in 1986 and 1988, to more than $30 during the Gulf War and winter of 1997. A key element in the price setting mechanism was inventory levels. If stock levels went up, fear of overproduction meant that prices fell. If inventory levels fell, operators feared shortages and prices rose. This became a more important influence on prices than the availability of crude oil or the growth in demand for oil products.

In 1998, the price of oil fell once more to $10/bbl. There were several reasons for that. OPEC had substantially increased its production quotas end of 1997. At the same time the Asian economic crisis hit Thailand and South Korea, both major oil consumers. There was considerable conflict between OPEC member countries; Middle East countries criticised Venezuela for its policy of increasing production at any cost, regardless of their quota. Rivalry between Iran and Saudi Arabia also weakened the organisation. OPEC's lack of unity meant that the decision they took in 1998 to reduce production lacked credibility.

- **Crude Oil Prices, Recent Developments, 2000-2014 (Fig. 19)**

Over the period, 1999 to 2003 OPEC's unity was re-established. A price of $10/bbl was a catastrophe for the oil-producing countries and it meant that they could no longer meet their financial needs. OPEC countries' debt was growing. A return to discipline among the OPEC countries was needed to increase prices. How could it be achieved?

The election of Hugo Chavez as President of Venezuela at the end of 1998 was the first sign of change. While the previous government had favoured maximising production, the new President favoured a policy of solidarity with third-world countries in general and with other oil-producing countries in particular. Aware of the importance of increasing oil prices, he argued for an agreement between Venezuela, Saudi Arabia and Mexico (a non-OPEC country) to limit production. This agreement would be strengthened by a strong improvement in relations between Saudi Arabia and Iran, the main Gulf producing-countries.

The commitments to reduce OPEC production, supported by clear signs of solidarity from the main non-OPEC producers, finally appeared credible to operators. In March 1999, the price of oil started an upward trend that would lead it to a peak level in 2000. The OPEC countries then decided to set an objective for the average price of a basket of crude oil of $25 per barrel, and a range of $22–$28 within which the price should remain: if the price went

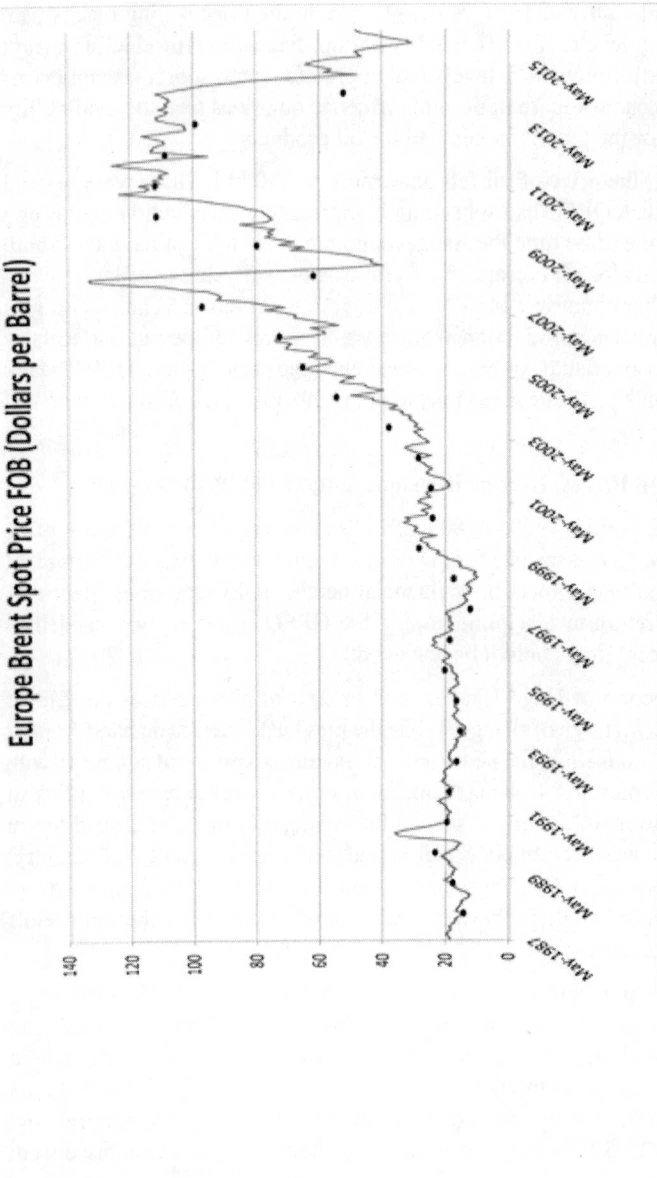

Source: US doe/eia, BP Statistical Review.

Figure 19: Brent Oil Spot fob Price – Recent evolution.

above \$28, production would be increased by 0.5 Mb/d, and if the price fell below \$22, production would be decreased by 0.5 Mb/d. This objective was largely achieved: during the first six months of 2001, the price of a barrel (OPEC basket) was \$21.

The terrorist attacks of September 11, 2001—destruction of the two World Trade Towers in New York by planes hijacked by terrorists linked to Al Qaida—caused a collapse in prices, with Americans greatly reducing their personal travel. But prices gradually recovered. Until 2003, \$25/bbl was generally agreed to be the "normal" price of crude oil, and this was OPEC's objective. But the threat of American intervention in Iraq caused uncertainty in the market and the addition of a "risk premium", which different experts estimated at \$5, \$10 or \$15/bbl. This theory was confirmed by the fall in the price of oil on March 20, 2003, the day on which President George W. Bush announced that the US rejected Saddam Hussein's response to the US ultimatum, and that the US-led coalition would attack Iraq. In London, the price of Brent crude fell from \$35 to \$25. Operators were not worried about the immediate consequences of the US action. Surplus capacity from countries neighbouring Iraq (Saudi Arabia, UAE, etc.) meant that lost Iraqi production could be made up and it was considered that, with surplus production capacity at 5 to 10 per cent of total capacity, there would be a return to "normal" market supply within a few months. It was also expected that investment in Iraq would once again become possible (plans were made to raise production capacity from 3 to 6 Mb/d), so a return to "normal" oil prices therefore seemed probable.

The Role of OPEC

Although supply and demand has had a basic role in the oil price setting mechanism since 1986, at least until 2003 it was OPEC's position that was decisive. Without OPEC, oil prices would have been much lower—probably of the order of \$10 to \$15 per barrel—over the period 1986–2003.

However, in periods of significant potential oversupply, OPEC cannot and does not wish to assume the sole responsibility for supporting prices. Thus, in 2001, OPEC reduced its production by 5 million barrels per day, i.e. by nearly 20 per cent, to prevent a sudden price fall. But, at the end of 2001, the organisation was faced with a dilemma: it could reduce its production further and see its market share decline dramatically and non-OPEC producers profit from higher prices without participating in the loss of production, or maintain its export volume and inevitably experience a fall in the crude oil price. In fact, at the start of 2002, the major non-OPEC producers (Mexico, Norway, and most importantly Russia) joined OPEC in their efforts to maintain prices.

(Cont'd...)

In the autumn of 2006, with the commissioning of new production capacity, a quiet political situation and mild weather, a tighter quota policy once again made sense. OPEC instigated massive production cuts in reaction to prices collapsing by a third, which stopped the decrease in prices and restored the organisation's credibility.

At the end of 2008, the worldwide recession and a further collapse in oil prices once again made the cartel's pricing policy a central issue. OPEC decided to reduce its quotas by 4 Mb/d over several stages, starting in September. It also tried to persuade other producing countries (Russia, Mexico, Norway, etc.) to join in. Russia agreed to a symbolic reduction since, during winter, Russian exports are reduced anyway because weather conditions limit tanker loading at the Novorossiysk and Primorsk terminals.

The collapse of prices in 2014 is clearly linked to a modification of the position of OPEC. To face the large excess of oil in the market, a consequence of the rapid development of the LTO (shale oil) production in the US but also of the increasing production of countries like Iraq and Iran (after 2015), OPEC could have, as usual decided to reduce its production. But the organisation refused to do so and at the OPEC meeting of November 27, 2014 Saudi Arabia, by far the leading country, decided to keep its production at the current level and announced it would defend its market share. Why reduce the production of countries with very low production costs (less than 20, sometimes $10/bbl just to allow high costs (typically the LTO – shale oil) productions to develop? The position of OPEC changed in 2017 and the organisation decided to limit production to increase the price.

Although countries like Brazil and Kazakhstan have envisaged joining, there are no guarantees that a larger OPEC could maintain its unity. Would Brazil with its biofuels really be welcome within the cartel? Would the complexity of relationships between the states surrounding the Caspian Sea allow countries such as Kazakhstan or Azerbaijan to join the cartel, without adversely affecting OPEC's relationship with Russia? Would Russia be ready to compromise its foreign policy goals, particularly with respect to Iran, by participating in OPEC? Given their relations with Europe and the US, is it conceivable that Norway and Mexico could join OPEC? Wouldn't the integration of Sudan within OPEC carry the risk of dragging the organisation into regional African conflicts? A more reasonable solution to any fall in demand seems to be OPEC working with "associate" members.

From March 20, 2003 to July 11, 2008, pressure on the market grew. After the fall of March 20, 2003, the price of oil quickly started to increase again, reaching $60 per barrel in 2005 and $75 in May 2006. After a decrease in the last months of 2006, it shot from $50 per barrel in January 2007 to $147 per barrel (Brent price) on July 11, 2008. There were many reasons for this. The situation in Iraq and the Middle East was not as had been expected. Iraqi production remained far below its level under Saddam Hussein. Attacks in Saudi Arabia were worrying. Some countries could not stop their production declining. Oil consumption rose strongly while the surplus production capacity that had resulted from the fall in demand and increased non-OPEC production after the second oil shock had disappeared. There was no shortage of oil in the markets, but the balance of supply and demand was precarious. Costs, particularly capital costs, were rising steeply. Arguments regarding levels of oil reserves added to the concern. These arguments were misdirected since the immediate problem was not the reserves underground, these were still sufficient for many years. It was rather above the ground, particularly the lack of sufficient capital investment for geopolitical reasons: producing countries were reluctant to invest massively to produce more oil for a market that did not seem guaranteed. Why invest to supply Western consuming countries who wanted to reduce their oil consumption because of their supply security concerns and to reduce greenhouse gas emissions? There was great concern about forecasts of an oil production ceiling of 95–100 Mb/d, while the needs of China and other emerging countries seemed unlimited. The market was desperately trying to balance future supply and demand.

Many specialists did not understand why the price increases did not reduce the increase in demand. The explanation is simple, the income effect—when revenues double, gasoline consumption increases by 70 per cent, is more important than the price effect—when prices increase by 100 per cent, gasoline consumption only decreases by seven per cent. Economic growth was extremely strong (four per cent per year from 2003 to 2007), while the fuel price increases seen by consumers were "tempered" by the significance of taxes in consuming countries and by price controls in emerging countries.

A comment should be made on the impact of speculation. When it seems probable that economic growth will continue and the needs of emerging countries will rapidly increase, e.g. automobiles in China, an increase in oil prices appears inevitable. Commercial "funds" will therefore invest in oil and other raw materials, thinking that prices will continue to increase. They of course make the trend in price increases more pronounced.

There was a fall in demand and collapse in prices from $147/barrel on July 11, 2008 to $40 at the end of 2008. Economic growth tumbled while oil production remained strong. Even the conflict in Georgia in August 2008 failed to slow the fall (however, the Russians bombed both sides of the Baku-Tbilisi-Ceyhan pipeline, the only outlet route outside the control of Moscow, to show that if they wished, they could stop exports from the Caspian).

The fact that oil was abundant and consumption was stagnant or even declining, was finally recognised. OPEC reduced its production quotas by 0.5 Mb/d in September, 1.5 in October, and 2 in December. This stabilised prices in the $40–$50 range. Investment funds withdrew from the oil markets (and those for other raw materials) en masse. This seemed logical considering the price forecasts, but only strengthened the trend to lower prices.

The fall in prices from $147 to less than $40 between July and December 2008 was in every respect similar to what occurred in 1986 at the time of the oil counter shock, when Saudi Arabia launched a price war to recover market share and prices fell from $28 to $8 between January and July. The reasons in both cases were the same: an oversupply of crude oil. The market forgets long-term considerations (anticipation of increasing and strong demand confronting limited future production) and focuses on short-term fundamentals.

In mid-2009 prices rose to $70 per barrel, close to the $75/barrel considered to be the "right price" by the King of Saudi Arabia and that needed to ensure the production of marginal supplies, i.e. for instance synthetic oil from Canadian oil sands. The price of oil continued to increase up to $ 120 $/b at the beginning of 2011. Then the price remained between $100 and 120 $/b up to 2014, as a supposed consequence of the "Arab Spring". The largest producing countries in the Gulf were not affected by the Arab Spring but a kind of "geopolitical risk" threatened these countries.

2014—The Collapse of Prices—The Impact of Light Tight Oil Production.

Mid June 2014, the Islamic State (now commonly called Daech) attacked Iraq and came close to 40 kilometers of Bagdad, threatening to take control of several Iraqi fields. The price of the barrel of oil spiked and increased by several dollars. However, quickly Daech withdrew by a few kilometers and the threat disappeared. And all of a sudden, the market discovered that there was a potential oversupply of oil in the world, especially in the US: the production of shale oil (Light Tight Oil) has increased from a few hundred thousand barrels a day to more than four million barrels a day in 2014, while the production of the other countries remained fair. The potential situation of oil oversupply was not new but had been hidden by the threat of geopolitical events provoking the collapse of the production in some major producing countries. The price of oil started to decrease rapidly. No decision was taken by OPEC, whose production continued unchanged, up to the traditional meeting of November 27 in Vienna. Saudi Arabia, by far the most important producer and the most influential country of the organisation declared that Saudi Arabia—and OPEC—wanted to keep their market share, that they did not want to reduce their low cost production just to allow high cost production to develop. (As already mentioned, production costs in OPEC countries, especially in Saudi Arabia are less than 10 dollars per barrel, while they are, although quite variable, more than 40 in the US).

The future of oil prices is not easy to forecast: the increase in the demand and the decrease to come in the oil production outside the US and OPEC because of much reduced investments (from more than 700 billion dollars in 2014 to less than 400 in 2016) should progressively rebalance supply and demand. But this could be slow. Probably prices will increase again in the next years but will not come back to the 100 dollars per barrel—considered a threshold a few years ago—before many years.

In summary therefore, the price of oil is mainly determined by the balance of supply and demand. "Speculative" movements only support underlying trends. Other factors—stock levels of crude oil and products, as well as geopolitical events—can play a determining role.

- **How Do Oil Prices Affect Demand?**

Oil prices of course play an important role in the economic activity. When the price of oil was 100$/b a few years ago, the value of oil traded internationally was more than $3 trillions. Today, assuming a 50 $/b this value is still $1.5 trillion or half the German GDP. This is significant, but small when compared with 2007–2009 stock market "losses" amounting to $25 trillion, or the amounts available in investment funds (these funds include in particular the pension funds which receive contributions from American employees to fund their retirement), which amount to tens of trillions of dollars.

Variations in the price of oil result in a significant shift of resources from producing countries to consuming countries.

Impact of prices for the major consuming countries: When the price of oil fell from about $100 in 2008 ($97 to be precise) to 60 in 2009, France's oil bill fell from roughly $70 to $40 billion p.a. This decrease represented more than one per cent of the GDP. The gas bill was also lower because gas prices are still linked to the price of oil.

The impact on inflation is also significant. The increase in oil prices was of great concern to European authorities since it brought inflation to a level of nearly three per cent in the year 2000. While this was still reasonable compared to the level of the 1970s (more than 10 per cent), it was far above than the inflation in recent years. The decrease in the price of oil—and of many raw materials—has decreased inflation to a level of nearly zero.

Impact of prices for poor countries: Although emerging countries found it relatively easy to tolerate a significantly higher energy bill, the same was not true for less advanced countries for which the increase in prices was stifling. Their oil bill, for example, in West African countries, frequently exceeded 10 per cent of the GDP, a level far greater than the few percentage points of GDP covered by governmental and privately funded aid. The bill remains high but more acceptable with current prices.

Impact of prices for producing countries: A high price is desirable for producing countries, since most depend almost exclusively on their oil and gas revenues to balance their budgets, and the minimum oil price needed to achieve this varies considerably from one country to another. The necessary oil price is relatively low for the Gulf countries with a limited population. These countries have accumulated significant financial reserves and their sovereign funds have hundreds of billions of dollars. $50 or $60 is sufficient for the UAE, Kuwait or Qatar (not taking into account the gas exports of Qatar). It is much higher for countries with a higher population. Saudi Arabia can make for a limited time for the low oil price because of the large financial reserves. But many countries need $100 to balance their budget. The worst situation is probably the situation of Venezuela. Russia also depends significantly on its exports of oil and gas. The fall in the value of the ruble at the beginning of 2009 reflected the importance of oil for Russia. Today, another loss of value of the ruble has allowed reduction in production costs to mitigate the impact of reduced prices.

Although the two oil shocks of 1973 and 1979 resulted in demand falling by 15 per cent, the increase in the price of a barrel from $10 to more than $100 between 1999 and 2008 had effects on demand that were slower and more limited. Several explanations for this have been advanced:

- The weight of oil in the economy is less than it was 20 years ago and so the importance of the energy bill is also less. France spent nearly six per cent of its GDP on its oil at the beginning of the 1980s but only one per cent in 2016 after four per cent in 2008. More efficient use of oil, and an increase in the service sector's share in the economy (services consume little energy) explain this. However, although oil has less weight in developed economies, it remains very significant for the poorest developing countries: in 2007 Senegal spent more than 8 per cent of its GDP to purchase the oil it needed (four per cent in 2015).
- The proportion of taxes in the price of gasoline and diesel fuel lessens the impact of crude oil price variations. Generally in France (as in many European countries), if the price of crude oil quadruples from $25 to $100 per barrel, the price of fuel at a service station only increases by € 0.50 per liter, which is 30 per cent of the consumer price.
- The price of a liter of gasoline represented half an hour's earnings at the French minimum wage in 1981, but less than 15 minutes in 2015.

- **High Oil Prices—How Do They Affect Supply?**

Non-OPEC production seems to be reaching its ceiling in many countries except for the CIS (in both Russia and countries of the Caspian region—

Kazakhstan and Azerbaijan in particular), West Africa and Latin America (Brazil). Only OPEC countries—and in particular the countries of the Middle East—seem to be able to increase their production significantly. Saudi Arabia is the only country with a fair excess capacity (around 2 million barrels per day), and has an actual production capacity of more than 12 Mb/d. This excess capacity is a political decision of the Saudi government which wants Saudi Arabia to be able to replace the exports of the second largest exporting country in case an event prevents this second country to export.

What is the "Right Price" for Oil?

While it is difficult to answer this question, there are several possible benchmarks that can be considered:

– Production costs (excluding costs of capital) are less than about \$10/barrel in the Middle East, and \$15 to \$20 in other producing countries. However, they are \$60 or more for the highest cost oil from difficult zones of the North Sea and synthetic oil obtained from the very heavy crude oil of Orinoco or oil sands (also called tar sands or crude bitumen) from Athabasca. Production costs of Light Tight Oil (LTO) are very dependent upon the production area (Eagle Ford, Permian, North Dakota…) and are also quite variable within the same production area. They are probably between 40 and 70 dollars per barrel. Anyway, LTO production costs put a "ceiling" on the oil price since as soon as the price reaches 50 dollars, LTO production starts to increase again.

– Most oil-producing countries who are members of OPEC depend on oil for 80 per cent to 90 per cent of their national revenue. Until roughly 2005, they prepared their budgets assuming an oil price of \$20–\$25/bbl. For example, Algeria used \$19/bbl for many years. Any revenue from higher prices was then used for exceptional expenditure (debt repayment, new equipment projects, etc.). This situation has changed and many producing countries now "need" a much higher price to balance their budgets. The price "needed" varies considerably from one producing country to another, but often exceeds \$50/bbl .

It should be noted that, if oil price increased up to 147 dollars per barrel in 2008, this was also a consequence of the huge increase in production costs which had increased by a factor of 2 or 3. De facto, between 2003 and 2008 all costs increased everywhere (cement, steel, manpower) including the oil industry. The collapse of oil prices from 2014 has obliged both the oil companies and the service companies to drastically reduce their costs and many international oil companies have posted objectives to be profitable with a \$60/bbl price of oil or less.

– *Who will make the necessary investments in exploration and production?*

The five largest international oil companies (Exxon Mobil, Shell, BP, Chevron and Total) have jointly earned more than $110 billion in profits every year from 2005 until 2013 except in 2009 (total fell to under $70 billion). Over the total period some of these profits were used to reduce their debt, which became very low, and to reward shareholders.

Today the situation of the IOC is of course more complex. They must continue to distribute fair dividends to keep their shareholders and of course to invest in new production projects to compensate the depletion of their fields. However, the most promising basins are often not accessible to major international companies. OPEC member countries control 80 per cent of reserves, and they are the lowest cost reserves to exploit. Since the nationalisations of the 1970s, and notwithstanding the few exceptions which are discussed later, most OPEC countries have no intention to re-open their oil and gas industries to major international companies. Saudi Arabia and Kuwait are completely closed. Outside the Middle East, Venezuela has only opened marginal fields and reserves of extra-heavy crude oil to foreign companies. Outside OPEC, Russia has shown that it wishes to keep tight control over its reserves.

The situation is slowly changing in Mexico where the energy business, totally closed to foreign companies, has been reopened after long discussions. In Iran, the lifting of the sanctions after the agreement between Iranian Authorities and the 5+1 group (US, Russia, China, France, UK—the permanent members of the UN Security Council plus Germany) should allow the foreign companies to participate in oil exploration and production. However, the design of the new contracts, which have to be voted by the parliament takes very long since it is very difficult for representatives to accept to "abandon" part of the nation wealth to foreign companies. Moreover some risks of reinstallation of the sanctions could also slow the process of opening.

Let us recall here that producing states adapt oil taxation levels when oil prices vary to leave the foreign companies' portion broadly constant (in dollars per barrel). This policy is consistent with a dominating political approach which sees mineral resources as an asset belonging to the nation and its people whose benefits (and sometimes the exploitation—see the case of Mexico in particular) must be reserved for nationals.

State-owned companies (Saudi Aramco—Saudi Arabia, NIOC—Iran, PDVSA—Venezuela, Pemex—Mexico, Sonatrach—Algeria, NNPC—Nigeria, etc.) get only part of the revenues from crude oil sales. Their government only returns a portion of the oil revenues to them and retains the rest to finance

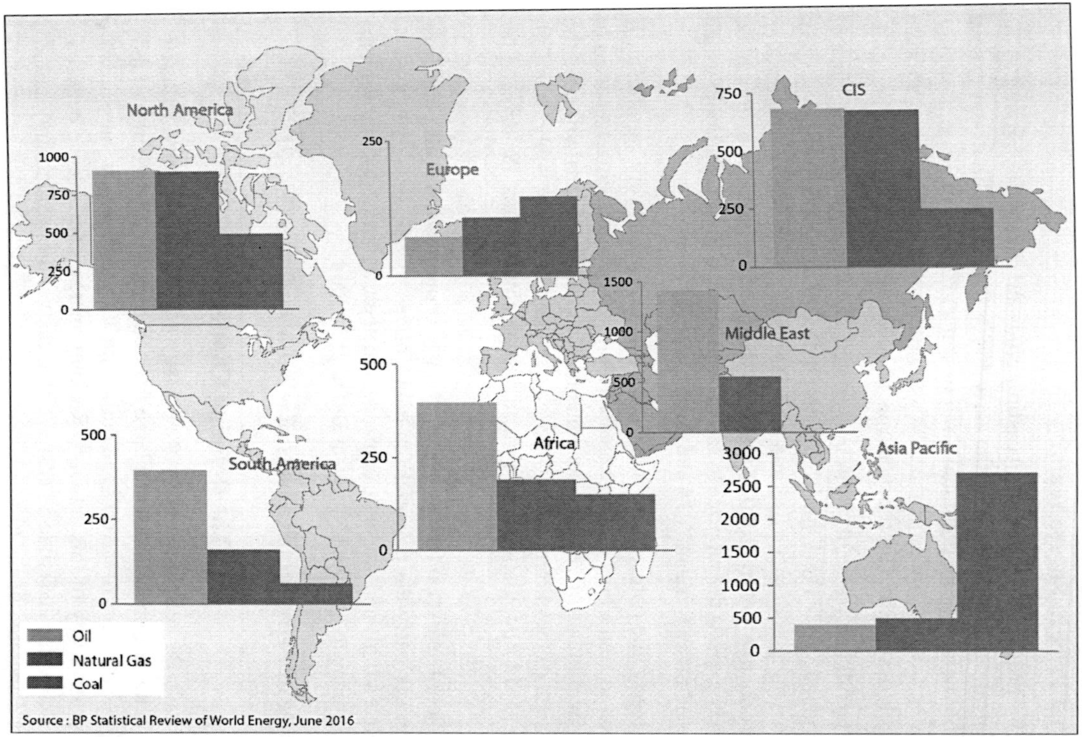

Figure 20: World 2015 Primary Energy Production (Mtoe).

their budgets. In many cases the amounts left for the national oil companies have been insufficient for them to maintain and develop their oil production capacities. This is certainly the case in Venezuela and from time to time in Mexico, Nigeria or Algeria.

- **What Price in Future Years?**

The process of experts forecasting crude oil prices has proved to be self-defeating. The forecast in the early 1980s that the price would exceed \$100/bbl before 2000, promoted a fall in demand and an increase in supply. Similarly, the low prices of the 1990s discouraged investment and so were indirectly responsible for the increases of 2003–2008.

The fall in price in 2014 was unexpected. It is clearly the consequence of the production of LTO (Light Tight Oil–Shale Oil) in the US. Nobody, except a limited number of specialists and the LTO producers themselves believed in this production before 2010. I wrote in the previous version of this book "Nobody expects the oil price to fall back to levels of below \$60/bbl" which happened many times in 2015 and 2016.

Clearly, the potential for increased demand remains very significant. If we want to "put China on four wheels", i.e. allow Chinese citizens access to the same number of vehicles per inhabitant as the US, China will need the equivalent of the current worldwide consumption of oil, for "only" one-fifth of the world's population. But climate change could reduce the demand for oil.

The oil market remains subject to basic economic laws: all periods of high prices carry the potential for future prices to fall, since they tend to stimulate supply and moderate demand. Nonetheless, future price movements will continue to be both significant and unpredictable.

- **Price of Petroleum Products: Ex-Refinery Prices** (Fig. 21)

The Refining Challenges

For long, the refining industry was mostly part of an integrated industry (up to the nationalisations of a large fraction of upstream activities of the majors at the end of the 60's and during the 70's, there was no measure of the profitability of this activity). Refining margins (difference between products value and crude oil cost, which measures the profitability) started to be calculated in the 70's.

(Cont'd...)

Historically, refining margins have been low and the profitability of refining was low due to persistent over capacities. The profitability improved by 2002–2007 due to near total saturation of world refining capacity.

Today the situation is better. However refining margins, calculated with market prices, never cover the full refining cost, which includes the financial depreciation. This financial depreciation is in the range of $10 per barrel of oil processed (the other costs are around $3) while refining margins are often around $5/bbl.

The reason for low margins is simple: excess capacities exist and there is a very strong competition between the refining companies. In Europe large capacities have been closed. New refineries were built, especially in the Middle East (Saudi Arabia built recently two large refineries, 400,000 b/d each in association with Total and Sinopec respectively). Large capacities were also built in Asia, to face the increasing demand. The largest refinery in the world is in India. This 1.2 Mb/d refinery (nearly the capacity of a European country) can export large volumes up to Africa where many refineries closed recently.

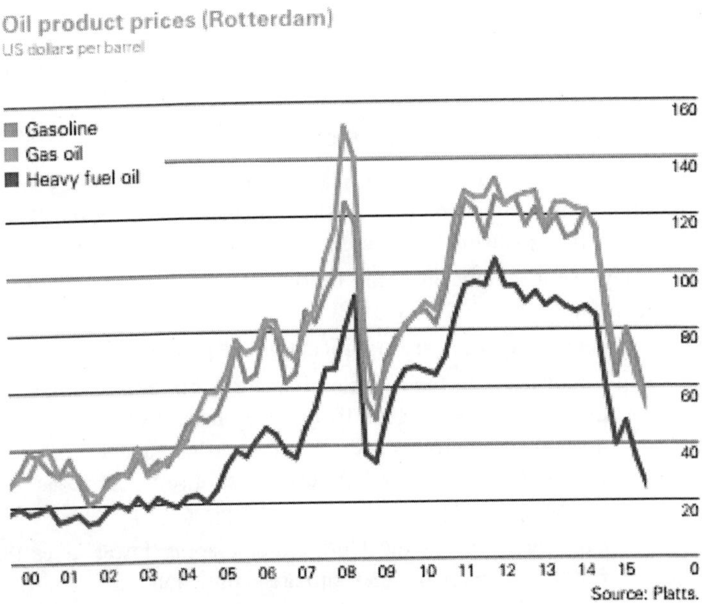

Source: Platt's (2016).

Figure 21: Rotterdam Spot Product Prices.

It is the prices of gasoline, diesel fuel, home heating oil, heavy fuel oil ... that are most important for consumers. These products are manufactured in oil refineries from crude oil. If a barrel of oil loaded onto a tanker in the Gulf costs in 2017, roughly $50, the cost of its transport to Europe, to Japan or even to the US, is only a few dollars (e.g. $3–$5) and its processing cost is of the same order of magnitude. The "composite" barrel of products (average value of products obtained from a barrel of crude oil) will therefore cost around $60. On average, crude oil represents 80 per cent of the value of the finished products.

The prices of petroleum fuels used for heating (liquefied petroleum gas, home heating oil and heavy fuel oil) are linked to those of competing energies. The price of heavy fuel oil partially depends on the price of coal or gas and the price of home heating oil is also linked to that of gas. On the other hand the price of motor fuels is not limited in that way since they do not currently compete with other products.

- **Pump Price–Taxes on Petroleum Products**

Globalisation of petroleum product markets has meant that, in much of the world, ex-refinery prices for gasoline or diesel fuel vary only by the transport differential. Even when transport costs are included, the difference is only a limited percentage.

The position of end consumer (i.e. pump in the case of motor fuels) prices is very different. They are based on these ex-refinery prices plus distribution costs and taxes.

Taxes on petroleum products vary considerably:

- They are generally low on heavy fuel oils whose prices are an important component of industrial manufacturing costs. Taxing heavy fuel oils would reduce industrial competitiveness.
- They are also low on home heating oil, an important item in a household's cost of living.
- On motor fuels they vary significantly. The practices used are:
  - Countries with high levels of imports, tax both gasoline and diesel fuel heavily, even though they may discount part of the taxes for taxi drivers and road transporters, again to maintain competitiveness. For other customers, in some countries taxes can be up to 70 per cent of the pump price.
  - Countries such as the United States apply lower taxes than Europe or Japan, but they still are significant.
  - Oil-exporting countries have abundant resources of fuel and up to recently sold it at a very low price, often lower than

> cost. They considered that oil belonged to the people and, as a resource available in the ground, it should not be expensive. In Venezuela and some Gulf countries, fuel was sold for a derisory sum. The Iranian Oil Minister once jokingly remarked that it would be preferable to give gasoline to automobile drivers for free, provided that they came to pick it up in the refineries thereby at least saving the distribution costs. However, prices in Iran have been strongly increased later to reduce consumption.

The very low prices practiced in major exporting countries encouraged excessive consumption, resulted in increased pollution and impoverished the country as they reduced the resources available for export. But even moderate increases in these prices sometimes led to protest movements or even riots with tragic consequences (in Venezuela in the 1990s, several hundred people died in riots following a decision to increase gasoline prices).

The situation changed recently. Most producing countries increased the prices and reduced subsidies. This was possible because of the lower price of oil. This was necessary to reduce the huge burden on the budget of the country created by the subsidies. On the other hand, the very high taxes on motor fuels in consuming countries are a major source of government revenue. In France, these taxes represent roughly 15 per cent of the nation's budget. This form of taxation is relatively painless and service stations are good tax collection agents. In addition, these taxes are supposed to take into account the outside effects (pollution) arising from the use of petroleum products.

- **Oil and Taxation**

The large taxes collected on oil products by some large consuming countries are a recurring subject of contention for producing countries, who criticise consuming countries for engine fuel taxes that they deem excessive, since these taxes slow consumption of a product vital for producing countries. To which the consuming countries reply that the distribution of tax levies between VAT, corporate taxes, income taxes, and taxes on petroleum products is an internal matter for them and they have the right to decide that as they wish.

Producing Countries: Oil Revenues and their Use

The oil revenues of producing countries are very significant. In 1980, OPEC countries' revenues amounted to \$260 billion, and in 2008 they were roughly \$1 trillion. Today they are close to \$500 billion. In most of these countries, revenues from oil (and gas in the case of Algeria, Qatar, Russia and Norway) represent most of the state's revenue.

(Cont'd...)

The use of this revenue varies depending on the country. Prior strong economic development and an established democratic tradition favour a "good" use of oil revenue. The classic example of that is Norway, which has created a fund for future generations and was wise enough to avoid the problems of "Dutch Disease".

What is Dutch Disease? When the natural gas deposit of Groningen, in Holland, was put into operation at the start of the 1960s, revenue from gas exports led to inflation (additional financial resources without simultaneous growth in production), increased wages and production costs, worsened the competitiveness of Dutch products and therefore destroyed some local businesses.

Similar phenomena have been observed throughout history. The conquest of Latin America by the Spanish filled their pockets with the continent's gold and silver. But the galleons filled with gold that brought wealth to privileged Spanish families did not bring economic development to the Spanish nation. On the contrary, it was the large Italian cities (Genoa and Venice), followed by the major ports of Northern Europe (Holland, Belgium, etc.), that became the drivers of the European renaissance.

Many oil-rich countries have problems in converting their subterranean wealth into a real development tool. Venezuela remains highly dependent on oil, despite having been a producer for a hundred years. With the fall in price, the situation of Venezuela is extremely difficult. The situation is similar in African countries. In Nigeria, oil revenues have destroyed part of the country's economic activity. For example, crop cultivation has been discouraged because oil wealth can easily be used to import food that could be produced locally. An extreme situation is that of Nigerian refineries, which are perfectly capable of producing at full capacity but in fact operate at very low levels since importing refined products provide the much sought after currency commissions. In Angola and the Congo, countries which have experienced brutal wars, oil money has made the situation worse because it has facilitated arms purchases.

In the Arabian Peninsula, oil money has completely transformed Saudi Arabia and its neighbours. It has paid for the development of major infrastructure (roads, water and electricity distribution networks, etc.) and the creation of health services, education etc. The various countries of the Gulf Cooperation Council are attempting to develop other activities to diversify their economies: these include developments in the gas sector such as Liquefied Natural Gas (LNG), or GTL (Gas To Liquids) fuels manufacture in Qatar, and development of the petrochemicals industry in Saudi Arabia.

(*Cont'd...*)

However, diversification away from hydrocarbons remains difficult even if in small countries (Dubai) services and commerce have become important.
In the case of the poorest countries, where government structures are the weakest, oil resources represent a very significant increase in wealth. Firm political will is needed in order to make the best use of these resources. In this regard, good examples include EITI (Extractive Industries Transparency Initiative) and Publish What You Pay initiatives, strongly promoted by NGOs with a strong presence in West Africa.

- **Price of Natural Gas** (Fig. 22)

Since gas and oil are closely related and, at least as far as their use in the residential and industrial sectors is concerned, substitutable products, the price of gas is—or was for long— linked to that of crude oil or petroleum products.

The reason is simple: when huge reserves of gas were discovered in the 50s in North Africa for instance, and when Algeria wanted to produce and sell the gas, European consumers through companies like Ruhrgas, Gaz de France or SNAM were very prepared to buy the gas. But the costs of production, transportation (from the center of Sahara to the coast of Algeria), liquefaction, transportation by ship (from the coast of Algeria to European ports) and regasification of the gas was simply huge and the investments could not be repaid quickly. So long term contracts had to be agreed upon between sellers and buyers. Sellers would commit to sell determined quantities of gas over 25 years or more and of course buyers would commit to take the gas. In order to make the price of gas competitive, it had to be linked to the price of energies in competition, heating oil and fuel oil. Some countries asked for premiums, underlying the cleanness of the product. But they did not succeed even if at some time the European Commission prohibited the use of gas for electricity generation, arguing it was a waste of a very privileged fuel. This prohibition was removed later.

The gas consumption developed very differently in the main markets. In the US, and in North America, there was always a large production of gas and gas was produced by a large number of—small or big—companies. So the price emerged from a gas to gas competition. In Europe, the market for natural gas developed in the 50's after the discoveries in Italy (Po Valley), France (Lacq), Netherlands (Groningen), but imports from North Algeria (later Russia and Norway) were quickly necessary. In Asia, the gas market developed first in Japan, then in South Korea and Taïwan and later in China, India. In both cases (Europe and Asia) imports were necessary and long term contracts were the solution to make these exports economical. Prices were linked to oil products prices.

Although the transport cost of crude oil is a low proportion of its price, this does not hold true for gas. So, for the present, there is no world market for gas, but rather three regional markets: one for North America, one for Europe and one for Northeast Asia.

For a long time, the price of gas in North America remained low since local production, augmented by imports from Canada, was sufficient to meet local needs. The price of gas then resulted from what was called "gas-gas" competition. However, there was a tight link between gas and petroleum products' prices, since, when the price of gas increased (as was the case in 2000 during the crisis in California), consumers switched to home heating oil. In addition, it was recently seen that some industries operating on natural gas simply cease operations when the price of gas becomes too high.

On the other hand, Europe has quickly become dependent on imports from Russia, Algeria, and more recently Norway. These imports required the construction of gas pipelines, liquefaction facilities, methane tankers and re-gasification units. To justify the high capital investment necessary it was essential for customers to have a contract for the purchase of gas over periods of as long as 20 years. But to do this, customers needed to ensure that the gas would remain competitive against home heating oil or heavy fuel oil. This led to the development of indexing formulas linking the price of gas to the price of competing petroleum products.

North Asia, particularly Japan, the world's leading importer, imports all its gas from Indonesia, Malaysia, Australia and the Middle East. Here again, formulas indexing the price of gas to that of petroleum products are necessary to ensure that the fuel is competitive.

Traditionally, the price of gas has been higher in Europe than in North America, and higher in Asia than in Europe, since Asia could only be supplied with LNG which is more expensive than conventional gas. During the 1980s and 1990s the price remained relatively stable from: \$1 to \$3/MMBTU[6] in the US, \$2 to \$4/MMBTU in Europe and \$3 to \$5/MMBTU in Japan. From 2000 to 2008 prices doubled, or even tripled, in these markets. Prices also tended to converge and become more volatile, because of the trend for liberalisation in gas markets. The increase in the price of gas was especially strong in the US because the growing demand could not be met by the local production. Imports from Canada were limited because Canada wanted to keep a good fraction of its production for the production of oil sands. So (see also Chapter 5-North America) the US anticipated growing imports and started to build a number of LNG re-gasification terminals.

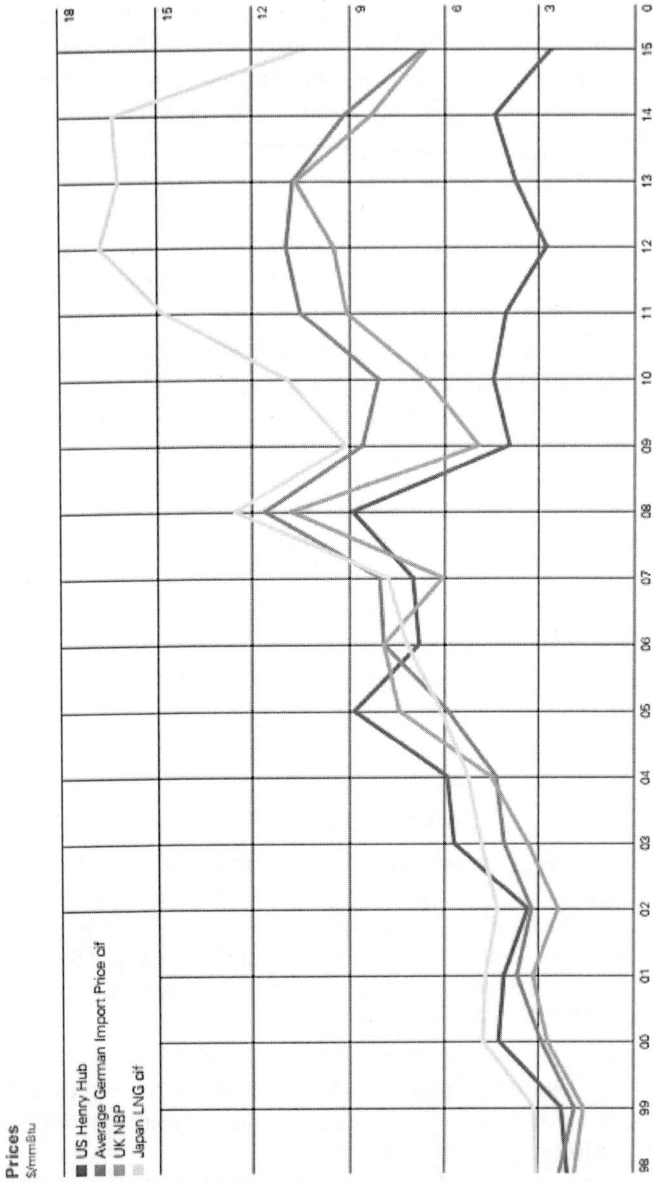

Source: BP Statistical Review, 2016.

Figure 22: Natural Gas Prices in Major Consumption Regions.

These terminals were only used at a very limited scale because of the sudden development of the production of tight gas and shale gas which in 2017 represent more than 50 per cent of the US production. Today, the US is net exporter and the first LNG cargoes were exported at the beginning of 2016. Some of the LNG re-gasification terminals were transformed into LNG exports terminals (at the cost of building liquefaction capacities). Starting in 2008, the price of gas in the US fell quickly to very low levels and is now around $3/MMBTU.

Reversely in Europe and in Asia after the fall of 2009 the price of gas increased in 2010 following the increase of the oil price. The price of gas remained extremely high in Asia and especially in Japan because of Fukushima. Additional quantities of gas were required to make up for the loss of nuclear electricity production.

In 2014–2015, the price of gas started to fall in Asia and in Europe. It is in the $4–$5/MMBTU range. As a consequence of the shrinking of the difference between US prices and European prices, the profitability of US exports can probably be questioned. The difference between the Henry Hub price (reference price in the US—Henry Hub is at the centre of large production facilities in Louisiana) and the European prices (German border price typical of imports coming from Russia or NBP—National Balancing Point, typical of the spot price in the UK) can probably not fully cover liquefaction, transportation and re-gasification costs between the US and Europe.

On a calorific base the price of gas is about 50 per cent of the price of oil in the US and 60 per cent in Europe in 2017.

An OPEC for Gas?

"Cartels …are illegal, unjustified and unjustifiable", at least for several antitrust bodies such as the Department of Justice in the US or the European Commission. There are many examples of sanctions being imposed, including in the industrial and raw materials sectors: the breakup of Standard Oil in 1911, and penalties imposed for cartels in the plasterboard sector in 2002, glass in 2007, steel in 2008, etc.

The idea of a gas cartel (OGEC) is nonetheless often discussed, particularly by countries like Russia, Algeria, Iran and Venezuela. Moreover, "OGEC" and OPEC would be very similar since they would both deal with the same family of products (hydrocarbons).

(Cont'd…)

Knowing the possible members of "OGEC", i.e. gas-exporting countries, is easy, since several of them are already members of OPEC (Algeria, Iran, Qatar and Nigeria). As for gas-exporting countries who are not members of OPEC (Bolivia, Egypt, Russia, Trinidad, etc.), their ability to join would largely depend on their economic position. Although Russia is sufficiently powerful and autonomous to join a gas OPEC with no risk of commercial reprisals, Trinidad and Egypt are very different as they are both very dependent on their American commercial partner. In Bolivia, support from the "Bolivarian" front within OPEC (Venezuela and Ecuador) would also facilitate the country's entry into a cartel. However, beyond the political will which already exists via the Gas Exporting Countries Forum (GECF), the potential value of a gas OPEC raises questions that depend on the nature of the gas industry. Because gas is mainly transported by pipeline, there is a strong mutual dependency between producer, transporter and consumer, and this results in the use of long-term contracts. Moreover, since gas competes with oil, petroleum products, coal, etc, the price of gas is often indexed to that of the alternative energy to ensure the gas is competitive and that the consumer's demand is robust. It will be clear that, in such market conditions, there is little chance that a gas OPEC could "determine" gas prices. The development of LNG and the internationalisation of gas flows could decrease the mutual dependency between consuming countries and producing countries. In such circumstances a gas OPEC would become feasible, but it would not necessarily be without commercial risk for the gas industry: were long-term contracts to be abandoned and price transparency decreased, would consuming nations and private players be prepared to promote gas and make the massive gas infrastructure investments needed?

- **Price of Coal** (Fig. 23)

Since the potential supply of coal was greater than demand, prices have been stable and remained relatively low up to the beginning of the 2000's (between \$15 to \$20/toe in the US, \$17 to \$25 in Europe and \$20 to \$30 in Japan). The price of coal follows the same trend as the price of oil. It increased up to 2008 but has fallen now to low levels, from \$50 per toe for coal in the US to \$100 for the best quality of coal imported in Japan.

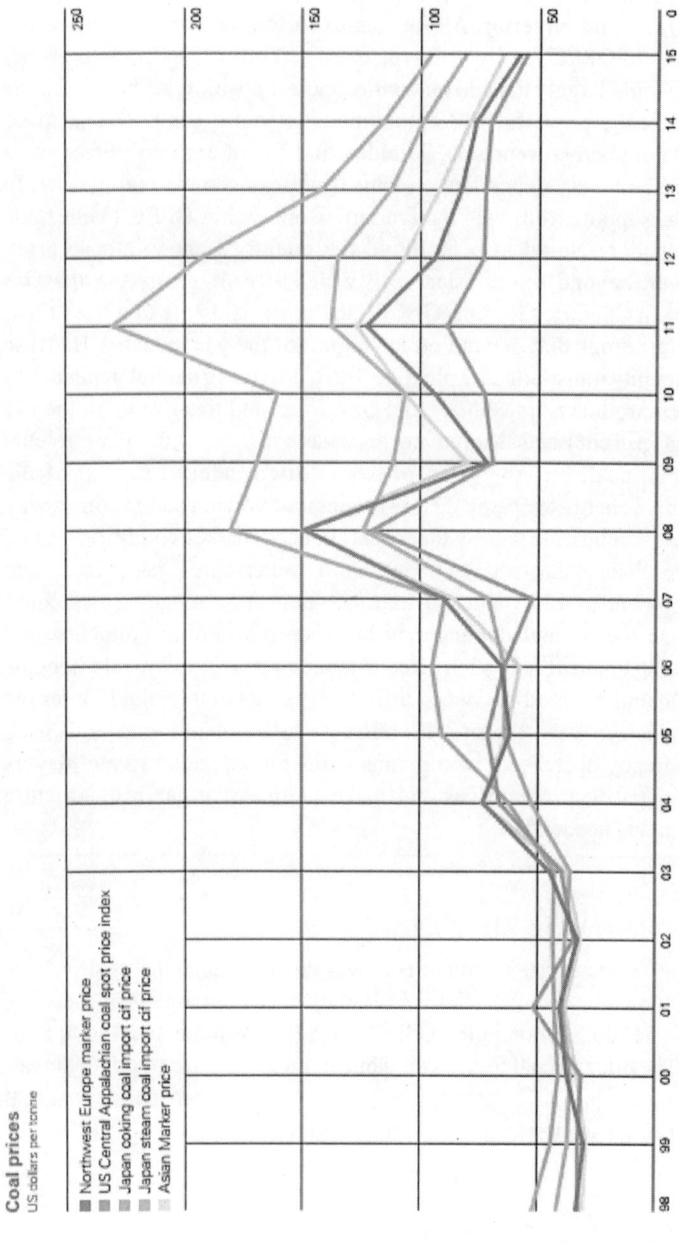

Figure 23: Coal Prices in Major Consumption Areas.

Source: BP Statistical Review, 2016.

The Uranium Market

Following the launch of nuclear programmes in Europe and Japan, the price of uranium rose from $6 to $43/lb over the 1970s. But overproduction in the 1980s caused prices to tumble so much that, by 1994, they had fallen back to their 1970 level.

Since mid-2003, prices have increased by a factor of 2.5, reaching $29/lb in 2005. They rose sharply to a peak of over $130/lb in mid 2007 before falling back more slowly. Since the fourth quarter of 2008 they have fluctuated around the range of $40 to 60/lb. The reasons for these changes are different from those in the oil sector and are linked to changes in availability and in the uranium industry. OECD's Nuclear Energy Agency cites, among other reasons, the Australian Olympic Dam Mine fire at the end of 2001, affecting one of the largest producers worldwide, and flooding of the McArthur River Mine in Canada the same year.

Uranium prices are not set by free markets; they are negotiated under contracts between buyer and seller that generally last for three to five years. In 2013, the world produced roughly 60,000 tons of uranium (or 130 million lbs). The main producers are Australia (28 per cent), Kazakhstan (12 per cent) and Russia (8 per cent). This production only satisfies half of the world demand, the deficit being made up by sales of uranium recycled from nuclear bombs.

The fact that uranium recycled from nuclear bombs is exhausted means that a sustained increase in the price of uranium can be expected, particularly since no new mines have been opened in the past 20 years and demand over the next few years is expected to grow by one per cent to two per cent per year because of the large number of nuclear power plants under construction.

However, there is an important difference between nuclear electricity generation and the use of coal, oil or gas, which is that the cost of the electricity is not dependent on the price of uranium which accounts for only five per cent of the production cost.

- **Price of Electricity**

The cost of electricity depends on many factors: the production route, the size of the plant and whether the production is at base or peak levels.

Base-load production (the production provided most of the time) is theoretically the least expensive. It comes from either nuclear powered plants or coal-fired plants.

Production required for shorter periods (semi-base-load and peak) is provided by gas-fired power plants, or even those using fuel oil. Generation costs at plants burning gas or fuel oil and operating only some tens of hours per year are significantly higher than those at nuclear or coal base-load plants.

The price of electricity varies according to the type of consumer, the level of competition in the market and, above all, on the time it is supplied. The cost volatility of prices is staggering: during some fortunately rare times of the year, the price of electricity may be several dozen times that of a period of low demand. This is because electricity cannot be stored, and very costly generation plant must be brought on line for short periods to meet peak demand.

Order of magnitude electricity generation costs in new plant are as follows (in Euros per MWh):

	Cost (Euro/MWh)
Nuclear	52
Gas-fired combined cycle power plant:	
— Price of gas $8/MMBTU	80
— Price of gas $4/MMBTU	50
Coal:	
— Price of coal: $120/T	74
— Price of coal: $60/T	51
Wind Onshore	84
Wind Offshore	150
Geothermal	75
Hydraulic	60
Solar PV	150
Solar CSP	250

Source: IEA/NEA 2015 (median case).

Generation costs in gas and coal fired plants mainly depend on the price of the fuel. The low price of gas at the start of the 2000s explains the trend for gas-fired combined cycle power plants.

These costs do not take into account the pollution caused by use of the various energy sources. Were high "costs" to be imposed on CO_2 emissions that would, of course, make coal far less competitive.

FOSSIL FUEL RESERVES

Since 80 per cent of energy needs are met by non-renewable fossil fuels, the question of their reserve levels is critical.

- **Oil Reserves**

Proved worldwide reserves of conventional crude oil are on the order of 240 billion toe—around 1700 billion barrels, or 51 years of production at the current rate. Additional reserves (roughly 140 billion toe) can be expected to be discovered and also found from improved knowledge of existing reservoirs. In addition, today's average recovery rates of roughly 30 per cent to 35 per cent (which means that 65 to 70 per cent of oil is left in the ground—the recovery rate can be as high as 60 per cent or more in favourable fields in the North Sea and as low as less than 10 per cent in extra heavy oil fields in Venezuela) could increase to 50 per cent in the future and thus add further to reserves. The total contribution of these additional reserves will depend on the price of oil and the extent of technological advances, and will take some time to be realised.

Since the start of the twentieth century, there had been many alarmist predictions that reserves would soon be exhausted. The large discoveries in Texas at the beginning of the 1930s, then in the Middle East around 1940, made these fears temporarily disappear. But they re-emerged in the 1960s. In 1970, the ratio of proved reserves to annual production was only 30, which suggested that reserves would be exhausted by the beginning of the twenty-first century. This was one of the reasons for the oil shocks, when the price of oil increased by a factor of ten. The fall in consumption and substantial level of exploration that followed meant that the forthcoming end of oil could be forgotten, until in the years 2000–2010, debates regarding oil reserves returned to the news.

Years 2000–2010: The Controversy over Oil Reserves and Peak Oil

There have been controversies as to the level of oil reserves for many years. The BP Statistical Review estimate for the end of 2016 is 1707 billion barrels. But these figures are sometimes contested.

Firstly, it should be noted that 85 per cent of these reserves are located in OPEC countries or other producing countries where access to information is difficult. In many countries, reserves are simply announced every year by the government. Private oil companies which are non-State owned and listed on the New York Stock Exchange must submit their figures to the

(*Cont'd...*)

SEC (Securities & Exchange Commission), which carefully evaluates these reserves: but the reserves of the five largest international oil companies (Exxon Mobil, BP, Shell, Total and Chevron) correspond to less than five per cent of the worldwide total.

Overall figures for reserves are thus doubted by pessimists, often members of ASPO (Association for the Study of Peak Oil), who contest the reserve levels published by many countries. They recall that, between 1986 and 1989, most Middle East OPEC countries multiplied their actual reserves by a factor of 2 or 3 to obtain higher production quotas, since these quotas were linked to reserves. There was intense controversy, fueled by well-known banker, the late Matt Simmons, regarding Saudi Arabia's reserves: according to him, these reserves were grossly overestimated, a fact denied by Aramco, which often stated its willingness to produce 12 or even 15 million barrels per day to meet market needs.

Basing its opinion on an evaluation of typical published reserves figures, ASPO announced that oil production would peak soon (2010, 2015) after which it would inevitably decline.

This concept of peak production is based on the work of King Hubbert, a petroleum geologist who worked for Shell in the US in the 1960s. Based on the fact that discoveries in America reached a maximum in the 1930s, he announced that American production would reach a maximum in 1969, which did actually occur. ASPO members have extrapolated this result to a worldwide scale and, since oil discoveries reached a peak in the 1960s, argued that production will peak in the very near future (Fig. 24).

The picture has been largely changed by the uprise of shale oil production (LTO– Light Tight Oil) in the US by 2010 (the first production of oil through combination of horizontal drilling and fracking was much earlier, in late 1940s).

As a conclusion, it is clear that hydrocarbon reserves are finite and therefore exhaustible. But little is known regarding the level of ultimate (i.e. total existing) reserves. The work of ASPO is now—at least for a while—forgotten. In any case, regardless of the amount of reserves, oil consumption and that of fossil fuels in general, cannot reach the level it has attained in developed countries in all regions of the world.

More Details about Reserves

A key distinction has to be made between resources, (i.e. oil in place), and the oil that can be extracted (recoverable reserves or simply reserves). Currently, on average only a little more than a third of the oil in place is recoverable, the recovery rate being about 35 per cent, which is an average of rates for particular fields that vary from less than 10 per cent to more than 80 per cent.

Proved reserves are reserves of oil in known reservoirs that are recoverable under current technical and economic conditions. Alternatively reserves are described as proved if there is a greater than 90 per cent probability that they can be produced. The term probable reserves is used when there is a 50 per cent probability of production, and possible reserves have a production probability of 10 per cent.

The distinction between proved, probable and possible reserves is only really of use to oil companies. At a worldwide level, it is more helpful to refer to the idea of ultimate recoverable reserves, which is the sum of:

- Reserves already used, i.e. the consumption of oil since 1859.
- Proved reserves.
- Reserves to be discovered.
- Additional reserves expected from improved recovery rates.

So the debate on oil reserves has restarted. "There are plenty of hydrocarbons", say the optimists (economists). "The abundance is false", say the pessimists (geologists), emphasising the fact that discoveries of giant oil deposits are now rare. In the 1990s, only 50 per cent of oil production was replaced by newly discovered oil. Although reserves increased by an average of just over one per cent per year between 1999 and 2009 (according to *BP Statistical Review*), this is because oil companies have significantly re-evaluated their reserves.

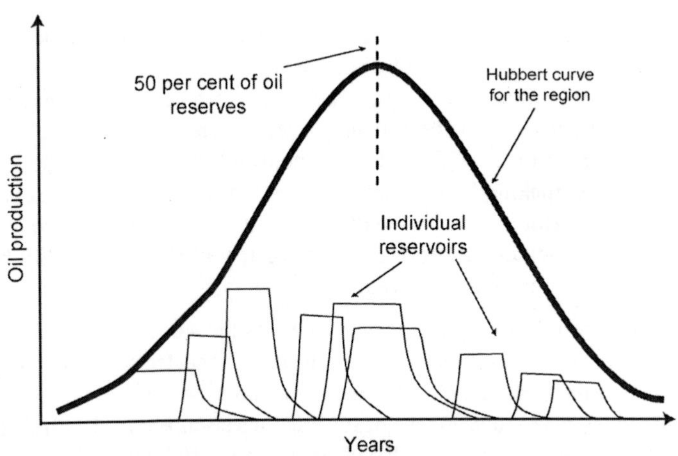

Figure 24: "Peak Oil" According to King Hubbert.

In summary, assessments of ultimate recoverable reserves vary from two trillion barrels according to ASPO, to nearly six trillion barrels according to the IEA. An average estimate is 4.7 trillion barrels, broken down as follows:

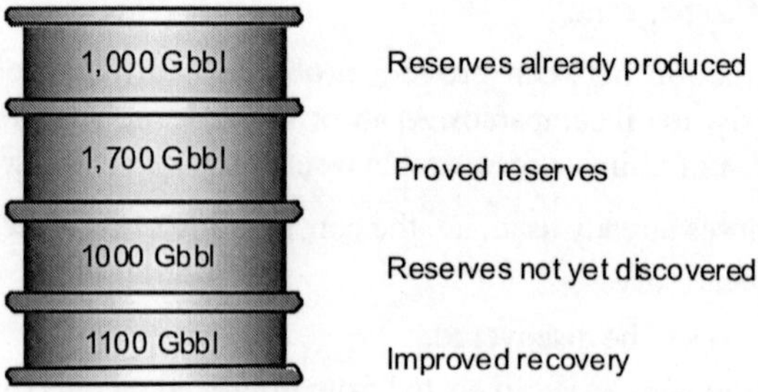

In total, remaining oil reserves (i.e. proved, not yet discovered and reserves from improved recovery) amount to over 100 years of current production.

Reserves of unconventional oil[7], i.e. the extra-heavy oils from Orinoco in Venezuela, and the oil sands of Canada, must not be forgotten. These reserves are significant.[8]

Unconventional Oil Reserves

Unconventional oil means oil that cannot be produced using "conventional" methods.

Extra-heavy oils are principally located in Venezuela, in the Orinoco oil basin, which holds more than 2000 billion barrels (in the ground) of extra-heavy crude oil. With a recovery rate estimated at ten per cent, this basin's recoverable reserves would be 200 billion barrels with current technology. At the beginning of 2011, Venezuela announced reserves of about 300 billion barrels, making Venezuelan reserves bigger than Saudi Arabia's reserves (265). But these extra-heavy crude oils must be pre-treated and transformed via cracking processes into lighter oil that can readily be transported and treated in a conventional refinery.

Tar sands, now usually called oil sands are—as the name implies—a mix of sand and asphalt or bitumen. The oil, formed in the depths of Canadian soil, rose to the surface in the absence of a cap rock. At the surface the light fractions evaporated and the heavy fractions became mixed with sand. There are two main techniques for its exploitation. If the asphaltic sands are at a shallow depth, traditional mining techniques are used: the sand mixed with asphalt is extracted by hydraulic shovels, mixed and heated

(Cont'd...)

with water, and the oil separated by decantation. If the oil sands are too deep for traditional mining, steam injection is used to liquefy the bitumen and recover it at the surface (SAGD – *Steam Assisted Gravity Drainage*). The bitumen must then be processed to produce a synthetic crude oil. These oil sands are mainly concentrated in Canada (in Athabasca and on Melville Island). Resources are currently estimated at some 300 Gt, of which 34 Gt are thought to be recoverable. Oil sands fields' development is costly and some projects can only be profitable if the oil price is $60 to $80.

Oil shale is organic matter in rocks, matter whose transformation into hydrocarbons is not complete and that can, at very high temperatures, yield oil comparable to certain crude oils. Oil Shale represent a significant resource, but the production costs are very high and current exploitation techniques are very harmful to the environment. Historically the oil shale industry pre-dated the conventional oil industry, but it became uneconomic after the discovery of crude oil in Pennsylvania in 1859 and practically no oil is currently produced from oil shale.

LTO (Light Tight Oil or Shale Oil) is also considered as non conventional Oil.

Production of oil will therefore continue for several more decades. As Sheikh Yamani[9] once said, "The Stone Age came to an end not for a lack of stones and the oil age will end, but not for a lack of oil." In any event, if we assume that automobiles continue to require gasoline and diesel fuel, and that oil reserves become exhausted, techniques for liquefying gas (GTL: Gas To Liquids) and coal will still enable these fuels to be produced[10].

- **Concentration of Hydrocarbon Reserves**

The geographical distribution of oil reserves (Fig. 25) is very uneven. Nearly 85 per cent of these reserves are located in OPEC countries, which therefore have a proved reserves to production (R/P) ratio of roughly 75, while for non-OPEC producers this ratio is only 17. North America and Western Europe, whose R/P ratios are 12 and 9 respectively, are the regions most directly affected by depletion of reserves.

Since more than 60 per cent of conventional oil reserves are located in the Middle East and 10 per cent in the CIS—mainly in Western Siberia—and because a quarter of natural gas reserves are located in Russia and 40 per cent in the Middle East, it is clear that 70 per cent of the world's hydrocarbon reserves are located in a small zone covering the countries bordering the Persian Gulf and extending towards Russia, including the Caspian region and Western Siberia (Fig. 26).

Conquest of the Arctic

The acceleration of global warming and increases in both the price and scarcity of natural resources has made the Arctic the centre of attention.

From a geostrategic viewpoint, the melting ice and shrinking icecap open new transport routes via the Northwest and Northeast Passages, which both opened for the first time in 2008. These new connections between the Pacific and the Atlantic could revolutionise marine shipping, putting Tokyo 14,000 km (8,700 miles) from London versus 21,000 kms (13,000 miles) currently. By claiming sovereignty respectively over the Northwest and Northeast Passages, Canada and Russia are attempting to control marine traffic in them.

The Arctic Circle is also strategically important in relation to hydrocarbons. According to a report by the *US Geological Survey* published in 2007, the Polar Circle could contain one-fifth of the planet's undiscovered recoverable hydrocarbon reserves amounting to 90 billion barrels of oil and 47 trillion cubic meters of gas, i.e. in total 60 billion toe or some 13 per cent of today's proved reserves. Although the majority of identified reserves are located near coasts, so in the territorial waters of the countries involved (the American state of Alaska, Canadian Beaufort Sea, Norwegian Barents Sea, Danish Greenland, and Russia's Siberian offshore), there is a significant possibility of Arctic reserves being in international waters or areas subject to disputed territorial claims (e.g. Western Greenland between Denmark and Canada, the Barents Sea between Norway and Russia, etc.).

Current competition for the Polar regions has included submissions filed with the UN and an increasing number of symbolic missions since 2007: Russia planting a flag 4,200 meters (14,000 feet) below the North Pole, cementing its hold over Franz Joseph Land, undertaking scientific studies on Wrangel Island, etc. In addition the US and Canada are investing heavily in icebreaker fleets and keenly negotiating commercial agreements with countries of the zone.

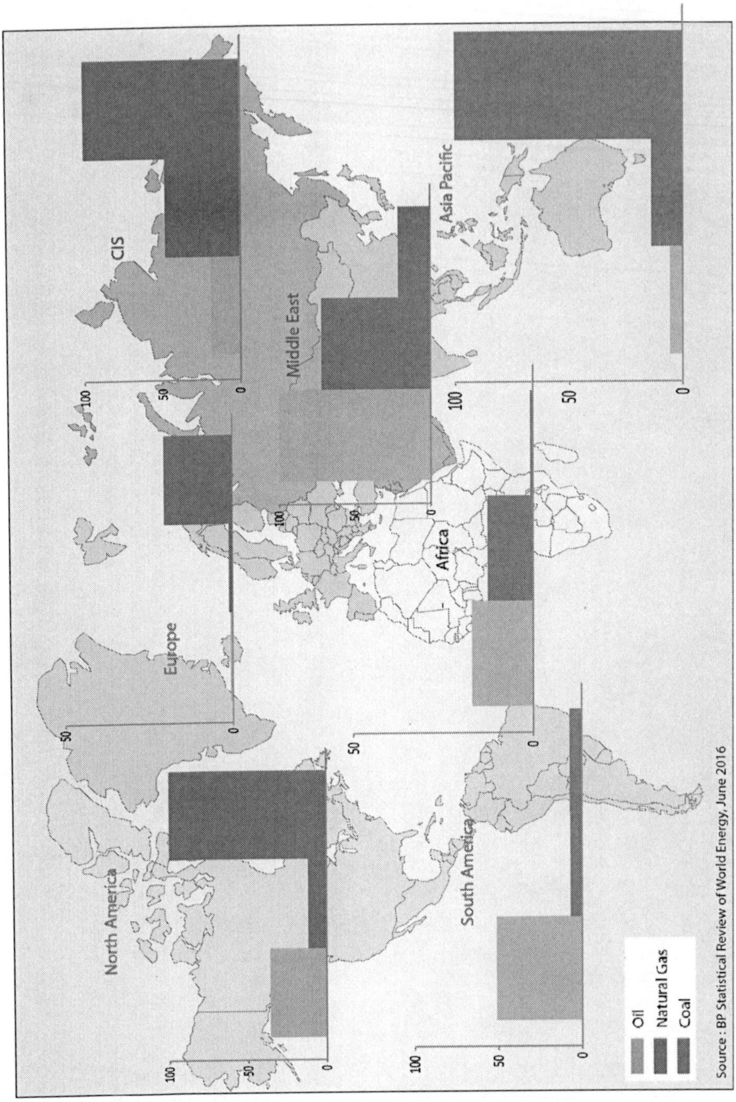

Figure 25: Energy Reserves

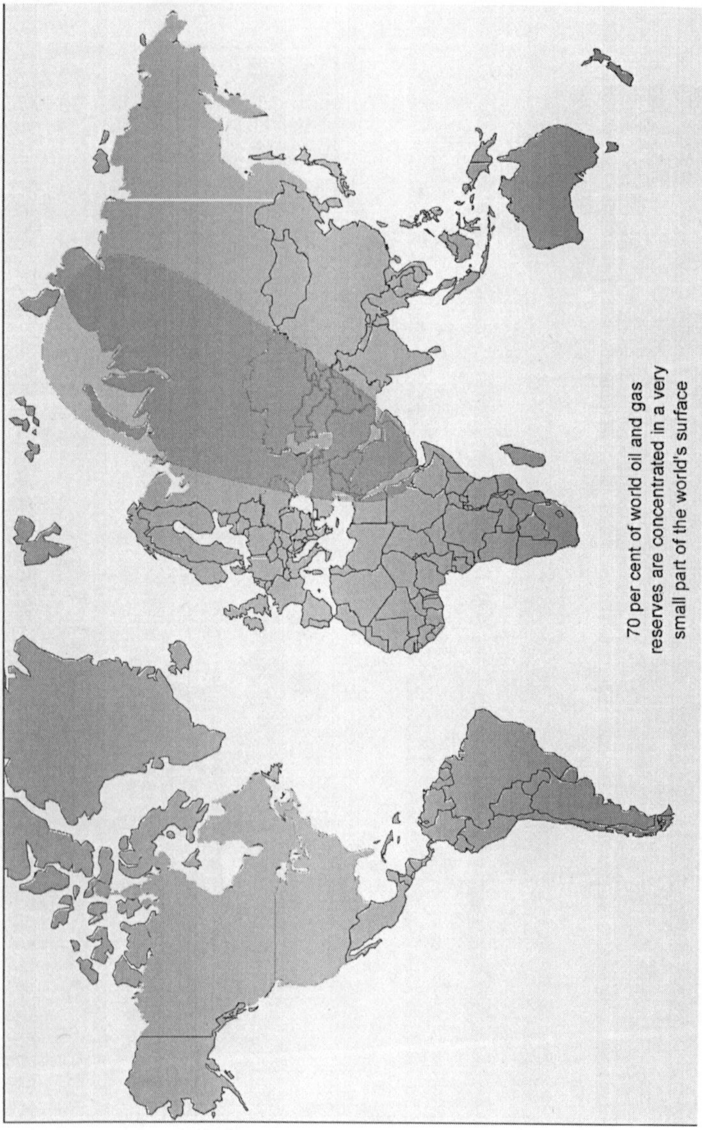

Figure 26: The Concentration of Worldwide Hydrocarbon Resources.

- **Exploitation of the Seabed's Soil and Subsoil Resources**

According to the 1982 United Nations Convention on the Law of the Sea, coastal nations have sovereign rights over resources from the soil and subsoil of their seabed, notably with regard to hydrocarbon resources. The continental shelf of a coastal nation comprises the sea-bed and subsoil thereof, up to the outer edge of the continental slope or up to 200 nautical miles from the coasts. Its boundary coincides with that of the maximum extension of the Exclusive Economic Zone (EEZ), the zone in which the coastal nation has the right to exploit all economic resources in the water, on the seabed and in the subsoil. Where two nations have coastlines that are adjacent or facing each other, a maritime delimitation agreement is necessary. When the continental margin extends beyond 200 nautical miles, nations are entitled to exercise their jurisdiction either up to 350 nautical miles from the coasts, or up to 100 nautical miles from the 2,500 meter isobaths, depending on certain geological criteria. In return, the coastal nation must contribute to a system for sharing revenue generated by the exploitation of mineral resources beyond the limit of 200 nautical miles, managed by the International Seabed Authority (ISA).

- **Border Disputes and Sharing of Energy Resources**

There are still numerous border disputes—often leftovers from decolonisation—and adjudication by international arbitration authorities, such as the International Court of Justice, is regularly required. In many areas, the discovery of hydrocarbon reserves has exacerbated tensions arising from disputed territorial claims. Examples are the Caspian Sea (Iran, Russia, Azerbaijan, Kazakhstan and Turkmenistan); Senkaku/Diaoyutai Islands (Japan, China and Taiwan); Sir Creek and Kashmir (India and Pakistan); Western Sahara (Morocco and Sahrawi Arab Democratic Republic or SADR); Sabah (Malaysia and Brunei); Mbanie (Gabon and Equatorial Guinea); Falkland Islands (UK and Argentina); Kuril Islands (Russia and Japan), Greenland (Canada and Denmark), etc. However, economic pragmatism coupled with diplomacy have already led to many settlements, or a peaceful acceptance of the status quo allowing development of raw materials, e.g. joint exploitation of the shared region (neutral zone) between Saudi Arabia and Kuwait, agreement between Russia and Japan regarding Sakhalin, Nigeria's restitution of the Bakassi peninsula to Cameroon, etc.

- **Natural Gas Reserves**

Proved reserves of natural gas amount to roughly 6600 tcf (185 bcm or 170 btoe) or an R/P (reserves to production) ratio of 53 years. This is sufficient for a substantial increase in natural gas's share of world energy supply. Additional reserves of roughly 100 billion toe can be expected from new discoveries. On the other hand, in contrast to oil, no increase in reserves will come from improved recovery rates as the recovery rates for gas already average

80 per cent. The very significant developments of unconventional gas raise important questions about reserves of tight gas, coal bed methane and, in particular, shale gas. These resources are probably very large but the potential for transforming them into recoverable reserves is still poorly understood.

Proved world reserves of natural gas are concentrated in two main areas: the CIS (28.6 per cent) and the Middle East (42.8 per cent). Three countries—Russia, Iran and Qatar hold more than 50 per cent of world natural gas reserves.

- **Coal Reserves**

Coal reserves are very large and well distributed throughout the world. Proved reserves (roughly 891 billion tons) are about 114 years current consumption, and probable reserves amount to 1,000 years.

- **Uranium Reserves**

Uranium reserves (assuming a relatively reasonable extraction cost of $130/kg are sufficient to enable existing or projected generation plants to operate for nearly 100 years.

In 2013, uranium reserves—reasonably assured resources, in theory accessible at less than $35 per Pound—were as follows (in thousands of tons):

Uranium Reserves–2013 (thousands of tons)

Australia	1706
Kazakhstan	679
Russia	505
Canada	493
Niger	404
Namibia	382
World total	**5902**

Source: World Nuclear Association.

OUTLOOK: FUTURE ENERGY NEEDS

As Pierre Dac[11] wrote, "The art of forecasting is difficult, especially when it involves the future". However, we need forecasts for the critical period required for the construction of new facilities (oil, gas and coal production, nuclear power plants, and development of new renewable energies) which can exceed ten years.

- **Overall Energy Demand**

  – *Increased Overall Energy Demand*

Economic and population growth will lead to higher energy demand. The size of the increase will depend on many factors, in particular the rates of economic growth, of increases in population and on environmental constraints. It will also depend on developments in technology. The price of energy will depend on the combination of these elements and be such as to equate its supply and its demand.

Many forecasts are made for future energy consumption but most of them pose the same problem: the increased energy and fossil fuel consumption forecast for 2050 is incompatible with the objective of reducing CO_2 emissions.

– *Factors that will Limit Growth in Energy Demand*

Lower population growth than expected will mean lower growth in energy requirements. In the 1990s, it was thought that world population—currently 7.3 billion—would reach 12 to 15 billion by 2050. The current estimate has fallen to 8 to 10 billion because of the very strong decline in third-world countries' birthrates. In addition, beyond a certain level of individual wealth, per capita energy consumption tends to stagnate (see Fig. 14). The fight against climate change will also influence energy consumption and lead to limits on the use of fossil fuels. Finally reserves, which by their nature are limited for oil and gas although for coal the timeframes are longer, will curb increased consumption. For example, if tomorrow China and India were to consume as much oil per head as South Korea does today, their joint consumption would significantly exceed current world production. If China's per capita consumption were the same as the USA's, its demand alone would also exceed current world production[12]. Beyond all moral or ethical considerations (would it be legitimate or not for every inhabitant of the planet one day to consume as much energy as an American citizen does today), the finite nature of resources will limit consumption de facto.

- **Energies for the Coming Century**

– *Outlook 2040*

In 2040, fossil fuels will remain the dominant energy sources. The International Energy Agency (IEA) forecasts that they should still meet between 60 per cent and 80 per cent of commercial energy needs. Oil consumption will continue to grow over the next few years since transport needs are increasing, but perhaps oil growth will be at a slower rate. The increase in the use of automobiles in North America and Europe will not be maintained but road transport sector consumption will be significant in China and India.

Oil will still be used as a fuel and as a raw material for the petrochemicals industry.

Gas will remain widely used, since it is the cleanest of the fossil fuels.

Coal should also continue to be widely used, meeting 30 per cent of energy demand. Fossil fuels in total will still meet 60 per cent of world energy demand.

The proportion of electricity generated using fossil fuels could increase from 60 per cent today to nearly 75 per cent in 2020, since neither hydroelectricity nor nuclear power will be able to meet the increase in demand. Coal will maintain its position as leader in electricity generation, accounting for 35 per cent to 40 per cent worldwide.

Because of the Chernobyl and Fukushima accidents and the problem of storing nuclear waste, public opinion in many countries will maintain its reservations on the use of nuclear power. The best prospects for the development of nuclear energy over the next few years are in Asia, where fossil fuel reserves and existing generating capacity are low and the demand for energy is exploding. However, the massive development of nuclear energy expected (currently there are 440 nuclear power plants throughout the world and some experts forecast more than 2,000) will require the use of a new, economical, Generation IV fast neutron reactors, since uranium reserves are only sufficient to fuel existing plants for some 100 years.

Renewable energies involve very different issues. The development of hydraulic energy is undoubtedly close to its limit; major dams (Three Gorges in China, Itaipu in Brazil, and Ataturk in Turkey) require the flooding of enormous areas and consequent population displacement that is increasingly unacceptable. The Inga site, near the mouth of the Congo River, has significant potential (of the order of 40 GW). Small-capacity dams (a few hundred megawatts) have already been built. The construction of additional dams at this site remains possible, but electricity demand in the region remains very low.

The use of biomass—i.e. wood—is very controversial in many regions of the world, particularly Sub-Saharan Africa, because of the deforestation and desertification of the regions involved that results and the very serious health problems for the inhabitants who inhale the smoke released during wood combustion (it is estimated that several million Africans die each year of respiratory illnesses). Finally wood combustion is very inefficient: less than 10 per cent of the wood's energy is recovered, although the quantities of wood used could be reduced significantly by improved kilns, which are simple to manufacture and use.

Finally, there are new renewable energies (NRE), the most promising of which are wind and photovoltaic energy.

Two scenarios prepared by IEA are shown below; the "New Policies Scenario" which takes into account energy needs, new technologies and the need to protect environment, and the 450 scenario which forecasts stabilisation of the atmospheric CO_2 concentration at 450 ppm, to limit the global temperature increase to 2°C by 2100.

Forecast Energy Consumption by Energy Source

G toe	*1980*	*2016*	*2040 New policies scenario*	*2040 "450" scenario*
Oil	3.1	4.4	4.8	3.3
Natural Gas	1.2	3.2	4.3	3.3
Coal	1.8	3.7	4.1	2.0
Nuclear	0.2	0.6	1.2	1.6
Hydro	0.6	0.9	1.5	1.8
Biomass and waste	0.8	1.2	1.9	2.3
Other renewables	–	0.4	1.0	1.7
TOTAL	**7.7**	**14.4**	**18.8**	**16.0**

Source: IEA and the Author.

– *Outlook 2050*

The forecast for 2050 is different. By then, hydrocarbon production will probably have started to decline and meet less than 50 per cent of demand. Other energy sources will have to take a much larger global market share, perhaps nuclear energy, if generation IV plants become available, since nuclear power does not contribute to the greenhouse effect. Renewable energies will undoubtedly play a far larger role as well. The use of hydrogen remains uncertain but it is probably not a solution. While its sole combustion product is very pure water, it is merely an energy vector and must be produced either using electricity, most logically from nuclear energy, or from hydrocarbons. However, this latter route has nearly all the same pollution problems as manufacture of hydrogen from hydrocarbons results in the production of carbon dioxide, the main cause of the greenhouse effect.

The twentieth century was unique in being a period of very cheap energy. It is probable that, in the medium term, the price of energy will reflect its scarcity. How will this transition take place: with or without a major economic and environmental crisis?

ENVIRONMENT AND SUSTAINABLE DEVELOPMENT

Environmental issues are of growing concern to Western public opinion, and thus of the political authorities as well. It is the duty of the latter to meet what appears to be the challenge of the twenty-first century: producing and consuming more energy while respecting the environment.

- **Local Pollution**

This is pollution emitted in a limited area, e.g. in a town. In the nineteenth century, this pollution resulted from the development of industrial activities.

In the twentieth century smog appeared (a contraction of the words smoke and fog). Smog is a particularly thick and toxic fog resulting from the condensation of water vapour into tiny droplets that form on the surface of microscopic particles making up smoke. When coal was the main urban heating source in London, smog was common; in 1952 more than 4,000 people died from respiratory problems caused by smog. Smog is also common above cities where automobile traffic is especially heavy.

Today, local pollution is mainly caused by transport. The principal pollutants in automobile exhaust gases are carbon monoxide, unburned hydrocarbons and nitrogen oxides. Unburned hydrocarbons and nitrogen oxides can react in the presence of sunlight to produce ozone. Ozone is an oxidising agent that attacks vegetation and irritates the respiratory system. Automobiles are now equipped with catalytic converters: devices installed on exhaust pipes that significantly reduce pollutant emissions. It is estimated that a vehicle manufactured now only emits one per cent of the pollutants from a vehicle manufactured in 1970.

Thanks to the measures taken, some experts believe that local pollution is disappearing. However, there are still problems to be resolved: nitrogen oxide emissions and nano particles by diesel vehicles. Nano particles are considered very dangerous and the future of diesel consumption looks bleak..

With the Auto Oil plan, launched at the start of the 1990s, the European Union set precise objectives for the reduction of polluting gas emissions. Better operation of catalytic converters requires a significant reduction in the sulfur content of engine fuels. Other measures have been initiated, e.g. the installation of particle filters on diesel engine exhausts, of service station nozzles that recover gasoline vapours, or simply setting standards for maximum CO_2 emissions (see below). Further improvements in air quality could be achieved by faster renewal of the automobile fleet and more inspections of engine operations.

Biofuels: These fuels are made from agricultural products and can be substituted for other higher-polluting fuels. Biofuels incorporate oxygen molecules that promote combustion and decrease emissions of pollutants such as carbon monoxide and unburned hydrocarbons. CO_2 is also absorbed by the plants used for the manufacture of biofuels during their growth. However, present biofuels only supply, and will only be able to supply, a low proportion of total consumption.

High-voltage Power Lines

Because high-voltage power lines generate magnetic fields it is sometimes claimed that they have harmful effects on the human body. An example is that, in June 2005, the *British Medical Journal* published a study demonstrating a relatively limited but real risk of childhood leukemia for children living less than 600 meters (2000 feet) from a high-voltage power line. No rational explanation has been found for this increased risk. In France, the International Agency for Research on Cancer (IARC), based in Lyon, classifies very low frequency magnetic fields produced by high-voltage power lines into Group 2B of potentially carcinogenic agents.

- **Regional Pollution**

This is pollution that is geographically far more widespread than urban pollution. It is caused by polluting gases emitted in one area being moved by the wind to other areas that may be several hundred or even thousands of miles away. Acid rain is a typical example of regional pollution: sulfur dioxide and nitrogen oxide emissions resulting from the combustion of heavy fuel oil or coal—both rich in sulfur—can affect areas over considerable distances. As an example, such emissions in Great Britain cause acid rain in Scandinavia. This acid rain is harmful to forests (destruction of vegetation) and lakes (destruction of fauna and flora). Emissions from Chinese power plants also cause acid rain over Japan. The extent of this regional pollution and its consequences depend largely on weather conditions (particularly wind speed and direction). It only involves gases with a lifespan sufficiently long for them to be carried over long distances: sulfur dioxide (SO_2), nitrogen oxides (NO_x) or ammonia (NH_3).

So regional pollution means that neighbouring states must negotiate to find concrete, effective solutions to avoid ecological disasters or even the loss of human life. In 1999, the United Nations therefore agreed on the Gothenburg Protocol, with its objective of a 75 per cent reduction in SO_2 emissions and a 49 per cent reduction for NO_x compared with 1990 levels. The European Union had reached a reduction in emissions by 80 per cent by 2010.

Refineries are the leading targets for projects aimed at reducing acid gas emissions. In fact, the combustion of heavy fuel oil is one of the leading sources of SO_2. Since 1980, lower sulfur content fuels have been used and that has reduced emissions by 35 per cent over the past 30 years. Today, refining plants are subject to very strict quota restrictions (the quantity of SO_2 per month was a maximum of 1,700 mg/Nm^3 [13] or less but that was lowered to 1,000 mg/Nm^3 in 2008).

The continuous progress made in improving the quality of petroleum products could give the impression that the problems of local and regional pollution are being dealt with in a better way. But a new issue is of increasing concern to the scientific community and civil society: climate change.

- **Global Pollution**

Global pollution is pollution whose effects are worldwide. The appearance of "ozone holes" over the South Polar Region, due to the destruction of the tropospheric ozone layer by so called CFC gases, was the first example. The elimination of CFCs, particularly in refrigerators, has stopped the growth of these holes.

There is another similar phenomenon, that of global warming, which the majority of scientists agree has existed since the 1990s. Hypotheses explaining this warming are still controversial: is it the result of natural phenomena or the consequence of human activities (greenhouse gases, deforestation, etc.)? The latter hypothesis is increasingly accepted, with roughly 90 per cent certainty, according to the IPCC (International Panel on Climate Change).

Global warming is probably linked to increased concentrations of greenhouse gases in the atmosphere. Heat from sunlight reflected off the Earth's surface is absorbed by greenhouse gases, instead of returning into space. The gases particularly concerned are carbon dioxide (CO_2, responsible for 40 per cent of the greenhouse effect) and methane (CH_4). CO_2—carbon dioxide or carbonic gas—is not harmful per se, but is the main contributor to global warming.

So it is very likely that the greenhouse effect causes global warming and is thus leading to climate change. There are several consequences: melting icecaps, rising seawater levels, risk of changes in the pattern of the Gulf Stream, climate change (cooling in temperate regions, warming at the equator), and the disappearance of some animal species. In addition, according to the IEA, the greenhouse effect may get worse since CO_2 emissions are forecast to increase by 1.7 per cent per year between 2002 and 2030, reaching a level of 38 billion tons. Most of this increase will come from developing countries as they consume increasing quantities of energy and particularly fossil fuels.

The temperature increase observed since 1950 is slightly less than 1 degree Celsius, but may reach several degrees by the end of this century. Certain signs—e.g. polar ice melting faster than predicted—are alarming.

Many experts agree in thinking that we must limit the global temperature increase to two degrees before the end of the century in order to avoid catastrophic consequences for the climate. To achieve this objective, CO_2 emissions need to be reduced by 50 per cent between now and 2050. Carbon dioxide emissions are about the same for industrialised and emerging (or developing) countries. To allow such countries to continue development that requires significant quantities of energy—and particularly fossil fuels, which are sources of CO_2—it would seem natural to allow them to continue to use the same quantities of energy as today. Industrialised countries therefore need to reduce their CO_2 emissions by 75 per cent. This is the purpose of the "Factor 4" objective in several European countries, including France, and of Barack Obama's programme to reduce CO_2 emissions by 80 per cent.

Figure 27 illustrates a scenario for the reduction of GHG emissions. Improving energy efficiency is certainly the most effective factor. The use of agrofuels and renewable energies, in addition to carbon sequestration, are also necessary.

The development of capture and sequestration techniques will also help in the fight against CO_2 emissions. CO_2 could be injected and stored in hydrocarbon deposits (either exhausted or currently being exploited), in deep geological layers, or in aquifer reservoirs. The energy stakes are enormous since significant development of such technologies would lead to increased use of coal, thereby changing the worldwide balance of power.

The Kyoto protocol (1997), the Copenhagen Conference were steps in the fight against climate change.

The COP21 Paris Agreement for climate change was opened for signature on 22 April 2016 at a high-level signature ceremony convened by the Secretary General in New York. At that ceremony, 174 parties to the convention signed the agreement and 15 parties also deposited their instruments of ratification. Currently, there are 191 signatories to the Paris Agreement. Of these, 63 parties to the convention have also deposited their instruments of ratification including US and China, acceptance or approval accounting in total for 52.11 per cent of the total global greenhouse gas emissions.

The Donald Trump decision to withdraw from the Paris agreement has an important but limited impact since a number of states and large cities in the US decided to keep policies designed to limit CO_2 emission.

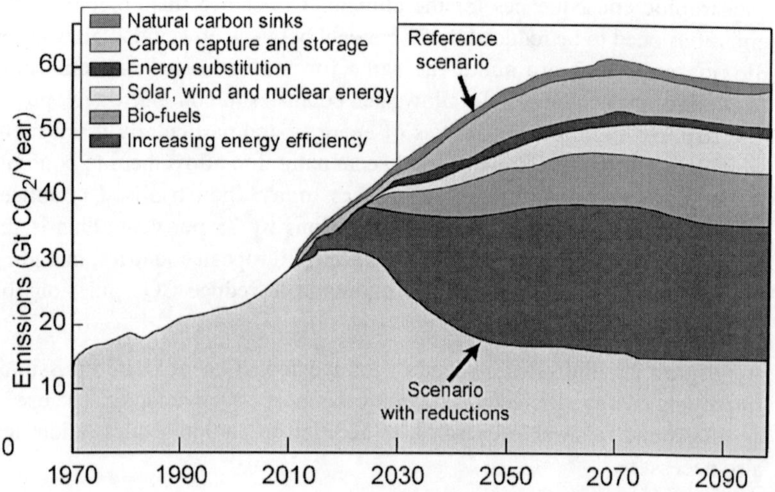

Figure 27: CO_2 Emissions.

- **Accidents**

The energy chain is by its very nature hazardous, and the possibilities for accidents are numerous. Producing oil or gas involves extracting matter that is often burning hot, corrosive and highly pressurised in an environment that can be extreme: North Sea waves of more than 15 m (50 feet), pressure of approximately 98 bars (100 kg/cm^2) at a depth of 1,000 m (3,300 ft) off-shore Africa, winds of nearly 300 km/hr (185 mph) in the Gulf of Mexico, etc. The distribution of gas or electricity requires very special care, since it involves substantial risks. And coal mining is hazardous as is shown by the many mining accidents in China and elsewhere.

Gas explosions also claim many victims:

- In Siberia, the movement of a train caused the explosion of gas that had leaked from a pipe and accumulated in a depression.
- In the United Arab Emirates (UAE), gas clouds exploded after a tank of butane was opened.
- In France, there was a gas leak at Feyzin refinery caused by incorrect manipulation of a valve and the gas exploded when a car passed by the side of the refinery.

But without doubt, the accidents having the greatest affect on the public are crude oil spills and the risk of a nuclear accident. Crude oil spills can have several causes: loss of well control (blowout), unauthorised ballast discharges, and oil spills caused by a shipwreck.

There has been significant pollution from well blowouts since the beginning of the petroleum industry: the Spindletop well drilled in 1900 was out of control for several weeks. More recently, in 1979 a blowout at the IXTOC-1 well offshore Mexico lasted nine months.

– The Macondo disaster

On 20 April 2010, there was a leak of hydrocarbons from a deep water well (the Macondo well) being drilled by Transocean's Deepwater Horizon rig for BP on the latter's Mississippi Canyon Block 252 in the Gulf of Mexico. The well was in 5,000 feet (1,700 meters) of water, 48 miles from the nearest shoreline, with a total depth of 18,360 feet (6,250 meters). The hydrocarbons ignited causing an explosion and fire on the rig, which burned for 36 hours until the rig sank. Eleven out of the 126 member crew on the rig were killed and 17 others injured. Despite a series of different attempts to stem it, oil and gas continued to flow from the well for 87 days. This spill was the worst oil spill in the oil industry's history. The total amount leaked has been estimated at between 4.1 and 4.9 million bbls; for comparison, the spill from the Exxon Valdez was estimated at 260,000 to 750,000 barrels. The well was finally capped by drilling two relief wells, to intercept and then plug the original well.

The three companies principally involved were BP, the lease operator; Transocean, the owner of the rig; and Halliburton, responsible for cementing the wellbore annulus to prevent hydrocarbons entering the wellbore. BP's internal investigation into this accident concluded that the disaster was the result of "a complex and interlinked series of mechanical failures, human judgments, operational implementation and team interfaces" coming "together to allow the initiation and escalation of the accident."

The US Government's National Commission on the BP Deepwater Horizon Oil Spill and Offshore Drilling, reported into the disaster and the future of offshore drilling to the President in January 2011.

The report was highly critical of BP's Safety Culture. BP, it said, has caused a number of disastrous or potentially disastrous workplace incidents that suggest its approach to managing safety has focused on individual worker occupational safety but not on process safety. These incidents and subsequent analyses indicate that the company does not have consistent and reliable risk-management processes and thus has been unable to meet its professed commitment to safety. BP's safety lapses have been chronic.

There is a striking discrepancy between fatalities in the U.S. and in European offshore oil and gas industry, with the former four times the latter per person-hour worked. This indicates that the problem is not an inherent trait of the business itself but results from the differing cultures and regulatory systems under which the industry operates. The U.S. federal authorities lacked regulations covering some of the most critical decisions made on the Deepwater

Horizon that affected the safety of the Macondo well. For instance there are no meaningful regulations governing the requirements for cementing a well and testing the cement used, nor for negative-pressure testing of the well's integrity—a fundamental check against dangerous hydrocarbon incursions into an underbalanced well.

In addition the government and industry were both woefully unprepared to contain or respond to a deepwater well blowout like that at Macondo. They lacked adequate contingency planning, and neither government nor industry had invested sufficiently in research, development and demonstration to improve containment or response technology.

The impact on the coastal zones of the Gulf of Mexico has been catastrophic. Tourism and fishing have been devastated. BP has pledged $20 billion to the Trust established to pay legitimate claims. The clean-up response involved approximately 43,100 personnel, more than 6,470 vessels and dozens of aircraft.

The disaster has transformed BP. To cover clean-up costs and compensation they took a pre-tax charge of $32.2 billion and sold a number of assets. Bowing to political pressure in America, they suspended dividend payments to shareholders. The Chief Executive and the Head of Exploration and Production at the time of the disaster have left the company. The financial impact on the company was such that its market capitalisation[14] fell by over $97 billion, i.e. more than halved, between the spill on April 20 and the low point for the share price on June 29. The new Chief Executive is an American, the first time that a non-British national has held such a position in BP.

The oil spill affected BP worldwide but the environmental concern raised by the oil spill has had percussions beyond BP. The American government imposed a six month moratorium on deep water (> 500 feet) drilling which meant that drilling at 33 off-shore wells was suspended. The oil industry has accepted that its ability to respond to such leaks is inadequate and, in July 2010, Chevron, ConocoPhillips, ExxonMobil and Shell announced that they had committed $1 billion to build and deploy a rapid response system to capture and contain oil in the event of a potential future underwater well blowout in the deepwater Gulf of Mexico. BP subsequently joined the scheme.

In government, the director of the Minerals Management Service resigned. There was considerable impact on US politics; the spill was even described as "Obama's Katrina". As BP's failure to contain it quickly continued, an opinion poll found that 53 per cent of adults thought that President Obama was doing a "poor" or "very poor" job handling the spill. The President was criticised, on the one hand for "a daily stream of negative publicity for the Gulf of Mexico" when less than 10 per cent of the coast line saw any oil at all. On the other hand, in late August the *New York Times* castigated the government for allowing too much uncertainty about lingering damage from the disaster.

– Other Spills

Unauthorised ballast discharges result from ship's tanks being cleaned with seawater and the cleaning water then being released into the open sea; ballast discharges represent one-third of marine pollution by hydrocarbons, or 2–3 times more than tanker accidents (Fig. 28).

Why Oil Spills?[15]

Considering the number of oil tankers in use and the quantities of oil and petroleum products shipped, shipwrecks are relatively rare. But they are still too frequent.

The cost of transporting oil is low compared with its selling price. Even for very long distances (e.g. from the Persian Gulf to the US or Europe) It is not more than a few dollars per barrel. But an operator's main concern is not whether he pays $10, $100 or $1,000; it is to not pay $101 if a competitor only pays $100, which is why he seeks the lowest cost transport possible. So very strict international regulation is vital to prevent the use of ships that are too old or in poor condition, and thus reduce the risk of accidents. Following the Exxon Valdez shipwreck (1989) nearly 40,000 tons of crude oil spread over the coasts of Alaska. The US then instigated a very strict inspection regime for ships entering their ports.

Following the Erika shipwreck off the coast of France (December 1999) and that of the Prestige (November 2002) off the coast of Spain, Europe enacted stricter standards albeit after long negotiations.

Determining the chain of responsibilities for oil spills is complex, as it is difficult to establish ownership of the ship and the cargo. Accusations are made against oil companies, accused of being careless, and against ship owners and flags of "convenience", charged with being lax. In response to the recent Erika (1999) and Prestige (2002) shipwrecks, the European Union has strengthened its legislation by requiring that all ships passing through its waters be equipped with double hulls. In doing so it has made common cause with American legislation, implemented following the Exxon Valdez shipwreck in 1989 off Alaska.

Although oil spills are infrequent, their consequences are such that they have a strong and lasting psychological impact on the local inhabitants.

Once the slicks have reached the shore, there are few cleanup techniques available other than mechanical ones. The repercussions are ecological (oil contamination of local fauna and flora), economic (tourism, aquaculture, etc.), political and psychological.

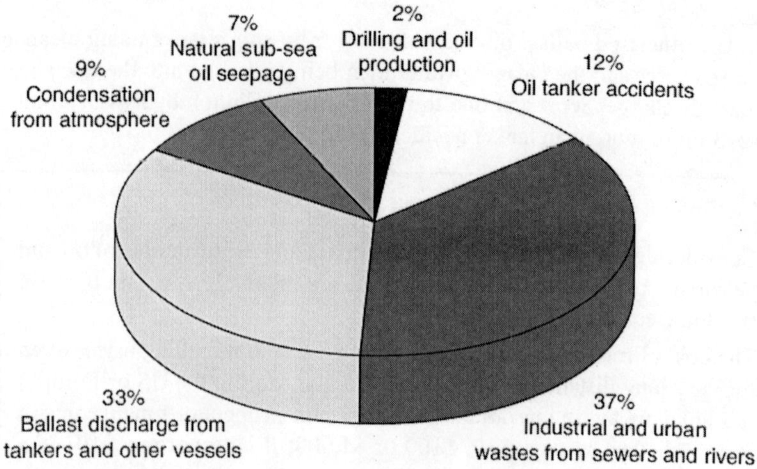

Figure 28: Sources of Marine Pollution.

– Nuclear Accidents

Accidents in nuclear power plants are similar to the extent that their probability is minute, but the scope of potential damage is such that the perception of the risk is increased and mistrust of this type of energy is heightened. The first major nuclear accident was that at Three Mile Island (depicted in a movie called *The China Syndrome* that invoked the theory that meltdown of the nuclear core would have released such enormous quantities of heat that the core would melt all the way through the Earth's core and emerge from the other side in China). This accident—which fortunately had no grave consequences—was undoubtedly caused by the reactor design. The Chernobyl accident was far more serious.

Principal Oil Spills

Date	*Ship/Vessel/Pipeline*	*Ship-owner country*	*Location*	*Discharge*
1967	Torrey Canyon	Liberia	Great Britain	119,000 t
1970	Othello	?	Sweden	60,000 to 100,000 t
1972	Sea Star	South Korea	Gulf of Oman	115,000 t
1976	Urquiola	Spain	Spain	100,000 t
1977	Hawaiian Patriot	Liberia	Pacific Ocean	99,000 t
1978	Amoco Cadiz	Liberia	France	223,000 t

(Cont'd...)

1979	IXTOC-1 platform	–	Gulf of Mexico	500,000 to 1,500,000 t
1979	Atlantic Express Aegean Captain	?	Trinidad and Tobago	280,000 t
1980	Irenes Serenade	Greece	Greece	102,000 t
1983	Castillo de Bellver	Spain	South Africa	250,000 t
1989	Exxon Valdez	United States	Alaska	40,000 t
1991	Mina al Ahmadi oil terminal		Kuwait	700,000 to 900,000 t
1991	ABT SUMMER	Liberia	Off Angola	260,000 t
1991	Haven	Cyprus	Italy	144,000 t
1999	Erika	Malta	France	20,000 t
2001	Oil platform	Brazil	Brazil	350,000 t
2002	Prestige	Spain	Spain/France	77,000 t
2003	Tasman Spirit	Greece	Pakistan	12,000 t
2006	Lebanese oil reserves	–	Lebanon	15,000 t
2007	Hebei Spirit	China	China	10,000 t
2010	Deepwater Horizon drilling rig	US	Gulf of Mexico	6 – 700,000 t
2010	Qua Iboe	?	Nigeria	95,500 t
2010	Xingang Port	China	Dalian, China	90,000 t
2012	Maturin Pipeline	?	Venezuela	41,000 t

Source: Wikipedia and http://www.itopf.com/

The Chernobyl Catastrophe: Ukraine 1986

When the coolant system in a nuclear reactor fails to reduce the heat produced by the nuclear reaction sufficiently, the core of the reactor starts to melt causing a massive release of radioactivity. The USSR design of the so called RMBK reactors, or graphite moderated reactors, had a number of deficiencies, one of which was the absence of an efficient system of containment. The Chernobyl accident occurred when the gas emissions caused by the melting reactor blew off the concrete slab covering it, which had not been designed to resist such pressures. The gases then condensed in the atmosphere, forming a radioactive cloud that the wind blew west and southwesterly for several thousand miles over the next few days. Much of Europe was affected by the radioactive cloud. As for most catastrophes, the causes were an unfortunate combination of human error and technical problems.

In the months following the accident, the number of cases of cancer and abnormal births increased in the Chernobyl region. Many agricultural products became unfit for consumption. Despite this having been denied by the Soviet authorities, the explosion directly caused the death of some 12,500 people over a 10-year period, while roughly 4 million people—

(*Cont'd...*)

both civilian and military—suffered consequences of varying seriousness from the catastrophe. More than 70,000 of them became disabled. Over 11,000 people, 1,800 in Chernobyl and elsewhere as far as eastern France, were treated for thyroid cancer. Globally, this accident cost the international community more than $1 billion.

As a temporary solution, the residual radioactivity was confined by pouring concrete around the ruined reactor. This was mainly financed by the European Union, with contributions from the United States, in exchange for which the operation of the nuclear reactor was abandoned.

The Fukushima Accident

On March 11, 2011 an earthquake provoked a tsunami, which flooded the Fukushima region. Immediately after the earthquake, the active reactors automatically shut down their sustained fission reactions. However, the tsunami disabled the emergency generators that would have provided power to control and operate the pumps necessary to cool the reactors. The insufficient cooling led to three nuclear meltdowns, hydrogen-air explosions, and the release of radioactive material in Units 1, 2, and 3 from 12 to 15 March.

The wave of the tsunami was thirteen meters high and over whelmed the plant's seawall which was ten meter high. The water flooded the low lying rooms in which the emergency generators were housed. After a while the circulation of water, necessary to cool the reactors, stopped, leading to the explosions.

There have been no fatalities in the accident but a number of people could die from cancer due to the radiations in the following years.

The Fukushima accident has led a number of countries to abandon the nuclear energy.

References

1. It is said that OPEC countries play the role of "swing producers". This role is due to economic—but also geopolitical—reasons. Following the 1973 embargo by Arab oil-producing countries against certain consuming countries, the major oil-consuming countries sought to diversify their supplies and obtain oil from non-OPEC countries.
2. The Seven Sisters were: Esso, which became Exxon in 1977, Mobil (which merged with Exxon in 1999), Socal (now Chevron), Texaco (which merged with Chevron in 2001), Gulf (bought by Socal in 1984), Shell and BP. CFP (which would later become Total) was sometimes called the Eighth Sister.
3. In virtually the sole type of concession system used until 1966, and up to World War II the State granted the companies the right to exploit the oil in exchange

for a royalty (typically 12.5 per cent of the price of crude oil). After WWII and starting in Venezuela the oil producing countries imposed the so-called 50/50 sharing. This was a tax, usually 50 per cent, on their profits, i.e. on the difference between the sales price and production costs, that had to be paid by the companies in addition to the royalty.

4. This was in fact the "posted price" used by companies and the producing states to calculate the royalties and taxes paid by the companies. The actual transaction price (the FOB sales price of oil by companies to third-parties or to their subsidiaries) fell throughout the 1960s, reducing the companies' profit per barrel (higher sales volumes compensated for this) while the posted price system maintained the revenue per barrel of the producing states.
5. In netback contracts, the crude oil producer's selling price was calculated to equate to the price of products obtained by the refiner when he sells the gasoline, diesel fuel, fuel oil, etc. produced on the markets, less the transport and refining costs incurred. Refiners, who had been making substantial losses at the start of the 1980s, could at last balance their books. So they started to process more crude oil, and flooded the product markets making prices tumble.
6. Millions of BTUs—British Thermal Units. This is the traditional unit used for natural gas pricing. There are roughly 40 million BTUs to one ton of oil equivalent.
7. For a long time, oil produced in very deep water (ultra-deep offshore, beyond 1,500 meters of depth) was considered to be an unconventional oil. Since the depth at which production is feasible has increased over time and with technological progress, there is no longer any reason for this distinction and such oil is now considered to be conventional.
8. A large part of the Canadian oil sands and Venezuelan Extra Heavy Crude Oil are now included in the reserves of conventional oil by *BP Statistical Review* and the *Oil and Gas Journal.*
9. Former Oil Minister of Saudi Arabia.
10. This does not mean that fuel consumption can be limitless. Hydrocarbon reserves are by their nature limited and reducing waste must be a priority—a priority strengthened by the need to fight climate change.
11. Niels Bohr and an ancient Chinese proverb said the same thing.
12. "To put China on four wheels, we would need five planets". In China, there are roughly 100 cars per 1,000 inhabitants, versus several hundred in the US or Europe. If tomorrow, Chinese households used the same number of appliances as American or European households, each Chinese would use as much oil as Americans, i.e. 3 tons per year. There are 1.3 billion Chinese so their consumption would be 3.9 billion tons of oil p.a., which is close to the current annual world consumption. And China represents "only" one-fifth of the world's population.
13. Nm^3 is a cubic meter measured under standard (normal) conditions of temperature and pressure.
14. Market capitalisation is the value of the company as seen by the investment market; it is the multiple of the company's share price and the number of shares issued.
15. Also see Chapter 2—paragraph 5.4.

Chapter - 3

Structure of Energy Industries

The creation and development of production capacity and transport and distribution networks in industries in the energy sector have often been undertaken by private enterprise. Coal production in much of Europe, for example, was long controlled by well known individual families such as Krupp in Germany. In the oil sector, the names of the founders of major companies are still well-known: John Rockefeller (Standard Oil), Henri Deterding (Royal Dutch, then Royal Dutch Shell), Marcus Samuel (Shell), etc.

Nonetheless, governments quickly became aware of the strategic importance of energy industries and decided to play a prominent role in their development.

NATURAL MONOPOLIES AND EFFECTS OF SIZE

There have been many examples of industrial development that have benefitted from the obvious advantages of a natural monopoly and economies of scale. Why build two parallel railway lines, two parallel gas conduits, or two parallel power lines to service the same customer? What could be more natural than making a single company responsible for gas and electricity distribution over a given territory? Although in many countries prior to World War II several companies were involved in gas or electricity distribution, only one company operated in a given zone: each company had its territory. This idea of a natural monopoly extends to rail transport, but also to telecommunications, water distribution, and in general all "network" activities.

The history of the leading oil company Standard Oil, illustrates the benefits of size. Over a ten year period (1870-1880), John Rockefeller created a company that held a near-monopoly in refining and distribution of petroleum products in the United States. The company's size allowed it to negotiate the lowest price for the crude oil that it purchased from many small producers, who had little bargaining strength in the negotiation. Similarly he obtained highly advantageous transport costs from the independent companies, far lower than the prices given to his competitors. Initially, Rockefeller did not get involved in crude oil production, preferring to benefit from competition between the very numerous producers operating in what was still a limited market. At the end of the century, because of the substantial growth in demand for petroleum products, Standard Oil found that it needed at least some control over its crude oil supply to give the supply security necessary for product manufacture.

Rockefeller therefore added crude oil production to Standard Oil's activities.

However, Standard Oil's size and strength were the subject of increasingly severe criticism from the media from the beginning of the twentieth century. In 1911, the company was broken up into 34 companies under the 1890 Sherman Act (antitrust law). Among these new companies was Standard Oil of New Jersey (which became Esso, then Exxon), Standard Oil of New York (which became Mobil after merging with Vacuum), and Standard Oil of California (Socal which became Chevron).

The end of the twentieth/beginning of the twenty-first centuries were marked by a new wave of inter-company consolidation: BP-Amoco-Arco, Exxon-Mobil, Total-Fina-Elf, Chevron-Texaco, Conoco-Philipps, etc.

This wave of mergers and acquisitions continued with Statoil-Hydro, Chevron-Unocal, Conoco-Burlington and Rosneft-Yukos.

THE PETROLEUM INDUSTRY: INTERNATIONAL OIL COMPANIES AND NATIONAL OIL COMPANIES

As soon as the break-up of the Rockefeller Empire was complete, the new companies found themselves competing with other major companies that had been formed in the early stages of the oil industry. These included Gulf and Texaco which developed the oil fields in Texas around 1900, Royal Dutch in Indonesia, Shell (which would merge with Royal Dutch in 1907), and Anglo-Persian (today's BP) in Persia (Iran). The seven largest companies—the "Seven Sisters"[1]—according to the expression coined by Enrico Mattei, head of Agip and then of ENI (the Italian petroleum company), came to exercise control of the oil industry throughout the entire world. To avoid "excessive" competition, they met in 1928 at Achnaccary Castle in Northern Scotland. Under the agreement reached ("As Is" agreement) they divided existing markets between themselves and limited competition to new markets only.

Although the American companies cited above were established through private enterprise, the development of other international companies owed much to decisions taken by the governments concerned. In 1914, the British government, who had concluded a long-term contract with Anglo-Persian for the Royal Navy's fuel oil supplies, made a major investment in Anglo-Persian which made it the majority shareholder[2]. In 1924, the French State created Compagnie Française du Pétrole (CFP). This company took over Deutsch Bank's shares in the Turkish Petroleum Company as part of German reparations for war damage. That company, active in Mesopotamia, had been created before World War I to explore in what has since become Iraq.

After World War II, the French state created Elf- Aquitaine[3] to merge the equity stakes it held in several different companies. So the French government was responsible for the creation and development of two major companies: CFP which became Total, and Elf which merged with Total at the end of the twentieth century. The same government also established the Institut Français du Pétrole[4] (French Petroleum Institute), a research and training organisation known throughout the world and intended to ensure that France was not dependent on American oil industry technology. These actions also resulted in the creation of a powerful para-petroleum industry based on the development of companies with robust technical competence in the upstream sector, i.e. seismology, drilling, engineering, etc. (CGG, Technip—which merged with Coflexip, Axens, etc.).

Petroleum companies concentrate on different strategic objectives depending on their country of origin and their relationship with its government. Broadly speaking North American companies' main objectives are financial profitability, while European state-owned or formerly state-owned companies—Total, ENI, Repsol, etc.—were created to ensure their countries' security of supply. Their privatisation have nonetheless led them to adopt the same management objectives as their competitors who have always operated under a free market system.

NATIONALISATION OF GAS AND ELECTRICITY IN EUROPE

• Origins of the Gas and Electricity Industries

Gas and electricity supplies during the nineteenth and start of the twentieth centuries was largely developed by local private companies setting up production facilities and local distribution networks in large cities, often with the aid of foreign capital. In France, up to the eve of the Second World War, private companies produced gas, generated electricity and distributed them over areas that sometimes covered several towns. The same system was used for rail transport, with several different companies sharing the rail network between them. It was as though France had been cut into slices like a cake, with Paris at the centre. One of these companies was the famous PLM (Paris, Lyon, Marseille).

Although the use of gas for heating and lighting had been known to the Chinese for thousands of years, the industrial manufacture of gas in Europe only started around the end of the eighteenth century, with the development of "town gas". Produced, initially as a by-product from the manufacture of coke for the steel industry by the destructive distillation of bituminous coal in a closed vessel, this "synthetic" gas was first used for lighting during the nineteenth century.

In 1821, in Fredonia (United States), William Hart, considered to be the "father of natural gas", dug the first North American well, after noticing gas bubbles rising to the surface of a creek. The first known natural gas company, Fredonia Gas Light was formed in 1858. The invention of the Bunsen burner in 1885 led to new prospects for gas: heating, cooking, etc. Nonetheless, its consumption was restricted to small areas because the lack of a transport system made it difficult to ship large quantities of natural gas over long distances. In 1890 there was an important development: the invention of leak-proof couplings. Their use meant that a pipeline could be built to deliver gas to Chicago from a reservoir in Indiana.

But it was only after World War II that natural gas consumption made real progress, due to the development of pipe networks and storage systems. It then finally replaced town gas. In Europe, gas deposits were discovered in the Po Plain of Italy, in Lacq, France and Groningen, Netherlands in the 1950s, and then in the North Sea in the 1960s.

The history of the electric power industry started at the end of the nineteenth century. In 1869, a Belgian called Gramme developed the first industrial dynamo (a generator using electromagnets), only a year after Siemens's production of an experimental dynamo. In 1877, it was again Gramme who succeeded in the industrial manufacture of alternators. In 1879, direct current became available from a power plant for distribution in London. In 1882, Edison built a power plant in New York with a distribution network at competitive prices serving 59 customers equipped with electric light bulbs. At the end of the decade, the use of electric motors meant that demand extended over a full 24-hour day. Several US cities had an electricity production and distribution system, but the use of direct current strictly limited the area that could be served due to increase in power losses over long distance lines. The use of power lines for alternating electric current transmission was commercialised by Westinghouse, who had a hydroelectric dam[5] in New York State. So alternating current became the industry standard.

In 1900, privately-owned companies called IOUs[6] provided 90 per cent of electricity production. Competition between them for city center consumer markets was fierce. But the increasing cost, size and efficiency of generating plant made their consolidation inevitable. Electricity distribution networks were developed beyond city limits and soon outside states. Federal rules were initiated to regulate the rates and accounts of utilities— municipal production and distribution companies. Electricity distribution was recognised as being efficient as a natural monopoly so controlling standards were established for it. The federal government had to intervene to promote rural electrification because of inequalities in distribution between different areas and this was extended to electricity generation and distribution generally. This trend accelerated during the Great Depression and the discovery of IOUs abusing dominant market positions. By the end of 1941, the major hydroelectric programmes of the Tennessee Valley Authority had made the state and federal governments responsible for a significantly larger share of production.

- **Rise of Interventionism Following WW II**

From 1938, private gas producers in the United States sold to a single buyer who had a monopoly of transport and distribution in defined geographical areas. World War II marked a turning point in industrial organisation, particularly in Europe. In some countries, e.g. France and the Netherlands, the government opted to grant this monopoly to government- owned companies. In contrast, in the US the government preferred to grant the monopoly to private companies. In any case, as the sole buyer, the monopolistic company had control over the balance of supply and demand. The companies that resulted, like Gaz de France (GDF) in France and Gasunie in the Netherlands, were a great success. Vertical integration, which enables companies to have a global vision of available production capacities and distribution, and thus permits investment for both base and peak-load supply to be optimised, was predominantly used in Europe, but not in the US.

After the war, many industries were nationalised in a number of European countries, particularly in the rail, gas, electricity, and later the telecommunications sectors. This policy was for economic, political and social reasons:

- *Economic*: Government-owned companies have a monopoly, which allows them to reduce costs.
- *Political*: Nazi resistance movements, within which the communists played an important role, were generally hostile to the economic liberalism of the interwar period, a liberalism that favored the rise of Nazism; at times, nationalisation was seen as a way of punishing private owners accused of having collaborated with the German occupying authorities.
- *Social*: Government-owned companies seemed best able to meet the public service obligation of supplying all consumers at comparable prices, regardless of cost. Keynesian economic ideas were then dominant and state intervention in the economy seemed natural and beneficial to the social welfare.

The structure of the gas industry therefore changed in Europe after World War II. In France, the Nationalisation Law of April 6, 1946 created Gaz de France, which combined 615 gas businesses representing 550 coal gas plants (94 per cent of French gas assets).

As for gas, the development of electricity production and distribution was initially undertaken by private companies, operating locally. In 1946, in France, there were 154 companies operating 86 thermal power plants and 300 hydraulic power plants. Over 1,200 companies were concerned with transport and distribution. The Nationalisation Law dated April 6,1946 transferred all the electricity generation, transmission and distribution companies' assets to Électricité de France (EDF).

This economic structure worked well. The large, government-owned gas and electricity companies seemed best able to develop production capacity, transmission and distribution networks satisfactorily and meet the strong growth in consumer demand.

The 1960s seemed to mark the start of a new "golden age" of humanity, based on strong and uninterrupted economic growth. GDP increased by five per cent to six per cent per year and the application of Keynesian theories led to the belief that economic recessions had now been overcome. The increase in demand, particularly energy consumption[7], generated sustained economic growth.

But the sunny landscape of endless growth—and the significant consequence of near full employment in industrialised countries—started to darken at the end of the 1960s. Worries about the exponential increase in consumption grew. A group of experts, calling themselves the Club of Rome, published, *Limits to Growth*, in which they warned of the coming exhaustion of raw materials (see Chapter 2). At the same time, a new generation appeared which did not identify with consumerism and sought a new model for society.

PRODUCING COUNTRIES: CONTROL OVER THEIR OIL RESERVES

- **The 1960s: Creation of OPEC**

Because they were unhappy with the reductions in the oil price imposed by the Seven Sisters at the end of the 1950s, five of the largest oil producing countries—Saudi Arabia, Iraq, Iran, Kuwait and Venezuela—met in Bagdad in 1960 and, on September 14, created the Organisation of Petroleum Exporting Countries (OPEC)[8]. Initially OPEC's objective was to ensure price stability. This objective was achieved and the price of oil remained stable for 10 years. Moderate increases were agreed between OPEC and the oil companies over 1969–1972; then OPEC unilaterally increased prices by a factor of three in

1974 (the first oil shock), and once again by a factor of three between 1979 and 1981 (the second oil shock).

- **The 1970s: Nationalisation of the Petroleum Industry**

The model of a state monopoly discussed above was also widely adopted in the 1950s, 1960s and 1970s by third-world countries. In these developing countries, the most commonly held theories favoured the creation of large state-owned companies, as this was the sole means of obtaining the resources needed for the significant investments required[9]. These state-owned companies were responsible for the main sectors of economic activity and developed the production and distribution of water, gas and electricity. Similarly metalworking, oil and chemicals were transferred to state monopolies. This is the theory of cluster industrialisation, or an "industrialising industry": from one strong heavy industry, the rest of industry is built.

The 1960s movements towards the affirmation of third-world country status and independence of the former colonies came to include the re-appropriation of national resources by oil producing countries. In the 1970s, the petroleum industry assets, i.e. the oil fields and the facilities, were nationalised: by 1972 in Algeria, Iraq and Libya, in 1976 in Kuwait and Venezuela and, starting in 1976, in Saudi Arabia.

Governments of oil producing countries established state-owned companies to manage their interests in the exploitation of the country's resources. These companies were required to transfer the majority of their revenues back to the State, but they retained a portion to invest or at least renew their equipment.

The International Energy Agency

The International Energy Agency was created in 1974 by most member-countries of the OECD, with the notable exception of France, which only joined in 1992. This was in reaction to the events of 1973, in particular the embargo ordered by the oil-producing Arab countries against several other countries, including the United States and the Netherlands, accused of supporting Israel in the Yom Kippur war. The main first objective of the IEA is to implement a system of reallocation of oil in case of reduction of oil supplies. This includes setting up strategic stocks and publishing regular and reliable statistics and studies on energy markets.

Today, however, IEA responsibility has expanded to include energy policy making in terms of economic development and environmental protection, as well as energy security. Its work covers diversification of energy sources, renewable energy, climate change policies, market reform, energy efficiency, development and deployment of clean energy technologies, energy technology collaboration with major consumers and producers of energy like China, India, Russia and the OPEC countries. IEA undertake a broad programme of energy research, data compilation, publications and public dissemination of the latest energy policy analysis and recommendations on good practices.

- **The Years 1980–1990: OPEC's Loss of Power–Members' Interests Diverge**

At the beginning of the 1980s, the increase in the price of oil had resulted in a fall in demand and the development of significant non-OPEC production. In the 1980s the cartel lost control of the market and its market share fell, by the mid-1980s, to less than 30 per cent from more than 50 per cent of world production in the 1970s (today it is around 40 per cent). This was despite the cartel's member-countries holding 80 per cent of world reserves and benefitted from production costs that were among the lowest on the market.

The fall in prices had been inevitable because of the significant capacity surpluses that resulted from the drop in demand. In response, OPEC established a quota system to reduce the production of the (then) 13 member countries in an agreed way. From 1982, OPEC accepted the role of swing producer: the other countries produced at maximum capacity and OPEC adjusted its production to demand. This situation lasted until roughly 2003, when surplus capacity had largely disappeared and OPEC could benefit from very high oil prices without having to reduce its production.

At times of low crude oil prices, there will always be differences of opinion between countries that seek to curb production in order to raise prices and countries that, having greater need for revenue, seek to maximise their production.

Toward Mutual Dependency

The crisis of 1973 and the embargo that was imposed made industrialised countries, the major consumers of oil, aware how dependent they had become on oil exporting countries. But since the 1970s, the reality has become more complex:

- The major exporting countries remain highly dependent on their oil revenues, which provide most of their budgetary income. Any interruption in exports would quickly have fair consequences for the exporters themselves.
- The exporting countries import massive quantities of finished goods and agricultural products. The European Union is the main trading partner of the producing countries of the Gulf.

– The exporting countries have numerous financial assets ("petrodollars" or "petroeuros") in Western economies. The yield on these assets depends on the economic growth of the countries in which they are invested, i.e. the energy-consuming countries. But historically this growth is in inverse proportion to the growth in crude oil prices. In addition to this, there is the risk that assets could be frozen, as was seen in the United States in the anti-terrorism programme that followed the attacks of September 11, 2001.

The producing countries, OPEC in particular, are therefore dependent on their sales of oil—and gas—to balance their budgets. Producing countries (which need revenue) and consuming nations (which need oil and gas) are thus increasingly mutually dependent.

- **The Recent Situation: Openings to New Ideas?**

After the creation of all-powerful national companies by nationalisation during the 1970s, the trend was reversed in the 1980s and 1990s. State-owned national companies were under pressure because oil prices were low; they reacted by gradually liberalising their policies and deciding to benefit from the technological expertise and financial capacities of the international companies. Some companies like Petrobras (Brazil), Lukoil (Russia) or subsidiaries of state-owned national companies like Petronas Gas (Malaysia) went so far as partial privatisation and became listed on their national stock exchanges.

The new oil bull market of the 2000s meant that, for some companies such as Sonatrach and Pemex, this liberalisation trend has been frozen. Moreover oil producing states have used the strength derived from their increased revenues to impose tougher taxation regimes and, rather than co-operate with international companies, had their state-owned company rely on the expertise of para-petroleum companies or particularly dynamic national companies that are developing their own expertise and using it at an international level: Petrobras towards deep offshore West Africa, Petrochina, Petronas, Petrovietnam and ONGC, setting off to win new business in Africa, Asia and Latin America, etc. When faced with significant opportunities for the development or recovery of national assets, some of these national companies (Rosneft and Petrochina) will even go as far as strengthening their capital by getting listed on local or foreign stock exchanges. Other state-owned companies in Kuwait, Libya, Saudi Arabia and South America (particularly PDVSA) have also been very active abroad, taking equity stakes in companies operating downstream in consuming countries[10].

POST THE 1970S: LIBERALISATION, PRIVATISATION AND NEW REGULATIONS

- **Problems of Keynesianism and the Return of Liberalism[11]: Weakening of the State's Role**

At the beginning of the 1970s, economic growth in Europe started to slow down, with an increase in unemployment following the first oil shock of 1973. Despite all the measures taken by the various governments of North America, Europe and Japan to stimulate their economies, a new phenomenon appeared: stagflation[12]. Since the war it had seemed possible for governments to manage the economy to avoid unemployment and high inflation, but it did not work. Inflation exceeded 10 per cent in many countries. Unemployment also reached nearly 10 per cent in a number of countries during the 1980s.

Liberal economic theories, ignored during the period when Keynesian-inspired economic policies had seemed successful, returned to fashion. According to these theories, Western economies were suffering from excessive state intervention. Deregulation and privatisation were required.

The purpose of *deregulation* was to eliminate barriers to competition. Price controls must be abolished, monopolies replaced by companies operating competitively, customs barriers must be lifted. Deregulation is often based on the theory that, because of technical progress, production facilities that are lighter and more flexible can compete with natural monopolies and show better performance. Greater competition between economic players is supposed to promote progress and benefit the consumer in the form of lower prices. Consumers can then consume more and/or invest more: in either case, economic activity is increased. This is a virtuous circle whose positive effects should benefit everyone.

Privatisation is above all a means to achieving greater efficiency: private companies subject to control by their shareholders are supposed to perform better than state monopolies. The state is not the most competent organisation to manage production operations. There is another objective, albeit less respectable: filling the coffers of the state.

State control was, until recently, very strong in the downstream sector, refining and marketing, of most countries apart from the US and a few European countries. Deregulation took place in the 1980s with the objective of increasing competition and thus lowering prices. It was implemented first in Europe, subsequently in countries like Japan, and finally in developing countries. In France, the last price controls on fuels were abolished in 1986, and in 1992 a new law was enacted significantly reducing the government's control over the petroleum industry.

- **Example of the British Energy Sector**

At the start of the 1970s Chile, a country that had gone from the socialist regime of Salvador Allende to the military regime of Augusto Pinochet, was where Milton Friedman's "Chicago Boys" put their economic theories into practice. But it was the 1979 arrival of Margaret Thatcher, the Leader of the Conservative Party, in power in the United Kingdom that marked the beginning of the liberalisation of Western economies. The British Prime Minister's fight against regulation reached its zenith during the coal miners' strike. Despite impressive mobilisation by the miners, the strike was defeated by the government. That weakened the trade unions to the extent that deregulation and privatisation could rapidly follow.

In the oil sector, the privatisation of BNOC (British National Oil Corporation) was the first step. Deregulation of the gas industry started in 1982 and, with the 1986 *Gas Act*, competitors of British Gas, which up to then had been a monopoly, were authorised to use its network to supply consumers using more than 25,000 therms per year. Next, British Gas was required to separate its gas transport and trading operations into two independent companies: Transco and British Gas International. This principle of separating activities was known as "unbundling". In addition, an independent regulatory body, the Office of Gas Supply (Ofgas) was created to promote competition, and the gas industry was placed under the authority of the Office of Fair Trading, responsible for ensuring compliance with competition legislation. Several years later, British Gas had to separate its exploration/production activities (which remained in the hands of British Gas International) from marketing and distribution which was passed to a new company, Centrica, currently a key player.

Deregulation of the electric power sector started in 1990. A pool of producers was established with a system of daily auction sales for wholesale supplies. However, prices increased in the initial years which, of course, was contrary to the objectives set. This shows the need to continue with some regulation, at least for the transition phase.

- **Example of the American Energy Sector**

In the US, regulation of the distribution of oil, gas and electricity between states is overseen by an independent government agency, officially linked to the Department of Energy: the Federal Energy Regulatory Commission (FERC). It was formed as a result of the 1977 reorganisation of the Federal Power Commission (FPC), itself created in 1920. It also oversees wholesale sales of electricity and oil, grants licenses for hydroelectric projects, and approves the construction of interstate pipelines, storage infrastructure and liquefied natural gas terminals. It ensures non-discriminatory third-party access to the network and can force a company deemed to have an excessively dominant position to be broken up into autonomous companies.

When he became President of the United States in 1981, Ronald Reagan modeled his economic policy on that of Margaret Thatcher. At that time the structure of the natural gas industry in the US was simple: gas producers sold their product to distribution companies, who were granted licenses by the Federal government for particular routes in order to promote the construction of interstate networks. Wellhead gas prices and the price for sales to LDCs (Local Distribution Companies) had been regulated by the Federal government since 1956. The price to the end user was set by the states.

In 1985, it became possible for users to buy gas directly from producers, independently of any transport contract. Then in 1992, the separation of transport and sales activities was decreed by law. These sectors were opened to competition: users could now freely choose their service providers. At the same time, a spot market for gas developed starting in 1982, and wellhead prices were completely deregulated by 1989.

FERC also initiated the movement for restructuring the electric power market. In 1992, the Energy Policy Act opened electricity production to competition, authorising a new category of independent producers to sell energy outside their state of origin. Thus, the US went from a system of territorial licenses to a free market in which customers were no longer reliant on a single supplier.

In 2017, the position in the US is that the structures from one state to another are very different, but these different structures co-exist. Some states have totally deregulated the power sector, while others have not, and the variety of players remains very large.

- **Developing a Single Energy Market in the European Union**

In Europe, the trend toward deregulation and privatisation is consistent with the outlook mapped out by the founding fathers,[13] who wanted to create a single economic market which would be open to competition. Nevertheless the European Commission has maintained the concept of public service, describing it as "general interest service".

In the energy sector, the abolition of all price controls on oil products was the first step. Then, gradually and following the British example, gas and electricity were deregulated. In 2007, the gas and electricity markets including sales to private individuals were opened to competition.

The European Union Gas Directive, enacted in 1997, was intended to create a competitive market for natural gas around common rules for transport, distribution, provision and storage. It is based on the right of third-party access to the transport network and storage in order to give eligible users the capability of purchasing their gas directly from producers. The directive requires integrated gas companies to separate their various activities into different corporate companies.

In practice the implementation of this directive by the member states, i.e. its incorporation into national legislation, took time. Member countries dragged their feet for various reasons: attachment to the concept of public service, social pressure to maintain the status quo and protection of jobs, the desire to put their national "champion" in the best position possible to confront competition, etc.

- **Results of Deregulation and Privatisation Policies**

Deregulation of the oil sector has posed no major problems: privatisation of companies operating in the downstream sector is virtually complete; where privatisation has not been implemented in the upstream sector that is often because ideological reasons have been given priority over economic efficiency.

Deregulation of the gas sector is more difficult. Because this industry is dependent on a pipeline network, the natural monopoly concept fits it well as it would be illogical to construct two networks for the same customer. This has given rise to the concept of "third-party network access", based on the telecoms model, allowing any supplier to service a customer through existing networks without having to build new infrastructure, which would obviously be wasteful.

In the electric power sector, the policies have had very mixed results and it is not clear that the promised decrease in prices has been achieved. In many developing countries, the privatisation of power companies seems to have been adopted as the solution to the government's failure to make customers pay their bills, or to finance the development, or even just the replacement, of the infrastructure. Additional progress must be made[14].

SITUATION IN DEVELOPING COUNTRIES

The oil shock of 1973, reinforced by that of 1979–1980 and combined with the economic crisis of the 1970s, put many developing countries in a difficult economic position, typified by budget deficits and endemic external debt. The crisis would force these countries to turn to industrialised nations and international organisations for loans to make up their deficits. This was the start of the "structural adjustment loans", made by international institutions to these countries who could not use capital markets to finance their debt. But, for the poorest countries, a condition of these loans was that they agreed to transform the way their economies operated.

As in industrialised countries, their difficulties were attributed to excessive government intervention: national industrial companies with too large personnel, price freezes to avoid inflation, and frequently, currency exchange rates that were totally disconnected from economic reality.

In many developing countries, deregulation and privatisation policies were implemented under the influence of international organisations, like the IMF and the World Bank. The results were mixed. Although Asian countries achieved robust economic growth, sometimes without the help of international organisations, in South America, and particularly in Africa, the difficulties remained.

The Example of Ghana

At the beginning of the 1980s, Ghana's economic situation was catastrophic: agricultural exports were at their lowest, industrial production was low, and the currency exchange rate was completely distorted. The official rate was one dollar for three cedi (Ghanaian currency), while on the black market a dollar was worth ten times more. Because of this, the government, taxed imports and subsidised exports both by that factor of ten: so one ton of crude oil imported at 600 cedis at the official rate would incur 5,000–6,000 cedis tax and the exporter of one ton of products worth 700 cedis would receive a subsidy of 7,000 cedis. To get the system back to normal, the World Bank encouraged the Ghanaian government to hold "auction sales" of dollars that it could make available immediately; the "official" rate that resulted from these auctions approached the black market rate. Under the influence of the World Bank, the government—at the time headed by Flight Lieutenant Rawlings, whose political leanings were fairly leftist—implemented a policy of price deregulation and privatisation of several public companies. By comparison with other neighbouring countries, Ghana's position today can be described as favourable, in part because of the strong support given by financial lenders (international organisations, bilateral aid and private companies).

ETHICS AND ENERGY

We can live without many things, but energy is indispensable to our society. The production and use of energy poses many ethical and moral problems. The production of energy causes pollution, whether it involves exploration or field development of an oil or gas deposit, transport of hydrocarbons, or production and transmission of electricity. It can be a source of corruption. As in all sectors of activity, energy companies—particularly oil companies—cannot ignore the social and political context in which they operate. In fact, they maintain complex relationships with their environment: site development of a deposit may result in many people being hired for jobs and the development of a local transport network, but may also lead to corruption, the use of forced labour, and pollution.

This brings up the issue of company responsibility: is it legitimate for an oil company to seek to ensure "correct" use of the revenue it distributes to the state where it operates? Is that within its competence; is it part of its duty? Must it secure its production sites against outside attacks, contribute to local development by building roads and schools, or set up a health insurance or pension systems? Should it operate in countries where human rights are not respected? The answer would be easy if the deposits of oil available were infinite, but this is not the case. In a context of limited reserves—some of which are not accessible—relinquishing the exploitation of a profitable deposit would either result in it being exploited by a competitor, or in the supply being lost to the market and thus in increased prices which would penalise consumers. After long being criticised for interfering in national political life, companies are sometimes asked[15] to assume some of the state's responsibilities in the countries where they operate.

A duty of continuous vigilance is necessary for the companies, while governments have a dual responsibility: pressing for the implementation of effective international rules, and then monitoring their correct application. Civil society can play a crucial role in supervision and as referee of last resort by exercising its power of electoral sanction and its ability to carry out economic boycotts.

INCREASED COMPETITION

The re-appropriation of national hydrocarbon resources by producing states during the 1960s and 1970s hardened the competition between international companies. Competition has become even more intense over the past years with the arrival of new players on the international market (independent companies from countries whose oil reserves are mature, e.g. the United States; or national companies seeking to expand into new markets, e.g. China). Also relevant is the expected fall in the number of new fields discovered, which makes it difficult for companies to replace their reserves. Although they controlled 60 per cent of world reserves in the 1970s, international companies today only control a small percentage (about three per cent). On an average, the majors have a Reserves-to-Production (R/P) ratio of about 10 years. Access to new fields and the technology required to increase the production ratio of existing deposits has become of strategic importance.

Nonetheless, relationships between major oil companies are more complex than they appear. Behind the fierce competition between the companies to access resources and find outlets for the crude oil they produce, they also cooperate on major projects. Faced with the capital intensity of some of these projects, they form joint ventures operated by jointly owned subsidiaries. This enables the companies to invest in a wider range of projects and so spread their risk. Other forms of co-operation include asset transfers/exchanges to optimise companies' tax positions or achieve regional synergies.

A climate of increased competition combined with pressure from shareholders for higher profits led to a series of major mergers and acquisitions at the end of the 1990s. This was a follow-up to the cost reductions that had already been achieved internally, by reorganisation etc., to reach the critical size needed for optimum profitability. But the difficulties of integrating different cultures made one-third of these ventures fail.

These mergers and acquisitions have raised fears that the new stronger companies could again achieve dominant market positions. However, Exxon (following the merger with Mobil) has a share of only four per cent of worldwide production, although in 1973 it was three times that for Esso alone. Contrary to popular belief, the players with "market power" (the ability of a player to influence the entire market by using its strong position) are the large state-owned companies rather than the *majors*. Aramco, the national oil company of Saudi Arabia, has a 12 per cent share of production, while the five largest non-national companies combined have just 15 per cent.

Today, links between private (i.e. usually publically-quoted) international companies and their home countries are no longer close. Such companies operate autonomously and refuse to be used as tools for achieving national strategic objectives. Their home nations are now happy to play the role of market organiser and facilitator: creating a political and economic environment that favours competitive market operation and a climate of confidence that stimulates economic activity (Fig. 29).

Governments can still intervene "directly" to guide and support a company, particularly to help it access reserves that are closed for political reasons. It is in the best interest of a company's nation of origin for the company to be in good health, if only because this maximises the taxes the company pays each year. So it is no longer the company that acts for the state, but rather the state that acts for the company.

The companies involved in the natural gas market are often oil companies, either national or international, or electricity generating companies seeking control over their supplies (e.g. the union of E.On and Ruhrgas, or the GDF-Suez merger which improves Suez's access to its gas supplies). There are therefore a number of equity cross-holdings between oil and gas companies. Does this presage a move towards multi-energy companies? Whatever the case, competition with the other energy companies is increasing upstream and also downstream with other companies using network distribution (water, telecoms, etc.).

There is less vertical integration in the gas sector than in the oil, coal or power industries. For example, the US the gas industry is highly diversified and no company plays a dominant role. There are roughly 1,400 local distribution companies and 23,000 gas producers, with the seven largest producing approximately a third of total domestic production. There are more than forty separate interstate transport companies. The transport companies and local distribution networks have different owners, either major oil companies or independent companies or they may be owned by municipalities.

In electricity generation, there are a few giant companies and a multitude of micro-producers. In the longer term, the European market is expected to be shared between a few multi-energy companies, probably including EDF, Suez, the German companies RWE and E.On…

The main players in the nuclear energy business consist of a few large companies, based in countries with the necessary technical expertise, and

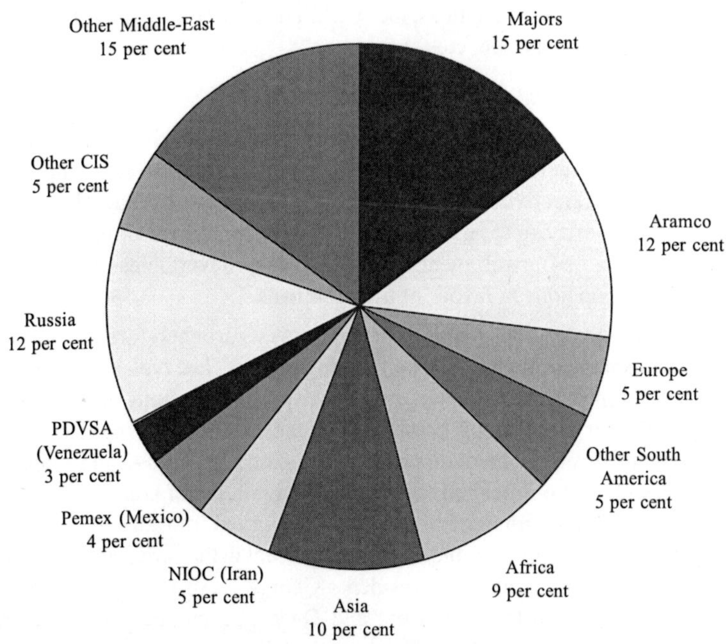

Source: IEA.

Figure 29: World Oil Production.

originally receiving government support. Some companies are very active in this market niche.

OTHER OFTEN FORGOTTEN PLAYERS

Apart from the players operating directly on the energy markets, there are others who have an influence on the general environment and thus have the ability to affect the markets' operation.

- **International Organisations**

The UN, a major forum for discussion and an organisation for the resolution of problems between nations, has the right to consider all international issues. Thus, it plays a role in armed conflicts (direct intervention or by mandate) and in embargos, for example the Iraq "Oil for Food" programme.

The International Monetary Fund and the World Bank affect the structure of the economies of the many developing countries who have obtained finance from them. These institutions have helped to launch the liberalisation and deregulation programmes in many parts of the world (see above).

The International Maritime Organisation (IMO) is responsible for international maritime regulations; the World Trade Organisation (WTO) agrees rules of international trade, etc.

- **Economic and Political Interests: Lobbies**

When energy prices increase, the consequences are felt throughout the entire industrial sector and so, in the end on retail prices. In some industries profitability is directly linked to changes in the price of crude oil, e.g. the automobile industry, or to coal e.g., the steel industry. Where companies today are independent of government authorities, they nevertheless try to guide government decisions in favour of their interests.

Pressure groups representing special interests are therefore organised to be omnipresent in political decision-making centres. The typical actions they take are attempts to make tax rules favourable to them or, inversely, unfavourable or penalising for competitors; the enactment of regulations that are advantageous for them or disadvantageous for competitors; and economic diplomacy (use of political power abroad to obtain major contracts). Indeed even heads of state on international visits are turned into salesmen for their national industries. Innumerable lobbies are present in the corridors of Brussels. The family of both American presidents George Bush is very close to the powerful Texas petroleum industry, and Dick Cheney, the American Vice President up to 2009, was for a long time the CEO of Halliburton, one of the worldwide leaders in the para-petroleum sector.

The view that people take of these practices depends on their culture. In the United States and in much of the European Community, allowing these special interests free expression is thought to be the best means of counteracting them. On the other hand in other countries, lobbying sometimes takes the form of clandestine power-plays that are subject to no democratic oversight.

- **Civil Society**

Non-governmental organisations (NGOs) such as Greenpeace or Human Rights Watch are players who act against what they see as "collusions of interest between the powerful" and have to be taken seriously. They influence public opinion, particularly because they are seen as independent from political or economic powers. They expose political and environmental scandals: for example Halliburton was accused of having benefitted from the preferential awarding of contracts in Iraq by American authorities; details of corruption by oil companies in Africa were revealed during the 1980s.

In July 1985, the ship Rainbow Warrior, belonging to the environmental organisation Greenpeace, docked in Auckland. It had intended to go, with other ships, to the Mururoa archipelago to protest against French nuclear tests. On July 10, France's foreign intelligence service (DGSE) sunk the ship. Unfortunately, a Portuguese photographer, Fernando Pereira, was onboard the ship that day and drowned. The two French agents responsible for the attack made a series of blunders which led to their arrest by New Zealand police.

So public opinion is of increasing importance in the debate. Indeed the major obstacle to the development of nuclear energy is the public's reservations concerning the environmental and health risks associated with nuclear power.

- **Research and Training Institutes**

Independent research institutes develop technology in parallel with the major energy companies' research centres. IFP Energies nouvelles (formerly IFP—Institut français du pétrole), was formed in 1944 to promote the development of French technology during an era when American technology was virtually all that was available. Other institutes (the Institute of Petroleum – now merged into the Energy Institute in London, the American Petroleum Institute, etc.) have the mission of creating links to industry, promoting information exchange, training, improving standards, etc.

- **Criminal Movements**

Because of the money it generates and the potential damage it can cause, the energy industry naturally attracts some illegal and even some criminal activities. The Strait of Malacca is, for example, the worst channel in the world for piracy. Fees paid by oil companies can be diverted by powerful mafia groups; the destruction of oil pipelines can be threatened or used to apply political pressure, etc. (see Chapter 4).

We must distinguish between groups whose prime objective is financial (e.g. the mafia) and who use political means to that end, and those who are totally politically motivated. But the latter do not hesitate to use illegal means to finance their terrorist activities. It was clear from the attacks of September 11 that petrodollars from the Arabian Peninsula can be diverted *via* various buffer organisations (shell companies, so-called charitable organisations, etc.) to finance terrorist activism. In response western countries—led by the United States—froze various financial assets that had come from this region. As a result, a number of financial assets were transferred from the US to Europe, or even Asia or the Middle East.

Today's major fear is that a supertanker or LNG tanker could be high-jacked and used as a bomb to attack a port or, even worse, an oil terminal or gas liquefaction or re-gasification terminal. This has lead to the reinforcement of maritime security over the past few years.

CONCLUSION

Private companies and national governments have had a shared objective: the need for the energy sector to be integrated to take advantage of the economies of scale available and the benefits that accrue to natural monopolies. But within that each has played the game of advancing their individual goals.

The oil industry's origin was the simple exploitation of a raw material and its structure was based on private companies. Then, in accordance with the accepted ideology of the time and because oil's increased strategic importance raised the question of security of supply, governments became involved and sought to control the business. Finally, as economic ideology changed, governments accepted the need to deregulate and allow the market to operate as it had in the industry's early days. The oil market has seen the spot market develop, and then the futures markets. The oil price is now determined by the free operation of these markets, without political interference; it is transparent and so is used for financial and industrial dealings. These developments came as a response to operational problems; the extent to which the industrial and commercial players participated in the decisions varied.

The structure of the oil sector has changed throughout its history. Initially private companies were dominant, governments then intervened when oil's strategic importance became apparent, the end of the twentieth century saw privatisation and deregulation, and the last few years there has been a return to some level of interventionism.

The fundamental objective of the gas and electricity industries is liberalisation of the market, including the application of the oil market's rules.

All policies are subordinated to that end. Governments are determined to apply the economic theory that liberalism and competition are the keys to economic progress.

References

1. Esso, Mobil, Socal, Gulf, Texaco, Royal Dutch Shell and BP.
2. Under this agreement the government undertook not to intervene in commercial policy but was given the right to appoint two non-executive directors to the Board, a right it retained until the sale of the government's holding under Margaret Thatcher.
3. See *Oil and Gas Exploration and Production*–N. Bret-Rouzaut and J.-P. Favennec, Ed. Technip, 2011.
4. Now IFP Energies nouvelles.
5. Niagara Falls, in 1896.
6. Investor Owned Utilities.
7. The doubling of electricity consumption every 10 years became both an objective and an assumption and the petroleum industry continuously scheduled the construction of new pipelines, tankers, refineries, and service stations.
8. Today, OPEC includes 14 countries: Saudi Arabia, Iran, Iraq, Kuwait, Qatar, United Arab Emirates, Algeria, Libya, Nigeria, Angola, Gabon, Equatorial Guinea, Venezuela and Ecuador. Indonesia left the organisation in 2016.
9. Remember that the post-war era was also marked by the advent of the USSR as the second dominant power in the world to the United States. The Soviet economic model—often described as the Socialist model—was used as a reference by countries that had just won their independence after conflicts, many of them violent, with the former colonial power which was seen as in the camp of imperialist and capitalist countries. The Soviet model, founded on collective ownership of the means of production, is based on state-owned companies managing all sectors of the economy. This model was widely admired in the third world, so much so that Nikita Khrushchev, General Secretary of the Communist Party, could declare at the end of the 1950s that "the USSR's wealth will surpass that of the United States by 1980" and this statement did not seem incongruous.
10. Also see Chapter 2.
11. In this book, the terms liberal, liberalism and liberalisation are used in the economic sense of meaning freedom from state interference or control. They should not be taken in the sense that the word liberal is currently used in political debate in the US.
12. The word stagflation is a contraction of stagnation and inflation.
13. The "small steps" doctrine of Robert Schuman and Jean Monet, which started with the European Coal and Steel Community (ECSC) and Euratom, two organisations designed to coordinate European policies, particularly in the energy sector.
14. See the conclusions of the Energy Summit in Africa, held annually since 2002.
15. For these topics, refer also in particular to the chapter on Africa, the problems in Nigeria and initiatives like *Publish What You Pay*, EITI, etc.

Chapter - 4

Energy Policies and Security of Supplies

Energy plays a fundamental role in economic and social activity, particularly in the transport sector. Two examples illustrate this well:

- During World War II, the availability of crude oil for the manufacture of fuels was the priority for the German army. After seizing the Romanian oil fields one of Germany's objectives in declaring war on the Soviet Union and invading Russia, was control of the oil deposits of Baku and the Volga. In fact, the German troops were defeated at Stalingrad and so failed to take control of Russian oil. A little later, Rommel headed toward the Middle East where giant oil deposits had just been discovered, but British troops and a lack of fuel prevented him from reaching his goal. Germany had to resort to coal liquefaction for the manufacture of fuel.
- In third-world countries, any shortage of petroleum products makes it more difficult to harvest food supplies and more importantly impossible to transport them to cities and thus feed urban populations. In the 1970s, the higher oil prices had particularly harmful consequences for many African countries: unable to buy oil they had to let the harvests wither because there was no transport available for them.

During the 1973 crisis, the OPEC countries' (Organisation of Petroleum Exporting Countries) embargo on oil deliveries to western countries that supported Israel during the Yom Kippur war, led these countries to take drastic measures to reduce their oil consumption. The fact that both the scope and duration of the embargo were limited did not change the fact that, in Western eyes, oil supplies from Arab countries were considered not secure and other sources must be sought. To reduce their dependence on OPEC oil, western governments promoted the development of new oil fields in Alaska, the North Sea, and later the Gulf of Mexico, the Gulf of Benin, and the Caspian region.

Although in 1973, Western countries depended on Gulf countries to make their economies run (up to 70 per cent of energy requirements in some countries were met by oil, mainly imported from the Middle East), the position in the twenty-first century is quite different. Oil's share in energy consumption has decreased, and OPEC's share of these supplies has also decreased. In addition, although consuming countries still need oil and gas, producing countries also need the revenues they provide.

Security of energy supplies remains anyway a priority. However, although 40 years ago it seemed that recourse to military means might be necessary, today the operation of an active and transparent market is seen as an alternative method for having secure supplies.

SOLUTIONS OFFERED BY THE MARKET

Starting from the observation that embargos like that of 1973 have never reoccurred, in 2000 John Mitchell (Royal Institute of International Affairs, Chatham House, Great Britain) told a European summit dedicated to the topic that it was now exporting countries and no longer importing countries that are vulnerable to the risk of disruption in supplies for political reasons. In fact, recently it was exporting countries that were subject to embargos (Libya, Iraq and Iran). Thus, over a period of thirty years, the nature of the risk has changed; what was a physical risk has become an economic risk.

Until the second oil shock, most oil was bought and sold under a rigid system of long-term contracts. After 1980, the development of a spot market was made possible by the increasing flexibility of contracts (particularly spot contracts, negotiated for single cargoes on a cargo by cargo basis). This now achieves an almost instantaneous balance between supply and demand by changes in the price. The risk has therefore become a financial risk. To meet the risk that arises from possible price changes, increasingly varied and complex financial coverage products have been developed, to the extent that the oil market has now become a financial market. This system enables physical risk to be anticipated and taken into account by financial means.

However, monitoring developments in the market can be difficult because of the lack of data. The availability of better statistics progressively improves knowledge of market mechanisms and so increases understanding of the question of supply security. Proposals[1] were made in Europe to improve oil supply security. One was for bimonthly publication of statistics on commercial and strategic oil stocks in Europe to improve market transparency in this respect. The impact of American statistics on stock levels on market prices is well known and a matter of common observation.

There is also a trend towards the development of a spot market for gas, particularly for LNG even if importing countries still use long-term contracts to ensure supply security.

The trend towards the integration of markets to give improved supply can be seen in all energy sources. But in the period of geopolitical tensions, the military tool is once again being used.

HOW TO IMPROVE SUPPLY SECURITY

The best way to ensure supply security is by controlling consumption, i.e. by improving energy efficiency. An increase in demand makes improving energy efficiency an even more important challenge. It has also meant that diversification of energy and supply sources are more and more indispensable.

- **Energy Efficiency**

In 2005, the European Union published a "Green Book" on energy efficiency, in which several measures were proposed to reduce waste as much as possible. It was stressed that success cannot be based solely on technological advances; it must also come from increased awareness encouraging citizens to change their behaviour as consumers. In 2012, EU Energy Efficiency Directive established binding measures to make European countries energy efficient.

On a worldwide scale, initiatives to improve energy efficiency and reduce fossil energy consumption remain limited. The IEA has prepared measures to change consumer behaviour, but they are measures that could only be adopted when there was a serious supply crisis.

Energy Efficiency in the European Union

The EU has set itself a 20 per cent energy savings target by 2020 roughly equivalent to turning off 400 power stations.

In 2016, the European Commission proposed a 2030 binding energy efficiency target of 30 per cent for the European Union. The new target is part of the Commission's proposal to update the Energy Efficiency Directive to make sure the new target is met.

The key policies under the EU directive for energy efficiency are annual reduction of 1.5 per cent in national energy sales, the preparation of National Energy Efficiency Action Plans every three years by EU countries, the planned rollout of close to 200 million smart meters for electricity and 45 million for gas by 2020 and large companies conducting energy audits at least every four years.

The main objective of this programme is clearly the wish to involve as many players in the energy business as possible and mobilise them in its support. The European Union believes that, at an international level, it should drive the instigation of measures to promote sustainable development and therefore intends to strengthen cooperation with nations (the US, Russia, China, etc.)

- **Diversification of Energy Sources**

The breakdown of total energy consumption into the different forms of energy used varies greatly from country to country. Industrialised countries use varying proportions of oil, natural gas, coal, nuclear energy and renewable energies.

Canada's and Norway's electricity generation is mainly hydraulic, while France uses its massive nuclear energy development.

Gas meets some 55 per cent of Russia's energy needs, but a much lower proportion in France and Spain. The main reasons for these differences that arise even between developed countries are the chances of the country's geology and their different national energy policies.

The situation in developing countries is even more diverse. The least advanced countries of course rely overwhelmingly on biomass and, among commercial energies, oil plays a predominant role. Natural gas and coal are not widely used since gas requires a massive and costly infrastructure and coal would require thermal power plants too large for local markets.

The diversification of energy sources is essential if excessive dependency is to be avoided: e.g. dependency on oil, which may be from unstable sources and with variable prices; and dependency on gas with its disadvantage of generally having a limited number of sources. Diversification reduces the consequences of one of the supply sources failing but its possibilities have at least one limit: oil meets 95 per cent of transport sector demand.

- **Geographical Diversification of Supply Sources**

There were two different reactions to the 1973 oil shock: one was a reduction in energy consumption; the second was the substitution of gas and coal for fuel oil to the maximum extent possible[2]. The second oil shock in 1979 reinforced this trend and led to a substantial reduction in world oil consumption. Both oil shocks made consuming countries aware of the absolute necessity of avoiding dependence on Gulf countries, or on any limited number of suppliers. Apart from the substantial increase in prices, western countries were faced with the strong psychological shock of suddenly realising the heavy financial burden that oil posed for their economies, and that the oil embargo imposed on some of them threatened the operation of their entire economic system. Diversification of oil supplies was made easier by the ten-fold increase in the price of oil, which made possible the development of oil fields (Alaska, the North Sea, offshore production in Latin America and Africa, etc.) that had previously been unprofitable.

This supply diversification is now even more necessary as, although OPEC's share of world oil production fell from 50 per cent in 1973 to under 30 per cent in the mid-1980s, it rose once again to about 45 per cent in 2015 and IEA estimates that it will exceed 50 per cent between 2020 and 2030. So the world's dependency on OPEC will again be considerable, and that is because the Gulf countries have nearly 60 per cent of global proved oil reserves.

Although the diversification of oil supply sources may be considered simple, it is far more difficult for gas. Central and Eastern Europe, for example, is highly dependent on Russia; the level varying from country to country, e.g. it is 50 per cent for Germany and 100 per cent for the countries bordering Russia.

Over the short to medium term, gas supplies cannot be as flexible as oil. Oil is transported by ships which can change destination several times during a voyage. Gas is shipped either by pipeline, whose routes cannot be changed, or by ship. However, the destination of LNG carriers is often fixed because the product can only be delivered to a re-gasification plant. In compensation for this, gas sellers are also dependent on their purchasers supplied by the gas pipeline, so they cannot simply cut off supplies unless they have a diversified export infrastructure.

Coal remains important for world energy supplies because of its substantial reserves. These reserves are fairly uniformly distributed: 28 per cent in North America, 32 per cent in Asia, 26 per cent in the CIS, 6 per cent in Europe (outside the CIS), and 4 per cent in Africa. Only the Middle East (0.1 per cent) and Latin America (2 per cent) have no significant reserves. This means that there are interesting possibilities for supply diversification.

Finally, it is difficult for countries in an unfavourable geographical position to diversify their electricity supplies. In Europe, for example, this is the case for peninsulas such as Spain, Portugal and Italy. Peninsulas have fewer options for importing electricity and so typically are dependent on one supplier, or at least one network. However, unlike the commodities discussed above, electricity has the advantage that it can be produced wherever appropriate, i.e. close to the area of consumption.

MEANS OF SUPPLY

- **Oil: A Pipeline Strategy**

  Pipelines are used for two reasons:

  – Because a pipeline is necessary to transport crude oil from its production site to a refinery or a coastal export terminal.

- For economic reasons, e.g. to reduce costs and/or to diversify export routes and thus decrease risks.

In all cases the development of infrastructure facilities helps to improve supply security.

– Where Pipelines are a Necessity

Where oil pipelines, of whatever length, have been laid within a single country, the risk is limited to possible terrorist attacks (Iraq and previously Colombia). Although Algerian oil deposits are located hundreds of miles from the coast, and thus require the construction of long pipelines, that does not increase the risk. It simply means that the cost incurred by the producer when the oil reaches the coast includes that transport cost and so the producer's margin over the FOB price is reduced. Similarly, while there are naturally occurring and technical risks in the operation of underwater pipelines, they generally are not at risk from terrorist acts or political disputes.

The case of some landlocked countries whose oil can only be exported by a pipeline that runs through another country is different. Such exporting countries are exposed to political risks through the actions of the transit nations.

– Alaskan Oil

Oil was discovered in the north of Alaska in the 1960s but production only started in the late 1970s. After considering shipment by icebreaking vessels, the producers decided on a pipeline across Alaska as the solution. When Alaskan oil was discovered, there was fair oil production in the United States, in fact oil imports into the US were limited by government regulations (see Chapter 5).

So Alaskan oil was not seen as strategically important and opposition to pipeline construction from the environmentalists was sufficient to prevent its construction. One of the grounds for this was that it would interrupt the caribou migrations. The fact that a considerable portion of Alaskan oil was owned by a foreign company (BP), did not help the cause of pipeline construction. Then there was the 1973 oil shock and the Arab boycott of oil supplies to the US. Alaskan oil was recognised as a strategic necessity. Congress, despite the opposition which was still considerable, passed the necessary legislation. The pipeline was built (and the caribou are still migrating happily).

But construction was complex: the environment is fragile and it was essential to ensure that the oil's high temperature did not melt the permafrost (a permanently frozen layer that covers the ground in this region). The pipeline therefore had to be raised. The construction was long and costly, and only completed in 1977 (Fig. 30).

– *Exploitation of Russian Oil*[3]

Most Russian oil is produced in Western Siberia. The Siberian oil is routed to the West by a network of pipelines delivering to the Baltic Sea at Primorsk, and the Black Sea at Novorossiysk and Odessa (Ukraine). Russia now has two problems: first, its loss of influence over its "near abroad" – as shown by the events in Georgia and in Ukraine and second, the immensity of its territory and remoteness of the oil fields.

Belarus, Ukraine, Poland, Hungary, the Czech Republic and Slovakia are supplied by the *Druzhba* (friendship) pipeline. This pipeline was formerly entirely within the Soviet zone of influence, today it supplies the Leuna refinery in Germany (formerly East Germany) and crosses several EU member states.

– *Export of Oil from the Caspian* (Fig. 31)

Except for Russia and Iran, the countries bordering the Caspian Sea – Azerbaijan, Kazakhstan and Turkmenistan – are landlocked and are therefore entirely reliant on their neighbours, particularly Russia, for access to the open sea. For some time, Kazakhstan's hydrocarbon production could only be exported via Russia using a network of oil and gas pipelines from the Soviet era. The network includes the CPC (*Caspian Petroleum Corporation*) oil pipeline, which can transport 50 million tons of crude oil per year from Tengiz to Novorossiysk. New pipelines are currently being studied to open the market to Kazakhstan supplies. These include a trans-Caspian oil pipeline connected to either the BTC (*Baku-Tbilisi-Ceyhan*) pipeline that links Azerbaijan to the Turkish Mediterranean coast, or to the pipeline linking Baku to Soupsa on the Georgian coast; there are also projects for pipelines to Iran or through Iran to Turkey, and a pipeline under construction leading to Chinese Xinjiang. There is a similar problem for Turkmen gas. Turkmenistan, which has a great deal of gas but little oil, was hit hard by the collapse of the Soviet Union. Before 1990, it exported large quantities of gas to Russia, which was used either for Russia's own consumption or exported to Europe.

Turkmen production fell from 80 billion cubic meters in 1990 (3 Tcf or 72 million toe) to 12 (0.4 Tcf or 11 million toe) in 1998. Over 2006–08 it exceeded 60 (2 Tcf or 54 million toe) and rose to 72 in 2015 (2.5 Tcf or 65 million toe). Similar projects to those for oil from Kazakhstan are being considered for gas from Turkmenistan, and also a gas pipeline to Pakistan via Afghanistan.

For the time being, Kazakhstan and Turkmenistan, whose resources are very significant, cannot avoid oil and gas export via Russia. Pipelines via Iran would be a solution, but this would raise great political uncertainties and encounter vehement opposition from the Americans.

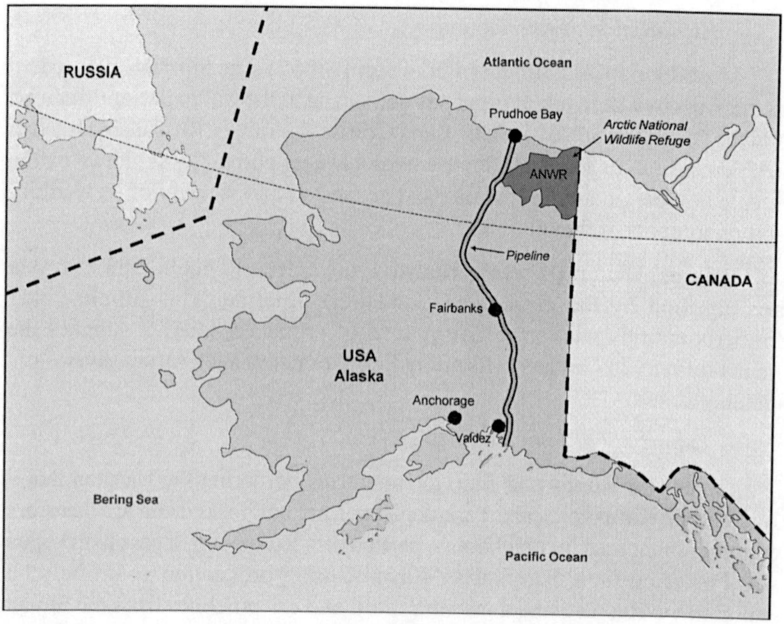

Figure 30: The Trans Alaska Pipeline.

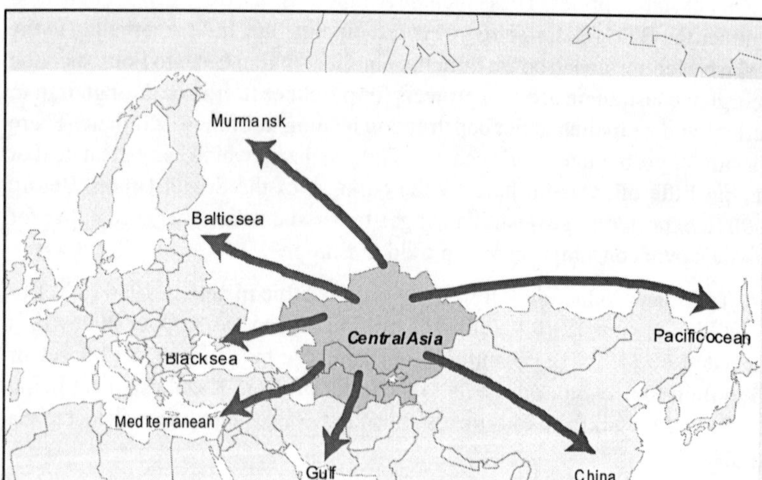

Figure 31: Possible Routes for Exporting Oil from Central Asia.

– *Chad-Cameroon Pipeline* (Fig. 32)

The exploitation of oil reserves discovered in southern Chad required the construction of a 1,070 km (665 miles) pipeline between the Doba fields and the port of Kribi in Cameroon. The development of this pipeline was the subject of long negotiations between the government, oil companies and NGOs, who were concerned about the consequences of pipeline construction for people, (Pygmies, etc.) living near the route and for the ecologically sensitive environment. It was thanks to the World Bank's intervention and their involvement in securing finance for the project that the pipeline could be built.

The agreement stipulated that revenues from the project would be allocated to social and educational projects financed by the state budget, and to a fund for future generations. This agreement was breached (see Chapter 9).

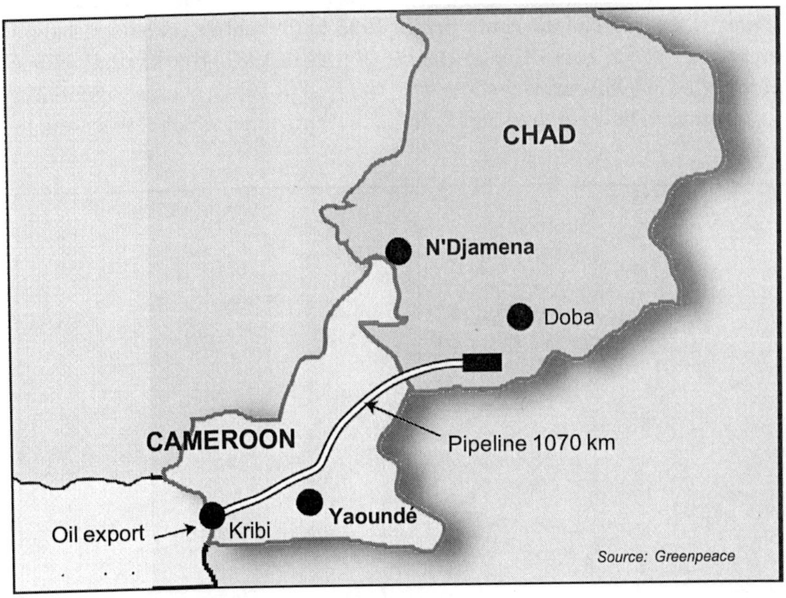

Figure 32: Chad-Cameroon Pipeline.

– *Pipelines Built for Economic Reasons*

The cost of crude oil transport to Europe or the US is critical for exports from the Middle East.

The lowest cost route is via pipeline to the Mediterranean, but this involves considerable political risks. The TAP (Trans-Arabian Pipeline) was built in 1950 and transported Saudi Arabian crude oil, via Jordan, to the Lebanese port of Az Zahrani. But, because of political conflicts in the region, it had to be closed by the end of the 1970s and Saudi Arabia now exports its crude oil by tanker from the Gulf and the Red Sea. The Petroline pipeline, built in 1981 and connecting the eastern Saudi Arabia oil fields to Yanbu on the Red Sea can reduce transport costs, provided of course that the Suez Canal is open. This is why, after the canal's closure in 1967, the Sumed pipeline was built (in 1974) between Suez and Alexandria, with a capacity of 120 million tons per year and a length of 330 km (200 miles). Its Mediterranean terminal is at Sidi Kerir, where the crude oil is reloaded and shipped to Europe and America.

The case of Iraq is particularly interesting. Part of Iraqi production comes from two northern regions: Mosul and Kirkuk. Oil produced from the Kirkuk field, discovered in 1927, was, from the 1930s, carried by twin 12" pipelines one terminating at the port of Tripoli in Lebanon (to accommodate French interests), the other at Haifa, then in Palestine (to accommodate British interests). Iraq closed the Haifa line in 1948 to prevent its oil being used by Israel and opened a new line to Banias (Syria) in 1952. But these pipelines were closed in 1982 during the Iran–Iraq war (1980–1988), because of political disagreements between Iraq and Syria[4]. A new pipeline, which flows north to

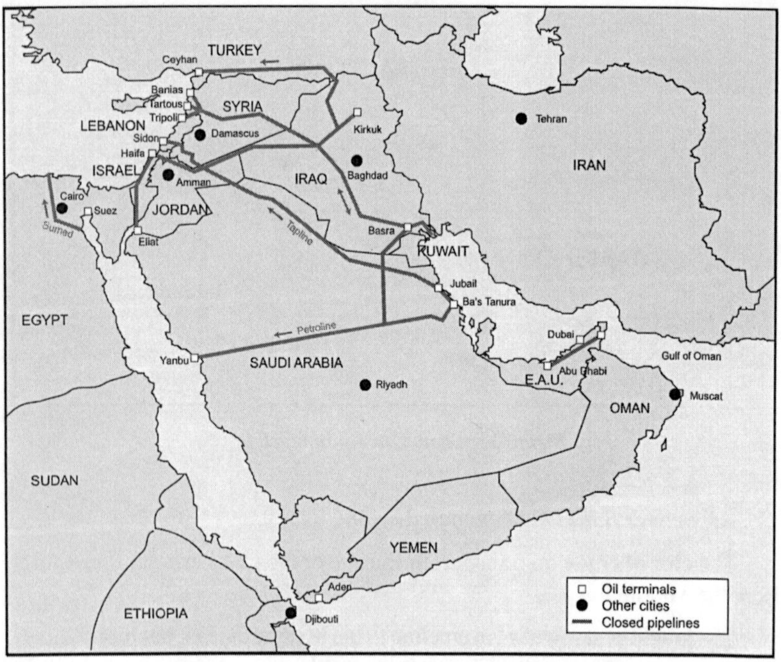

Figure 33: Principal Oil Pipelines in the Middle East.

the Turkish port of Ceyhan, was built more recently; it carefully avoids Syria. Its operation of course depends on the goodwill of Turkey. Oil from the south of Iraq is exported from the port of Al-Faw, at the head of the Gulf, in Iraq's small window of access to the sea. In addition to the risks of military conflict associated with this terminal, exports via Al-Faw have the disadvantage of a higher transport cost, particularly to western markets, compared with exports via Ceyhan (Fig. 33).

- **Gas: Gas Pipelines, Source of Conflicts?[5]**

The rapid increase in natural gas demand and the need for supplies from sources that are increasingly remote from major markets, is leading to the increasing shipment of natural gas in the form of LNG (currently nearly 30 per cent of international trade). Nevertheless pipeline transport remains very important. But this type of transport is inflexible: supplies by pipeline from Russia to Europe cannot be diverted to Asia. So for a pipeline to operate successfully there must be an ongoing partnership in the project between the producing countries, the consuming countries and the transit countries.

- **Electricity: the Different Questions that Concern Power Networks**

The supply of electric power is more dependent on simple geographical factors: mountains, forests, peninsulas, etc., than any other source of energy. In Italy there are two natural features that restrict an optimal national supply system. First, the northern mountains require the use of power transmission lines that are more expensive and more susceptible to damage. Next, the fact that Italy is a peninsula limits supply routes from the rest of the continent. Access to the power network is thus limited by these geographical considerations. Networks are interconnected to facilitate exchanges but this adds to the risk of blackouts (see Italian blackout of 2004).

- **Coal**

The main coal producers (China, US, India, etc.) are also the largest consumers and generally local production satisfies demand. So the main issues involved in the supply of coal arise at a national level. Inland transport of coal is by road (via truck), rail or inland waterway barges, the risks involved and the responses that can be made to any supply disruption are the same as for any other product transported under the same conditions. Coal is exported by sea. Increased coal demand and the problems that occurred in China, particularly in 2003 (several mines closed due to accidents) have resulted in a considerable increase in freight rates.

THREATS TO ENERGY SUPPLIES: THE RISK OF PHYSICAL FAILURE OF TRANSPORT NETWORKS

Energy supplies are most vulnerable during transport.

- **Ground Transport Infrastructure**

Pipelines are an easy target. In Colombia, the main oil fields, Cano Lemon and Cusiana, are inland. Rebel movements, the FARC (Revolutionary Armed Forces of Colombia) and more particularly the ELN (National Liberation Army, Guevarist movement), have often blown up pipelines. However, although sabotaging a pipeline is relatively easy, it can also be repaired quickly: teams from Ecopetrol, the national Columbian company, promptly repaired the damage and interruptions to supply were limited. The situation is normal after the peace agreement which was signed in 2016.

Since 2003 the situation in Iraq has been very similar: movements opposing the new regime regularly blow up the two main pipelines: Kirkuk-Ceyhan and Rumaila-Fao. Each of these attacks causes a reduction in exports for several days, although these pipelines are quickly repaired. Iraq is reported to have lost $12 billion as a result of more than 500 attacks that took place between 2003 and 2008, which would mean their average loss was over 0.5 Mb/d. However, the situation has improved.

The destruction or sabotage of one or more pipelines in a producing country does not endanger the hydrocarbon supplies to any consuming country. The problem would clearly be more serious if such an attack affected a hub[6] close to a centre of consumption, for example, on Slovak territory, through which much of Eastern Europe's gas supplies are transported.

The Case of Electricity

The problems of supply security for electricity are quite different from those posed by the supply of hydrocarbons and they relate to the condition of the national infrastructure rather than international trade. Electricity demand varies considerably, both throughout the day and throughout the year. Demand at its peak is far greater than the average so high production capacity, most of which remains unused at other than peak times, must always be available. Most cases of power failure, e.g. in California, Northern US, Italy, London, etc., are caused by a lack of investment.

- **Strategic Geographical Channels (Straits and Canals)**

More than two-thirds of world crude oil production is transported by sea. Ships are most exposed to the risk of terrorist or criminal (piracy) attacks during their passage through straits or canals where they must significantly reduce their speed and mobility. In the Straits of Malacca, piracy is rampant and oil tankers and other vessels are attacked. Once onboard, pirates rob the crew and leave the ship with no one in control. There is a great risk of the ship running aground on one of the many reefs or small islands scattered throughout the archipelago (Fig. 34).

The Straits of Malacca are not the only strategic channel for the transit of hydrocarbons. Nearly 90 per cent of oil and gas exports from the Middle East pass through the Straits of Hormuz. Although ground-based transport, e.g. pipelines for delivery of crude oil to ports in the region's northwest, have been considered, tankers are still the most logical method because of the proximity of the oil fields to the Gulf, low shipping costs, the need to supply Asian markets, etc. However, dependency on the Straits of Hormuz gives considerable strategic strength to Iran, who controls the straits. Closure of the Straits of Hormuz would undoubtedly lead to a sustained disruption of hydrocarbon supplies. Initially, this shortage could be mitigated by consuming countries drawing down their strategic stocks, but were the crisis to be prolonged, the consequences would be severe.

That is why, in 2008, tensions between Iran and the west regarding the Iranian nuclear programme was one of the factors resulting in increased crude oil prices.

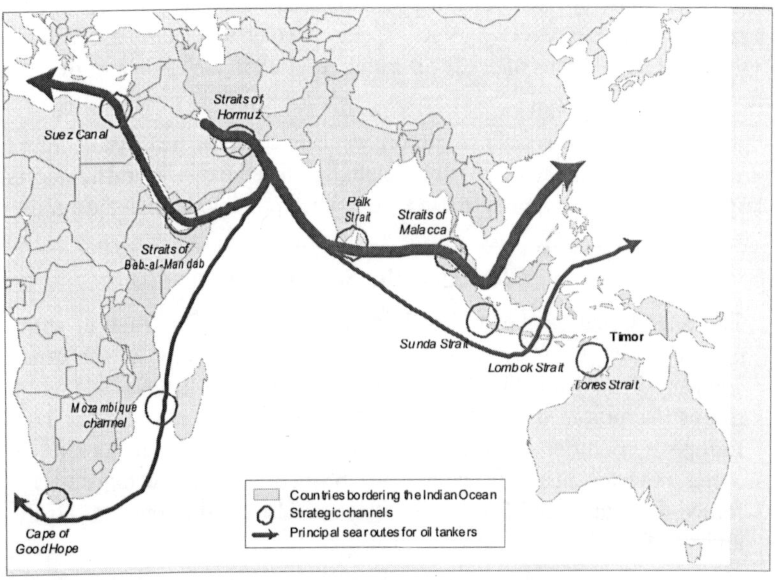

Source: Le Monde Diplomatique, Philippe Rakacewicz, October 1995.

Figure 34: Main Strategic Channels.

Slightly more than 3 Mb/d Gulf crude oil pass through the Straits of Bab-el Mandeb and the Suez Canal heading for Europe. For several years now, terrorist activity has grown along the coasts of Yemen, near the Straits of Bal-el Mandeb (bombing of the French oil tanker Limburg in October 2002, attacks in Yemen and in the Horn of Africa, etc.). In response, the US opened a military training camp with more than 3,000 soldiers in Djibouti, traditionally an exclusively French preserve. For the Suez Canal, the best way to prevent its closure, which would force tankers to take the Cape of Good Hope route, would seem to be the development of good relations between the European Union and Egypt. Another important development is that of piracy off the coast of Somalia. At the end of 2008, a Saudi Arabian oil tanker was captured and not released until payment of a ransom several weeks later. Since then, the situation has improved.

Finally, the last of the bottlenecks is the Bosporus and the Dardanelles Straits. The former is approximately 32 km (20 miles) long and 1.0–2.5 km (0.6–1.5 miles) wide, and bisects the city of Istanbul; the latter is 65 km (40 miles) long and 1.6–6.4 km (1.0–4.0 miles) wide. The terrorist threat appears to be minor but the Turkish authorities are far more concerned about environmental risks. The Bosporus is considered hazardous because of its rapid currents that make navigation difficult and, with continuing increases in the passage of oil and methane tankers via these two straits, the probabilities of an accident are growing[7]. Blockage of either of these straits would temporarily interrupt European, and perhaps even American, supplies. In 1994, a collision between two Cypriot ships, one of which was a tanker, caused the spillage of 20,000 tons of crude oil which resulted in the closure of the strait for a week.

The Turkish government therefore wants measures to be taken in order to limit these risks as far as possible, including a reduction in traffic and the largest ships being required to use a pilot when passing through the straits.

Closing of the Suez Canal

The Suez Canal has been closed on two occasions. The first, of short duration, was in 1956 following Nasser's nationalisation of the canal company. Shortly after the nationalisation, joint action by British and French troops, supported by the advance of Israeli troops, allowed the two European countries to take back control of the canal. But the United States, not wanting a conflict with the USSR (Nasser's protecting power), forced the British and French to withdraw. The canal re-opened shortly afterward.

On June 5, 1967 at 7:45 am, an Israeli air attack destroyed Egypt's air force. The Hebrew state wanted to prevent an attack by Arab countries, which it saw as imminent. In reprisal, Egypt decided to close the Suez Canal. It did not re-open until 1975. Oil consuming countries took measures to counter the situation, and the advent of supertankers carrying large quantities of crude oil, reduced the costs of the longer voyage. In 1974, an oil pipeline, Sumed, was built parallel to the canal so that some tankers could avoid the voyage around Africa. Today Egypt is further dredging to enable the largest tankers to use the Suez Canal.

SECURING HYDROCARBON SUPPLIES MILITARILY

Faced with all types of threats of (terrorism, rebellion, etc.) at both the international and national levels, it would seem that military force is necessary to ensure the world's continued hydrocarbon supplies. The Americans, thanks to their large military capacity, are virtually alone in taking on the task of securing supplies. Thus, other countries benefit from the American umbrella without directly participating in maintaining order.

- **The American Military Monopoly**

Today, only the United States has the military power to send troops and equipment several thousands of miles from its own territory to operate in several theaters of action simultaneously.

The US has signed a number of bilateral agreements with other countries, in all corners of the globe, giving them the right to set up military bases. Wikipedia reports that, in the Middle East, there are about 26000 men. US forces, previously numbering some 7,000, were withdrawn from Saudi Arabia in 2003 because it was no longer necessary to enforce the no-fly zone over Iraq. These forces mean that the US can ensure production from the reservoirs, its dispatch via gas and oil pipelines and its loading for export.

Another region that is crucially strategic for the US is that stretching from the Caspian Sea to the Dardanelles Straits. To secure hydrocarbon exports from the Caspian Sea, and from the Russian port of Novorossiysk, the US has signed agreements with several Black Sea coastal countries (Bulgaria, Georgia and Romania) to set up bases or provide military training. The US has also had a military base in Turkey (Incirlik) for several years.

The US navy is present on all oceans and seas throughout the world and can be used to secure the marine transport of hydrocarbons, particularly in coastal regions and in the strategic channels where it is most vulnerable. So the 6th American fleet is present in the Eastern Mediterranean (close to the Black Sea, the Bosporus and the Dardanelles Straits and the Suez Canal), the 5th fleet in the Gulf with its command centre in Bahrain, and the Diego Garcia base in the Indian Ocean. All this naval deployment is intended for the protection of American interests in the Gulf region.

Finally, the US has opened a naval base in the Philippines to secure the Straits of Malacca against piracy and the growth of radical Islamist groups (Abu Sayyaf, GAM, Jemaah Islamiyah, etc.) in this region.

The US also intervenes indirectly. The Islamic Republic of Iran advocates a division of the Caspian Sea that is rejected by the other littoral nations, and it therefore disputes Azerbaijan's ownership of several oil fields. Iranian naval forces have therefore launched sorties to intimidate Azeri ships and foreign oil companies working in the sector.

Because of this prospect of armed conflict with Iran, the US helps finance Azeri naval forces, thus providing the Azeri government with a means of military deterrence to prevent tension rising uncontrollably (Fig. 35).

- **Being a "Free Rider"**

With their smaller military resources, the other major oil consuming nations do not have the means to secure hydrocarbon supply routes. The European Union is experiencing real difficulties in making European defense viable; despite interesting military-industrial programmes, results are not yet satisfactory. China is still restricted by weapons embargoes imposed by the EU and the US after Tiananmen Square in 1989. Japan remains dependent on American military forces. The other consuming countries, developing countries and emerging countries can only provide security for their own territory.

This situation is worrying. The European Union cannot even exercise responsibility for security in the Black Sea, the route for a significant portion of European crude oil imports and so strategically vital for its hydrocarbon imports. Even traditional European spheres of influence have been taken over by the Americans (military base facilities in former French areas e.g. Djibouti or the Gulf of Guinea). The advantages for the US and disadvantages for other consuming countries are obvious. In times of peace, at least in times of market stability, the situation need not be worrying. But should a crisis erupt, the US can give priority to ensuring their own supplies over the need for an equitable distribution of resources. No American imports pass through the Straits of Malacca but the American military deployment there could allow them to put pressure on supplies to China (a future major competitor?).

China seems aware of its vulnerability. That is why it is trying to construct facilities for imports from the Caspian Sea region and from Russia. China also claims sovereignty over the Paracel and Spratly islands, this may well be to have a maritime outpost there to limit American military influence, rather than because of an interest in the possible reserves. Finally, good relations between the Chinese government and the government of Myanmar mean that China has a military base at the entry to the Strait of Malacca.

A military solution may appear to be the last resort to dealing with supply disruptions, but there is an alternative way of managing a sudden drop in the supply of hydrocarbons, and particularly oil: that is stocks.

A SPECIAL ISSUE: STRATEGIC STOCKS

- **Principles of Setting up Strategic Stocks and their Role**

After World War I, several European countries established reserve stocks of petroleum products. These were intended first and foremost to meet the army's fuel requirements in the case of an emergency. Although the importance of this objective was reinforced during World War II, gasoline played a decisive role in the outcome of some of the battles, policies later started to change. Now stocks are no longer set up just to ensure military supplies, but rather for protection against a sudden and sustained drop in supplies from exporting countries.

With its Strategic Petroleum Reserve (SPR), the United States has the largest reserves in the world. The SPR's storage capacity is 727 million barrels and, in September 2016, the inventory was 695 million barrels. With American consumption currently at 19 million barrels per day and imports at 7 million, this stock represents nearly 37 days consumption and 99 days imports. Although strategic stocks must be sufficient to make up for a shortage of crude oil imports for a certain period (the length of which varies), they cannot, however, compensate for a total disruption of supplies.

Nevertheless holding these stocks is a crucial and strategic part of the defense policy of the countries that do so. Faced with increasing political danger from countries such as Venezuela and Iran, as well as the capability of terrorists to disrupt consuming countries' supplies, no major oil importer can neglect the need to hold strategic reserves. This is why China, the world's second largest oil consumer, announced at the start of 2005 that it would increase its storage capacity. It will go from 30 to 90 days consumption from some 200 to 630 million barrels by 2020, based on new demand assumptions in a three phase development. These stocks will be held on four sites: Zenhai, Daishan, Huangdao and Xingang.

Japan is reported to have a capacity of 583 million barrels.

There are three principal systems for holding strategic stocks. Firstly, there are private stocks, held by private companies that are each responsible for managing their obligation, using either their own reserves or by "leasing" reserves under a contract with other operators. Next there are national stocks for which the government is entirely responsible. This is the system used in

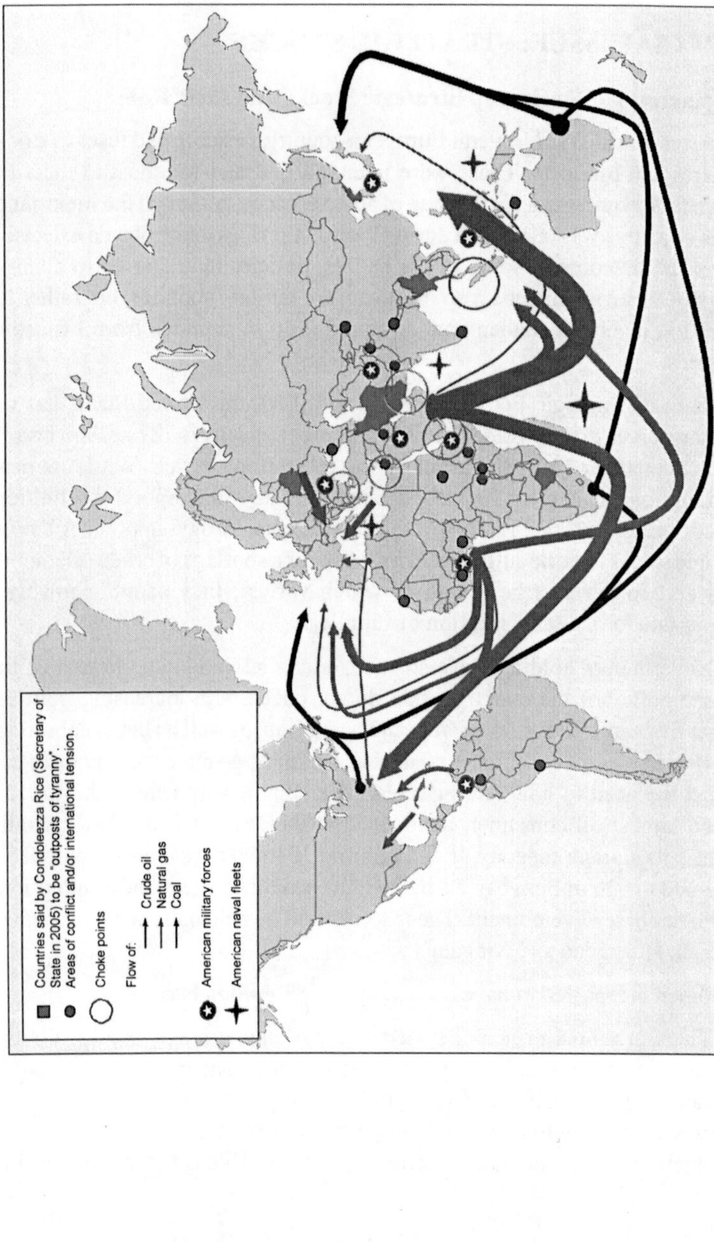

Figure 35: Military Security for the World's Fossil Fuel Supplies.

the US and Japan. Finally there are agency stocks, i.e. stocks managed by either a public or a private body, with operators paying the agent a fee in proportion to the obligation that the agent meets for them. These three systems are not incompatible and some countries use all of them.

- **International Energy Agency and European Union Compulsory Stock Obligations**

– *"International Energy Program"*

Following the establishment of the International Energy Agency, it prepared an international energy programme including rules for levels of strategic stocks.

Each member state is required to hold oil reserves equivalent to 90 days (originally it was 60 days) of net oil imports. In addition, each participating country must "at all times have ready a programme of contingent oil demand restraint measures enabling it to reduce its rate of final consumption" (Article 5, Chapter II).

Chapter IV covers the implementation of emergency measures. When a group of member states suffers or is threatened with a reduction in oil supplies equal to seven per cent of final consumption over the last four quarters for which data are available, each country must reduce its demand by seven per cent and oil taken from the reserves is allocated among the countries affected.

When the reduction in supplies amounts to 12 per cent of final consumption, the countries are only required to reduce their consumption by 10 per cent.

IEA stocks amount to roughly four billion barrels, two-thirds of which are held by the oil industry. These stocks are made up of 58 per cent crude oil and 42 per cent petroleum products.

– *European Union Compulsory Stocks Obligation*

European strategic stocks were first established in 1968, prior to the first oil shock. Three directives govern the regulation of oil reserves.

These require member states to maintain stocks equivalent to 90 days (65 days until 1972) of average internal consumption during the previous calendar year for each category of petroleum products (automotive gasoline, diesel fuel, kerosene, jet fuel, etc.). Two comments are relevant in comparing this to the IEA system discussed above: first the 90 day obligation relates to consumption, not just imports, and second, the directives clearly specify that the requirement applies to crude oil as well as several petroleum products—intermediate or end products—designated by name.

The directives also specify various ways in which these stocks may be held, e.g. by an agency, and that a country may, through intergovernmental contracts, set up stocks on behalf of companies, organisations or agencies located in another member state. Such stocks are entirely at the disposition of the government that owns them and the "host" country cannot prevent that government from transferring all or any part of them.

Finally, regarding the use of these stocks, the European directives are less precise than those of the IEA and simply stipulate that if there is a supply problem, the Commission will organise a meeting. Member states do not have the right to draw down their stocks without holding such a meeting. In addition the EU has recently proposed that reserve levels be increased to 120 days consumption, this is still being debated but it does not have the support of private oil companies (Fig. 36).

France's Strategic Stocks

As a member of both the EU and the IEA, France is subject to the strategic storage regulations of both organisations: 90 days of internal consumption and 90 days of imports. In fact, France's strategic reserves represent 95 days of internal consumption.

These requirements were effected by a law of December 31, 1992 which applies to "registered operators", i.e. the companies that sell the products. It requires them to hold stocks equivalent to a quarter of the products they sold in the previous year. There are various ways for an operator to meet its requirements. It can physically store the products itself, or discharge part of its obligation by paying a fee to the French Committee for Strategic Oil Stocks (Comité professionnel des stocks stratégiques pétroliers or CPSSP). The CPSSP itself has stocks held for it by the Private Corporation for the Management of Security Stocks (Société anonyme de gestion des stocks de sécurité or SAGESS). The latter was formed in 1988 and its shareholders are the registered oil operators. Its role is to purchase and hold stocks of crude oil and petroleum products on behalf of CPSSP.

These stocks are subject to continuous monitoring by the government. Each operator must provide the head of the Directorate for Energy and Mineral Resources (Direction des resources énergétiques et minérales or DIREM) with a monthly report specifying the levels of the stocks it holds. Any operator not meeting its requirements is liable to a fine.

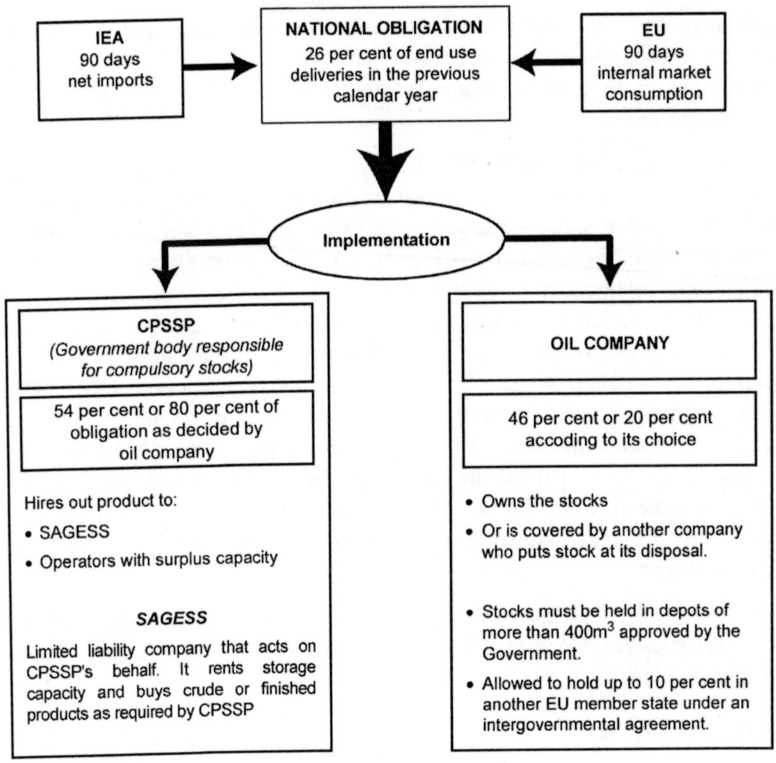

CPSSP : *Comité Professionnel des Stockages Stratégiques Pétroliers*
SAGESS : *Société Anonyme de Gestion des Stocks Pétroliers*

Figure 36: The Strategic Stock System in France.

- **The Special Case of the American Strategic Petroleum Reserve (SPR)**

During the 1970s, following the first oil shock, President Gerald Ford signed the *Energy Policy and Conservation Act* (December 22, 1975) and authorised the creation of the Strategic Petroleum Reserve already described above. Its storage capacity (727 million barrels as already stated) consists of hollow cavities in salt domes along the coast of the Gulf of Mexico. It is the world's largest oil reserve and it holds a significant part of American strategic stocks.

The SPR has a major role in American policy. Its strength comes from the fact that draw-downs from this stock are rare. It was established to deal with a supply disruption, or the threat of disruption which is basically the same thing, but it can also be used to lower prices. The American President announced the recourse to SPR oil in 1991 during the first Gulf War to contend with the disappearance of Iraqi and Kuwaiti production from the market.

In September 2005, Hurricane Katrina destroyed a significant portion of production capacity in the Gulf of Mexico. The increase in crude oil prices was limited by the announcement of—and the actual—sale of oil withdrawn from this reserve.

The value of the SPR is limited in two important ways. First, the concentration of storage on the coast of the Gulf of Mexico could pose a problem should massive recourse to it be necessary in an emergency. Lifting the crude oil and its national distribution would undoubtedly require a great deal of time, particularly as the storage is not close to the financial, economic and political centres of the US. Secondly, the SPR only contains crude oil. However, when there is a serious crisis what matters immediately is the rapid shortage of petroleum products that occurs. The hurricanes of September 2005 destroyed both oil production capacity and refineries in the Gulf of Mexico. Although the announcement of recourse to SPR stocks strongly limited the increase in crude oil prices, the lack of product stocks meant that nothing could be done to limit the very strong increase in the price of products, particularly the spike in the price of gasoline, which increased by 30 per cent in a few days.

Strategic stocks can therefore provide a solution to the risks of disruption in energy supplies. However, this solution only works for a crisis of limited duration.

CONCLUSION

Supply security is a political, economic, strategic and military issue. There are two different approaches to the problem. The first is that of the US, which gives priority to supply and ensuring the stability of producing areas, particularly the Middle East. The main objective is to ensure that there are plenty of supplies for the American market, with environmental issues being given second place. The US is sufficiently powerful to resist calls from the international community that is more sensitive to pollution problems.

The European Union's approach goes in a different direction; it is based on the need to reduce energy demand. The advantage of this policy is that it complements policies that respond to environmental risks. However, it seems that the European Union has abandoned the task of ensuring the physical security of supplies to the US.

References

1. Improve the transparency of oil statistics in Europe; promote the development of investments in refining; re-launch energy savings; institute a dialogue with producers and discuss the consequences of possibly using the Euro as a means of payment for purchases of crude oil.

2. Although industrialised countries absorbed the effects of the first oil shock relatively easily, developing countries had far more difficulty. From 1974–1975, they simply no longer had the means to pay for the oil they needed. In any event, all countries sought to make energy savings after 1973.
3. The geopolitics of the evacuation of hydrocarbons from Russia, but also from Central Asia, is described in further detail in Chapter 8 dedicated to the CIS.
4. The Kirkuk-Banias pipeline was used again from 2001 by Saddam Hussein in order to breach the oil embargo, until 2003 when it was damaged by US air strikes.
5. This topic is discussed again in Chapter 8 on the CIS and the periodic crises between Russia and Ukraine concerning the transit of Russian gas through Ukraine.
6. A depot used for reception, storage and dispatch of supplies.
7. Every year, nearly 50,000 ships cross through this zone with more than 100 million tons of oil and other hazardous materials.

Chapter - 5

The North American Continent

The three countries that make up the North American continent: Canada, the United States and Mexico, are linked by the North American Free Trade Agreement (NAFTA). Within NAFTA, the US is predominant: its GDP amounts to 85 per cent of the total. The US is the new Rome: a superpower for some, a hyperpower to others. American power—particularly its military power—remains dominant at the beginning of the twenty-first century even if the growth of China, India will limit the influence of the US. During the 1991 Gulf War to end Iraq's occupation of Kuwait, the US deployed an army of

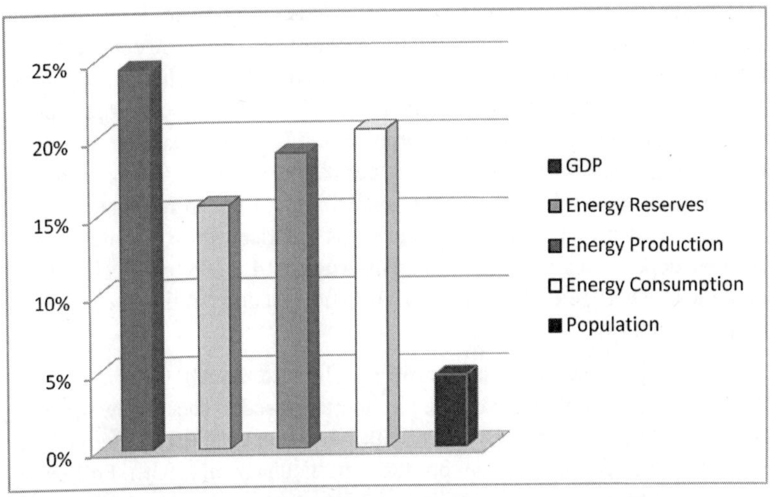

Source: BP Statistical Review 2016.

Figure 37: United States World Rankings 2015.

600,000 men, 90 per cent of the coalition's manpower. The Yugoslavian conflict in 1999 was settled by America even though, logically, the solution should have been found within Europe. Finally, the army that invaded Iraq in March 2003 was very largely American (Fig. 37).

VERY HIGH ENERGY CONSUMPTION

Energy consumption in the United States is substantial: with five per cent of the world's population the US uses some 17 per cent of world primary energy production and half of the world's motor gasoline consumption. The US accounts for 20 per cent of the world's consumption of oil, 23 per cent of gas, 10 per cent of coal, 33 per cent of nuclear energy and 22 per cent of generated electricity. On an average each US citizen consumes about 7 tons of oil equivalent per year. That is over twice per capita European consumption and over three times that of China (Fig. 38 and 39).

American power is largely based on intensive energy production and use: coal in the eighteenth century, oil after 1859—date of the first discovery of crude oil by Colonel Drake in Titusville, Pennsylvania—and more recently, gas and electricity. Despite some progress in terms of energy optimisation and use, the US has doubled its consumption over the past 40 years.

There are two aspects to this very high energy consumption: the level of demand itself but also the amount of resources. American fossil fuel reserves, which were originally substantial, have allowed the US to develop industries and transport on an extremely large scale (Fig. 40).

Canada has reserves of gas and heavy crude oil, and very large reserves of oil sands; it is the world's leading producer of hydroelectric energy. It is a net exporter of crude oil, natural gas, uranium and hydraulic electricity, mainly to the US. The size of its resources means that Canada is also a large user of energy: despite a low population (32 million), it is the sixth largest consumer in the world. It has the world's highest per capita electricity consumption—about 16,000 kWh—because of the availability of cheap hydroelectricity. Energy exports from Canada (oil, natural gas and electricity) are vital for the US. This dependency was highlighted on August 14, 2003 by the electricity blackout which affected large areas of the Midwest and Northeast of the US, as well as Ontario.

Mexico was one of the largest oil suppliers to the Allies during World War I. But when the Western companies there refused to accept new national regulations, the government reacted with a law that established the nation's ownership over all subterranean products, particularly oil (1938). Following this nationalisation, the international companies boycotted Mexican oil and increased exports from Venezuela. Oil production in Mexico collapsed and did not become significant again until the 1970s.

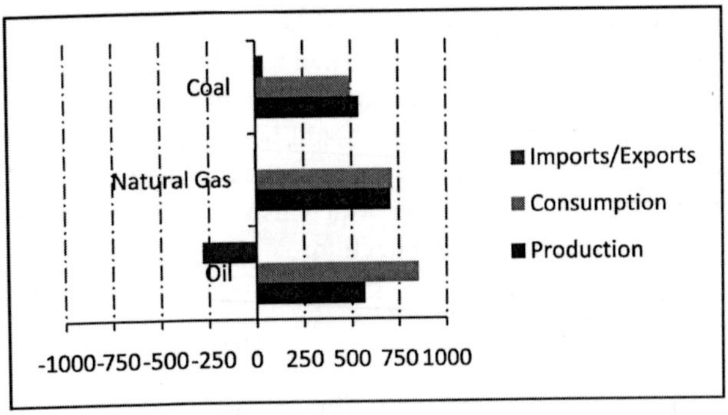

Figure 38: Overall US 2015 Energy Balance (Mtoe).

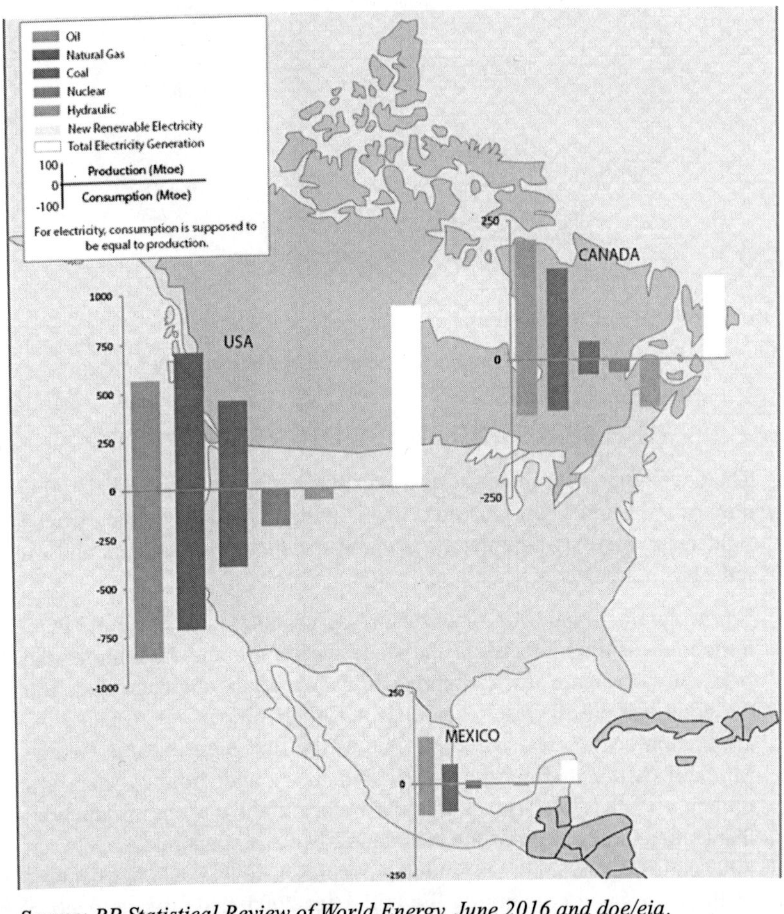

Source: BP Statistical Review of World Energy, June 2016 and doe/eia.

Figure 39: North American Energy Balance by Country in 2015.

Today, Mexico has moved away from the resource nationalisation policies towards investor friendly policies which includes introduction of service, profit sharing and production sharing contracts in the oil and gas sector. Therefore, the principle that natural resources should be controlled by the people, so effectively enforced by the government has finally changed with the introduction of new energy policies which also have the potential to address country's rapidly declining oil production.

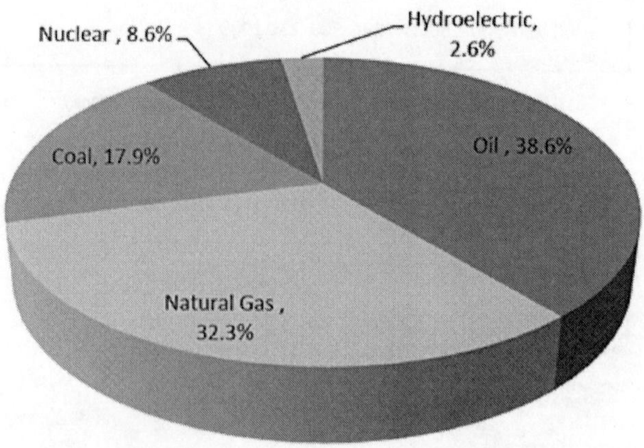

Source: BP Statistical Review, 2016.

Figure 40: US Energy Consumption by Source in 2015.

SHALE GAS AND SHALE OIL REVOLUTION

The development of shale gas and later shale oil production (shale oil is now called Light Tight Oil, since this is a light crude oil coming from a tight reservoir) has completely changed the picture of the gas and oil industry in the US.

The technology used for shale oil or gas production is not quite new: horizontal drilling—to reach the shale reservoir—and fracking of the reservoir—to create artificial permeability—are very old techniques. But the combination of these techniques and their proper use to make the production economical is recent. One of the first pioneers was George Mitchell (Mitchell Energy) who started to try and produce shale gas probably in the 70's. But it was not before 2000 that the production, thanks to an adaptation of the techniques, became economical. Between 2000 and 2005 the shale gas production represented less than five per cent of the total gas production in the US. After 2005 shale gas production developed very quickly and is now more than 50 per cent of total gas production in the US.

The "story" of shale oil is still more recent since the production of LTO became significant only in 2010. Production increased up to 2015 (more than 5 Mbd) before falling in 2015 and 2016 because of the fall in oil prices which made—temporarily—LTO less economical.

OIL

Oil is still the United States' main energy source. With consumption of about 20 million barrels per day they are by far the world's largest user. Until World War II, the US produced over half the world's crude oil. But in 1949 the US became an importer and the share of imports grew from 10 per cent of consumption in 1949 to 50 per cent on the eve of the overthrow of the Shah of Iran in 1979. A fall in oil consumption and the development of Alaskan (Prudhoe Bay) production resulted in imports declining to 30 per cent in 1985.

US production reached a maximum of 11 Mbd (the famous "King Hubbert's" peak announced ten years before) in 1970. This production declined first slowly then more rapidly down to less than 7 Mbd by 2005, making the US importing two-third of their oil requirements.

Production increased from this date, thanks to the development of offshore oil fields in the Gulf of Mexico, and of course because of the production of shale oil and so the US now depends on imports for only 33 per cent of its consumption compared to around 66 per cent ten years ago. Their oil reserves now are 11 years of annual production (Fig. 41) therefore supply security is better but is still a vital issue for the United States.

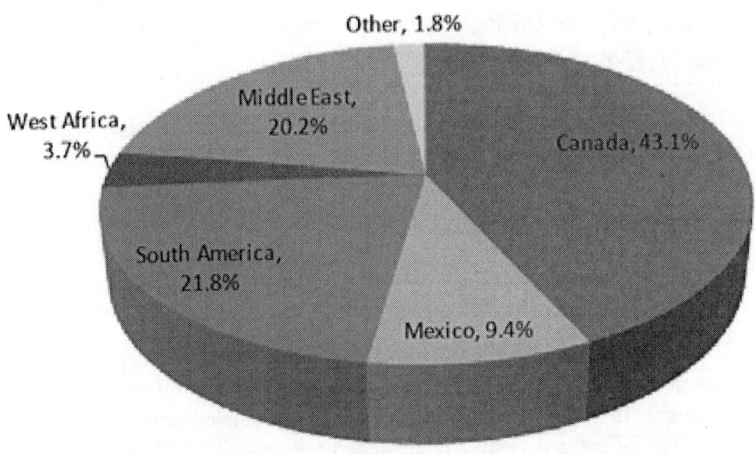

Source: BP Statistical Review, 2016.

Figure 41: US Oil Imports in 2015.

Canadian oil production is currently some 4.3 Mb/d. Canada is the leading supplier of oil imports to the US. A network of pipelines carries oil from Western Canada to the east coast of the US. After Canada the countries with the largest oil exports to the US are Saudi Arabia, Venezuela Mexico and Colombia. Canada's "conventional" oil reserves amount to about 5 billion tonnes (or 33 billion barrels), but unconventional reserves, mainly the oil sands[1] of Alberta, are far larger.

Although the quantities in place are significant (more than 300 billion barrels), recoverable quantities are lower, although estimates vary widely (from 10 to 200 billion barrels–170 billion barrels according to the provincial government). The oil recovered from these oil sands is limited by the enormous energy and water requirements needed for its processing.

Refining in the United States

In the end, what counts is the availability of end products (fuels, etc.). Although the US was self-sufficient in crude oil and finished products for a long time, from the beginning of the 1980s, falling product demand linked to increased prices led to a reduction in refining capacity. Many refineries closed, particularly the small ones which could not survive in an industry where economies of scale are important. Several inland refineries closed when the local oil fields that supplied them became exhausted. In total there are now only 140 refineries operating in America, compared with more than 300, thirty five years ago. Because of the severity of the anti-pollution regulations and opposition from environmental protection organisations, no refineries have been built for nearly 50 years. Consequently, the US imports large volumes of finished products from neighbouring countries, for example Venezuela.

Mexico is the world's twelfth leading oil producer: so it is a major non-OPEC player. Its proved reserves are estimated at 11 billion barrels, after being reduced from 50 billion barrels to meet the restrictive evaluation standards of the SEC (Securities and Exchange Commission, New York Stock Exchange). Actual reserves are therefore probably larger.

Pemex, the Mexican government and OPEC

The history of oil production in Mexico started at the beginning the twentieth century. The country rapidly became the main Latin American producer. In 1938, the oil industry was nationalised and the Mexican government created Pemex (Petroleos Mexicanos) which still has total control of the hydrocarbons industry. The proved reserves went down from 50.8 thousand million barrels in the year 1993 to merely 10.8 thousand million barrels in the year 2015. In nearly two decades, PEMEX recovered 78 per cent of the proved reserves, which indicates that limited effort was given to maintain the reserve replacement ratio.

Following nationalisation, oil production collapsed since American companies refused to buy oil from Pemex and developed production in neighbouring countries, particularly Venezuela. Mexican production did not return to levels sufficient for exports to become significant until the 1970s.

Sixty per cent of Pemex revenue is paid to the Federal government which is currently a third of the latter's budget. The size of these payments makes it difficult for the company to invest sufficiently to maintain production and increase the country's reserves. However, the Mexican government has recognised the problem this causes, since in 2004, the company's capital investment budget reached a record $12 billion. Seventy-five per cent of that was for production facilities. At the same time, President Vicente Fox agreed to provide more opportunities to private companies in the energy sector, while excluding the possibility that government-owned companies—Pemex for oil and gas, and CFE (Commission Federal de Electricitad) for electricity—would be privatised.

The 2012 presidential candidate Enrique Peña Nieto who became the president in December 2012 promised in his presidential campaign to further liberalise the energy sector by opening private investments in the oil and gas sector. Consequently, on 11th August 2016, secondary laws including 21 legislative changes were passed which opened the gates for private investment in the Oil and Gas sector helping PEMEX to seek partnership with International Oil Companies to explore Mexico's deep water and shale resources through service contracts, profit sharing and production sharing contracts. Under these secondary laws, PEMEX will also have to end retail monopoly on gasoline and diesel sales and PEMEX pays a lower tax rate of 65 per cent against 79 per cent previously.

Although Mexico is not a member of OPEC–the US even went so far in 1986 as to press for the resignation of a Mexican minister who was favourable to OPEC membership–the country has shown several times that it is willing to work with that organisation to ensure the global supply of oil and guarantee a price to producers. An example was in March 1999 when an agreement between Mexico, Venezuela and Saudi Arabia made acceptance of a new reduction in OPEC quotas credible and enabled the price of crude oil to rise. There have been similar agreements since. In addition, until 2005 Mexican Isthmus crude oil was the only non-OPEC crude included in the OPEC basket.[2]

Like Canada, one of the main characteristics of this country is the fact that most exports go to its American neighbour. Thus, in 2015, of the 2.5 million bbl/d produced, 1.9 million went to domestic consumption and 0.6 million to the United States (Mexico imports about 0.2 million b/d crude oil from the US). Mexican production is largely concentrated in the south of the country near the Gulf of Mexico. Two-thirds of production is from the Bay of Campeche region alone. It includes the giant offshore Cantarell deposit, commissioned at the end of the 1970s, which tripled national production in only a few years. But production from this field is in rapid decline.

- **Development of Rail Transport**

Pipelines have been the major source of transportation over the years but recently rail transport has become critical. Due to the surge in crude oil production in the US after the shale revolution, the crude oil cargo load on the rail network has increased from 44 Million barrels in 2010 to a peak of 316.7 Million barrels in 2014. The share of the crude oil transport in the year 2014 was 11 per cent of the total oil produced and transported. Given the geographical flexibility necessary to serve any refinery in the US, responsiveness to quickly expand infrastructure and efficiency of operations, rail transport will play a key role in crude oil transport in the US.

NATURAL GAS

US natural gas demand peaked in the early 1970s and then, when increased prices ("the gas bubble") led to its substitution by other fuels, fell sharply, the decline lasting until 1986. By the mid 1990s gas demand had returned to its 1970 level. It reached a maximum in 2000 but has remained reasonably steady at just below the 2000 level since. It may now grow further, particularly in the electricity generation sector where gas has clear advantages in terms of efficiency and cleanliness.

In the US, there are half-a-dozen large basins containing natural gas. American national production in 2015 was 705.3 Mtoe, meeting 99 per cent of national consumption. Limited quantities are imported from Canada and Trinidad and Tobago. The forecasts of gas production and demand made in 2000 indicated substantial deficits by 2010 which could only be met by imports of LNG. However, the extensive development of non-conventional gas, mainly shale gas (there are limited quantities of coal bed methane) has completely changed the picture. Non-conventional gas now represents 56 per cent of total US gas production (Fig. 42 and Fig. 43).

Canada's consumption has been relatively stable for the last ten years, at about 92.2 Mtoe. But the short term forecast is for sustained growth because of gas' increased use for the production of oil sands, whose recovery and processing are energy intensive. In Canada, natural gas is mainly found in the Western Sedimentary Basin.

Mexico's estimated gas reserves have, like those for oil, been revised dramatically downward. Ultimate Mexican gas reserves are probably far greater than those known today, but Pemex have not invested the resources necessary for a systematic study of the gas potential in the country's sedimentary basins. Mexico's gas production is therefore less than its internal demand so limited quantities of gas must be imported from the US.

The gas reserves of each of these North American countries are equivalent to some 10 years of current production.

Source: BP Statistical Review, 2016.

Figure 42: Natural Gas Production and Consumption in the United States.

Natural Gas Trading within North America

There are many pipelines connecting the American and Canadian markets and the increased US demand in the late 2000's has led to many projects to increase pipeline capacity over the past decade. An example is the Alliance gas pipeline, which cost $2.5 billion and is over 1,200 miles (2,000 km) long, the longest gas pipeline ever built in North America. Its capacity is 35 million cubic meters per day and it delivers gas produced in Western Canada to the Chicago region (Fig. 44).

- **LNG Imports**

The natural gas market in North America is undergoing sweeping changes. Although a structural gas surplus in the 1980s led to low prices, an increase in consumption, due in particular to the trend for gas-fired "combined cycle" power plants in the power sector, led to higher prices. However, because of the non-conventional gas referred to above, natural gas prices started to fall in August 2008 and they have been on a declining trend since.

The US Department of Energy (DOE) improved US supplies of natural gas by allowing drilling in areas under the jurisdiction of the Federal government. These are in mountainous and maritime zones: the Rocky Mountains, where reserves are estimated at 2 trillion cubic meters, offshore Florida, in the North Atlantic and in the Pacific, where estimated reserves are 2.2 trillion cubic meters. The development of unconventional gas has largely increased natural gas production and has reduced imports to merely 1 per cent of the total demand in 2015. Supply and demand are balanced in 2016. This has also led to expansion plans for the LNG export facilities: many terminals are under construction. More are planned.

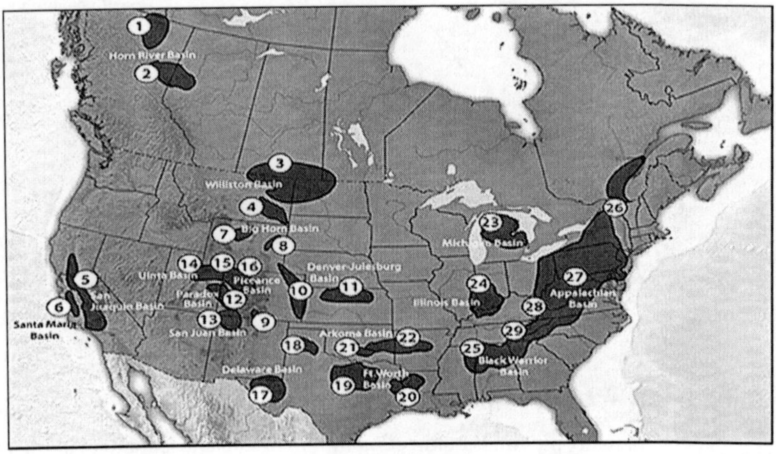

Source: Gastem.ca

Figure 43: United States Non-Conventional Gas Reserves.

The forecasts for increases in gas demand and therefore imports made before the development of non-conventional gas production led to nearly 40 new projects for re-gasification terminals being developed. However, because of the substantial growth in shale gas, utilisation rate of the import terminals reduced drastically and now many of the new export terminals are proposed at the site of existing import terminals.

- **Organisation of the Natural Gas Market in the US**

Deregulation of the US gas industry started in 1978. Since then, the US has experienced a period of overproduction, referred to as the gas bubble, as well as times when supplies have been under pressure. Each of these different phases has highlighted particular problems. Most federal controls over the industry have been abolished, except for regulation of the transport and storage system. This ensures third-party access to the transport and storage system and mandates separation of transport from marketing. Pipeline tariffs are in two parts, a fixed fee that entitles the user to capacity and a variable element based on his throughput.

Prior to deregulation, a producer had to sell to a transport company; following deregulation, he can now sell to an end user, local distribution

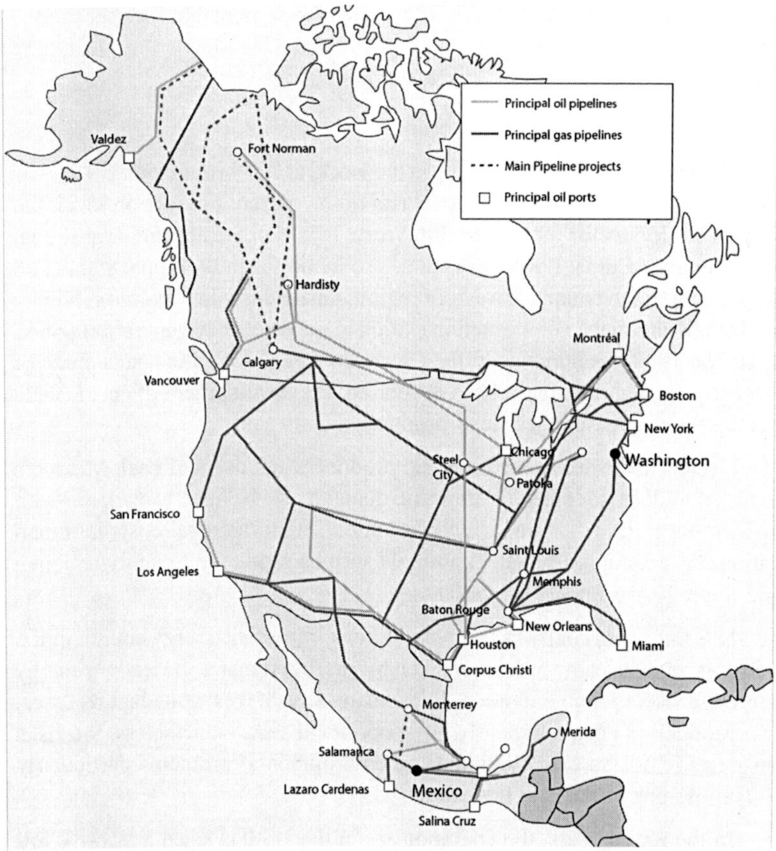

Figure 44: Principal Hydrocarbon Supply Infrastructure in North America.

company or broker. The selling price is no longer regulated. Previously, transport companies were responsible for supply security; it is now in the hands of purchasers. Users can purchase their gas from the seller that they choose and decide how delivery is to be arranged, i.e. they can contract for gas supply, transport, storage, etc. separately or they can purchase these services bundled. Deregulation means that many industrial and commercial customers who are served by a local distribution network can buy their gas directly from a producer or broker. It is possible to resell unused transport and storage capacity to the owner or on a secondary market.

Thus, the US natural gas market is open to all. Wellhead gas prices have been decontrolled since 1989. Interstate transport is regulated by FERC (Federal Energy Regulatory Commission), which ensures non-discriminatory network access for all competing suppliers, controls rates, and regulates the construction of new gas pipelines and storage sites. Distribution is regulated by commissions at the state level, which are also responsible for user rates.

COAL

A Dying Abundant Energy Source

US has the largest coal reserve in the world at 237 billion tonnes which is more than one-quarter of world total and at the current production level, the reserve could last for more than 300 years. It is also the second largest coal producer after China. Forty per cent of production is in the Appalachian and 50 per cent in the country's western region, particularly in Wyoming. Ninety per cent of national coal production is used in the electricity generation sector. Since the 1990 amendments to the Clean Air Act (CAA), the coal's share of electricity generation market has decreased; the development of cheap shale gas has also increased electricity production from gas.

Canada and Mexico are marginal producers and users of coal. Mexico's production does not meet all domestic demand, the balance is made up with imports from the US, Canada and Colombia. Imported coal costs less than national production. Canada exports its surplus production mainly to Japan and South Korea for steel manufacture.

Not long ago, coal was the second most important energy source in the US after oil. It has now been over taken by gas, but remains the leading energy source for electricity generation. It has many advantages: abundant reserves, low production cost, and nearly no geopolitical risk. Nonetheless, the risks associated with its extraction and the environmental problems particularly CO_2 emissions, make coal less attractive.

In the recent years, the coal industry in the US has taken a massive toll and the current production level is 31 per cent lower it was in 2008. The key causes for this crisis are the fallen demand, overcapacity, environmental liabilities and limited profitability. This has led to many coal mines in the US to shut their operations. Also, the coal price has fallen from over \$80/ton in 2011 US to only \$40/ton in 2016 which makes it difficult for some of the producers to even cover the marginal cost. A reduction of 132 million tons of coal demand is expected between 2014 and 2020. According to financial publications, the industry is expected to carry \$70 billion of liabilities in 2020 out of which it will have the capacity to cover only \$25 billion.

The equity holders have already taken the toll for the loss and the long term bond holders can't do much except waiting for the market to restructure and the price to rise.

- **Environmental Aspect**

The first US anti-pollution measures were enacted in 1955, but the principal air quality control measures started in 1970, with the Clean Air Act and the creation of the Environmental Protection Agency (EPA). In 1990, the Clean Air Act Amendment (CAAA90) brought in a group of measures to decrease pollutant emissions for power plants and also proposed measures concerning acid rain and alternative fuels like ethanol.

Further measures (Clean Skies Initiative) have been taken to limit pollutant emissions from major coal-fired power plants.

The EPA has also decided to tackle the veil of pollution which affects the views at more than 150 of the country's National Parks, particularly the famous Grand Canyon and Yellowstone Park.

ELECTRICITY

North America is the world's largest electricity market, with 19 per cent of world electricity production concentrated in just one country: the United States. Installed capacity amounted to 1,270 GW in 2016, of which 1063 GW was in the US.

The electricity production and transmission systems of Canada and the US are integrated within the North American Electric Reliability Council (NERC) and its ten regional reliability councils. Thus, the continent can be divided into five major interconnected systems:

- The Western Interconnection, which includes western Canada, American western states and Baja California in Mexico.
- The Eastern Interconnection, which includes the Canadian provinces of Saskatchewan and Manitoba.
- The Quebec zone.
- The Texas Interconnection.
- The Mexican system.

With implementation of the NAFTA agreement in 1994 and the move to greater deregulation in all three countries, electricity interdependency continues to grow.

- **Electricity Production**

In 2015, the US produced 4,087 TWh of electricity, 20 per cent from nuclear energy, 33 per cent from gas, 30 per cent from coal, renewable energies (hydro mainly but more and more solar and wind) developing quickly.

As in many countries, there has been a recent tendency in the US to replace coal-fired power plants with combined cycle power plants operating on natural gas. Gas-fired power plants have many advantages: ease and speed of construction, higher efficiency, and near-zero pollutant emissions apart from CO_2 emissions which are anyway lower than with coal (Fig. 45).

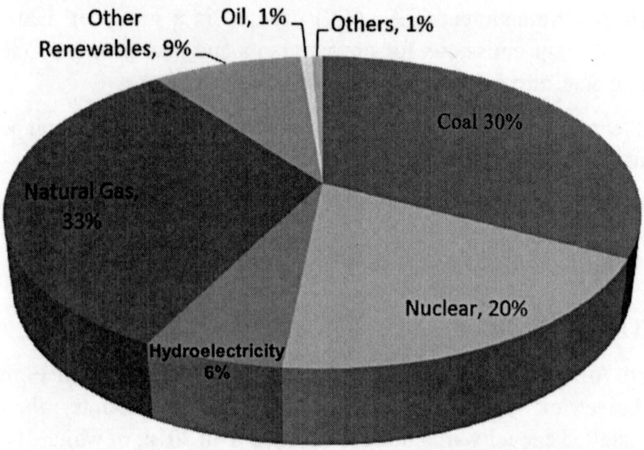

Source: DOE

Figure 45: US 2015 Electricity Production by Energy Source.

In Canada, over 60 per cent of electricity generation is hydraulic. Canada is the world's leading producer of hydraulic energy, which has a particularly interesting quality, it can be stored. Water retained in dams is used when demand is strong. Quebec is the largest electricity market and 93 per cent of the region's installed capacity is hydraulic-based.

In Mexico, fuel oil was the most widely used energy for electricity generation for many years. However, natural gas is now largely used. Mexican electricity demand is continuously increasing, with growth of roughly six per cent per year recently. Non-fossil fuels will generate an increasing share of electricity in the near future.

The current interconnection systems between Mexico and the US are largely insufficient; only Baja California has efficient interconnections with its American neighbour.

- **Nuclear Generation**

The 60 American nuclear power plants with 100 reactors provide 19 per cent of total electricity production. The nuclear industry was developed very early on in the United States: the first nuclear plants date back to the 1950s.

Recently four reactors were closed but one was built (Watts Bar Unit 2) which came online in June 2016. Four new nuclear reactors are actively under construction: Vogtle Units 3 and 4 in Georgia and Virgil C. Summer Units 2 and 3 in South Carolina.

However, the competition with gas and coal makes the development of new reactors unlikely in the near future.

Regarding waste storage, an important issue in the nuclear industry, on July 9, 2002 the US approved the creation of a permanent waste storage centre located in Yucca Mountain.

- **Renewables-Based Generation**

In the US, 15 per cent of total electricity is generated from renewable resources. A large fraction (42 per cent) is hydraulic-based. The Great Lakes, located in the mid-west region between the US and Canada, have a significant hydroelectric potential.

- **Agro-Fuels in North America**

Although a late entrant, the US has benefited strongly from its corn production and replaced Brazil as the leading producer of ethanol for biofuels. Their ethanol production has quintupled since 2000, amounting to nearly 31 Mtoe in 2015, thanks to a vast network of refineries in more than 20 states. The environmental benefit of these agro-fuels is limited. Their production is also used to subsidise the farmers.

- **Organisation and Regulation of the American Electricity Market**

Until recently, the American electricity industry was dominated by vertically integrated public monopolies, which were subject to state regulation. With the 1992 introduction of competition into the generation sector, this has changed. The market is totally deregulated in Texas, Pennsylvania, New Jersey, Maryland...but some states (for instance Alabama), where prices have always been low, are resisting the change.

Because the structure of operators and producers is highly varied, the coordination is complex. Control and regulation of the energy industry is divided between the federal level and the various states: the central (federal) government controls interstate commerce, while commerce occurring wholly within a state is controlled by that state. The main federal tool is the FERC (Federal Energy Regulatory Commission). At the state level, the regulatory institutions are PUCs (Public Utilities Commission).

In November 2001, FERC announced price controls for companies where this was justified by their size. The FERC could require a particular company to charge a price equal to its production cost rather than the market price. Despite the fact that deregulation led to the breakup of public monopolies, the increasing number of mergers means that private companies are again acquiring dominant positions.

There are roughly 5,000 companies operating on the American electricity market. Three-quarters of their total production comes from a few hundred private capital companies, while 2,000 public or municipal companies supply 15 per cent of the electricity market. There are also 1,000 companies which are owned by their employees and users. It is interesting to note that there is a fairly significant difference in prices between public and private companies— roughly 20 per cent on average—partly due to public subsidies and tax exemptions.

CHALLENGES FOR AMERICAN ENERGY POLICY

- **Oil Imports: Vital for the United States**

The US remains by far the world's largest oil consumer: imports are decreasing but in 2015, US oil imports were still 6.6 Mb/d second only to China which imports 7.6 Mb/d; 60 per cent are from non-OPEC countries (mainly Canada and Mexico) and 40 per cent from OPEC members. Three of the main suppliers of oil and petroleum products to the US are their immediate neighbours: Canada (3.1 Mb/d), Mexico (.7 Mb/d) and Venezuela (.7 Mb/d). Saudi Arabia (1.0 Mb/d), Iraq and Colombia are also significant suppliers.

Because the US represents over a fifth of the world's oil market, US imports alone represent seven per cent of world oil production, and the major crude oil exporters believe that their presence there is crucial. The geographical proximity of Canada, Mexico and Venezuela make them natural suppliers, but for Saudi Arabia, their decision to sell into the US market has a cost: crude oil to the US is sold in Ras Tanura at a lower price than the same crude oil shipped to the Asian market (Fig. 46).

- **The United States: The Failure to Become Energy Independent**

Up to the 1940s, the US produced more than half of the world's crude oil. But this position very quickly changed and imports became necessary. Because imported crude was far less expensive than local production, in 1949 the US established a system of oil import quotas to protect their high cost domestic producers. Small domestic producers campaigned under the slogan of: "keep out cheap foreign oil."

Whenever America is faced with the threat of shortages or an embargo, American energy policy yet again becomes a topic of discussion. Following the first oil shock in 1974, President Nixon launched "Project Independence", a plan to enable the US to recover the energy independence it had lost at the end of the 1950s: "Let us set as our national goal...that by the end of this decade we will have developed the potential to meet our own energy needs without depending on any foreign source." This project was unrealistic. In January 1975, Gerald Ford, who had replaced Nixon as President, proposed an impressive plan for the opening of 250 coal mines, construction of 200 nuclear power plants, 150 major coal-fired power plants, 30 oil refineries and 20 major new synthetic fuel production plants, all within ten years. Shortly thereafter, Nelson Rockefeller, Vice President and grandson of the Standard Oil founder, proposed a $100 billion programme to subsidise synthetic fuels and new energies. However, in practice these initiatives led only to the long-delayed construction of the Trans-Alaska pipeline, and fuel consumption standards for American cars requiring improved fuel economy with tax penalties for non-compliance[3].

Following the oil counter-shock of 1986 and abundant energy production in the 1980s and 1990s, American concerns about supply security faded. They returned to the forefront with the California crisis in 2000: that was the result of a shortage of electricity generating capacity in the western US but it developed into an American energy crisis with the price of electricity, and that of gas and home heating oil, skyrocketing. However, unlike the crises of the 1970s which were caused by justified fears of shortages, the crisis of 2000 was more the consequence of poorly managed deregulation of the energy markets[4].

Energy Policy: Trump vs Clinton

Donald Trump, the Republican candidate who won the elections in the United States and Hilary Clinton who was the nominee from the Democrats has very different views on the energy policies. They expressed their stand during the election campaign for the future of the energy policy in the United States. Key objectives of Donald Trump are:

- Support for the Keystone XL pipeline (a pipeline to transport oil from Canada to the Gulf of Mexico).
- Allow drilling on Federal lands wherever it is currently restricted.
- Revitalise the dying coal industry in the US.

Key Policies of Hilary Clinton were:

- Focus on the clean energy generation and making US the superpower of clean energy.
- Modernisation of the energy grid.
- Replacement of coal by natural gas which can act as a bridging fuel and 25 per cent of electricity coming from renewable sources by 2025

In short, Donald Trump has a pro fossil fuels stand when it comes to energy generation while Hilary Clinton had a pro renewables stand with a long term strategy to replace fossil fuels with renewables.

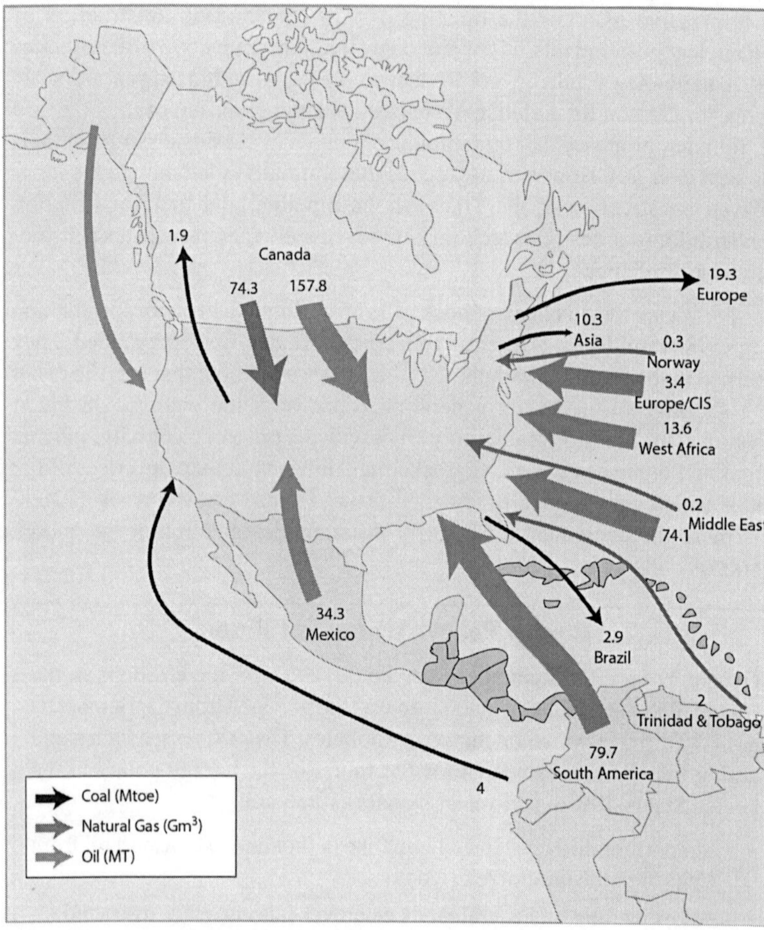

Source: BP Statistical Review of World Energy, June 2016.

Figure 46: US Energy Supplies in 2015.

- **Local Solutions**

For a long time, the US has prohibited the development of hydrocarbon deposits located in federal National Parks and National Wilderness Areas. The quantities involved can be significant: one American geological study in 1998 estimated the technically recoverable reserves of ANWR (Alaskan National Wildlife Refuge) at about 10 billion barrels, with a production capacity of up to, or even exceeding, one million barrels per day. So American policy faces a dilemma: to choose between environmental concerns and security of supply. This has been highlighted by the BP oil spill in the Gulf of Mexico (see chapter 2) which caused the government to try to impose a moratorium on off-shore drilling.

- **Energy Policy Outlook**

The US government seeks to limit American oil dependence by diversifying supply sources and energy sources. Development of shale gas and shale oil has reduced dependency. Attempts are also being made to limit fuel consumption, a difficult task in a country where the individual automobile is king.

This administrative approach to managing energy problems is highly contested by economic liberals, who believe in allowing market forces to predominate and recall that all previous attempts at government intervention have failed.

Despite the reduction of oil imports from the Gulf, the concentration of oil reserves in the Middle East encourages the US to develop a foreign policy for that region intended to ensure reliable long-term supplies, for the US and for the rest of the western world.

AMERICAN FOREIGN POLICY AND SUPPLY SECURITY

At the end of the 1990s, a report by George Tenet, then head of the CIA, describing the increasing difficulties with the Middle East, particularly due to the Israeli-Palestinian conflict, affirmed the need to reduce dependence on this zone by focusing efforts on the Caspian and above all the Atlantic: Latin America (Venezuela and Mexico) and Africa (Gulf of Guinea and the Maghreb). The objective was to find new resources in order to put pressure on Middle-Eastern producers. This American energy policy was thus consistent with measures taken by Presidents Carter and Reagan: develop the global oil business and ensure it can function correctly by securing transport routes and developing new supply sources.

- **Relations with Neighbouring Countries**

Canada plays a central role in the region's energy balance since it is the only country exporting all forms of energy: it is the leading supplier of oil to the US and electricity trading between the two countries is significant.

NAFTA is helping to develop trade particularly trade in energy, in the region. But Canada may, in the near future, prioritise conserving its national reserves for domestic consumption.

With regard to oil, the development of the immense oil sands reserves should readily enable Canada to continue to supply the US. In contrast, Canadian natural gas reserves (one per cent of world reserves versus nearly five per cent for the US) are limited and the development of oil sands production will make necessary the use of increased quantities of gas.

Concerning electricity, the Energy Ministers of the region's three countries met in March 2001 to agree a common strategy, particularly regarding projects for integrating their national grids. Although trading between the American and Canadian markets is significant (Canada's net exports to the US were 58.4 TWh in 2014, or nearly 10 per cent of its production), electricity trading between Mexico and the US remains very limited due to a severe lack of infrastructure.

The prognosis for Mexican oil supplies remains mixed. With the current rate of production, its reserves are declining rapidly. Although the potential for further reserves is thought to be significant, Mexico has not recently had sufficient financial resources to invest the amounts required to develop oil and gas production, since a large portion of Pemex's income must be paid to the government. The "opening" of the exploration and production activities to foreign companies should facilitate the development of energy (including electricity) production.

- **Chaotic Relations with Saudi Arabia**

Saudi Arabia supply to US has fallen to five per cent of American crude oil imports from 15 per cent in 2011. Nevertheless it is a key partner of the United States. It co-operates with American security policy and has allowed three US military bases on its territory in order to reduce instability in the region and the impact that would have on crude oil prices. Overall the two countries are tightly linked by common strategic and energy interests (see chapter 11 on the Middle East). Since the Kingdom was founded in 1932, the terms of the deal have been clear: the United States ensures the security of the Wahhabite Kingdom, in exchange for which the latter supplies the West with oil. The US intervention in Kuwait in 1991 was aimed at preventing Iraq from controlling 20 per cent of world crude oil reserves (the total reserves of both countries) and threatening two other countries: Saudi Arabia and the United Arab Emirates, which hold 16 per cent and 6 per cent of world reserves respectively. The result of the Iraqi invasion was intervention by a coalition of 34 countries to liberate Kuwait, and also protect Saudi Arabia.

However, this alliance between the world's largest democracy and one of its most absolute monarchies is not always harmonious. The events of September 11 helped exacerbate the grievances accumulating between the two partners. Washington accused Riyadh of using its oil wealth to finance terrorist groups (15 of the 19 terrorists that hijacked the planes and crashed them into the World Trade Center towers and the Pentagon carried Saudi identity cards, and Osama bin Laden himself is of Saudi origin), and the regime's lack of democracy seemed incompatible with the US Greater Middle East project. On the other hand, the Saudis are irritated by the criticism of them in the American media and unconditional support the US gives to Israel.

Yet the pact that links them does not seem to be questioned. Saudi Arabia is the only country whose large production volume gives it a dominant power over the market and whose reserves are of a size that would enable it to destabilise the world economy. While it is possible that America's Gulf oil supplies could come from other sources, that physical independence could not shelter the US from political upsets in the Middle East: the oil market is worldwide and an incident on an oilfield or at a refinery in the Middle East affects prices worldwide. In addition, although the power of the US is astounding, it still needs the support of other countries, whether industrialised or emerging. This means that it needs to protect the economic interests of its allies.

Thus, the Washington-Riyadh axis continues to be one of the keys to oil geopolitics at the beginning of the twenty-first century. However, the numerous visits by Chinese leaders to Riyadh and Saudi leaders to Beijing show the extreme importance given by Beijing to the only country whose oil exports are large enough to meet Chinese needs.

- **Intervention in Iraq**

After initially supporting Saddam Hussein's regime in Iraq as a protection against communism, and subsequently against the neighbouring Iranian regime, in March 2003 the US launched a pre-emptive strike to destroy it; the threat posed by weapons of mass destruction—which in fact did not exist—was the official reason. The main reason was rather the desire to eliminate a dictatorial regime accused, wrongly, of aiding terrorism, and particularly Al-Qaeda. The US government, strongly influenced by neo-conservatives, abandoned the policy of multilateralism that had governed international relations since 1945 and sought to re-establish democracy in Iraq through the elimination of Saddam Hussein. This, by a reverse application of the domino theory[5], would lead to flourishing democratic regimes in neighbouring countries.

Oil of course was relevant to this invasion. At the end of the 1970s, the Carter Doctrine, named after President Jimmy Carter, stated officially that the US would do everything possible, including the use of military force, to ensure that it would receive the energy supplies it needed and that the oil flow to the US would continue unhindered. So an additional motivation for this armed intervention was to have an alternative favoured partner to Saudi Arabia.

Clearly in 2017, the result of the US intervention is a disaster. Iraq has always been a complex country to manage. The country is split between an important Kurd minority, a Shia majority and a Sunni minority and Saddam was relying on this Sunni minority to ensure his power. The decision of the US authorities directed by Paul Bronner to fire all the soldiers and the hierarchy of Saddam Hussein was a huge mistake. The creation of the Islamic State (Daech) is one of the consequences of this decision. The Sunni generals fired by Bronner turned their feet towards Daech.

The government in now in the hands of the Shia majority, but Ali Malikki as a prime minister could not manage the country and eradicate corruption. Terrorism has not been stopped, indeed thousands of people have died through terrorist acts since 2003. One of the worst attacks killed more than 200 people in 2016.

Oil production remained low for many years after 2003 because of insecurity in the country. In 2009, the government allocated to various companies (IOC, Chinese companies) fields already discovered but which were never developed because of the political situation (war between Iran and Iraq,1980–1988, embargo on Iraq exports after the invasion of Kuwait by Iraq on August 2, 2010, and the consequent sanctions which lasted up to the end of Saddam. Production could have been expected to grow to 10 Mb/d, based on the potential of the fields. Present production in only 4.2 Mbd, which is much higher than the production after the fall of Saddam, but much lower than the target. This is mainly because of technical problems but also for geopolitical reasons: could Iran and Saudi Arabia accept Iraqi production rising to between 5 and 10 Mbd?

- **Tensions with Venezuela**

Since coming to power in 1999, up to his death in 2013 President Chavez has increased his criticism of US policy, which even led to economic sanctions being imposed by the Clinton administration. The close relations between the Venezuelan President and the Castro regime only made things worse.

The developments of the LTO production in the US and the fall in the Venezuelan production have made the US much less dependent on Venezuelan crude.

- **Russia: Complex Relations**

With oil production approaching—and sometimes exceeding—that of Saudi Arabia, Russia could be a particularly interesting partner for the United

States, although the remoteness of Russian hydrocarbon deposits as well as antiquated transport facilities which are largely restricted to delivering to the European market, limit the possibilities of supplying the US. However, the situation could change fairly soon with projects for the development of pipelines terminating on the Pacific coast.

US-Russia relations have changed, at least for a period of time, since the September 11 attacks: Russia took advantage of the situation to emphasise its return to the concert of great powers. Criticism of the Russian government's actions in Chechnya abated and a coalition against terrorism was formed. However, George W Bush's second term, which he devoted to the fight for democracy, including American financial support for peaceful revolutions in Russia's neighbouring countries (Georgia in 2003, Ukraine in 2004, and Kirgizstan in 2005), marked a return to mutual mistrust. The crisis in Ukraine (2014), the annexion of Crimea by Russia further deteriorated the situation.

- **The Caspian Sea: a Good Swing Supplier**

Although, this area is no longer considered to be the "new Saudi Arabia", the US remains very active in this complex region, which is a good swing supplier. Their strategy is preventing the development of any project for the delivery of hydrocarbons via Iran, and not allowing Russia to maintain the monopoly it has always enjoyed over the pipeline infrastructure from the Caspian region. To do this, it obtained agreements to establish military bases on the territory of former Soviet republics bordering the Caspian, and provides financial support for the democracy movements in these countries, thus contributing to their emancipation from the tutelage of their Russian neighbour. This policy led to the construction of the Baku-Tbilisi-Ceyhan pipeline, inaugurated in 2006, which delivers Azeri oil to the west via Georgia and Turkey, carefully avoiding Iran and Russia.

- **The Lifting of Sanctions Against Some Producing Countries**

On April 23, 2004, sanctions against Libya, imposed 20 years earlier because of the bombing of the Pan Am Boeing 747 over Lockerbie and the Libyan government's support of groups considered to be terrorists, were partially lifted.

Libya probably has the largest oil and gas reserves in Africa with the potential to increase its production substantially. Oil (and subsequently gas) production in Libya started in the 1960s with American companies participating. After the 1969 revolution, Libya's new strongman, Colonel Kadhafi, decided to restrict production, before driving the negotiations with the oil companies that resulted in the Tripoli Agreements. That led to a substantial increase in crude oil prices in 1971. Kadhafi subsequently nationalised the Libyan assets of all foreign oil companies.

American companies were the first to benefit from the new exploration-production contracts offered by the government when sanctions had been lifted. The experience they had gained from forty years of working in Libya meant they had good knowledge of the fields and they also have the favourable opinion of their former Libyan partners.

Since 2011 and the death of Muhamar Khadafi, the situation in Libya is chaotic. The country is split between the western part (Tripolitaine around Tripoli) controlled by General National Congress the Eastern part (Cyrenaïque around Benghazi) controlled by Libyan National Army and the Fezzan in the South. A new government supported by the international organisations came to power in March 2016 but it has to face different oppositions and its real influence is far from clear.

Daech established a second implantation in Syrte, the place where Khadafi was born and a main exportation port for oil. Today the oil production, which was close to 1.8 Mbd before 2011, is very limited and volatile, on average around a few hundred thousand barrels per day.

- **The Relations with Iran**

Unlike the position in Libya, the D'Amato Law, enacted in 1996 and renewed in 2001 for a further five years, continued to provide for sanctions on Iran for several years (the law penalised any non-American company that invested more than $20 million in Iran). However, the relationships improved when President Hassan Rohani was elected in 2013 and replaced the radical Mahmoud Ahmadinejad. Iran's nuclear programme and Tehran's support of Hezbollah were sources of tension between the two countries. Long negotiations on the nuclear programme came to an agreement on July 14, 2015. In exchange for the freezing of the military nuclear programme of Iran, the "5+1" (US, Russia, China, UK and France—permanent members of the Security Council of the UN—plus Germany) accepted to progressively suspend the sanctions. Iran immediately announced that its oil production would increase quickly by 0.5 and then by 1 Mbd. But reaching these objectives will probably take some time because of relatively old fields and installations. Another obstacle is the necessity to design new laws and contracts to allow the participation of foreign companies in the oil and gas exploration and production.

- **The Keen Interest in Africa**

Following the increasing difficulties encountered in the Middle East, the US wanted to increase oil imports from Africa in the 2000 years (oil imports were up to 60 per cent of US consumption). For example, Walter Kansteiner, Assistant Secretary of State for African Affairs, stated in 2002 that "African oil represents a national strategic interest for the United States". The stated objective was to see Africa's share of US oil imports increase from the current 17 per cent to 25 per cent in ten years. There were several reasons for this interest: the size of probable reserves, the quality of African oil (light and low in sulfur), the proximity of African coasts to the US market, and finally the offshore location of many deposits, a factor that reduces geopolitical risk.

However, the strong development of Light Tight Oil production in the US has largely reduced oil imports (from 12 to 6 Mb/d in about 10 years). Moreover the quality of LTO (light and low sulfur) is quite similar to the quality of the African crudes. So in a few years US oil imports from West Africa have fallen to a very low level and oil from Nigeria or Angola (and of the other producing countries) is now exported to Asia.

CONCLUSION

North America is still the largest energy consumer in the world, but the situation has changed. Now the US and Canada are producing increased quantities of oil (and gas) through oil sands in Canada and LTO in the US. With very large reserves of coal and substantial quantities of shale oil and gas to be produced, the continent could be more or less balanced in terms of production and consumption.

This is also good news for the rest of the world. The risk of a competition, for instance between the US and China for the control of energy reserves thus strongly reduces.

References

1. The original name was tar sands or bitumen, since these deposits are truly bitumen mixed with sand. The name was changed to oil sands, which is more "politically correct", since "tar" is a by-product of the destructive distillation of coal and highly carcinogenic.
2. The OPEC basket is a group of crude oils deemed to be representative of production.
3. CAFE standards (Corporate Average Fuel Efficiency). These standards were suddenly imposed and led to American automobile manufacturers releasing small cars onto the market which had been designed too quickly and were unreliable, resulting in US consumer resistance to them. Manufacturers succeeded in avoiding these rules by getting large vehicles, although they were for domestic use, considered as trucks and thus exempt from CAFE standards.
4. *"Failure by design"*. The main reason for the California crisis was the maintenance of price caps on retail electricity sales, while local operators had to buy their electricity wholesale at a prohibitive rate due to insufficient production.

5. In the 1960s, the domino theory was used to justify US intervention in Vietnam. The Americans thought that if Vietnam fell to communism, neighboring countries would also fall. Neither the fall of the Vietnamese regime, until then supported by the Americans, in 1975, nor the fall of Saddam Hussein's regime in 2003, had the predicted results.

Chapter - 6

The South American Continent

Since the end of the nineteenth century, the countries of Latin America have been large producers and exporters of raw materials. Historically, the significant hydrocarbon reserves discovered in Mexico and Venezuela at the start of the twentieth century led international companies, particularly American and British, to invest in these countries. However, relations between these companies and the governments rapidly deteriorated when the companies were seen as abusing their position and failing to pay just compensation to the host governments for their resources. In addition, foreign companies and their respective governments have always tried to put in, at the head of South American countries, people in whom they have confidence, to ensure that the countries adopted the "neo-liberal" policies that conformed to their interests. For a long time, this attitude has prevented the development of democratic regimes and weakened those that have been established. It has resulted in the nationalisation of mineral extraction (Mexico, Bolivia) and the development of guerilla warfare (Peru, Columbia). Despite significant progress, a large share of the population in these countries currently lives below the poverty line. When this is compared to the continent's wealth in natural resources and in terms of biodiversity, the contrast is startling.

In fact, South America has significant natural energy resources. There are large oil reserves (19 per cent of proved world reserves), mainly located in Venezuela and Brazil, more modest natural gas reserves, very limited coal reserves but considerable hydroelectric potential which currently provides 17 per cent of world production and 60 per cent of electricity in South America. So the region is self-sufficient in all forms of energy, particularly as its own primary energy consumption is low, amounting to five per cent of the worldwide total. Oil and hydraulic electricity provide almost three-quarters of this (Fig. 47 and Fig. 48). However, the very high share of hydraulic energy in the continent's production of electricity can be a handicap in times of drought, as was the case in 2001, particularly in Brazil and in Venezuela (a drought led the Venezuelan government to close some offices because of the lack of electricity recently). Nuclear electricity generation is very small and limited to Argentina and Brazil (Fig. 49).

OIL

- **Venezuela**

Venezuela's oil reserves were for long estimated at around 80 billion barrels but the government decided by 2010 to increase the reserves to 300 billion barrels, by incorporating the huge reserves of the Orinoco Belt. So, Venezuela has now the largest oil reserves in the world, before Saudi Arabia. However, this is more a political than a technical decision since oil production in Venezuela (2.6 Mb/d) is less than 25 per cent of the Saudi production. And also, because of the extremely difficult situation of Venezuela, the production is declining.

Following the nationalisation of oil in Mexico in 1938, western oil companies made Venezuela their main source of oil in South America. The country then became the world's leading exporter. Its role in World War II was particularly important: it supplied 60 per cent of the oil consumed by the Allied forces. But the wealth that came from this only reached a limited number of people and, although private capital was brought into the industrial and service sectors, the economy remained largely dependent on oil.

After the war, the majority of Venezuela's population was very poor and there was increasingly open opposition to the dominant position of the interests of western capital. Following the populist uprisings that led to democratic elections in 1947, Venezuela introduced a new petroleum tax on

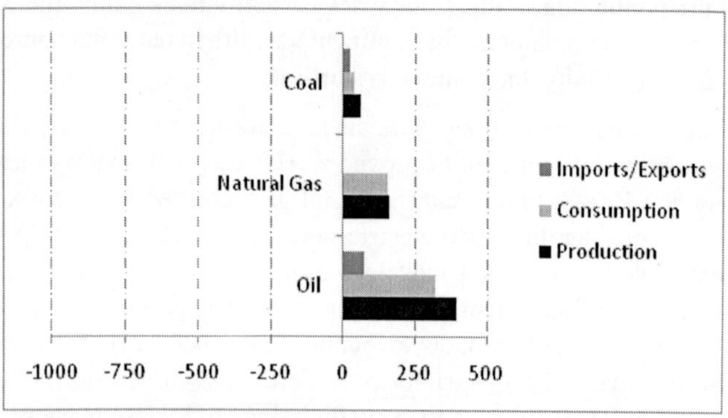

Figure 47: Total South American Energy Balance 2015 (Mtoe).

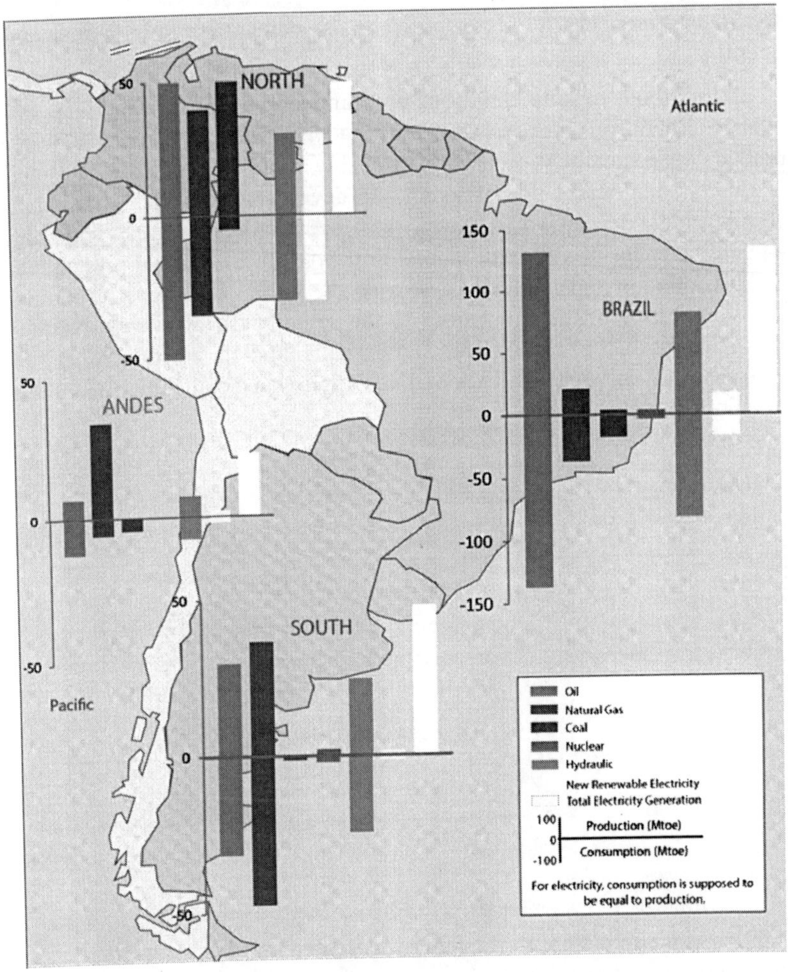

Source: BP Statistical Review of World Energy, June 2016 and doe/eia.

Figure 48: South American Energy Balance 2015.

oil profits: profits were split 50/50 between the government and the oil companies. The—mainly American—oil companies accepted this new situation after discussions with the US government. These companies had to pay taxes to the US government and the new taxes paid to the government of Venezuela were deducted from the taxes paid to the US government. The US government accepted this decision in order to keep good relations with the producing countries. This fifty-fifty system was quickly enforced in most of the producing countries. However, during this period, the Venezuelan (and more generally the South American) oil sector continued to depend on foreign financial interests.

In addition, despite ambitious programmes for social initiatives and industrialisation, oil revenues had a very negative influence on national industry productivity generally. Venezuela was probably one of the first cases of "Dutch Disease", even before the discovery and development of the Netherlands Groningen gas deposit would provide the best example: these new "windfall" mineral revenues encouraged imports to the detriment of local production, created inflation and gradually destroyed the basis of the local economy. Many countries would fall victim to the same chain of events. Neither the nationalisation of oil facilities and deposits in 1975, nor the creation of Petroleos de Venezuela SA (PDVSA), the state-owned company, altered this situation.

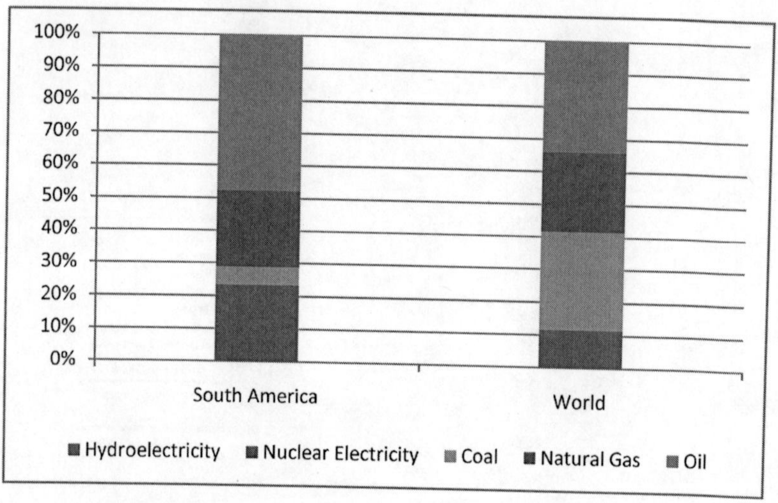

Source: BP Statistical Review, 2016.

Figure 49: Primary Energy Consumption 2015.

Like all the producing countries, Venezuela had to endure the hardships resulting from the fall in oil prices after 1986. At the start of the 1990s, the government's and PDVSA's policy was to maximise oil production. Venezuela ignored OPEC's production quotas and adopted an objective of increasing its market share, relying on the size of its reserves and its proximity to the US, the world's largest crude oil importer.

The 1998 collapse in oil prices, with a barrel traded at less than $10 by the end of the year, put an end to this policy. The election of Hugo Chavez as the country's President in January 1999 radically changed the situation: soldier, former putschist and head of a failed coup in 1993, he made absolutely clear his resolution to achieve a social transformation in Venezuela. His sympathies were with the third-world and he was determined to restore discipline within OPEC. His visit to every OPEC member capital and the agreement between Venezuela, Mexico and Saudi Arabia that followed, gradually convinced the markets of OPEC's determination to control prices.

Venezuela's Oil Reserves: Orinoco Extra-Heavy Crude Oil

In total, these extra-heavy crude oil reserves (see Chapters 1 and 2) are estimated at more than 222 billion barrels (Oil in place is probably close to 2000 billion barrels but recovery rate is low). Although 30 years ago these resources were deemed to be non-recoverable and so could in no way be included in the reserves figures, from 1998 such unconventional crude oil has actually been produced. Four joint-ventures were formed between the state-owned company PDVSA and foreign partners to develop production of this unconventional crude oil (ConocoPhillips (as the sole foreign partner), ExxonMobil and BP, Total and Statoil, ConocoPhillips with ChevronTexaco).

The basis of these four projects was to extract the oil (which in the reservoir is at a high temperature and so liquid) and transport it to the coast. As the extra-heavy crude oil solidifies at ordinary temperatures, it must be diluted with a light solvent to remain fluid. At the coast, the crude oil and the solvent are separated. The heavy crude oil is processed into a lighter crude (so-called synthetic crude oil)—which can easily be used—in an upgrading unit, a complex refinery where heavy molecules are transformed into lighter molecules and most of the impurities are removed from the crude oil.

In 2007, Venezuela, taking the opportunity of the huge increase in oil price, increased PDVSA's equity in the extra-heavy crude oil partnerships to 60 per cent. In response, ExxonMobil and ConocoPhillips withdrew from the joint-ventures and filed a lawsuit against the Venezuelan government.

Today Venezuela has called new foreign companies (Petrovietnam, Chinese companies) to develop new acreages in the Orinoco. But the production of oil in Venezuela is still decreasing. Despite the largest reserves in the world, Venezuela produces barely 25 per cent of the oil produced in Saudi Arabia or Russia.

Hugo Chavez died in 2013 and was replaced by Nicolas Maduro. The political and economic situation has largely deteriorated, and this of course was exacerbated by the collapse of oil prices in 2014.

- **Brazil**

Up to the beginning of the 2000s, Brazil's oil production was more or less enough to meet domestic demand. Most of the production was coming from the Campos basin, an area offshore Rio de Janeiro and San Paolo, with 2,000 meters water depth.

By 2007 and 2008 two very large fields, Tupi (later called Lula) and Carioca were discovered in the "presal" (in English pre-salt). The fields were offshore, below 2,000 meters of water, 1,000 meters of sediments (where lie the Campos fields) and 2,000 meters of salt. The salt deposits were the result of water evaporation when the Atlantic ocean was formed at the time of the opening between South America and Africa, 120 million years ago.

The Lula and Carioca fields have given Brazil the potential to become a major oil exporter. The reserves of these two fields alone are estimated at 12 billion barrels (some estimates exceed 50 billion barrels) and should be capable of producing an additional five million barrels per day in a few years. Total undiscovered reserves in the presal could exceed 100 billion barrels.

Development and production have started. More than 40 FPSO (Floating Production Storage Offloading platforms) will probably be set up. Total investment is several hundred billion dollars. Petrobras borrowed a large fraction of this amount and the debt of the company is more than 100 billion dollars.

In 2015, Brazilian oil production amounted to 2.5 million barrels per day. Oil production will increase but probably slowly due to the situation in Brazil, largely a consequence of the Petrobras corruption scandal which involves several politicians.

- **Other Oil Producers**

Production in Argentina (0.6 Mb/d) is in slight decline. The state-owned company YPF (Yacimentos Petroliferos Fiscales) was privatised in 1990.

Major oil discoveries were made in Columbia in the 1980s. Production was subject to interruptions because of guerilla warfare and peaked in 2002. It declined for several years but has now been rising since 2006 and reached 1 Mb/d in 2015. Production is forecast to increase, at least over the next two years and will do so for longer if the current increase in exploration activity is successful.

Ecuador was an OPEC member until 1993 and rejoined in 2007. Its production is currently below 0.6 Mb/d in 2015 (Fig. 50). Ecuador nationalised its resources and converted historical production sharing contracts to service contracts in 2010.

A Fight for Oil: The Chaco War[1]

Oil was the cause of the bloodiest war of the twentieth century in South America. In the 1930s, Chaco, a vast desert territory on the borders of Bolivia and Paraguay, was thought to contain significant oil reserves. Two major companies, Standard Oil in Bolivia and Shell in Paraguay, were involved in exploration for this oil. The rivalry between the companies and the countries resulted in a war, which lasted from 1932 to 1935. Despite their greater numbers, the Bolivian troops, mainly native American soldiers from the mountains who were unfamiliar with the desert, could not prevail against a Paraguayan army which was better adapted to the war's conditions. After three years of fighting and heavy losses for both countries (60,000 Bolivian deaths out of a population of 3.5 million), it was discovered that the oil was nothing but a figment of the imagination of both countries' nationalists, stimulated by that of the oil companies.

- **The Role of State-Owned Companies**

In all South American oil producing countries in the 1980s, the oil industry was in the hands of a state-owned company which held a monopoly over production, refining, and even marketing of oil products.

In Venezuela, the foreign oil companies were nationalised on January 1, 1976. Lagoven took over the assets of Esso, Maraven the assets of Shell and Corpoven the assets of the other foreign companies. They were combined into a single state-owned holding company: Petroleos de Venezuela SA (PDVSA). Lagoven, Maraven and Corpoven have now disappeared following the restructuring of PDVSA, which still controls most of the country's oil and gas activities. By law, foreign companies are only authorised to be involved in "marginal fields" or the exploitation of "extra heavy" crude oil.

In Colombia, Ecopetrol groups together the state's interests in the hydrocarbon sector, but acts jointly with foreign companies in the production sector. Thus, the Cusiana Field, the largest discovery of the 1990s, has been developed jointly with BP.

In Brazil, the role of Petrobras has always been a matter of controversy. Petrobras has a monopoly in the refining sector, but the production sector is open to other companies, although the most attractive exploration zones are always available for Petrobras. What is unique to Brazil is that Petrobras is recognised as a very efficient operator, particularly in respect of its technological advances in ultra-deep water exploration and production. At the other end of the spectrum, i.e. in marketing, other companies can operate and are free to import the products they wish to sell.

In Argentina, YPF (Yacimentos Petroliferos Fiscales) the national oil company was privatised by Carlos Menem in 1990. Later, the company was bought back by Repsol in 1999. However in 2012, as a sanction against the—supposed—too limited investments of the company, the government of Argentina decided to nationalise the Argentinean affiliates of the company. As a consequence, the YPF national oil company was again created.

- **Refining**

South America is a very important refining zone. Although most countries' refineries have export capability, the region encompassing Venezuela and the Caribbean islands play a key role in supplying the United States, particularly, with gasoline. Indeed more than half of Venezuelan crude oil production is

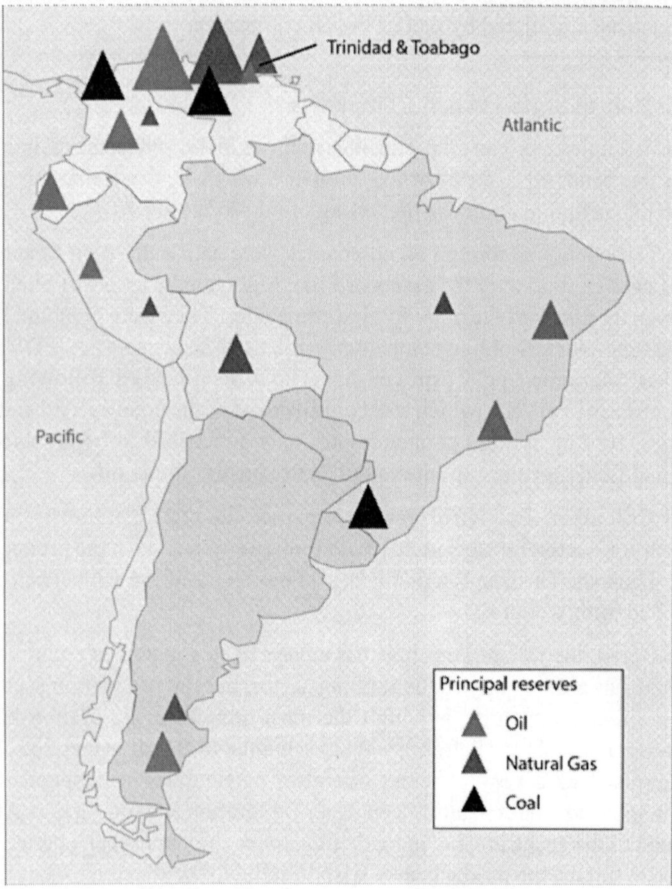

Figure 50: Main Fossil Fuel Reserves in South America.

locally refined and it is the finished products that are sold. The enormous Punto Fijo/Paraguana complex has had the world's largest oil processing capacity, nearly 1 Mb/d, since the two former refineries at Amuay and Cardon were connected by pipelines to become one plant. Citgo, acquired by PDVSA, has several refineries in the United States and a large distribution network for petroleum products.

PDVSA, similarly to Aramco, has a very specific refining strategy. These two state-owned companies, belonging to two of the largest OPEC producers, have deliberately developed substantial refining capacity in the US and Europe that can process the heaviest crude oils they produce to facilitate the disposal of crudes that could otherwise be difficult to sell.

NATURAL GAS

The known natural gas reserves of South America are limited, comprising only four per cent of the world total, possibly because little investment has been made in exploring for a fuel for which, at least until recently, the market was limited because the standard of living in South America does not allow for the massive use of natural gas and in several South American countries electricity is mainly hydraulic based. However, the situation is changing with the development of gas networks in the wealthiest areas and the construction of gas-fired combined cycle power plants.

Venezuela has the largest reserves, but the production largely associated with that of crude oil, is mainly re-injected into the reservoirs to sustain the production of crude oil. Several other countries also have large reserves: Bolivia, Argentina, Brazil, Peru, and Trinidad and Tobago.

For long Argentina was exporting gas to Chile and Brazil. However, because of the very low price of gas imposed by the government, exploration was very limited and Argentina is an importing country. Two countries in Latin America are gas exporters: Bolivia exports by pipeline to Brazil and Argentina; Trinidad and Tobago exports by LNG to Argentina, Chile and Brazil (plus more limited quantities to North America, Europe and even Asia).

COAL

Colombia is one of the largest coal exporters. It has by far the biggest production in South America and is the only South American country to be a world scale player in coal trading. Revenue from coal exports is second to that from oil exports. The coal mines are owned by foreign privately-owned companies like BHP Billiton (Great Britain/Australia) and Glencore (Switzerland). The latter controls the largest coal mining operations in South America and the world's largest open-pit mine. Columbian coal is exported to the US, Europe and the rest of South America.

On the other hand Brazil, whose coal reserves are very limited and of poor quality, imports some 15 million tons per year, mainly for the steel industry, with small quantities for electricity generation.

ELECTRICITY

South America has abundant resources for electricity generation. It has both significant oil reserves and also uranium resources. Two countries—Brazil and Argentina—have nuclear power plants. Finally, South America has significant renewable energy potential: hydroelectricity, biomass, wind and solar. Hydroelectricity is the major source of electricity and that should continue, even though gas-based generation is expected to increase.

Brazil's electricity consumption represents more than 40 per cent of the South American total. This country's electricity generation capacity is about 137 GW nearly 70 per cent of which is hydroelectric, giving Brazil 9 per cent of worldwide hydroelectricity generation. Until the commissioning of the Three Gorges dam in China, the Itaipu Dam jointly controlled by Brazil and Paraguay, was the largest hydroelectric production complex in the world. There is still a fair development of hydro production in the Amazon and a direct current transmission line, the longest in the world, has been built to transport electricity from the Amazon region to the south of Brazil where consumption is concentrated. Apart from hydraulic generation, Brazilian electricity comes from coal and increasingly from gas. Brazil has suffered from major droughts in recent years, which have reduced electricity generation, weakened the economy and made the development of gas-based generation necessary.

After Brazil, Venezuela is the continent's second leading electricity consumer, closely followed by Argentina. Venezuela also depends largely on hydroelectricity. Despite its resources, Venezuela has recently suffered from considerable electricity shortages mainly because of the poor rainfall in some years which has led to short supply of water in the dams used for hydroelectric power generation.

The Ethanol Experiment in Brazil

In 1981, after the second oil shock, oil prices had never been so high. Brazil, a major crude oil importer, was being economically strangled. So Brazil instigated an ethanol fuel programme to reduce its need for oil imports.

Two new fuels were developed for spark-ignition engines: pure ethanol and a mix of 80 per cent traditional gasoline and 20 per cent ethanol. Of the 11 million lightweight vehicles on the road in Brazil, 6 million operate on pure ethanol and 5 million use the 80/20 mix. The other fuel distributed, diesel fuel, is all petroleum based but it is reserved for commercial vehicles and heavy trucks.

Today Brazil is the second largest biofuels producer globally with an annual production of 17.6 Mtoe, second only to the US.

Half of the area (6 million hectares) that Brazil devotes to sugarcane are sufficient for the production of 6 billion US gallons (25 billion liters) of ethanol per year. There is criticism of the increase in industrial sugarcane cultivation at the expense of food crops and concern as to the possible danger of aldehyde exhaust emissions from ethanol fuelled vehicles. But the production of ethanol from sugarcane remains one of the least controversial ways of biofuel production.

- **Regional Integration**

Although, the north of the continent, separated from the south by the vast Amazon rainforest, is more orientated towards the North American continent and the United States, there is a very clear integration movement within the "Southern Cone" (Argentina, Chile, Brazil, Bolivia and Paraguay). Brazil has large resources of oil and hydroelectricity. Although self-sufficient in oil, it must import gas. Bolivia, is very well placed to supply its large neighbour.

The development of this inter-regional network of energy distribution includes the construction of gas pipelines (between Bolivia and Brazil, Argentina and Brazil, and Argentina and Chile) and of power transmission lines between Argentina and Brazil, and between Argentina and Chile.

In South America as elsewhere, deregulation and privatisation is underway in the electricity sector with the privatisation of several power generation plants and many companies being broken up to separate their different activities. But in some cases it has led to re-integration, i.e. when American and European firms have been authorised to expand their share of both the electricity sector and the gas sector and so their businesses in these different sectors have been merged.

DYNAMICS AND CHALLENGES

South America is confronted by the challenges of regional integration and that of reducing the poverty that affects a large fraction of the population. Its role in supplying the world with energy, particularly hydrocarbons but also coal to a smaller extent, is a fundamental element in the geo-politics of this region.

- **Omnipresence of the Large American Neighbour**

Total oil supplies to the US from Venezuela, Colombia and Ecuador are large. In addition Venezuelan oil, in the form of products manufactured at their local refineries, plays a role in balancing the US oil supply system. So a United States objective is to maintain the power to influence the South American oil producing countries in order to defend the USA's geostrategic interests, particularly those involving energy. The US also supports the enlargement of NAFTA so that, as part of a future Free Trade Area of the Americas (FTAA), it would cover the entire American continent. The objective is to substitute economic and financial interdependence of South American countries for the political tutelage of the past as a means of ensuring US access to the subcontinent's resources.

Conversely, South America is attempting to acquire genuine independence from the United States. The Mercosur, Andean Community and Union of South American Nations (UNASUR) projects are an alternative that is completely South American and excludes the US. They advocate a form of cooperation beyond just a free trade area, more on the lines of the European Union. Such ideas are particularly supported by Venezuela and Brazil. The latter aspires to establish a role as the subcontinent's dominant, and future world power, and so is in competition with the US for leadership in the region.

The members of Mercosur are Brazil, Argentina, Uruguay and Paraguay. Although considerable progress has been made, there is tension between the small countries (Paraguay and Uruguay) and the large ones (Brazil and Argentina). Within the Andean Community (Venezuela, Colombia, Ecuador, Bolivia and Peru) the strength of Venezuela's oil revenue had for some time significantly increased its influence. Venezuela joined Mercosur six years after its application in the year 2012. However, participation of Venezuela in Mercosur has been suspended.

- **Venezuela's Gamble**

Hugo Chavez's policies have provoked strong opposition, both internally and externally. At the beginning of 2002, there was a damaging strike within PDVSA that stopped a large part of their production. As a result, Hugo Chavez urgently appointed Ali Rodriguez, whose name was widely respected in the oil world and who was Secretary General of OPEC at the time of the strike, as head of the company. But once the situation was under control, several thousand executives were fired, so PDVSA lost their valuable skills and, since then, production has still not returned to its former levels. PDVSA suffers from a structural deficiency in its investment capacity: the contribution it is required to make to the needs of the national budget is such that the resources left to it are insufficient to allow for production maintenance and development. Facilities are aging and deteriorating and reserve replacement is low. The international operators present are not motivated to invest more than the strict minimum because of the uncertainty as to how future legislation will develop.

After the death of Chavez and the fall of oil price, the situation has become worrisome.

On an international level, Venezuela is trying to reduce its dependence on the US market by diversifying its trade outlets geographically and as a result its exports to the US decreased from 1.5 Mb/d in 2005 to 0.7 Mb/d in 2014. On the contrary, US exports of refined products to Venezuela increased from 14,000 bbl/d in 2005 to 76,000 bbl/d in 2014. Chinese companies have acquired several concessions as well as signed a loan agreement with Venezuela and simultaneously a mutual trade agreement has been signed with Iran. The company IHS estimates China's cumulative loan to Venezuela at $56 billion since 2007.That should allow Venezuela to sell its oil in Asia via Iran in exchange for facilitating the sale of Iranian oil in Latin America. This has resulted in China and India becoming the second and third largest importers of Venezuela's crude oil. Nevertheless the more or less open conflict between Venezuela and the American government cannot disguise the reality: the US needs Venezuelan oil and Venezuela needs the US market. The PDVSA has too many interests in North America to contemplate a radical change in their alliance: there are significant exports of crude oil and products and Citgo, a PDVSA subsidiary based in the US, has nearly 1 Mb/d refining capacity, mainly supplied by PDVSA under long-term contracts, and a large network of service stations. The extra-heavy crude oil production projects illustrate the importance of the links between the two countries, since the main US companies (Conoco and Exxon) were leaders in two projects before they withdrew when PDVSAs equity share was increased.

- **Colombia: The end of the civil war**

Another oil producer where the level of production was previously in decline, Colombia still exports large quantities of oil to the US. The government has been in confrontation with extreme left-wing guerilla movements (Revolutionary Armed Forces of Colombia – FARC, National Liberation Army – ELN, etc.) for decades and they controlled part of the country. Far right paramilitary organisations (United Self-Defense Forces of Colombia – AUC) were formed to oppose these movements and protect the interests of large landowners. The conflicts between the government and these movements were virtually continuous. The rebel movements were based on the production and trafficking of drugs which were the source of financial resources and it is these activities which are at the heart of these conflicts.

There has been significant improvement in the security situation since the election of Alvaro Uribe as President in 2002 and with the increasing involvement of the United States within the framework of the "Colombia Plan". Financing the fight against guerillas and drug trafficking helps the US achieve several objectives: a direct attack on the source of cocaine that is flooding the

US market; stabilising the country to facilitate maximum and continuous production of oil. Also, the return of peace combined with a US presence in Columbia allows the United States to "encircle" and apply pressure on Venezuela, Ecuador and Bolivia.

A historic agreement was signed between the government and the FARC (the main organisation of opposition).The citizens recently voted against the peace treaty but the peace process will continue.

A number of pipelines are transporting the crude to Covenas, the export terminal on the Atlantic ocean. Some crude oil is also transported to the Pacific.

- **Bolivia: the "Gas War"**

Privatisation of the energy sector in the 1990s led to an intensive exploration programme and, between 1998 and 2001, proved gas reserves quintupled. However, in 2003 the expected foreign currency bonanza from this led to a veritable "gas war", questioning its optimal exploitation. The population, one of the poorest in the region, asked for renationalisation of the industry in order to take advantage of a significant portion of the revenues. In addition, many Bolivians remain hostile to Chile and prefered to see a gas pipeline built to Peru rather than across Chile, even if this route would not be very profitable. Social problems flared again in the spring of 2005, forcing President Mesa to resign. No agreement can be reached on the route for the gas pipeline or the location of the liquefaction facilities. With development of the reserves being blocked by these disputes, the southeast regions, where most of the gas reserves are located, are tempted by separatism.

Gas Nationalisation in Bolivia

In April 2006, the newly elected, President Morales, decided to nationalise the hydrocarbons industry and sent the army to take control of oil and gas production facilities. This spectacular measure was more important for the message it carried than for its real consequences. Bolivia's gas reserves amount to 0.2 per cent of worldwide reserves. The main victim of this nationalisation was Brazil, which is the largest importer of Bolivian gas. Up to now, only part of the gas was used because of the abundant hydroelectricity generation in Brazil. But the recent droughts have led to an increase in gas imports, which is why the measure taken by Bolivia was serious for Brazil.

There is also a project to export liquefied gas. But this proposal has raised concerns in Bolivia among people who do not want to "squander" a precious national resource. Another difficulty is that the gas pipeline would cross part of Chile, which separates Bolivia from the Pacific coast, which was once part of Bolivia prior to the conflict between the two countries from 1879 to 1884.

- **Self-sufficient Brazil?**

Brazil is, probably with Iraq and perhaps the Gulf of Guinea, the region where oil production has the largest potential for growth over the next few years. Presal discoveries and production has increased oil availability from 1.7 Mb/d in the year 2005 to 2.5 Mb/d in 2015. Brazil could become an oil exporter. Interestingly, the then President, Lula, declared that Brazil should not export crude oil as a raw material but exports should be in the form of refined products. This view reflects the old "industrial development" theory that it is better for an emerging country to export finished products rather than the raw material from which they are derived. However, this is now very questionable; when refining margins are low—which is often the case—refining products for export can reduce, rather than add, value.

Brazil wants to develop natural gas based electricity generation to reduce the use of hydraulic electricity and so limit the impact of droughts on the country. The major challenge remains the development of the internal market in order to consume all of the Bolivian gas purchased under a take-or-pay contract. Brazil has been hard hit by the recent nationalisation of Bolivian gas and the increase in the price of gas purchased from there (see above).

Finally it should be noted that the Brazilian energy system has one of the lowest rates of CO_2 emissions in the world, thanks to the massive use of hydroelectricity and the many incentives to develop biofuels.

- **Argentina: Energy and Economic Crisis**

After Argentina's 2001-2002 financial crisis, debt restructuring was vital for the country to have the capacity to borrow the capital it needed for investment in the development of its infrastructure.

In such a difficult economic climate, the national energy situation influences the country's general situation. Thus, the energy crisis of 2004, linked to a sudden increase in demand resulting from artificially low prices, resulted in delaying the economic recovery that was taking shape: the government had to introduce rationing and break a gas supply contract with Chile. To prevent such a situation from reoccurring, the Argentine government has formed a new state-owned company called Enarsa (to replace YPF, bought in 1999 by the Spanish company Repsol), and plans to liberalise energy prices. Additionally, Argentina has implemented reforms to allow private investors to invest in offshore and unconventional geological plays especially the shale reserves.

CONCLUSION

South America will soon have to come to terms with several major issues and first, how to organise the different national energy sectors: the regulations needed, liberalisation, and the status of state-owned companies. This first point will determine the region's ability to attract the foreign investments needed to develop energy production, and to make the creation of a major South American integrated network possible.

Such a network depends on the extent to which the region's countries are prepared to cooperate with each other, and with their large North American neighbour, as well as how the balance of power develops, particularly with regard to Brazil, which is the major regional power.

There are many uncertainties that will affect the region's future: political tensions in Venezuela, Colombia and Bolivia; the levels of national debt and the weakness of the economic situation, particularly in Argentina; and finally the inability of a number of countries to achieve satisfactory economic development from their oil revenues.

References

1. See Tintin's comic book adventure "The Broken Ear" ("L'Oreille Cassée") by Hergé.

Chapter - 7

Europe

INCREASING ENERGY IMPORTS

Whether by "Europe" we mean the European Union, which has had 28 members since 2007[1], or "geographical" Europe, which includes the European Union (EU), Iceland, Norway, Switzerland, the countries of the former Yugoslavia, Albania and Turkey, the continent is characterised by very high energy consumption and substantial dependency on foreign supply sources.

Geographical Europe as a whole is less dependent on energy imports than the EU as Norway is one of the largest producers and exporters of oil and gas in the world.

In the period following World War II, Europe's main energy source was locally produced coal. The explosion in the demand for petroleum products at the end of the 1950s and during the 1960s resulted in great dependence on producing countries, particularly the Middle East, since Europe produced only very limited quantities of oil.

At the beginning of the 1970's, oil was the largest source of energy and Europe was very dependant on oil producing countries especially after the oil shock. In the mid-1970s the position improved and the rate of energy independence increased; for the EU from less than 40 per cent to 50 per cent in 2000, and for Europe overall from 45 per cent to more than 60 per cent.

This was for several reasons:

- Strict energy conservation measures and a structural change in the European economy from manufacturing towards services, which are less energy intensive.

- Development of hydrocarbon deposits in the North Sea.
- Development of nuclear electricity generation.

On the other hand, the growth in gas consumption rapidly increased Europe's dependence on external suppliers, even though production from the Netherlands starting in the 1960s, followed by the North Sea in the 1980s, provided some relief.

EU's energy demand in 2015 was 1.63 billion toe, i.e. about 12 per cent of worldwide consumption. It is the third largest centre of consumption, after Asia and the United States. Oil accounts for 37 per cent of consumption, gas 22 per cent, coal 16 per cent, nuclear energy 12 per cent, hydroelectricity 5 per cent, and new renewable energies 8 per cent.[2] The current energy demand is 12 per cent lower than the peak demand in the last decade and is now lower than it was in 2006.

Europe is the world's fifth regional energy producer, production amounting to nearly one billion toe, or eight per cent of worldwide production. Natural gas is approximately a quarter of this, oil, nuclear and coal around 20 per cent each and hydroelectricity about 13 per cent, the rest is solar and wind. Primary energy production has probably peaked since European production costs are often higher than the price of imported energy.

Energy Balance – Europe 2015 (Mtoe)

Mtoe	*Consumption*	*Production*	*Balance*	*Self sufficiency*
Oil	662	164	–498	25 per cent
Natural Gas	450	285	–165	63 per cent
Coal	303	174	–129	57 per cent
Nuclear	198	198	0	100 per cent
Hydroelectricity	170	170	0	100 per cent
New renewable	142	142	0	100 per cent
TOTAL	**1925**	**1132**	**-792**	**50 per cent**

Energy Balance – EU 2015 (Mtoe)

	Consumption	*Production*	*Balance*	*Self sufficiency*
Oil	600	72	–528	12 per cent
Natural gas	362	108	–254	30 per cent
Coal	262	145	–117	55 per cent
Nuclear	194	194	0	100 per cent
Hydroelectricity	76	76	0	100 per cent
New Renewables	136	136	0	100 per cent
TOTAL	**1630**	**731**	**-899**	**45 per cent**

The four largest producing countries are: Norway (225 Mtoe, largely oil and gas), the UK (121 Mtoe, mainly oil and gas), France (119 Mtoe, mainly nuclear) and Germany (115 Mtoe, mainly coal and new renewables) (Fig. 53).

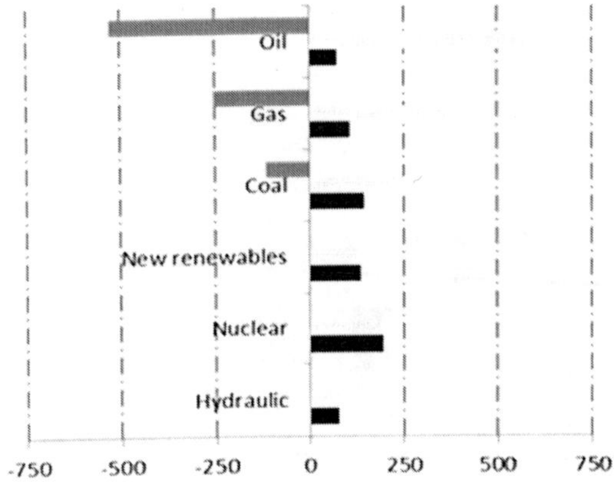

Figure 51: EU Energy Balance 2015 (Mtoe).

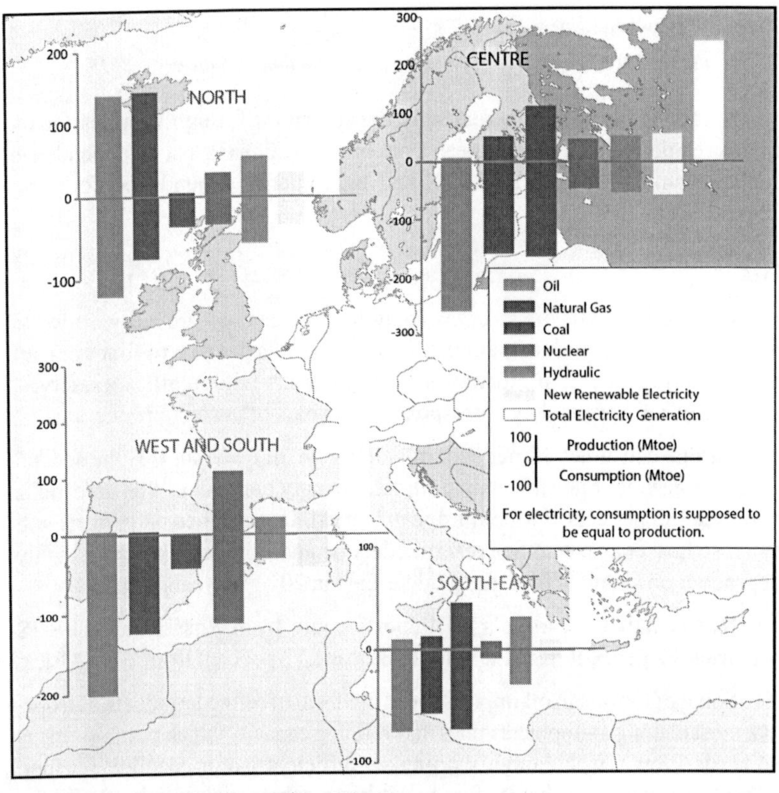

Source: BP Statistical Review, 2016 and doe/eia.

Figure 52: Europe: 2015 Energy Balance by Zone.

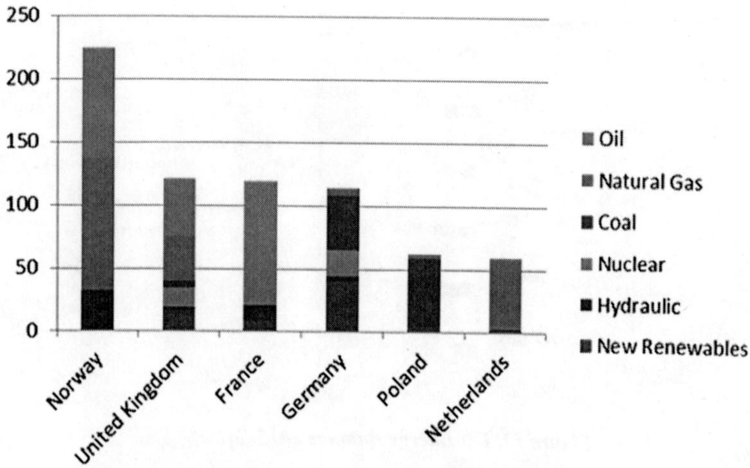

Source: BP Statistical Review, 2016.

Figure 53: European Primary Energy Production by Country – 2015.

Europe is becoming increasingly dependent on foreign supplies for its energy requirements. The European Commission estimates that oil dependence could reach 90 per cent by 2020, and total energy dependence could be 70 per cent in 2030.

OIL

Despite its small oil reserves (only 0.3 per cent of proved worldwide reserves), Europe produces about 3.3 million barrels per day, or four per cent of total world production. Norway is the only country with significant reserves, at eight billion barrels they correspond to 11 years of current production.

Europe consumes 18 per cent of worldwide oil demand. It is the second biggest consumer after the United States. Seventy per cent of this demand is imported (88 per cent for the European Union). Dependence on imports will increase further as North Sea reserves decline and Europe risks being highly dependent on supplies from the Middle East in 20 or 30 years time.

Nearly half of Europe's oil imports come from Russia and the CIS countries, 22 per cent from the Middle East and 17 per cent from West Africa.

Some of European oil imports are in the form of refined products. Europe, like most major geographical zones, has refining capacity which roughly covers its needs. However, although it produces sufficient motor gasoline, jet fuel, home heating oil, and heavy fuel oil, it has a substantial deficit of naphtha (raw material used in the manufacture of plastics, synthetic fibers, etc.) and diesel fuel. So these products are imported, principally from Russia and, to a lesser extent, from North Africa. Following the fall in both their production and consumption of oil at the beginning of the 1990s, Russia has a large surplus of refining capacity and can export petroleum products cheaply. Their quality does not always meet the desired standards, but they can be re-processed and improved in European refineries. Algeria is also a major exporter of petroleum products.

Norway

Norway has a very special position in Europe because of its significant North Sea oil and gas reserves. In 2015, it was the world's 15th largest oil producer and 10th largest oil exporter. Oil and gas represent 22 per cent of GDP. Norway is a major player on the European energy stage.

Thanks to oil and gas production, Norway has become one of the wealthiest nations in Europe. Although the country's oil reserves are in gradual decline (40 per cent have already been produced), its future looks fair thanks to the recent discoveries of natural gas. The gas production has increased in the recent years and in 2016 Norway exported 117 bcm mainly to Europe through pipelines and LNG terminals. Norwegian gas accounts for 20 per cent of European gas consumption. Gas sales are expected to reach 130 bcm by 2020.

Norway is a member of the European Economic Area (EEA), but it has not joined the European Union. So there are no restrictions on its decisions as to the use of its petroleum wealth. To ensure sustainable economic development, in 1990 it set up the Petroleum Fund, now the government Pension Fund, with assets equivalent to US$ 890 billion in August 2016.

NATURAL GAS

Gas demand grew at an average rate of 2.5 per cent per year from 2000 to 2008, faster that the growth rate for oil. Then the demand fell because of the competition from renewables for electricity production. It should remain stable in the future. Although Europe's gas reserves are small (only 1.7 per cent of proved world reserves in 2015), European production is 7.8 per cent of the world total (versus 16 per cent for Russia and 22 per cent for the US).

But this high rate of production, largely coming from Norway, Great Britain and the Netherlands, is only sufficient to cover 40 per cent of European demand. Europe is thus heavily dependent on foreign supplies which come mainly from two countries: Russia (roughly 60 per cent of the total European Pipeline Imports) and Algeria (roughly 7 per cent). Norway also exports large quantities of gas to the EU. Supplies from Russia and also from internal

European sources are all made by pipeline. When deliveries were first made from Algeria in 1965, they were in the form of LNG (liquefied natural gas), but a large portion of these deliveries are now made by underwater pipelines. Algeria imports have decreased from a peak of 65 bcm in 2005 to just below 35 bcm in 2015 owing to termination or suspension of contracts with Belgium and Italy.[3] EU imports from Norway, Russia and North Africa will continue to grow.

The size of European demand has attracted other potential suppliers such as Nigeria and Qatar. Over the medium-term, imports may also be made from South America (Trinidad and Tobago), Angola and other Middle Eastern countries. The extent to which gas imports continue to grow will largely depend on their costs. US LNG imports started in 2016.

Gas consumption in Great Britain, Germany and Italy is between 60 and 80 million toe per year for each country or, in total, nearly half of total European demand.

COAL

Coal is Europe's historical source of energy. It fueled economic development from the start of the industrial revolution until the end of the 1950s. In Great Britain, France, Germany and even Poland, the development of many industrial regions was based on coal, indeed the vestiges of this mining era can still be seen there today.

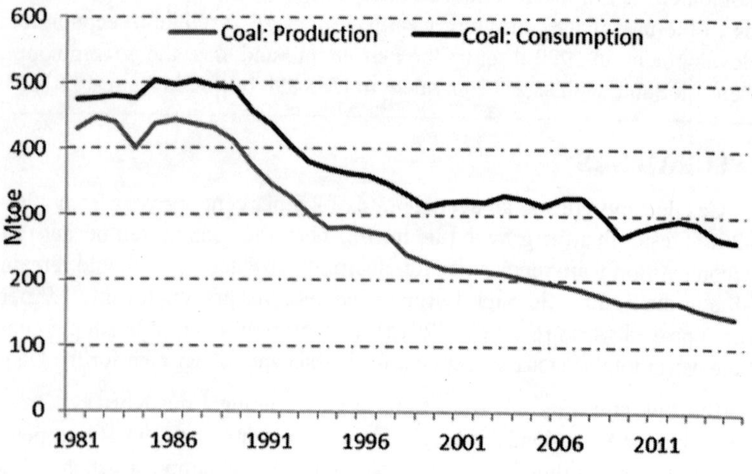

Source: BP Statistical Review, 2016.

Figure 54: European Coal Production and Consumption 2015.

Europe has six per cent of both proved worldwide coal reserves and of world production (behind China and the US). These reserves correspond to 112 years of current production.

European demand is 7.4 per cent of the worldwide total and is declining. So, 40 per cent of consumption is imported. Production in European countries with large reserves (Germany, Poland, Great Britain, etc.) has been declining since the start of the 1990s, for economic reasons. European coal is Costlier to produce and its quality is lower, so it has gradually lost market share. Germany is the biggest coal consumer in Europe using 78 million toe in 2015, principally for electricity generation. Next are Poland and Great Britain.

European coal is currently uncompetitive on two counts: compared with its international competitors and compared with other energy sources. That is why British production, intended mainly for electricity generation, has dramatically fallen, it was more than 200 Mt/y in the 50's but now it is only 5 Mt/y; combined cycle power plants operating on natural gas and imported coal, are both less expensive (Fig. 54).

ELECTRICITY

The European Union generated 3,261 TWh in 2013, or 14 per cent of the worldwide total. Based on its calorific value, 3,300 TWh is broadly 280 million tons of oil equivalent, but if it were produced entirely from thermal sources (coal, oil or natural gas), it would amount to 700 million toe.

Within Europe, the national power grids are fairly widely interconnected, but the means used for electricity generation vary greatly from one country to another. Hydroelectricity remains dominant in Scandinavia, nuclear energy is the main source in France and Belgium, while coal is mainly used in Germany and Poland.

Globally, the EU produces 33 per cent of the world's total nuclear electricity, just behind North America. It is the leader in electricity generation from renewable energies – excluding hydroelectricity—(37 per cent), the third in thermal energy (ten per cent), and the fourth leading producer of hydroelectricity (nine per cent) (Fig. 55).

- **Nuclear Generation**

With 423 TWh in 2015, France produces 49 per cent of European nuclear-based electricity, Germany 11 per cent, and Great Britain 8 per cent. The very high percentage in France results from an energy policy decision taken in the aftermath of the first oil shock. At that time, France relied on oil for 70 per cent of its total energy demand and a substantial portion of its electricity generation was from heavy fuel oil. In November 1973 the French government accelerated France's nuclear programme and, recently, between 70 per cent and 80 per cent of electricity produced in France has been nuclear. In 2014, this was 77 per cent, because total electricity consumption in France fell. Sixteen European countries (including fifteen EU members) currently have nuclear power plants, but four of them (Germany, Sweden, Belgium and the Netherlands) have, at least in principle, decided to phase out nuclear energy, although Sweden is now reversing this decision and the phase out in Germany appears to have been delayed.

Nuclear energy helps reduce greenhouse gas emissions and so at least in that way contributes to sustainable development. It may also be considered as a factor in energy independence (the uranium consumed by power plants is mainly imported, but the production sources are diversified and the supply of uranium poses no major problems). Nuclear energy is reducing CO_2 emissions

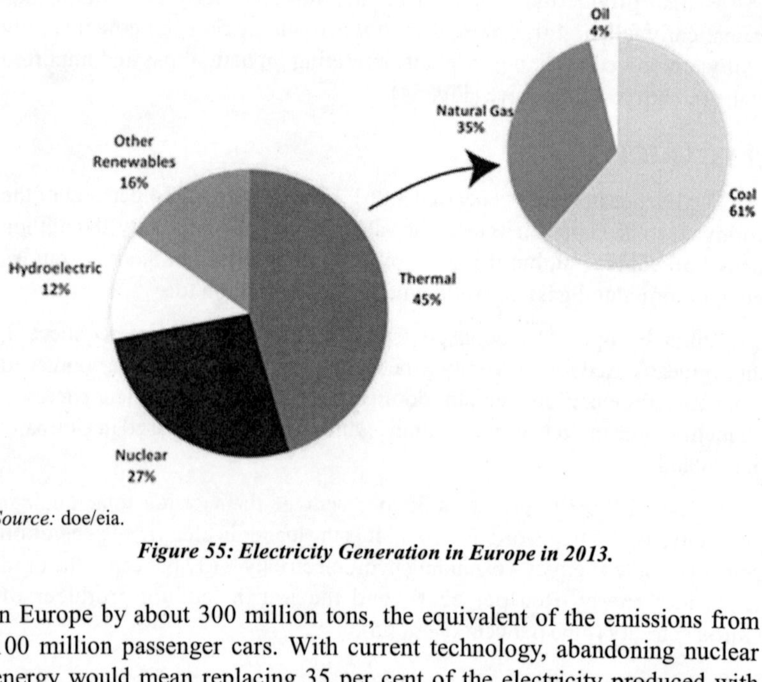

Source: doe/eia.

Figure 55: Electricity Generation in Europe in 2013.

in Europe by about 300 million tons, the equivalent of the emissions from 100 million passenger cars. With current technology, abandoning nuclear energy would mean replacing 35 per cent of the electricity produced with conventional and renewable energy. Also expertise in nuclear power plant construction can be exported. It can be a source of revenue for the European Union and its businesses if the difficulties encountered in the construction of the Olkiluoto (Finland) and Flamanville (France) reactors are overcome.

The debate over nuclear energy continues, particularly in the light of the accident at Fukushima. A limited number of nuclear plants are under construction. In Europe, one each in Finland and France is under construction but the share of nuclear electricity production in Europe will go down. Countries like Belgium, Germany, Sweden, the Netherlands and Switzerland could phase out nuclear power and France has a target to reduce the nuclear share in the energy mix to 50 per cent by 2025.

- **Renewables-Based Production**

In Europe, renewable energies (hydraulic, geothermal, biomass, solar and wind) provide 25 per cent of energy consumption, with half of that being hydraulic-based.

There is now only very limited potential for the expansion of hydro-electricity. On the other hand, the development of new renewable energies (wind, solar, biomass and geothermal) must be a priority for any improvement in supply security and the environment.

In December 2008 the EU agreed measures to reduce the EU's contribution to global warming and ensure reliable and sufficient supplies of energy aiming to make Europe the world leader in renewable energy and low-carbon technologies. The intention was to achieve a 20 per cent reduction in greenhouse gas emissions by 2020 compared with 1990, mainly by increasing the use of renewable energy and curbing energy consumption. This also reduces dependence on imported oil and gas.

Increasing the use of renewable energy requires subsidies in favour of wind, solar, geothermal and biomass even if the cost of some renewables (solar for instance) is decreasing.

Wind is still the most widely used renewable energy. In 2015, there was 235 TWh wind-based electricity production. Germany has 25 per cent of this and Spain 23 per cent.

Energy Efficiency: The EU Objectives

Now, EU regulators are poised to propose a more binding target to cut energy use by 30 per cent by 2030, a more ambitious goal than previously discussed, according to some sources.

A draft law, which the European Commission is expected to publish soon, is part of a set of proposals to implement 2030 goals on cutting emissions, increasing renewable energy use and preventing energy waste.

A preliminary agreement was reached in October 2014 when the 28 member states agreed to increase energy savings by at least 27 per cent compared with business as usual.

Since then, political momentum for a deeper cut has grown as using less energy curbs dependency on imports from nations such as Russia, while creating jobs in construction and insulation.

Following Britain's vote in June to leave the European Union, the EU executive has also been keen to promote the social benefits of its policies.

Climate and Energy Commissioner Miguel Arias Canete has said every one per cent improvement in energy efficiency could lift seven million people out of energy poverty because their homes would be better insulated with lower energy bills.

The 30 per cent compares with an existing target of 20 per cent for 2020, which initially was not binding and that EU was far from achieving until a law in 2012 forced progress.

The EU Commission could be keen to use the target as a step towards implementing the Paris Agreement on climate change.

A proposal to share out a 2030 target to cut greenhouse gases by at least 40 per cent was published in July 2016. It has to be debated by member states and the European Parliament before it can become law. These elements show that the main objective of the EU is energy efficiency and reduction of emissions, at the expense of economic development and reduction in unemployment, according to some experts. This is an open debate.

ORGANISATION AND REGULATION OF GAS AND ELECTRICITY MARKETS

The EU's liberalisation of electricity and gas markets has several objectives:

- To lower energy prices by abolishing monopolies and restoring free competition. Competition should, according to liberal economic theory, reduce costs.
- To promote the development of a single European energy market.
- To increase the ability of European companies in the energy sector to compete with their international competitors.

As well as the benefits in terms of efficiency that are expected from the above, the creation of a single energy market is also intended as a mechanism for reviving the construction of Europe, in a way that coal and steel can no longer achieve.

Taking advantage of the experience gained in other countries (US and Great Britain), the European Commission has asked each member state to re-organise their gas and electricity markets to abolish monopolies in countries where they existed; to separate production, transport and distribution activities; and, where possible, to create competition between operators. This organisation is to be completed by:

- Setting up an electricity exchange where the players can trade kilowatts (Powernext).
- Creating a body for the regulation and reorganisation of former public monopolies so that transport and distribution activities are legally and functionally separated from production. For example, France has set up a regulatory body called "Commission de régulation de l'énergie" which is an independent administrative body in charge of the French electricity and gas markets.
- Setting up a gradual programme to open national markets to international competition, while taking differences between the various countries into account.

The European internal electricity market Directive of June 26, 2003 increased the extent to which the electricity market was open to competition by giving all non-household consumers the right to choose their supplier from July 1, 2004, and the same right to households from July 1, 2007.

- **Electricity Market**

In the past, operators on the European electricity markets have had a variety of structures and strategies. Électricité de France (EDF) was an entirely state-owned, vertically and horizontally integrated electricity monopoly; there was hardly any equivalent except in Portugal and Greece. In comparison, the German power system is structured into three levels: municipal, regional and federal, with a number of different companies active at each level. Two German companies, E-On and RWE operate on all three levels.

Europe is divided geographically into five electrical sub-continents, with varying levels of interconnection by aerial high voltage (VHV) lines or underwater cables. Obviously the British Isles are only connected to the continent by underwater cable. Spain and Portugal formed an "electricity peninsula", but now are connected to the continental shelf via VHV powerlines that cross the Pyrenees.

– *Electricity – the British Example*

The deregulation of the British market and liberalisation of prices started on April 1, 1990. It was one of the first examples of price competition in the wholesale electricity market and was copied in many countries. It worked by a price determination system operated by "the Pool". This was a daily auction sale at which producers submitted price/quantity offers for supplying electricity for every half-hour of the following day. In theory prices should have fallen, but in fact they increased by 40 per cent (in money of the day) over the first four years and stayed well above marginal costs until 2001. A group of users, retail and industrial consumers therefore put pressure on the government and OFGEM (Office of Gas and Electricity Markets), the regulatory body formed by the 1999 merger of the Office of Electricity Regulation and the Office of Gas Regulation, for measures to be taken to lower the process charged by the Pool.

Finally, in 1998 it was agreed that the Pool should be replaced by a market similar to traditional raw material markets. NETA, the New Electricity Trading Arrangements, would become operational in 2001. In 2000, during the period provided for final consideration of and the establishment of NETA, pool prices started to fall. Unfortunately, this caused such problems for the electricity generating companies that the DTI (Department of Trade and Industry) had to grant them emergency loans. Of course, if considered separately, the creation of NETA and the fall in prices could be seen as connected since they took place at the same time. But in fact the establishment of NETA was but the last of a series of regulatory measures initiated prior to market liberalisation and all of these had an influence on the fall in wholesale prices.

Currently prices are regulated by OFGEM. They protect consumers by promoting competition, wherever appropriate, and regulating the monopoly companies that run the gas and electricity networks. In doing so they should take account of the interests of consumers as a whole, including their interests in the reduction of greenhouse gases and in the security of the supply of gas and electricity to them.

– *Gas – the British Example*

The UK's Oil and Gas (Enterprise) Act of 1982 gave third-parties access to the British Gas distribution network. In 1986, the Gas Act allowed eligible customers, i.e. those consuming more than 25,000 therms p.a. to purchase their gas from competitors of British Gas (BG), via the BG network. In return, the law made sales to customers buying less than 25,000 therms p.a. a BG monopoly. The law privatised BG and created a gas regulatory body called OFGAS. In 1992, OFGAS decreased the threshold for BG's monopoly from 25,000 to 2,500 therms p.a., which decreased BG's market share for industrial and commercial consumers from 75 per cent at the end of 1992 to less than 25 per cent at the end of 1995.

British Gas is now part of Centrica, which is publically quoted. In the residential market BG's market share is currently 37 per cent for gas and 24 per cent for electricity.

- **Deregulation: Contributor to Energy Security?**

The challenge is not the physical transmission of electricity from one end of Europe to the other, but rather to allow electricity generators to locate themselves where they wish, so that, as a result, the best interconnections for the networks are achieved. For gas, the objective must be to ensure free circulation of imports within the single market. In both cases, the objective is to ensure availability of the energy needed in all places and at all times, so that the economies of EU member states and the operations of companies within the EU are not disrupted and, in particular, that any re-occurrence of incidents like the 2003 electricity blackout in Italy is prevented. It is also argued that a further objective of deregulation should be to strengthen energy supply security.

Switzerland

Switzerland occupies a unique strategic position right at the centre of the European energy transport network. With no indigenous fossil fuel resources, its electricity generation is hydraulic, nuclear and from wood fired traditional thermal plant. It is dependent on imports for 59 per cent of its energy supplies and, as there is no sea access, these energy supplies depend entirely on transport routes through the EU.

But Switzerland does export electricity and 70 per cent of these exports go to Italy. So the European Commission has expressed its interest on several occasions in integrating Switzerland into the European electricity supply system. Swiss network operators control some of the key interconnections on which Italy relies for its electricity requirements. The blackout that Italy experienced at the end of 2003 because there was no effective system to coordinate the Swiss and Italian network managers' operations is evidence of how important this question is.

SECURITY OF EUROPEAN UNION SUPPLIES

- **Increasing Future Energy Dependence**

In the future, Europe will have to import an increasing proportion of its energy needs (Fig. 56), i.e. at least 75 per cent by about 2020.

Dependence rate	*2007*		*2015*	*2020*
	Europe	*EU*	*EU*	*EU*
Oil	69 per cent	85 per cent	88 per cent	90 per cent
Gas	43 per cent	62 per cent	70 per cent	75 per cent
Primary energy	45 per cent	58 per cent	70 per cent	75 per cent

However, not all analysts find the EU's position worrying. Energy imports as a proportion of the EU's total imports remain limited. Recently 15 per cent of the imports made by the EU member states came from major oil exporting countries, while these imports represented 30 per cent of the total exports made by the same countries. The oil exporting countries are thus more dependent on the EU than the reverse. Also the importance of the trade between the EU and CIS is radically different for the two partners. In 2015, Europe was responsible for taking about 64 per cent of CIS oil exports and supplying a large proportion of CIS imports. But the CIS only furnished 44 per cent of the European Union's imports.

The European Union and Russia have a common interest in increasing the continent's energy security. In 2000, a dialogue started which is intended to pursue the establishment of an EU-Russia energy partnership: nuclear safety and waste processing, the INOGATE (Interstate Oil and Gas Transport to Europe) and TRACECA (Transport Corridor Europe-Caucasus-Asia) programmes to develop and renovate oil and gas pipelines in former Soviet Union countries, etc. The objective is a gradual integration of the EU and Russian energy markets.

RELATIONS BETWEEN EUROPE AND RUSSIA – THE CASE OF GAS

CIS's abundant hydrocarbon reserves and their proximity to Europe make Russia and the European Union natural partners in relation to energy. Their interdependence is shown by the fact that 64 per cent of CIS oil exports and 65 per cent of its gas exports go to the European Union, and that these make up 44 and 42 per cent of EU imports of oil and gas respectively (Fig. 57). In 2020, Russian gas imports will be higher both in volume and in the percentage of European consumption they meet.

Russia is Europe's longest standing gas supplier. This gas comes from deposits in Siberia, particularly those in the north of the Tyumen region in Western Siberia. The length of the gas pipelines supplying Europe is considerable, and they cross several countries between Russia and the customers. During the period of the Soviet Union, the position was simple: gas passed through the Ukraine, at that time part of the USSR, then through Czechoslovakia, at that time one country and a USSR satellite, before reaching its East German destination. Since 1990, the transit countries have no longer been under Russian dominance, and this has made the position more complex; neither the Warsaw Pact nor the USSR still exist and many of their former members are today part of the European Union.

The role of Ukraine was especially crucial: until the construction of the Nord Stream pipeline about 80 per cent of Russian gas exports to Europe were transported by pipeline through this country.

In the 2000's Ukraine was crushed by its burden of debt vis a vis Russia. Ukraine made repayments by ceding equity shares in Ukrainian companies to

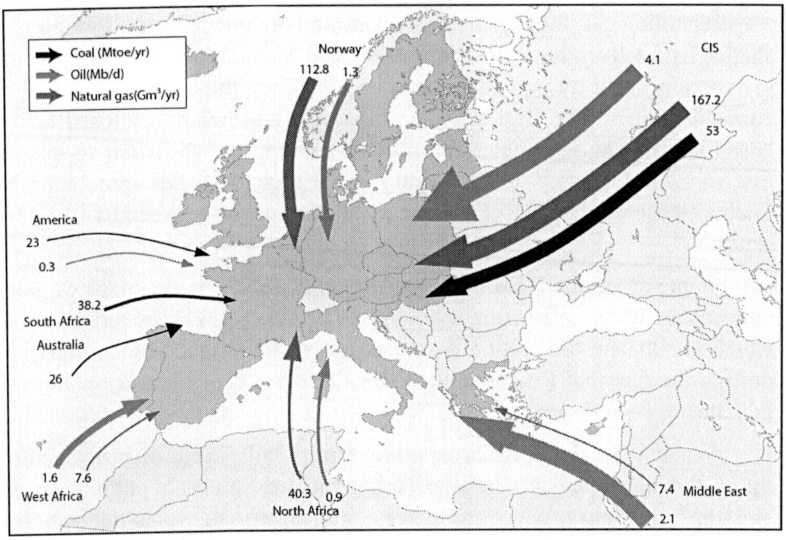

Source: BP Statistical Review 2016.

Figure 56: European Union 2015 Energy Supplies.

Russia, and continued to misappropriate some of the hydrocarbons crossing Ukraine by pipeline for its own consumption. This put the Russian government and Gazprom in a dilemma: should they send gas to Europe, with the risk that some of it would be siphoned off without payment, or interrupt deliveries and deprive itself of Western currency. To resolve this problem, in 2000 Russia commissioned a gas pipeline linking it to Germany via Belarus and Poland. The next step was the Nord Stream project, a twin gas pipeline under the Baltic Sea from north to south that enables Russia to supply Western Europe directly while avoiding any transit countries. The first line was commissioned in 2011 and the second in 2012. Based on the success of the Nord Stream, a Nord Stream 2 project has been planned. As detailed in Chapter 8 (CIS) another pipeline, South Stream was planned by Russia to supply Europe with a pipeline starting from Yamal, passing through the Black Sea and arriving in Bulgaria before delivering gas to central Europe. This project was abandoned following the 2014 crisis (Maidan Revolution and conflict between Ukraine and Russia), replaced by a Turkish Stream pipeline, but this pipeline got frozen because of a military incident between Turkey and Russia. As Europe is highly dependent on Russian gas supplies, it is a stakeholder in the conflict between Moscow and Kiev. It must handle Russia carefully while also supporting the Kiev regime. Note that American interests are never far off, as shown by the financial support received by partisans of the Orange Revolution in Ukraine and by the strong support given to the Maidan Revolution (February, 2014).

Regarding gas, long-term supply contracts are intended to allow for risk sharing between producers and consumers, and encourage construction of new production capacity and infrastructure, but they must comply with EU competition law. The Brussels Commission is particularly opposed to the "destination" clause sought by producing countries who want to ensure that gas sold to a consuming country is not re-sold by this same country. Such a clause would prevent the free circulation of gas between EU member states.

On the question of dealing with Russia, there is a marked lack of unity between the EU countries on the policies to be pursued. This benefits Russia, which is reluctant to accept any measure proposed by the EU Commission despite the fact that Russia is economically more dependent upon Europe than the reverse.

The future level of Russian exports to Europe will depend on many factors: the cost of developing new transport infrastructure, the cost of putting new oil and gas fields into production, increase in Chinese and Asian demand and Russia's trade arbitrage between exporting to the west (Europe) and exporting to the east (China, Japan, etc.), competition from Caspian Sea oil and gas and, finally, the rate of Russian economic restructuring and its consequences on the level of internal energy demand.

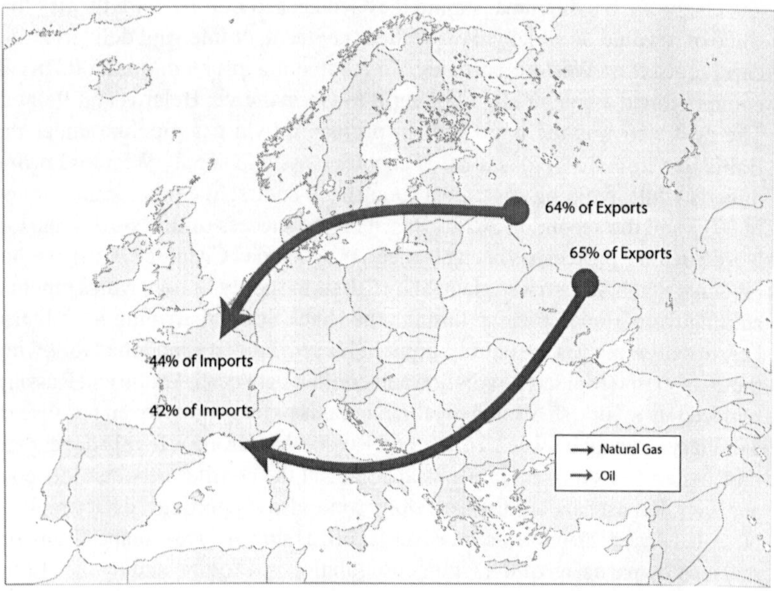

Figure 57: EU and Russian CIS Hydrocarbon Trade 2015.

A key parameter is also the objective of EU to reduce both fossil fuels consumption and dependency on Russian gas.

- **Relations with North Africa**

Historically, North Africa has had close links with European countries through the colonisation of Algeria by France, Libya by Italy, French protectorates in Morocco and Tunisia, and also through the British presence in Egypt until the mid-twentieth century. Today two of these countries, Algeria and Libya, play an important role in European energy supplies because of their strength in hydrocarbon resources, particularly in gas.

The proximity of the Mediterranean's two shores makes Europe and North Africa natural economic partners. The Euromed programme is a new global and multilateral approach, intended to create a zone of stability and mutual prosperity by gradually replacing traditional bilateral trade agreements with an area of free trade with the single European market.

Algeria, whose first gas exports were made in the 1960s, has developed a dual export system. Initially, because technology for laying deep sea gas pipelines had not been developed, the decision was made to export LNG (Liquefied Natural Gas). However, Algeria has, more recently, built three gas pipelines to deliver its Saharan gas to Europe. The Trans-Mediterranean Enrico Mattei pipeline, built in 1983, which crosses Tunisia, then the Mediterranean, arrives in Sicily, and finally reaches Italy via the Strait of Messina. The Maghreb-Europe (Pedro Duran Farell) gas pipeline, completed in 1999, crosses Morocco, then the Strait of Gibraltar, to reach Spain. The Medgas pipeline, between Algeria (Beni Saf) and Spain (Almeria), is a new link between the two countries. There are other pipeline projects being studied: Libya-Italy; Algeria-Sardinia-Italy, possibly doubled by Sardinia-Corsica-France. In total these projects would enable Algeria to supply more than a third of the EU's gas imports. However, the decrease in gas availability for export from Algeria, the competition with Russia and Norway, the stagnation of the European demand make these projects less likely.

The development of these pipelines of course helps to ensure European supply security since, to make the investment profitable, the producing countries have an interest in making the gas pipelines they have built operate at full capacity. Nevertheless there are risks: trans-border tensions between Algeria and Morocco, or between Algeria and Tunisia, could affect European supplies, but the depth of the mutual interest shared by the countries in question does give some guarantee of security.

Electricity Interconnection

An underwater power connection between Morocco and Spain was commissioned in 1998. It is about to be doubled to give a capacity of 1,400 MW. In the long term, an electricity ring should connect all the Euromed programme countries.

- **Remote Gas Sources**

Additionnal sources of gas for Europe exist. As an example, Nigeria's first liquefaction train was put into service in 1999. The prohibition of gas flaring should accelerate development of that West African giant's resources. It is worth remembering that originally the main buyer of Nigerian gas was to be the Italian company Enel. As a result of the Italian government's decision to prohibit the use of nuclear energy, this electricity generating company had commissioned a significant thermal generating plant using fuel oil. So Enel wanted to diversify its fuels, particularly so as to protect the environment. The proposed imports of LNG from Bonny required the construction of one (or more) re-gasification terminal(s) as there were none in Italy. But the construction of such facilities was strongly opposed by the local authorities in the areas where they were to be built.

To justify construction of the liquefaction facilities at Bonny, Enel had entered into a take or pay agreement with the Nigerians, so it found itself in the absurd situation of being obliged to pay for gas that it could not possibly receive. The problem was resolved by a swap agreement with Gaz de France; the Nigerian gas was delivered to GDF's terminals at Fos-sur-Mer (near Marseille) and Montoir (near Nantes), and GDF in exchange delivered equivalent quantities of Norwegian gas to Italy via the French gas pipeline network.

Another source of gas is now Qatar, which exports fair quantities (about 25 Bcm in 2015) to Europe.

Portugal received the first cargo of LNG coming from the US in May 2016. Additional cargoes from the US are expected. There could be a strong competition with the traditional suppliers (Russia, Norway, Algeria).

- **Relations with the Middle East**

The influence of the European Union over events in the Middle East is limited, particularly by the omnipresence of the US military in the region. However, it does have certain advantages. Its historical links have made the EU the main trading partner of Gulf countries: it furnishes a large fraction of Saudi, Kuwaiti and UAE imports. Saudi Arabia is the leading buyer of French weapons.

However, the EU is harmed by its lack of a common foreign policy and lack of strategic vision for energy: the EU does not take part in diplomatic activity relating to the Israeli-Palestinian conflict. Effectively EU cooperation with Gulf countries is largely limited to declarations of intent and exchanges of information to improve the way the market functions.

Europe will also need to consider the use of its member states' military forces to secure seaways. This will become a priority as oil imports from the Middle East increase considerably.

Within this context, would the prospect of Turkish membership of the EU change the situation? In guaranteeing EU access to oil pipeline routes from the Caspian region, it could help to improve supply security. The existence of a common border with major producing countries of the Gulf (Iraq and Iran) could constitute an opportunity for the development of over-land delivery routes, once relations between Turkey and its neighbours return to normal and stable governments are in place in those two producing countries. However this is not likely to happen soon.

- **What European Strategy for Supply Security?**

Europe today seems to be restricting its interest to questions of network construction, the fight against pollution, and deregulation of the gas and electricity markets. Member states are at an impasse in developing a global approach to achieve supply security for all European countries.

On March 8, 2006 the European Commission published a Green Book on the development of a common and consistent European energy policy. This Green Book was designed to help the European Union to establish the foundation for secure, competitive and sustainable energy (see Chapter 4).

It starts by noting that Europe depends on imports for a large percentage of its energy demand and that this dependence can only increase. Hydrocarbon reserves are declining. Energy is becoming more expensive. The infrastructure requires improvement. Over the next 20 years, 1 trillion Euros will be needed to meet anticipated energy demand and replace ageing infrastructure.

These challenges are common throughout Europe, and they require a European solution. EU member states still hesitate about transferring decision-making powers on energy policy to Brussels so that a truly Community-wide energy policy could be developed. But such a common policy is increasingly necessary (Fig. 58). The European commission has proposed long-term strategic steps like increasing energy efficiency, increasing energy production and diversifying supply routes, building missing infrastructure links and strengthening emergency and solidarity mechanism to combat the supply security issue.

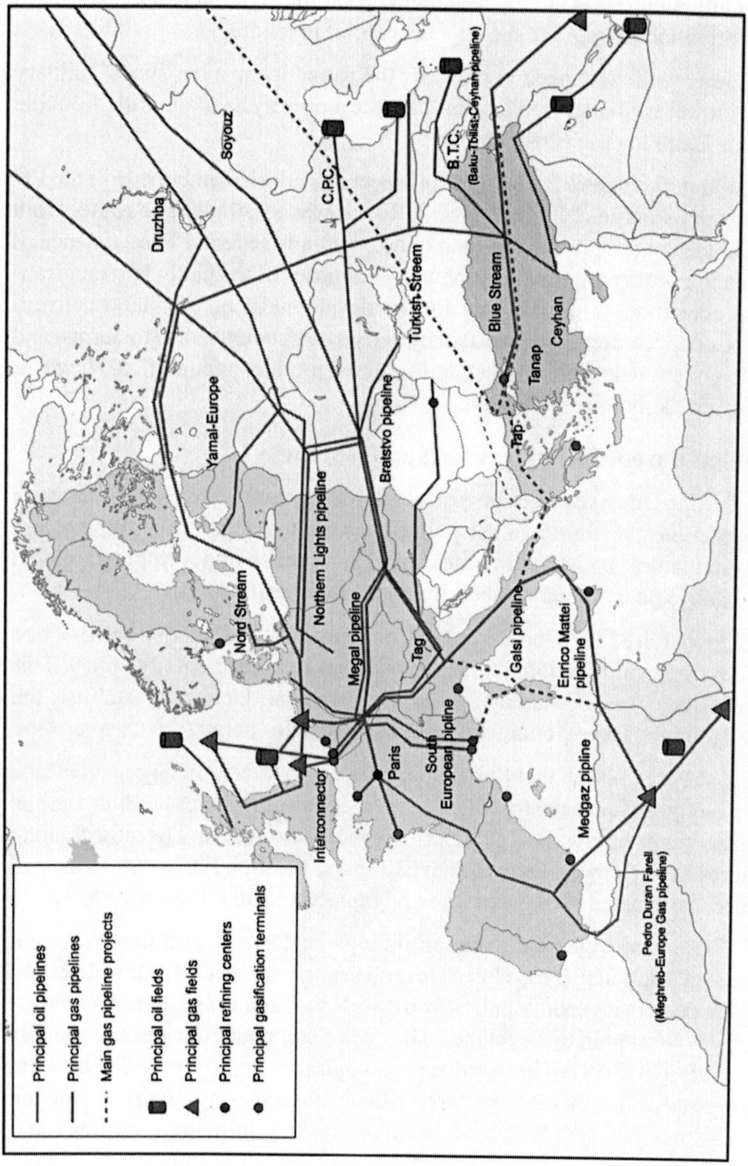

Figure 58: Source: Principal European Hydrocarbon Supply Infrastructure.

- **Europe and the Issue of Sustainable Development**

Sustainable development is an additional factor to consider in the development of European energy policies. It can help in the development of strategic choices. For example, nuclear electricity generation can simultaneously reduce Europe's energy dependence and CO_2 emissions.

In Western Europe, the carbon intensity of GDP (the ratio of quantities of CO_2 emitted as compared to GDP) has decreased by roughly 1.6 per cent p.a. since 1990. Carbon emissions only started to decrease in 2007 and thanks to an increase in the electricity production from wind and solar, the emissions in Europe are expected to decline further in line with the 2020 target to reduce greenhouse gas emissions by 20 per cent.

CONCLUSION

Plans for an EU-wide Energy Union are taking shape, following the European Commission's adoption in February 2015 of a 'Framework Strategy for a Resilient Energy Union with a Forward-Looking Climate Change Policy'. The strategy underlines the EU's ambition to attain 'secure, sustainable, competitive, affordable energy for every European'. The initiative seeks to transform energy markets and energy/climate policy across the EU.

Its goals include cross-border coordination and integration in energy security, supply, market operations, regulation, energy efficiency, low-carbon development, and research and innovation. There is an important foreign policy aspect to the Energy Union, given the imperative of managing security and supply risks in Europe's neighbourhood. By addressing structural divisions between member states, the Energy Union could have a marked beneficial effect on the EU's capacity to conduct a unified and effective foreign policy. Development of the Energy Union presents abundant challenges, however.

Policy and legislative changes will need to be coordinated across 28 countries. Variations in EU member states' attitudes to security and energy policy may lead to differences in priorities. The wider context is also complicated. Interrelated challenges rooted in broader policy issues include the partial transition to low-carbon energy, and concerns over competitiveness relative to other major economies.

Last but not the least, the markets for coal, oil, gas and renewables are changing significantly. The shale oil and gas 'revolution' in the United States has altered the economics of hydrocarbon fuels, and the plunge in oil prices since mid-2014 is causing energy businesses in the EU to reassess investment plans.

References

1. Austria, Belgium, Bulgaria, Croatia, Cyprus, Czech Republic, Denmark, Estonia, Finland, France, Germany, Greece, Hungary, Ireland, Italy, Latvia, Lithuania, Luxembourg, Malta, the Netherlands, Poland, Portugal, Romania, Slovakia, Slovenia, Spain, Sweden and the UK. UK will leave EU in the next few years. For this edition, the calculations and analysis are done considering UK as part of EU.
2. The estimate of 8% for new renewable electricity generation in European energy consumption is based on a figure of 143 Mtoe for 2015.
3. https://www.oxfordenergy.org/wpcms/wp-content/uploads/2016/05/Algerian-Gas-Troubling-Trends-Troubled-Policies-NG-108.pdf

Chapter - 8

The Commonwealth of Independent States

On, December 8, 1991, following the collapse of the Soviet Union, the Minsk Treaty established the Commonwealth of Independent States (CIS). Two weeks later, the first three signatories—Russia, Belarus and Ukraine—were joined by eight former USSR countries—Armenia, Azerbaijan, Kazakhstan, Kirgizstan, Moldova, Uzbekistan, Tajikistan and Turkmenistan and by Georgia two years later. Only the three Baltic States, Estonia, Latvia and Lithuania, refused to join former Soviet socialist republics in the CIS, and in fact they joined the European Union in May 2004. The CIS is and will continue to be dominated by Russia because of its geographic, historic and particularly economic importance.

Georgia left the CIS in 2008, after the war with Russia. Ukraine and Turkmenistan are only associated members. But the role of the CIS must not be overestimated: there is no common or community-wide policy. Russia prefers bilateral agreements, in which it takes advantage of its predominant weight, to multilateral arrangements. There is clear diversity in the different forms of regimes: for example, the systems of government found in Belarus and in several countries of Central Asia have little in common with the governments that have resulted from the Ukrainian "revolution". To consider the principal energy issues, the main fossil fuel resources are found in Russia, Azerbaijan and the Central Asian republics. Kazakhstan is rich in oil, Turkmenistan has large gas reserves, and Uzbekistan has a small quantity of oil and gas. Azerbaijan also has substantial hydrocarbon resources. It was of course in Baku, on Azerbaijan's Caspian Sea coast that the great oil adventure began in 1870, only a few years after the first wells were drilled in the US. In 1900, the city became the world's main oil production centre. But the production rate declined until the October 1917 revolution and the industry moved further north, toward the Volga. It was this region's oil fields that

Hitler was after when, in 1941, he aimed an offensive at the Caucasus. But the defeat at Stalingrad prevented Germany from seizing the Russian oil reserves, and the German economy suffered from the very high cost of the substitute fuels it had to produce. It was one of the main reasons for the defeat of the Third Reich.

Historically, energy has always played a key role in Russia, both economically and indeed generally. From the earliest days there were entrepreneurs seeking to develop the country's resources to supply what was still a small oil industry. The armies of workers employed later took part in the first major socialist revolution in history. The oil industry left its marks on this revolution. The cruel war between the White Armies, supported by the Western powers, and the Red Army led by Leon Trotsky, was only won by the latter thanks to the fact that the Soviet armies had sufficient fuel, particularly for Trotsky's famous headquarters train. Following the Red Army's victory, during the period of the New Economic Policy (NEP) at the start of the 1920s, Lenin declared: "Socialism is the Soviets plus electricity". Today, Russia is the largest country in the world, possesses substantial oil reserves, has the world's second largest proved reserves of gas, and very large quantities of coal.

Russia has always been an important energy exporter. Foreign sales of hydrocarbons are a major source of foreign currency. Oil and gas exports amounted to 356 billion dollars or 68 per cent of total Russian exports in 2013. Most of the revenues were from oil and only 14 per cent from gas. Natural gas is the most widely used energy domestically and the trend is for

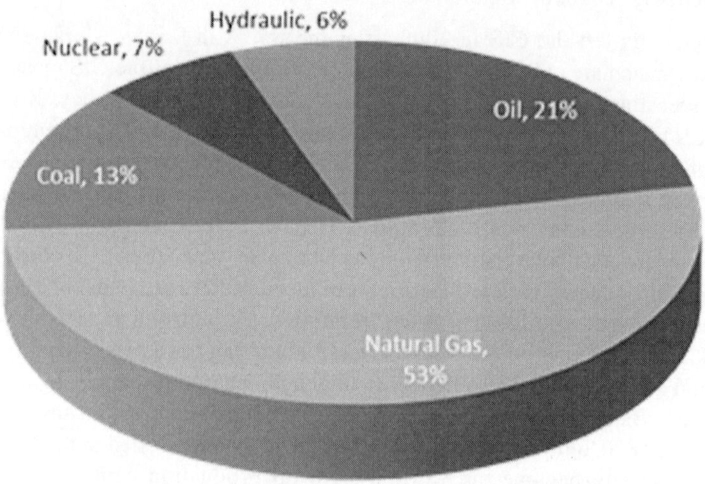

Source: BP Statistical Review, 2016 and doe/eia.

Figure 59: Russian Consumption by Energy Source (2015).

its proportion to grow since Moscow prefers to export oil rather than gas, simply because the revenue is greater. Although at present most exports go to the European Union, Russia is ideally positioned at the crossroads of Europe, North America and Asia. Russian exports to the Europe or China, or even just the potential for them, will have an influence on world energy balances (Fig. 59 and 60).

THE ENERGY SCENE IN THE COMMONWEALTH OF INDEPENDENT STATES

- **Oil**

– *CIS Reserves*

Russia has by far the largest oil reserves in the CIS (102.4 billion barrels) and the sixth worldwide, but Kazakhstan's reserves are also substantial (30 billion barrels, ranked eleventh worldwide). Adding the reserves of the other states (Azerbaijan, Uzbekistan and Turkmenistan), makes the CIS sixth in the worldwide rank for oil reserves, with less than half the reserves of Saudi Arabia but with 89 per cent of the reserves of Iran.

In 1900, Baku was the main oil production centre in the world. Nearly a century later in 1988, the Soviet Union was the world's leading crude oil producer, with 600 million tons per year (including 500 million for Russia alone). The fall of oil prices in 1986 is considered by many as the main reason for the collapse of the Soviet Union, since most of the export revenues were coming from oil exports. The end of the communist regime led to a collapse in oil production; in 1995, the CIS oil production was 350 million tons (300 million in Russia). However, the consumption of petroleum products also fell and so the level of exports was maintained. But CIS production was overtaken in 1992 by Saudi Arabia which became the world's leading oil producer (Fig. 61).

– *The Situation of the Oil and Gas Industry in Russia before the Collapse of the Soviet Union*

Before 1990, the oil and gas industry was fully controlled by the state (as most of the other industries). In 1989, the Soviet Ministry of Gas Industry was converted to a corporation, named Gazprom in 1989, retaining all of its assets. Although it is a private company, the Russian government holds a majority stake in the company.

Gazprom's production fields are located around the Gulf of Ob in Western Siberia. Plans have also been made to develop the Yamal Peninsula. Gazprom's gas transport system includes 158,200 kilometres of gas trunk lines. In 2015, Gazprom produced about 418 billion cubic meters (14 trillion cubic feet) of natural gas, more than seventeen per cent of global gas production. Gazprom

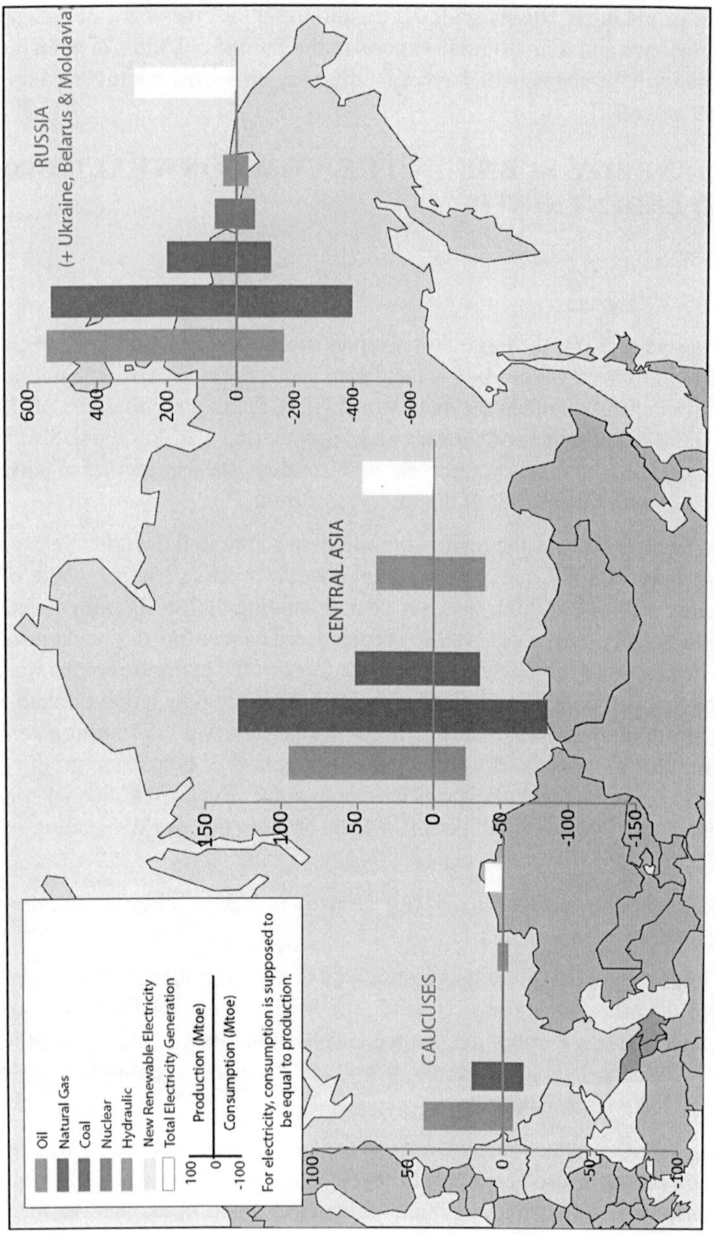

Sources: BP Statistical Review 2016 and doe/eia.

Figure 60: CIS Energy Balance Sheet 2015.

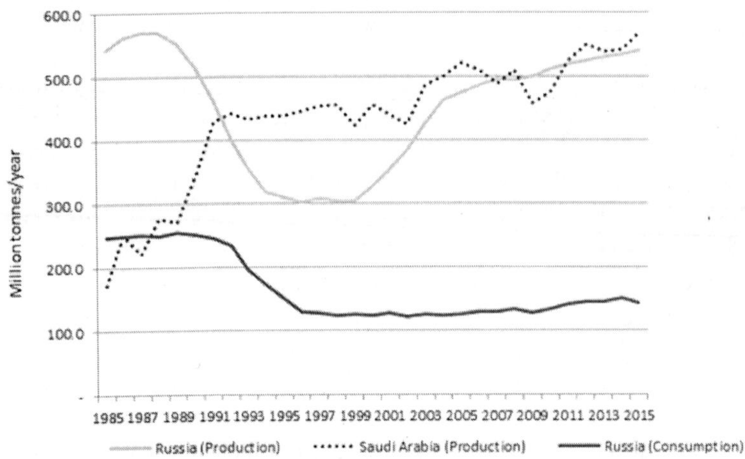

Source: BP Statistical Review, 2016.

Figure 61: Saudi and Russian Oil Production and Russian Consumption.

also produced about 36 million tons of crude oil and nearly 15 million tons of gas condensate.

Regarding the oil industry, within the USSR State Planning Committee (Gosplan), there was a State Committee for the Oil Industry which handled this area of the economy. Different ministers were appointed to deal with oil activities (Ministry of Geology, Ministry of Oil Construction, Ministry of Refining and Petrochemicals). After 1990, these ministries were abolished and the government created several integrated oil companies from the different parts of the ministries. Some of these companies were sold at very low prices to some oligarchs of the new regime.

–The Return of Russia to the International Oil Scene

As mentioned, the oil production in Russia fell from 500 mtpy in 1986 to 300 in 1995. The position of the Russian petroleum industry started to improve in 1998. Much progress had been made in restructuring and the devaluation of the ruble helped reduce the previously high[1] Russian production costs to a competitive level. Russian production increased, reaching 8 million barrels per day in 2002 and has been consistently over 10 Mbd since 2009.

The example of Yukos shows that spectacular increases in the Russian production was obtained largely by using more modern production techniques based on the most advanced technologies offered by western service companies.

After 2000, Vladimir Putin tried to get a better control of the oil and gas industry. Yukos, probably the largest company was eventually dismantled after his CEO, Mikhail Khodorkovski, was arrested in October 2003, on the grounds of fiscal misappropriation (in fact he was a potential competitor to Vladimir Putin in the political field). Rosneft[2] became progressively the national oil company of Russia. Today, the largest Russian oil companies are Rosneft, Lukoil, Gazprom Neft, Surguneftegaz. Interestingly enough, foreign companies, as at the time of Lenin, were interested in getting shares or developing associations with Russian companies. Just before being arrested, Mikhail Khodorkovski was negotiating with Exxon for this company taking a share in Yukos for several ten billion dollars. The negotiation failed.

BP was more successful with the creation of TNK-BP in 2003. This company reached a fair level of production. However, in 2012, Rosneft bought 50 per cent of equity interest held by BP in the joint venture. BP got 17 billion dollars cash and 12.5 per cent shares on Rosneft. Later BP managed to control 20 per cent of Rosneft shares.

There are also divergent views as to the CIS's potential oil reserves. Some analysts argue that, because the entire territory was explored methodically during the Soviet era, there are only limited reserves remaining to be discovered. In contrast, others believe that the use of more modern methods will uncover deposits that the older methods could not find. In fact, there are many regions still relatively unexplored; Eastern Siberia could contain substantial reserves, as the discoveries off the Sakhalin Islands tend to suggest.

Its geographical proximity and the existence of the pipeline system make Europe a natural choice as Russia's prime customer. However, this situation may well change in the future as Asia is increasingly interested in CIS oil and gas. The interdependence of Russia and Europe and the resulting geopolitical challenges will be considered at greater length later.

One of the Largest Discoveries in 30 Years: Kashagan

Discovered in 2000 in the Kazakh offshore Caspian Sea, Kashagan is estimated to contain recoverable reserves of more than 13 billion barrels and is considered—with Tenguiz, a nearby Kazakh field and probably the "presal" fields in Brazil—to be one of the largest discoveries over the 30 last years. The field is in the hands of by North Caspian Operating Company, a joint project between KazMunayGas, Eni, ExxonMobil, Royal Dutch Shell, Total S.A. (16.81 per cent each), China National Petroleum Corporation (8.4 per cent) and Japan's Inpex Holdings, (7.56 per cent). ENI is the field operator.

The production was supposed to begin in 2007. Initial investment for the development of the field was estimated around 10 billion dollars.

To produce oil it was necessary to build five artificial islands, 75 kilometers offshore from the coast. In addition to the difficult geographical conditions, the climatic conditions are extremely severe. The quality of the crude oil is also a reason for the difficulties of the development. The sulfur content of the crude oil and of the associated gas is high. When the production started in September 2013, the pipelines were quickly corroded by the sulfur in the gas. Production stopped very rapidly and all the pipelines needed replacement.

Production started in 2016, ten years after the initial forecast date. Total investment has increased from 10 to more than 50 billion dollars.

- **Natural Gas**

Russia has the second world's largest proved gas reserves after Iran and before Qatar and Turkmenistan. Until 2009 Russia was the world's largest producer of natural gas but, that year, its production fell and that of the US rose, so Russia lost its lead position. It remains the second-largest consumer, with demand at 50 per cent of the US level.

The natural gas industry in Russia is largely dominated by the state-owned company Gazprom. Although several non-government owned companies co-exist in the oil sector, in the gas sector, Gazprom controls more than 90 per cent of Russian gas reserves and production and it manages the 96,000-mile (155,000-km) network of gas pipelines. Production and reserves are primarily concentrated in the north of the Tyumen region in Western Siberia and, to a lesser extent, in the Astrakhan region, in European Russia. Four fields (Yamburg, Urengoi, Zapolyarnoye and Medvezhye) contain more than half of Gazprom's reserves, and the first two represent more than 60 per cent of Russian production. But these fields are now in decline and others are needed to take their place.

Production started at the Sakhalin field in 2009, and additional production is expected from Eastern Siberia and from the Yamal fields which are currently being developed. The Shtokman, in the Barents Sea, production, which was planned to commission in the 2010's years (with an LNG facility planned in Murmansk) has been delayed because of the present situation of prices and of the political context (tensions between Russia and the West over Ukraine).

– *Natural Gas in Central Asia*

Four other CIS countries have substantial reserves: Kazakhstan (0.9 Tm^3), Turkmenistan (17.5 Tm^3), Uzbekistan (1.1 Tm^3) and Azerbaijan (1.1 Tm^3). There are several problems in Kazakhstan because of the geographical division between the north and the south. The gas fields and the infrastructure for its distribution are in the north, so the country's southern section has to take gas supplies imported from Uzbekistan. For its exports, Kazakhstan remains very dependent on the Russian gas pipeline network controlled by Gazprom and built during the Soviet Union era.

Turkmenistan is in a similar position. Its production collapsed in the 1990s since the main customer was Russia, with some Turkmen gas being re-exported to Europe. Gazprom reacted to the decline in Russian demand after the fall of the Berlin Wall by favouring its own production for exports and significantly decreasing its off-take of Turkmen gas. The rebound of consumption in Russia and the increase in European imports led Gazprom to increase its lifting of gas from Turkmenistan.

Until recently Central Asian governments gave priority to the development of oil resources. Today, the different governments seem to have accepted the need for substantial investments in the gas sector, to strengthen their independence from big brother Russia. Turkmenistan is exporting gas to China and larger projects for gas exports from the Central Asian countries to Asia exist. Azerbaijan is developing gas exports. (Fig. 62).

- **Coal**

At nearly 160 billion tons, Russia's proved coal reserves are the world's second-largest after the United States (237 billion tons). However, domestic coal consumption is declining because of the low price of gas, coal's main competitor. The World Bank estimates that, in 1993, coal was subsidised by more than one per cent of Russia's GDP to ensure its competitiveness.

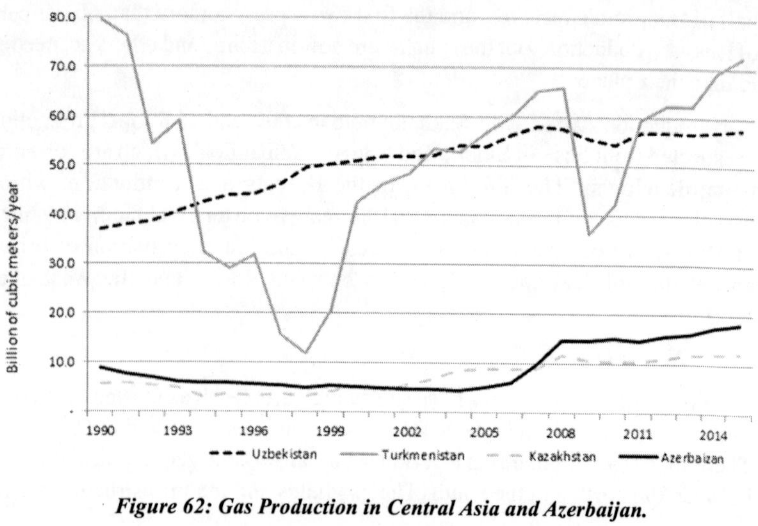

Figure 62: Gas Production in Central Asia and Azerbaijan.

The Russian government has been working with the World Bank for several years to restructure the coal sector. The first step taken was to dissolve the then state monopoly (*Ros Ugol*); now 77 per cent of Russian production is in private hands. But the same old infrastructure and an operating system that was established during the Soviet period and is unsuitable for an international market economy business, still affects other coal producing CIS countries. An example is the Ukraine, which also started to restructure this sector several years ago.

Russia's objective is to maximise its oil and gas exports. It is therefore increasing coal consumption in order to free up additional quantities of hydrocarbons to be sold abroad.

- **Electricity**

Like oil, gas and coal, the production of electricity in the CIS declined substantially after the collapse of the Soviet Union, and the decline lasted until 1999. Russian Federation generation in 2013 was 1058 TWh (fourth largest in the world); made up of over two-thirds thermal production, 17 per cent from hydraulic and about 16 per cent from nuclear. Russia has 31 nuclear reactors, all located west of the Urals: 50 per cent of them are identical to the reactor involved in the Chernobyl catastrophe, and nearly one-third date back to the start of the 1980s.

Transmission and distribution networks connect six of the seven electricity regions but they are old and very poorly maintained. Electricity losses are substantial—e.g. 7 per cent in Armenia—so some countries have to import electricity from their Russian neighbour. Russia has taken advantage of this to gain control over its partners' electricity sector by buying either generating capacity (UES– United Energy Systems, the 52 per cent state-owned Russian company acquired 80 per cent of generation capacity in Armenia and 35 per cent in Georgia) or the distribution network (purchase of 75 per cent of the Tbilisi power network). But Russia has also had problems in maintaining its own infrastructure. On May 25, 2005, a power cut plunged two million Muscovites into darkness and trapped 20,000 people in the subway. President Putin reacted by accusing the UES of giving priority to overall energy policy considerations rather than its principal role of maintaining the power network.

Reform of UES has been planned for several years. The proposal is that UES should be broken up into several regional electricity generation companies (known under the Russian acronym of OGKs). These will be privatised, with the government's stake not exceeding 40 per cent, but with the distribution network remaining in state hands. Since 2005, Russia has made progress to restructure the industry through $30 billion privatisation of generation infrastructure, implementation of a wholesale energy spot market, introduction of incentive-based economic regulation and open access arrangements for transmission and distribution networks. Also, developments are made towards retail market reform and more cost-reflective pricing; and the establishment and strengthening of key market and regulatory institutions. There are still reforms needed to improve the wholesale and retail market structure along with efficient and cost effective user pricing.

Hydroelectric Conflict in the Ferghana Valley[3]

"Divide and rule": this was the principle behind Stalin's plan when he drew up the borders of the five Central Asian Soviet Socialist Republics (SSRs). In other words, he wanted to prevent any single state in the region dominating the others. But after the fall of the Soviet Union, the interdependence of these states on each other became clear and tensions between them grew.

These tensions are particularly acute in the Ferghana Valley. This agricultural area, the richest in Central Asia, is divided between three countries: Uzbekistan, which has more than three-quarters of the valley, Tajikistan and Kirgizstan. Although Stalin gave Uzbekistan the benefit of the valley's fertile land for growing cotton, he left the other two with control of the water supplies. This is because the sources of the Syr Daria and the Amu Daria, the two largest rivers in Central Asia, lie in the mountains of these two countries. They are the poorest nations in the area but, under the USSR, there was a national plan under which they were required to supply water to the three downstream countries (Uzbekistan, Turkmenistan and Kazakhstan) for crop cultivation. In exchange, Tajikistan and Kirgizstan, whose sources of raw materials are limited, received coal, gas and oil for electricity generation.

However, since 1991, Uzbekistan, Turkmenistan and Kazakhstan have increased the prices for their fossil fuels to world market levels, which Tajikistan and Kirgizstan cannot afford to pay. In response, and also in reaction to an agreement of 1992 that brought in a system of quotas favourable to the downstream states, Kirgizstan increased the water flows from its dams during winter, so that its hydroelectric power plants could operate at full capacity. This enabled Kirgizstan to increase electricity generation from 9.2 billion kWh in 1980 to 13.8 billion in 2003, 80 per cent of which was from its hydroelectric sources. This led to serious tensions between the parties since not only was the additional water completely unnecessary for Uzbek crops, it transformed part of the Ferghana Valley into swamps making cultivation impossible. During the summer the position was reversed, Uzbekistan complained of not receiving enough water for its cotton and Kirgizstan merely responded by declaring that it had respected its winter quotas.

Tension rose still further in 2001 when Kirgizstan passed a law stipulating that, from then on, water would be considered a commodity and sold to the countries downstream. The Kirgiz government claimed that this was justified by the refusal of the other states to share in the very high cost of maintaining the hydraulic infrastructure (hydroelectric power plants, dams and reservoirs) that dates back to the Soviet era. In retaliation, Uzbekistan stopped its gas deliveries, to which Kirgizstan responded by releasing increasingly large quantities of water. Recently, in the region around Kyrgyzstan's village of Ala-Buka after 40 Uzbek soldiers backed by two armored personnel carriers appeared on 18 March 2016 and established a checkpoint on a road leading to the village. Uzbek authorities did not immediately provide a reason for the troop movement. In response, Kyrgyz authorities moved an equal number of troops and vehicles to the area. In the end, after talks between representatives of the two countries, most of the troops departed and the incident fizzled out. Such incidents have occurred along the borders in the Ferghana Valley—shared by Kyrgyzstan, Tajikistan, and Uzbekistan in the past as well.

Although the States agree on the principle and the need for an understanding on the question of water in Central Asia, tensions persist and no country seems willing to make the first step to break the impasse. Since the Ferghana Valley is already a very troubled region (terrorism, drugs, ethnic confrontations, etc.), these energy problems exacerbate the conflicts even further.

GEOPOLITICS OF TRANSPORTING HYDROCARBONS FROM CIS STATES

Many of the current geopolitical challenges affecting Russia and the CIS relate to the choice of the export routes for oil and gas. Although the territory of the CIS is vast, direct access routes to ice free ports are limited and do not allow for optimal routing of these exports. Since the breakup of the USSR the various governments in office have tried to find their own solutions to the problem, and this has been a real handicap for Russia.

One of the problems is that the infrastructure used to transport oil and gas and for electricity transmission between the various regions and countries of the CIS is more than 30 years old. So the CIS needs to modernise its transport facilities both to cover domestic consumption and for exports.

- **Ukraine and Belarus: The Former Keys to Russian Exports**

Russia is the leading oil and gas supplier to the European Union and to Europe in general. Europe takes 44 per cent of CIS oil exports and 42 per cent of its gas exports so its market is crucial for Russia and the interdependence

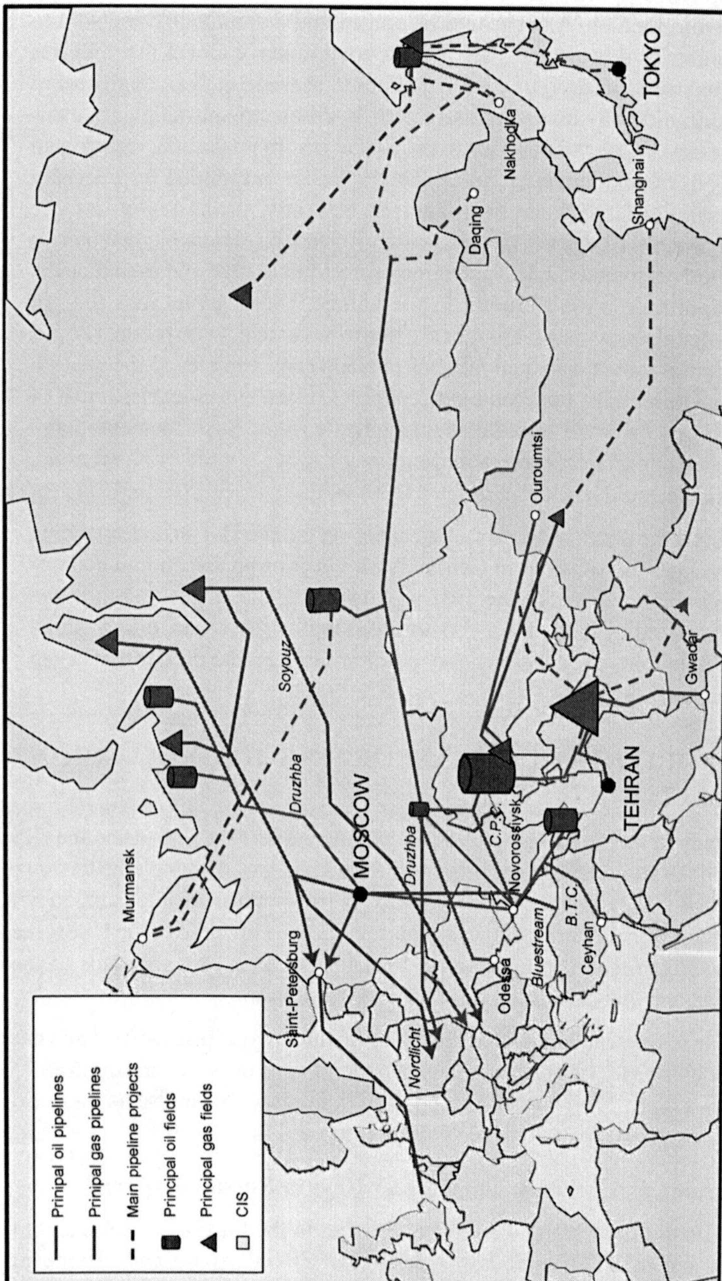

Figure 63: Main Hydrocarbon Export Routes from the CIS.

between Russia and Europe could continue to grow as European demand increases which will also depend on the political relations between Russia and Europe. However, there are few export routes from Russia and the Central Asian States, which makes the position of the transit countries, particularly Ukraine and Belarus, very important.

For oil, the Druzhba pipeline, which is over 3,500 km (2,200 miles) long and has a capacity of 1.2 Mb/d, separates into two branches at Mozyr, in Belarus. The northern branch continues through Belarus to supply Poland and Germany. The longer southern branch runs through Ukraine to the Czech Republic, Slovakia, Hungary and Romania. The other main export route is the Prydniprovski Main Pipeline, with a capacity of 2.1 Mb/d, delivering oil to the port of Odessa for subsequent export by sea. This is vital for Russia since it makes the Ukrainian port of Odessa a second major access point to warm seas, after the Russian port of Novorossiysk. (Fig. 63).

All gas exports are by pipeline, although LNG facilities are planned.

Up to 2010, around 80 per cent of Russian gas exports were made via Ukraine, with most of the rest going via Belarus. This benefited Ukraine since, in return, it received between 26 and 30 billion cubic meters of gas per year. Russia, Ukraine's leading trading partner at the time took advantage of the amount of debt owed to it by Ukraine, by negotiating transit agreements that were advantageous for its energy companies, e.g. Gazprom or Transneft.

Following the tensions and crisis between the two countries, Russia has devised a strategy to reduce its dependence on the countries of Eastern Europe, particularly Belarus and Ukraine. One way to do that is the Russian government's clearly stated ambition to participate in the privatisation of the energy industries of former Soviet bloc countries. The other solution open to Russia to limit its dependence on its neighbours as much as possible is the development of alternative export routes.

– Russian Gas Exports to Europe: Who Depends on Whom?

Until 1991, the gas pipelines crossed the USSR, then Czechoslovakia, and terminated in Germany. After the fall of the Berlin Wall, the "political" operation of these two gas pipelines became far more complex: Belarus and Ukraine became independent and these two countries are gas consumers. Although consumption in Belarus is limited by its low population, consumption in Ukraine was significant (however this consumption fell from around 60 bcm per year ten years ago to less than 30 bcm now, both for economic reasons and because of the difficult relationships with Russia, especially regarding gas supplies). During the USSR era, the price of gas was kept low. Socialist countries countries paid the same price for the Russian gas as the Russian consumers, roughly 25 per cent of the international price. Up to 2005 Ukraine continued to pay this low price because of the friendly relations between Russia and Ukraine.

From 2005, after the "Orange Revolution", there were recurring disputes between Russia and Ukraine: Ukraine had trouble paying for Russian gas, which was one of its vital needs. If Ukraine stopped paying for the gas it consumed, Russia was faced with a dilemma: stop delivering gas to Ukraine and expose itself to the misappropriation of some of the gas in transit, or stop all exports and suffer financial losses while running the risk of destabilising trade relations with the West (Fig. 64).

Different crises were illustrations of the dangers of the situation: at the beginning of 2006, Russia raised the price of gas sold to Ukraine from \$20 to \$230 per thousand cubic meters, in oil equivalent terms from \$3.3 to \$38/bbl. This was obviously politically motivated. Following the "Orange Revolution" which installed a regime much less well disposed to Moscow, the Kremlin was using gas as a weapon to demonstrate its strength. But decreased deliveries to Ukraine meant decreased deliveries to Western Europe, to the latter's great displeasure, particularly that of Italy and the new EU member states. During the winter of 2006–2007, it was a crisis with Belarus that disrupted Russian supplies to Europe.

The crisis of winter 2008–2009 was of an altogether different magnitude. At the start of January, Moscow demanded that Kiev pay the debt it owed for

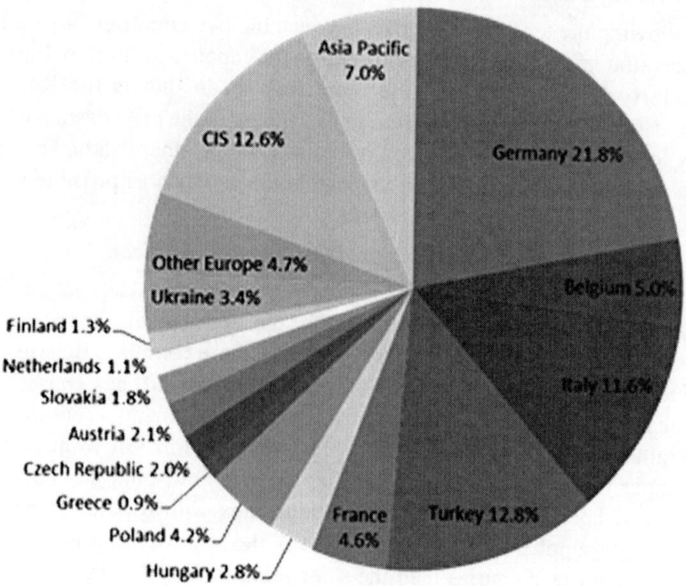

Source: BP Statistical Review, 2016.

Figure 64: Russian Gas Exports in 2015.

earlier, still unpaid, gas deliveries. The dispute then broadened to include the transit fees paid by Gazprom to Ukraine. Deliveries to Europe stopped for nearly three weeks. Several European countries, particularly those in the east who depend mainly on Russia for their gas supplies, were largely deprived of gas at a time when the temperatures were particularly low.

There were probably multiple reasons for the conflict: Moscow's desire to pressure the Ukraine government and favour a candidate who was an ally of Russia for the forthcoming elections, and to show Europeans the importance of limiting dependence on transit countries by speeding up construction of the Nord Stream and South Stream gas pipelines that avoid Ukraine and Belarus.

Their control of the gas pipelines gave Belarus and Ukraine means of exerting very strong pressure on their large eastern neighbour. But this position has been largely weakened affected by the construction of gas pipelines which avoid the two countries.

- **Russia: the Continuing Search for Viable Routes for its Hydrocarbon Exports**

The European Union exerts an increasingly strong attraction on Eastern European countries. This process seems to be irreversible, even though Russia maintains some influence on them; the "Orange Revolution" of November–December, 2004, did not put an end to Russian influence in Ukraine particularly in the economic sector. Only Belarus still remains solidly anchored to Russia.

To remedy the dependency on Ukraine (and Belarus), Russia developed several projects. For oil, a pipeline has been built connecting the West Siberian oil fields to the Primorsk terminal in the Gulf of Finland. With a capacity of 1 million b/d, this pipeline enables Russia to avoid crossing the Baltic States.

Regarding gas, the first project was the Blue Stream gas pipeline running from Southern Russia to Ankara, passing under the Black Sea and avoiding the potentially unstable Caucasus region and the countries north of the Black Sea where transit fees would have been payable. The second project was the Nord Stream (North European Gas Pipeline) project, with a length of 2,100 km (1,300 miles), including 1,200 km (750 miles) offshore, which supplies Germany. A first line was built in 2011 and a second one in 2012. The total capacity is 55 bcm per year but only 22.5 bcm can be used because of EU restrictions. Nord Stream goes under the Baltic Sea, and so reaches European markets without passing through the former satellite countries. To the south, the Europeans planned the Nabucco project; the name of the project came to its developers after seeing Verdi's opera of the same name, which depicts the Jewish resistance to Assyria in Babylonia during the time of Nebuchadnezzar (a situation which may seem somewhat analogous to European dependence on Russian gas). But this project was abandoned recently.

The project simply had not enough gas to feed the gas pipeline. Azerbaijan was willing to supply some, but not in the quantities needed. Turkmenistan has substantial gas resources but, to avoid passing through Russian territory, Turkmen gas must either go under the Caspian or via Iran. The problem with the Caspian is that there is no agreed legal status that would permit the passage of such a pipeline. Iran obviously has substantial resources, but the present situation still makes it difficult for that country to be used as a supply route for Europe by pipeline.

Russia has proposed the South Stream project, to run east-west across the Black Sea before climbing through Bulgaria and Serbia towards Hungary and Central Europe. South Stream would have avoided Turkey. Following the 2014 crisis between Russia and the West, and because of the opposition of the European Commission, South Stream was cancelled after which Russia proposed the construction of Turkish Stream which would connect Russia and Turkey under the Black Sea. However, after the destruction of a Russian plane by Turkey at the end of 2015, this new project was again cancelled. In 2017, better relations between Russia and Turkey could revive the Turkish stream project.

So for the moment the "Southern Corridor", another source of supply for Europe, will be the TANAP-TAP pipeline. This project will connect the giant Shah Deniz gas field in Azerbaijan to Europe through the South Caucasus Pipeline (SCP), the Trans-Anatolian Pipeline (TANAP) and the Trans-Adriatic Pipeline (TAP). This project is of strategic importance for both Azerbaijan and Turkey. It will allow the first Azerbaijani gas exports to Europe, beyond Turkey. It will also strengthen the role of Turkey as a regional energy hub. Construction of the pipeline began formally in March 2015 and is expected to be completed in 2018.

Turkey has announced that it may refuse to act merely as a transit country, and wishes to become a hub that purchases and re-sells gas. European supply security cannot be strengthened by any of these projects, unless Turkey becomes a member of the European Union.

Other export markets of interest to Russia are those of Asia. The Sakhalin Islands, with their estimated reserves of 14 billion barrels of oil and 2.7 trillion cubic meters (96 trillion cubic feet or 2.43 billion toe) of gas, are already supplying crude oil and LNG to Japan.

The East Siberia Pacific Ocean (ESPO) pipeline is a huge project aimed at delivering crude oil from East Siberia oil fields to Asia. The first section of ESPO (2757 kilometers) runs from Angarsk, on the shores of Lake Baïkal to

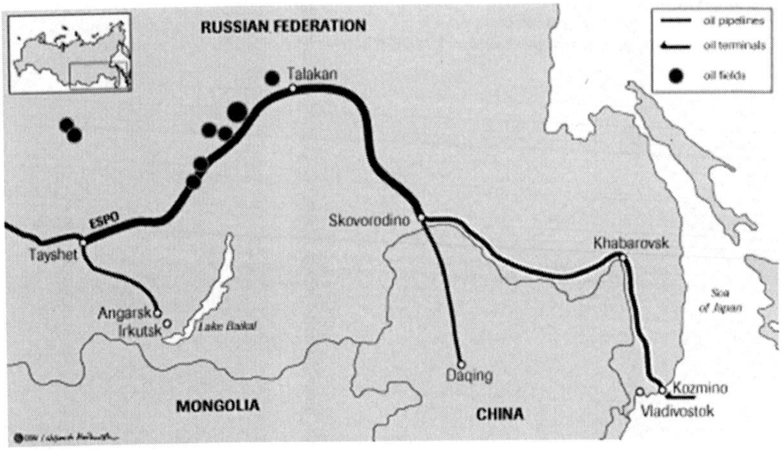

Source: osw.waw.pl.

Figure 65: Russian Oil Pipelines and Terminals - ESPO.

Tayshet and then to Skovorodino and was completed in 2009. The second section (ESPO 2) Skovorodino—Kozmino (or Nakhodka, close to Vladivostok) was completed at the end of 2012.

The ESPO oil pipeline is one of Russia's most expensive infrastructural projects. The total construction cost of its two sections exceeded US$23 billion. In 2012, ESPO transported 30 million tonnes of oil, including 15 million tonnes to China. The key recipients of Russian oil from ESPO are: Japan (31 per cent), China (24 per cent), the US (22 per cent), and South Korea, Singapore, the Philippines, Thailand and Malaysia.

A pipeline between Skovorodino and Daqing (China) has also been built to replace transportation of oil by rail. The Russian part, from Skovorodino to the Amur River—the border between Russia and China—was built by Transneft. The Chinese part was built by CNPC (China National Petroleum Company). Initial capacity was 15 million tons per year to be increased to 30 (Fig. 65 and 66).

- **Central Asia: what Solutions for a Landlocked Region?**

Three of the five Central Asian countries (Kazakhstan, Uzbekistan and Turkmenistan) also have major difficulties in exporting their hydrocarbon resources. The region remains an important strategic stake for the large countries surrounding it, i.e. Russia, China, India and in particular, Iran. Their geographical position (they are landlocked and Uzbekistan is even double landlocked) and their past (these are former Soviet socialist republics), made these three countries almost entirely dependent on the use of the Russian

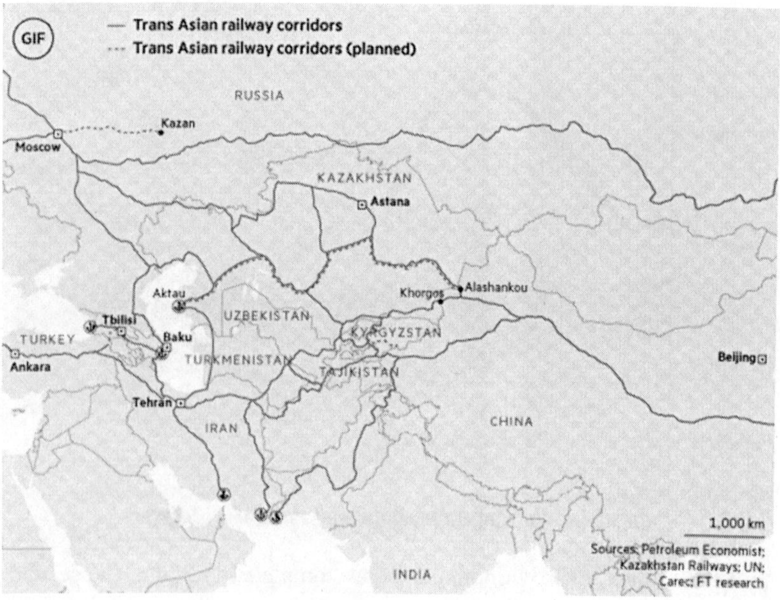

Figure 66: Railway Corridors.

infrastructure. Exports of Turkmen gas and Kazakh oil take the northern route, via Russia, by pipeline directly to the European market or to the Black Sea loading ports (Novorossiysk, Odessa, etc.).

However, these countries are developing exports to Asia. Kazakhstan is exporting crude oil to China. The oil pipeline starts from Aktau on the Caspian Sea and reaches Alashankou in China.

Turkmenistan is exporting gas to China through the Central Asia Gas pipeline which is going though Uzbekistan and Kazakhstan to Jingbiang in China. Capacity of the line is 55 bcm increasing to 85 bcm thanks to an agreement between China and the gas producing countries in Central Asia.

Another project is a gas pipeline connecting Turkmenistan to India via Afghanistan and Pakistan (TAPI pipeline). The TAPI pipeline stretches 1600 kilometers from the eastern Mary province in Turkmenistan, Herat and Kandhar province in Afghanistan, through Multan and Quetta in Pakistan to Punjab province in India. The pipeline is due to go on-stream in 2019 but several geopolitical factors can further delay the project.

Security is a major concern for the TAPI project. The pipeline passes through the Balochistan province in Pakistan which has recently seen escalated protests from the Baloch nationalists who have attacked pipelines in the past. Additionally, pipeline passes through some regions, particularly the Greshk district in Afghanistan which is under Taliban control and the recent events especially the killing of militant Burhan Wani by Indian Armed forces in Jammu and Kashmir have led to an increase in tensions between India and Pakistan. In the middle of all this, it will be a key challenge to finish the project on time. Iran could also offer a supply route out of Central Asia, through a swap arrangement under which Tehran would receive Caspian oil and gas, thereby "freeing up" the hydrocarbons produced in the south for export. But this project has encountered up to now strong American opposition. The last possibility is for oil pipelines going from Central Asia to Turkish ports either directly or via Armenia and/or Azerbaijan.

Whether or not these projects are undertaken depends on Russia, which would have to make certain choices, e.g. a strategic alliance with Iran. This option would benefit Iran, which wants to again become a key player in the international community, and it would benefit Russia which could play a role as a counterweight to the Baku-Tbilisi-Ceyhan pipeline that can deliver crude oil directly from the Caspian Sea via Turkey without going through Russia which was imposed by Washington. The advantage to Russia could make it worth them accepting the loss of some of its dominance over the former Soviet republics of Central Asia.

HYDROCARBON SECTOR: POLITICAL AND LEGAL CONSEQUENCES OF THE PUTIN ERA

The decade from 2000 to 2010 saw nationalism return to the energy sector. After the fall of the Soviet Union, the new Russian President, Boris Yeltsin, privatised the largest state-owned companies, particularly those in the oil sector. Some people, now known as the oligarchs, made their fortune by buying these state-owned companies for derisory sums. But Vladimir Putin quickly put an end to this liberalisation of the Russian energy sector. In 2003, Mikhail Khodorkovski and other leaders of Yukos were arrested and accused of fraud and other financial crimes, just as a merger between Yukos (20 per cent of Russian oil production, 2 per cent of worldwide production) and Sibneft (Russia's fifth-leading oil company) was about to be completed. In addition, he broke off negotiations underway with US companies (Exxon-Mobil and Chevron) for the sale of a substantial share of Yukos' capital for tens of billions of dollars. By this coup, Vladimir Putin achieved two objectives: he punished the head of Yukos for his obvious political ambitions, and sent a strong signal to other oligarchs. By requiring Yukos to pay fines amounting to billions of dollars, he forced the company to dispose of its most lucrative subsidiaries and regained control of a strategic sector. On December 19, 2004, the main subsidiary of Yukos, Yugansknefteg as, was put up for auction and bought by a financial group that was formed a few days prior to the sale and behind which stood Rosneft, the only oil company owned by the state.

Although the government did not seek to nationalise all companies in the oil sector, it tried to limit the possibilities for international companies to access Russian reserves. An example is the law of June 2003 on production sharing agreements (PSAs), which complemented that of 1996. That made it more difficult for an oil field to be included on the Duma-approved "List Law", which lists oil fields open to PSAs, so PSAs became the exception rather than the rule. Then in February 2005, the Russian Energy Minister announced that only companies with majority Russian ownership would have the right to obtain licenses to exploit the oil and gas resources of Siberia.

Vladimir Putin is thus seeking to strengthen state control over the Russian hydrocarbons sector. The problem remains how to reconcile such state control with liberalisation, particularly of the gas sector, to enable Russia to join the WTO.

Because Russian energy policy is an integral part of its foreign policy, the climate of international affairs also affects its energy policy. After the September 11, 2001 attacks there was reconciliation between the US and Russia that appeared to be sustainable. However, hopes for this mutual understanding were dashed when national interests, including those relating to hydrocarbons, diverged. Russia was opposed to the BTC pipeline (Baku-Tbilisi-Ceyhan) supported by Washington, although the Kremlin finally accepted it; and Moscow remains Iran's leading partner for their peaceful nuclear programme. A further cause of the divergence was the clear US presence during the peaceful revolutions in Georgia (2003), Ukraine (2004) and Kirgizstan (2005). Although the prime objective of US strategy is to encircle China, Russia nevertheless sees these moves as reducing its sphere of influence and freedom of movement.

CONCLUSION

Russia has regained influence in the world thanks to the oil and gas industry. Can Russia resist the decrease in oil and gas prices? This will make necessary diversification of the Russian industry, still largely dependent on hydrocarbon.

References

1. In Russia, in addition to the production costs, which are already high because of the field conditions, the transport costs are considerable because of the distances between the oil fields and the coast. A large part of the production comes from the Tyumen region which is several thousand miles from the Baltic or the Black Sea. Transport costs are particularly high when part or all of the transport is by rail.
2. Rosneft is Russia's leading oil producer with some 4.2 million barrels of oil equivalent per day production and reserves of 33,9 billion boe.

3. For further information, see Yann Balay, “La vallée du Ferghana: séisme au cœur du ‘Heartland’”, Master’s Thesis (in French), universite Pierre Mendes France—Grenoble II, 2002–2003.
4. This was done on completion of the Transalpine Pipeline carrying crude oil from the Mediterranean to Ingolstadt, in 1967. Ingolstadt had previously been supplied by pipeline from Karlsruhe, and the flow in that line was then reversed.

Chapter - 9

Africa

Africa is unique in having a very low consumption of primary energy (excluding firewood): of the order of 0.4 toes per head, compared with 1.7 globally and 7 in the United States. South Africa alone accounts for 29 per cent of Africa's total energy use and North Africa for over 40 per cent. On the other hand, the countries of Sub-Saharan Africa (West, Central and East Africa), from Mauritania to Namibia, and from Sudan to Mozambique, use very little commercial energy. This low energy consumption is, at the same time, both the cause and the result of the region's low level of development.

The main characteristics of Sub-Saharan Africa are its relatively sparse population, its poverty and the large distances that make communication between the north and south and between the west and east very difficult, indeed often impossible. There are hundreds of daily flights connecting Europe and America, or Europe and Asia, but communications between Africa and the other continents remain more limited and inter-African travel sometimes remain difficult. Flights are limited. The rail network remains embryonic. The road system is inadequate for rapid and safe travel from one country to another. Interconnections between the continent's different energy networks can develop (for example, the power pools), but progress has to be made.

Many countries are landlocked. Capitals which are very far from the coasts, e.g. Bamako (Mali), Ouagadougou (Burkina Faso), Niamey (Niger), N'Djamena (Chad), Bangui (Central African Republic), Kampala (Uganda), Kigali (Rwanda), Bujumbura (Burundi), Lusaka (Zambia), Harare (Zimbabwe), Lilongwe (Malawi),...can only be supplied with heavy goods via complex transport systems (at best by train over part of the distance, then by truck for the remainder of the journey, over roads that are often in poor condition). The costs are extremely high and bear heavily on the economies of these countries.

ENERGY FOR AFRICA: THE IMPORTANCE OF OIL

The continent's energy balance continues to be dominated by biomass which, in its various forms, represents two-thirds of total household energy consumption.

With the exception of South Africa, which consumes very large quantities of coal, and North Africa which consumes substantial quantities of natural gas, oil remains the dominant commercial energy[1], particularly in Sub-Saharan Africa (Fig. 67).

- **Oil in Africa: Recent Discoveries and Significant Reserves**

While oil production started in many of the world's regions in the nineteenth century (United States, Russia and Indonesia) or at the start of the twentieth (the Middle East and South America), hydrocarbons were only discovered in Africa much later. Production started in the 1950s. It is concentrated in two zones but several countries: the area surrounding the Gulf of Guinea, with the two major producers Nigeria and Angola, and several significant producers (particularly, Congo-Brazzaville, Gabon, Equatorial Guinea, Chad, Ivory Coast, Cameroon); and in North Africa (Algeria, Libya, Egypt, and, to a lesser extent, Tunisia). Production started in 1999 in Sudan, 2003 in Chad, 2006 in Mauritania, 2010 in Ghana. Oil production is waiting for development in Uganda. Kenya, Senegal and a few other countries could become oil producing countries over the next years.

Proved African oil reserves amount to 17 billion tons, nearly seven per cent of worldwide reserves, and are fairly equally distributed between North and West Africa. In 2015, the continent's production was 8.4 Mb/d, nine per cent of the worldwide total. Its production and reserves do not make Africa a new Middle East, but its role as supplier to Europe and especially Asia makes it a key player because Africa consumes only 46 per cent of the oil it produces. There are large volumes available for export and the continent is the third largest oil export zone, just behind the Commonwealth of Independent States but far behind the Middle East (Fig. 70).

– *Oil in North Africa*

Algeria and Libya are large suppliers to Europe. Egypt's production is stable but consumption is increasing and all its production is now used in its domestic market. North Africa has the advantage that France, Italy, Spain, Greece and Turkey are reached simply by crossing the Mediterranean. More than two-thirds of North African oil exports go to Europe.

The historic ties between France and Algeria, and between Italy and Libya, have played an important role in the way in which the oil industry in these two countries has developed. French companies discovered the Saharan oil deposits before Algeria became independent.

Libyan oil was first discovered and produced by independent US companies without European refining capacity, so large refineries were built in Sardinia, Sicily and Southern Italy to process it, which incidentally fulfilled the Italian government's pledge for economic development in these regions.

These countries' oil policies are closer to the Middle East oil producers than to those in West Africa. Algeria and Libya are OPEC members; they nationalised the oil industry in the 1970s and the state companies (Sonatrach and NOC respectively) still play a very important role and are highly sensitive to political tensions in the Arab-Muslim world.

Libya's production was about 3.5 Mb/d in the early 1970s but it then declined sharply as the restrictive terms that Colonel Gaddafi's government imposed on the oil companies reduced the capital they were prepared to invest

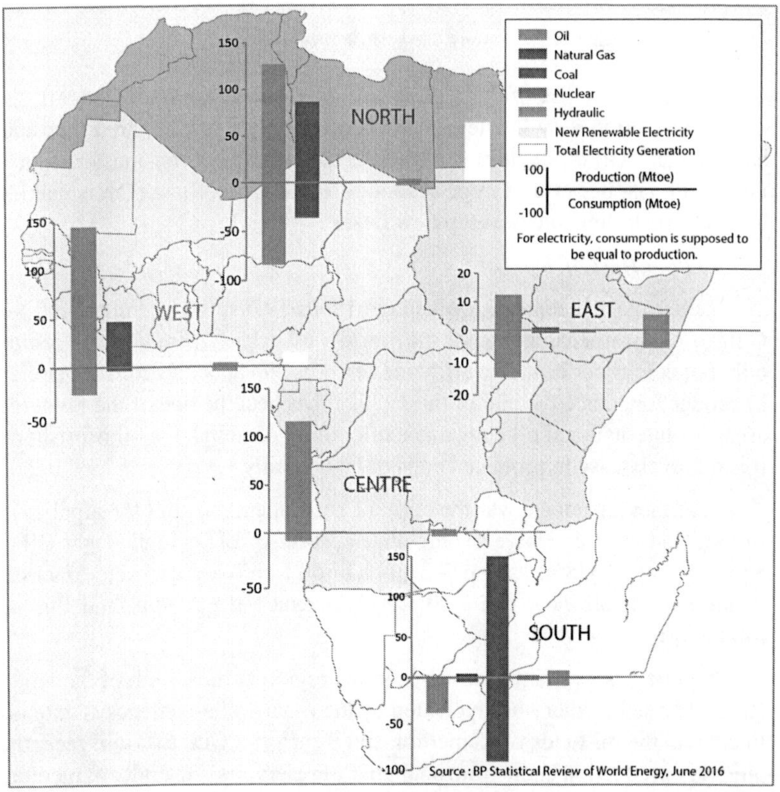

Source: BP Statistical Review, June 2016 and doe/eia.

Figure 67: Energy Balance in Africa, 2015.

and also because the government itself wished to reduce production. Production was then a bit less than 2 Mbd. After Colonel Gaddafi's contrition for the Lockerbie bombing and the halt to his nuclear programme, Libya was no longer subject to US sanctions and foreign oil companies returned to make massive investments in Libya. Companies who were in Libya before nationalisation, such as Occidental Oil, ExxonMobil, British Petroleum and Shell, have been joined by Sonatrach and Gazprom.

Oil in the Economies of Principal North African Producers – 2016

	Proved reserves (Gtons)	*Production (Mb/d)*	*Consumption (Mb/d)*	*Exports (Mb/d)*	*Oil's share of exports*	*Share of GDP*
Libya	6.3	.43	0.2	.2	50 per cent	60 per cent
Algeria	1.5	1.6	0.4	1.2	75 per cent	35 per cent
Egypt	0.5	0.7	0.8	0.0	N/A	N/A

Source: BP Statistical Review of World Energy, June 2016, and OPEC.

After the collapse of the regime and the death of Colonel Gaddafi, the production fell to very low levels and is often only a few hundred thousand barrels a day. Oil production in Algeria is now stable but the consumption is increasing fast because of large subsidies to oil prices. Sonatrach is making huge efforts to find and develop new fields.

– Oil in West Africa

Rather more recently, i.e. since the 1960s/1970s, the region around the Gulf of Guinea became part of the world's oil scene. Although this region only holds four per cent of worldwide reserves and accounts for six per cent of production, since the end of the 1980s it has become one of the favoured areas for international oil company exploration. Although the oil is offshore, it is relatively easy to produce and is of high quality.[2]

A further advantage was the region's convenient location for supplies to Europe and the US. However, the development of LTO (Light Tight Oil—Shale Oil) in the US has stopped exports of oil from West Africa to America. Crude exports are now mainly directed to Asia (50 per cent) and Europe (40 per cent) (Fig. 70).

Nigeria has substantial reserves in the region at the mouth of the Niger River. The sedimentary basin created by the river's alluvial deposits extends to contain the oil fields of Cameroon and Equatorial Guinea. Until recently, Nigerian production came from a number of reservoirs, generally of medium size. Their production is often mixed to give commercial crude oil blends that are exported from the terminals of Forcados, Escravos, and Bonny and named after the relevant terminal.

Is there a Move toward Tax Competition between Producing States?

The laws governing foreign investment in most of the countries in this region are relatively favourable to overseas investors in terms of their access to resources and the tax regimes applied. Obviously not all countries have the same production potential; the oil, and possibly the gas, prospects in Nigeria and Angola put their governments in a strong position in relation to the oil companies. Although these two countries may seem demanding in relation to revenue sharing and taxation, some small oil countries have revised their taxation laws to ensure that they remain competitive despite the stagnation in their level of reserves.

Angola's oil production, which started during the Portuguese colonial period in the Cabinda enclave, developed first thanks to discoveries made in offshore Cabinda and then thanks to discoveries in offshore Luanda, starting with Girassol in 1996. Now the attention is focused to possible presal discoveries, like in Brazil. As already explained, presal deposits are the result of the opening of "Pangea", starting 120 million years ago and creating large areas were sediments were covered by salt due to seawater evaporation. Since Angola was adjacent to Brazil historically, there are good chances that oil fields can be found in the "presal" of Angola. In neighbouring countries (Equatorial Guinea, Congo-Brazzaville, Gabon), production is constant or slightly declining.

Oil was discovered in the Jubilee field in Ghana by Tullow Oil in 2007. Production started at the end of 2010 with about 100,000 b/d. The expected production is 120,000 Bpd but problems with gas separation have risen. First oil flowed from the Tweneboa, Enyenra, Ntomme (TEN) fields offshore Ghana, to the FPSO Prof. John Evans Atta Mills in August 2016. Potential reserves could make Ghana an important producing country.

The area from Guinea-Bissau to Nigeria could become important for its sub-salt oil fields. Other discoveries have been made off-shore Sierra Leone in 2009 (Venus field), but no development occurred. Senegal and Mauritania made large oil and gas discoveries recently.

– *Central and East Africa*

Oil production started in Sudan in 1999. The oil fields in production are in the centre of the country and crude oil is delivered for export to Port Sudan on the Red Sea via a 930 mile (1,500 km) pipeline commissioned in 1999. The operating companies are the Chinese CNPC, India ONGC and Malaysia Petronas. There were western companies with Sudanese production but they withdrew under pressure from NGOs (Non-Governmental Organisations).

South Sudan became independent after 2011, as a result, the country has been divided. The oil reserves are mainly in the south, but the transport facilities are principally in the north. However, the situation remains extremely confusing. A civil war is dividing South Sudan. Moreover, the fields have suffered from the conflicts and South Sudan is landlocked. A new pipeline should be built to transport the crude oil up to the Tanzanian coast. (North) Sudan continues to export some crude but at a much lower level and revenues have dramatically fallen.

Production in Chad commenced in 2003, after the Chad-Cameroon pipeline was commissioned. Oil fields were first discovered around Lake Chad in the country's northern region in the mid-1970s, but they were too small to justify the oil pipeline to the Cameroon coast, over more than 2,000 km (1,200 miles), that was required to export the crude oil. Civil war also caused several delays to the realisation of Chad's dream of becoming an oil producer.

Source: BP Statistical Review 2016.

Figure 68: West African Oil Production.

However, the US oil company Conoco, moved the exploration effort that it had undertaken in the north, further south and, followed by Exxon, discovered substantial reserves in the Doba region. To produce the oil, it was necessary to build a 1070 km pipeline across Cameroon. The project was long delayed, particularly by NGOs protesting about the risks resulting from the need for the pipeline to cross environmentally sensitive zones, and the risks for the inhabitants, particularly the Pygmies, of these regions. The project was eventually commissioned at a total cost (production facilities and pipeline) of nearly $4 billion, thanks to the World Bank which, after detailed studies, finally approved it and financed a portion of the capital investment required.

The Chad production has fallen over the last years. However, new production has been developed by CNPC which also built in 2011 a 20,000 b/d refinery, extremely useful for the country which otherwise had to import products from Cameroon or Nigeria. Part of oil production could be exported by the existing pipeline. All the same in the neighbouring Niger, CNPC accepted to build a similar refinery in Zinder, in exchange for the development of oil fields in the Agadem region. Some oil could be exported, probably through the Chad Cameroon pipeline. But no decision has been taken so far.

The Doba-Kribi Oil Pipeline

The delays in starting the Chad project were due to Chad's partners' concern to ensure that the project's revenues were used well (see below), as well as the environmental concerns over construction of the 1070 km oil pipeline between Doba and Kribi in Cameroon, the location of the crude oil export terminal.

Because the pipeline had to be laid through environmentally sensitive zones, the NGOs asked for guarantees against the possibility of damage. The construction also led to the forced eviction of thousands of rural dwellers, who had to be compensated. After the pipeline had commissioned, there was a lot of lawsuits, with some rural dwellers complaining that their compensation was insufficient.

Oil in the Economies of the Principal East and West African Producers - 2016

	Proved reserves (Gtons)	*Produc-tion (Mb/d)*	*Consump-tion (Mb/d)*	*Exports (Mb/d)*	*Oil's share of exports*	*Share of GDP*
Nigeria	5.0	2.4	0.3	2.1	87 per cent	35 per cent
Angola	1.7	1.8	0.1	1.7	95 per cent	45 per cent
Congo-Brazzaville	0.2	.3	.014	0.28	N/A	N/A
Gabon	0.3	0.2	0.005	0.19	N/A	N/A
Equatorial Guinea	0.1	0.3	-	0.3	N/A	N/A
Sudan	0.2	0.1	0.08	0.02	N/A	N/A
Chad	0.2	0.08	0.001	0.079	-	-

Source: BP Statistical Review 2016 and OPEC.

While Chad's and Sudan's reserves are extremely important for their economic development, they are marginal in worldwide terms. However, for years now they have been the subject of intense international public debate due to the nature of the political regimes in office in Khartoum and N'Djamena, as well as the political and economic situation in these two countries.

Another country where oil has recently been discovered is Uganda, again by Tullow Oil. Large deposits have been found around the shores of Lake Albert. Interestingly enough most of the exploration wells have been successful. The government wants some of this oil to be processed in a local refinery to supply the local market, because the country is landlocked and has previously experienced severe fuel shortages, for example during the period of the dictator Idi Amin Dada at the end of the 1970s.

There are probably also similar quantities of oil in the Democratic Republic of the Congo on the other side of Lake Albert. But the government is reluctant to open the area to exploration.

Use of the Funds from Chad's Oil

Local and international NGOs were concerned about the use of funds provided by the World Bank, as well as revenues from oil sales. So Chad became the first country to accept a loan from the World Bank that was subject to conditions on the future use of oil revenues generated by the project. Royalties from crude oil production had to be paid into an escrow account.

Part of these government royalties (10 per cent) had to be paid into a fund for future generations. Eighty per cent of royalties had to be allocated to expenditure on health, education, rural development and other social services.

At the beginning of 2006, Chad's government challenged the agreement with the World Bank, decided to cease payments into the fund for future generations and to use the money "for security objectives", clearly to buy weapons to confront the threat from rebels installed in the border regions of Sudan. The World Bank reacted immediately by suspending all loans to Chad. An agreement between the World Bank and the Chad government was reached in July 2006. However, in September 2008, thanks to its oil revenue (estimated at $1.4 billion for 2008) Chad repaid the entire loan of $65.7 million granted by the World Bank for the pipeline's construction. The World Bank is therefore no longer in a position to put pressure on Chad in relation to their use of the oil revenues.

Today, the World Bank has returned to Chad. A fair amount of money has been used to build roads, universities and hospitals. However, universities and hospitals do not have all the required equipment/personnel to operate in good condition.

• Natural Gas: Good Potential for Export

The potential for increasing natural gas production in Africa is substantial. The continent has eight per cent of the world's reserves and much of this potential has not so far been developed.

North Africa has increased production since the 1960s to become the main player in the African gas world. Algeria alone accounts for 39 per cent of the continent's total gas production, and Algeria and Egypt together use over 64 per cent of African gas demand. Egypt's production potential is being increased by the discovery of new gas fields, Zohr and Nooros.

Algeria is one of the world largest gas exporters. Algerian gas is exported to Europe by three pipelines (the Enrico Mattei line to Italy, the Pedro Duran Farell line to Spain via Morocco and the Straits of Gibraltar, and the Medgaz line), or as LNG.

Associated Gas Flaring

All crude oil production has associated production of natural gas. Associated natural gas production can be either:

– Re-injected into the reservoir to maintain pressure and assist subsequent oil recovery.

– Used as fuel for industry or electricity generation.

Where gas re-injection is too costly and there is insufficient local demand, the surplus gas is flared. Such flaring wastes significant quantities of energy and is increasingly unacceptable because, apart from other reasons, flaring increases greenhouse gas emissions. Most producing countries, under international pressure, have decided to cease flaring with minimum delay. In several African countries, this means either massive re-injection or the development of liquefaction projects. Also, the World Bank initiative of "Zero Routine Flaring" brings together governments, oil companies, and development institutions to eliminate routing flaring no longer than 2030.

Libyan gas exports go mainly to Italy by pipeline, while Egypt has gas liquefaction facilities but due to the development of the local consumption these facilities are not used now.

Nigeria produces substantial quantities of associated and non-associated natural gas. An increasing proportion of this gas is liquefied in a plant at Bonny that was commissioned in 1999. Further expansion is being planned. Nigeria is one of the largest LNG exporters.

Some of the Nigerian natural gas is used for domestic industrial applications and there are two expansion projects to provide additional outlets:

- The West African Gas Pipeline (WAGP) can supply Benin, Togo and Ghana with Nigerian gas. The first objective was to supply the power plants in Ghana (Takoradi) and then in the other countries. The WAGP is now in operation. However, this pipeline transports only limited gas quantities. The reasons are many: Nigeria does not have enough gas to feed the pipeline (exporting gas as LNG is a preferred solution), technical problems arise (the pipeline is offshore and was broken a few times), the Takoradi plant is not always in a position to pay for the gas.
- The Trans-Saharan Gas Pipeline (TSGP), which would link Nigeria to Algeria over a distance of 4,100 km (2,500 miles). However, it should be noted that this project has now been under consideration for over 40 years; the failure to realise the project results both from its high cost and the fact that it would not give an alternative outlet for Nigeria should Algeria fail to take their gas for either political or commercial reasons.

There is an LNG unit operating in Equatorial Guinea. The LNG plant in Angola is affected by the fact that the project is supplied by a very large number of fields.

- **Coal: The Wealth of South Africa**

There is little coal in Africa but the reserves that do exist are largely concentrated in one country. South Africa has 88 per cent of the continent's reserves, and that makes it one of the major players in the world coal market. With an annual production of 140 Mtoe (250 million tons of coal), the country is the world's sixth leading producer. The Mpumalanga region alone is responsible for more than 80 per cent of national production.

Part of the South African coal is of excellent quality with low ash content and low sulfur. Although only a third of South African production is exported, mainly to the European Union and East Asia, South Africa is the world's sixth largest net exporter of coal. The country's exports of over 75 Mtoe make up six per cent of the coal traded on the international market. Coal is mainly exported from the terminal at Richards Bay, the world's largest, with an annual capacity of 91 million tons (or 45 Mtoe). Ninety-three per cent of South African electricity is generated from coal and 90 per cent of the coal consumed is used for electricity generation.

These abundant coal resources have enabled South Africa to develop a substantial industry in synthetic fuels (conversion of coal or gas into oil).

– Sasol, leading company in the manufacture of liquid fuels from coal

The South African company Sasol, privatised in 1979, is the world's leading producer of automotive fuels from coal. The apartheid policy practiced by the white minority regime in South Africa until 1994 led international authorities to impose an embargo on oil deliveries to South Africa. Pretoria reacted by having automotive gasoline and diesel fuel produced from coal, using the Fischer-Tropsch technology used for German production during World War II (see Chapter 4). Sasol was given the right to supply at least one fuel pump in all the service stations in their supply area.

Sasol's coal liquefaction plants are located in Secunda (east of Johannesburg). These very large manufacturing facilities are built above coal mines and provide a highly competitive supply of fuels.

- **Electricity: Rarely Available in Africa**

Both the production and consumption of electricity in Sub-Saharan Africa are particularly low. While most of the population in North Africa and in the Republic of South Africa has access to electricity, only 32 per cent of the Sub Saharan population is in the same situation.

The situation is serious in Sub-Saharan Africa. As said, more than two-thirds of the population has no access to electricity and rural electrification rates are desperately low. The majority of the world's population who lack access to electricity live in Africa.

Outside South Africa (where electricity is mainly generated from coal) and North Africa (where, particularly in Algeria, it is often produced from gas), electricity is hydraulic or generated from fuel oil. Petroleum products have a very substantial share of the electricity generation market in Sub-Saharan Africa, and that can be disastrous when the price of oil is high. The position in the poorest countries is the most critical since the small generation facilities used are powered by gas oil, which is twice as expensive as heavy fuel oil, and it is those countries that have the greatest difficulty on paying for their petroleum products.

There is hydraulic generation in many African countries. There is a very significant potential in and around Guinée-Conakry, Mozambique, the Nile region and especially Central Africa. Inga Falls, near the mouth of the Congo River, could generate the electricity needed for the entire region several times over. But the size of the capital investment needed and the low electricity demand close to the site are important obstacles. A plan to transmit electricity across the continent to Egypt and then to Europe was drawn up by NEPAD (New Partnership for Development in Africa), but it looks to have been abandoned.

The Aswan Dam

Started in 1962 and completed in 1971, the Aswan Dam (Sadd el-Ali) is one of the largest dams in the world. It is 11,800 feet (3,600 meters) long, 364 feet (111 meters) high. The thickness at the base is 3,215 feet (980 meters) and 131 feet (40 meters) at the crest. Its reservoir holds 169 billion m^3 of water and it is equipped with 12 generators each rated at 175 MW. It generates 15 per cent of the Egyptian electricity demand. This dam also provides for flood control, management of irrigation on the banks of the Nile and improved navigation. But even so, apart from the construction phase problems of population displacement and impact on the environment (biodiversity, archeological ruins, silt retention, rising water table, evaporation, etc.), control of the Nile is a cause of tension between the 10 countries that share it (Ethiopia, Uganda, Kenya, Tanzania, Burundi, Congo, Rwanda, Eritrea, Sudan and Egypt) and their 250 million inhabitants who depend on it. Although the continuing dialogue between the riverain countries maintains a relative consensus on use of the water, the hydroelectric projects being built by Ethiopia are complicating relations, particularly with Egypt.

- **Electrification of Africa**

Improving production and distribution of electricity in Africa had become an objective both for the governments and for international organisations (UN, NGOs). The objective is to increase the electrification rate from 32 to around 80 per cent at least by 2040/2050. We must be realistic: in its well prepared and released, *Africa Energy Outlook* (2040) the Internal Energy Agency expects the number of people with access to energy to increase from about 350 to 1350 million which means that the number of people without access will still remain at 650. But one billion inhabitants will get access to electricity.

How can we reach this objective? First, probably a fair number of large plants (dams, large gas power plants) will have to be built to improve the situation in the cities both from a quantitative and a qualitative point of view. Today in some cases more electricity is available, since progressively more and more IPP (Independent Power Producers—private companies) are delivering electricity to the former National Electricity Company. But the problem can be the maintenance of the transportation lines and distribution facilities. There is a lot of gas in West and Central Africa and there will be soon a lot of gas in East Africa which should be used for this purpose.

- **Oil: Africa's Main Energy Source**

– *Atypical Use of Oil*

Although the proportion of the energy sources in Africa is close to the world average[3], there is a key difference in the way in which oil is used. In the world the use of petroleum products is being confined to their captive markets more and more all over the world, i.e. mainly transport. In Africa, however, they are still widely used for electricity generation, the use of automotive fuels being limited by the underdevelopment of the continent's transport infrastructure (Fig. 69).

Oil is particularly attractive in an environment where consumption of energy is expensive and low because, as a liquid, it is easy to transport and store. Despite all of the interest in photovoltaic energy (environment and independence), small gas oil fueled generating plants can be a good source of electricity, indeed they can be very competitive in remote areas which are difficult for the electricity grid to access.

– *The Refining Paradox*

Because, except in South Africa, Nigeria and North Africa, market demand is small, only a few small refineries have been built, and they operate in difficult economic conditions. Nigeria's four "large" refineries make up 75 per cent of West African refining capacity. But these refineries only operate at very low levels.[4] Nigeria is in the paradoxical situation of being an oil producing country which has refineries capable of meeting the internal demand for petroleum products, yet needs to import very large quantities of automotive gasoline. This position, although very good for certain neighbouring competitor refineries (e.g. SIR in Abidjan), is preventing the establishment of a West African market for petroleum products, which is necessary if the region's supply costs are to be reduced.

The situation of the refining industry deteriorated quickly over the last years. Most of the refineries in East Africa (except in Sudan and South Africa) are now closed. The situation is hardly better in West Africa where most of the refineries face financial difficulties. Refineries projects exist in Nigeria but are unlikely to be developed soon.

Most of African refineries suffer from the competition of very large refineries in the Middle East and in India. The largest refinery in the world is in India, with a 1.2 Mbd capacity, which is several ten times the size of a typical Sub-Saharan refinery. Motor fuels can be imported in large quantities with low refining and transportation costs from these remote refineries in Asia. But a situation where most of the products consumed in Africa would be imported from other continents does not look sustainable.

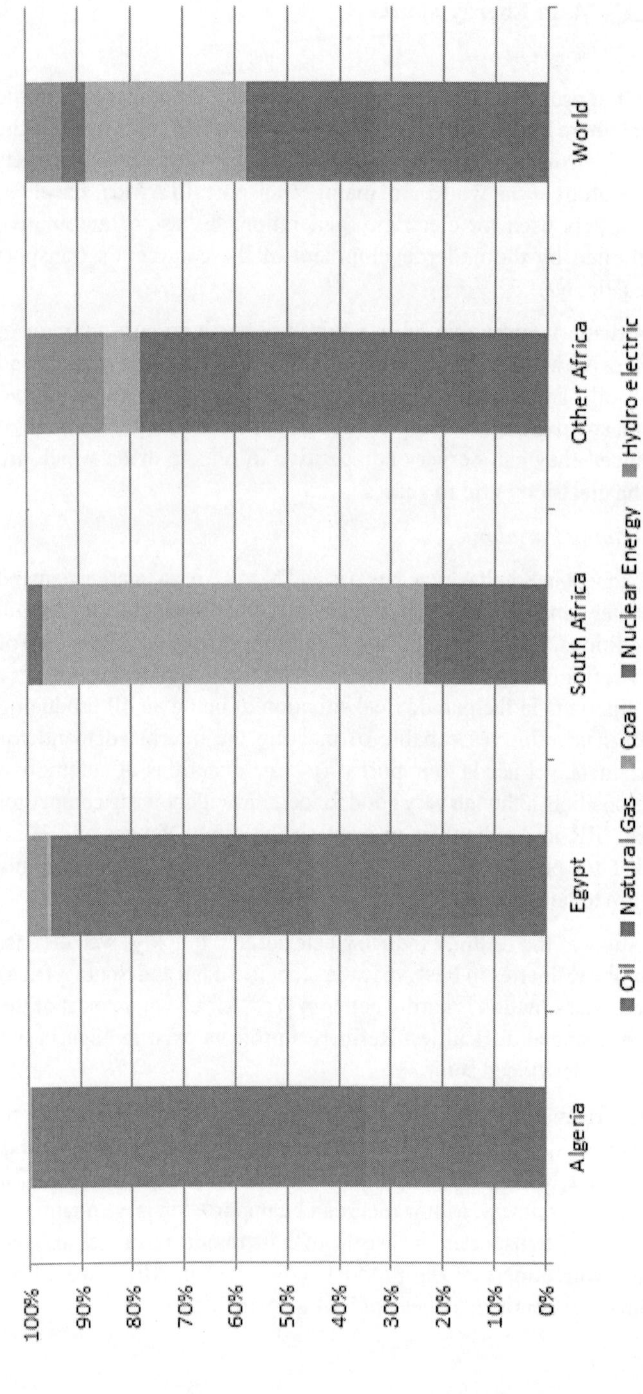

Source: BP Statistical Review 2016.

Figure 69: Energy Balances of Different African Countries 2016.

- **Oil Revenue and Development**

The exploration and production business has little connection with other commercial activities. Except perhaps in Nigeria, it creates relatively few jobs. The technology and the capital used nearly always come from overseas. However, it is a very significant source of income for oil producing states whose crude oil exports sometimes account for 90 per cent of their export revenue.

However, it is difficult to understand how this wealth is used. Several major African producing countries are in a poor economic, and even political, situation

The "Dutch Syndrome"[5] or "Dutch Disease" has run rampant in Nigeria, as in many other countries.

In producing countries like Equatorial Guinea and Chad, international organisations and NGOs pay very close attention to how oil resources are used. But verification is not simple, if only because it infringes on a country's sovereignty and the governments seek to keep the autonomy that hard currency from oil sales gives them.

Will Biofuels Permit Sustainable Development in Africa?

There is reasonable optimism in Africa concerning biofuels. Of particular interest are those based on jatropha, a shrub that is widespread in Sub-Saharan Africa and India, mainly used for hedging or as a medical balm, and highly drought-resistant. Capable of producing seeds for oil manufacture in less than a year and with its maximum production in three to four years, it can be harvested for 30 to 40 years. To date only a small area has been planted but oil has already been produced from it that is being used as an engine fuel. The residues from pressed seeds are also used as fertiliser. Apart from jatropha, other possibilities such as cassava peelings are also being tested.

Taking the initial experience with ethanol and biodiesel further, there is now biofuels production in a number of countries, e.g. Mali, Ethiopia, Kenya, Madagascar, Mauritius, South Africa, Zimbabwe, etc. At the Dakar Summit in 2006 the "Association Africaine des Producteurs de Biocarburants" (Association of African Biofuel Producers) was formed. Many African governments see their choice of a massive development of non-food crops such as jatropha and giving preference to local industries over exports, as the promotion of sustainable development and a contribution to the fight against underdevelopment. Tanzania, which is also developing jatropha, has announced that rural dwellers who practice subsistence farming and avoid monoculture should be guaranteed the right to remain on their land.

EXPLORATION AND PRODUCTION – PLAYERS IN THE GULF OF GUINEA

In many Middle East, Latin America and North African countries, state-owned companies either have a monopoly or at least play an active and determinant role in the upstream oil sector. However, the position is different in Sub-Saharan Africa. Here, the states and the major international oil companies are closely linked and their relationships, which have been forged over several decades, are complex. The national origin of the company in question is important in this relationship and can be a legacy of the colonial period.

- **Country-by-Country Overview**

In Nigeria, about 95 per cent of crude oil is produced by joint ventures (JVs), i.e. partnerships between the state-owned company NNPC (Nigeria National Petroleum Corporation) and foreign companies, the foreign companies being the operators in nearly all cases. The main JV, operated by Shell with NNPC holding a 55 per cent stake (and with Total and AGIP participation), produces nearly half of the country's crude oil. In other JVs (where the operators are ExxonMobil, Chevron, ENI/Agip and Total), NNPC has a 60 per cent equity. In a JV, each partner (i.e. NNPC and the foreign company) pays the proportion equivalent to his equity stake of the JV's costs. More recently the government has replaced JVs by Production Sharing Contracts (PSCs) for new exploration and production contracts. In PSCs all exploration and, if oil is produced, production costs are borne by the foreign company, which is paid for the costs it has incurred and its share of profit by a part of the production if the project is successful.

In Angola, the upstream oil sector is subject to the provisions of the 1978 hydrocarbon act. That makes the national company Sonangol the only company permitted to undertake the exploration and production of hydrocarbons. Sonangol, like NNPC, forms joint venture partnerships with foreign companies or, more frequently, arranges for a foreign company to make the investment and undertake the exploration and production work under Production Sharing Contracts (PSCs). The main overseas companies active in Angola are:

- Chevron, through its subsidiary Cabinda Gulf Oil Company is the operator for most of Cabinda's production, in partnership with Sonangol, Agip and Total.
- ExxonMobil, in partnership with BP, Agip and Norwegian interests, is the operator for a deep offshore block in which significant discoveries have recently been made.
- Total is the operator for another deep offshore block, in partnership with ExxonMobil, BP, and Statoil. A number of discoveries have been made in this block since 1996.

Total, which acquired Elf's assets, is the main operator in Congo-Brazzaville, with Agip, who have been there since the 1960s, in second place. Total operates here mainly in partnership with Chevron, Energy Africa (Engen—South Africa) and SNPC (Société Nationale des Pétroles du Congo), the state-owned company. Agip is also in partnership with Chevron and SNPC. Although Shell, ExxonMobil and BP only have very limited interests here, smaller companies—many of them North American like the very enterprising company Marathon, who also have a strong presence in Equatorial Guinea, or Anadarko—have recently made large investments in offshore Congo.

In Gabon, the two main operators are still Shell and Total, who have been operating there since the start of Gabonese production. But to an even greater extent than in the Congo, most companies making upstream investments are now small non-government owned companies like Amerada Hess, which is already producing. The largest oil producer in Gabon is now the independent company Addax (bought by SINOPEC in 2009). On three exploration blocks Agip, historically the number three operator in Gabon, has a joint venture with the Malaysian State-owned company Petronas, who are very active in the sector.

In Equatorial Guinea, the first discovery, and later the first production, was made by the Spanish firm Cepsa. This field (Alba) produces about one million tons p.a. of a very light oil known as a condensate; it is now owned by Marathon Oil and two small independent US companies (Noble Affiliates and Globex International). The largest field, Zafiro, is operated by ExxonMobil whose partner is Ocean Energy, an independent US company. The third large field, Ceiba, is now operated by Hess.

EXPLORATION AND PRODUCTION – PLAYERS IN THE EAST

- **Country-by-Country Overview**

Mozambique is a gas rich country which has key global oil and gas players like Statoil, ONGC, Petronas, Anadarko, Tullow and ENI who also are the main participants in the Offshore Rovuma basin. The estimated discovered natural gas is nearly 100 Tcf in Mozambique. Also, the gas reserves in Mozambique make it the third largest gas reserves holder in Africa after Nigeria and Algeria. Eni which operates in Area 4 with estimated recoverable gas resources of 85 tcf has partnered with Anadarko to develop a two train LNG facility with an annual capacity of six million tons. The final decision on the LNG project has been made in 2017 and the costs are anticipated between $15 billion and $17 billion. As an alternative market for the gas, the government is also considering a pipeline from Rovuma to Gauteng in South Africa which can distribute gas locally in Mozambique before the final delivery to South Africa.

Tanzania has evolved as an important country of the east with substantial gas reserves and presence of some International companies like Shell, Statoil, Petrobas, ExxonMobil, Ophir and Mubadala Petroleum. After a series of offshore natural gas discoveries in the southeastern coast, the country's reserves are now at 55 tcf. This makes Tanzania the second most prominent natural gas market in the east after Mozambique. The future of the gas lies in the development of LNG terminal for the export of the gas for which an agreement was made between the Tanzanian Petroleum Development Corporation and International Oil Companies operating in Tanzania.

Kenya on the other side is not producing any oil currently, but, the lead operator of the country, Tullow Oil, submitted a Field Development Plan to the government in December 2015 to develop nine fields in the South Lokichar basin from which the expected production is between 60,000 bbl/d to 100,000 bbl/d. The final investment decision depends on the finalisation of the export route through a pipeline whose development is not clear because the pipeline is planned from Uganda's oil-rich Albertine Graben area to Kenya's Lamu Port as agreed between Uganda and Kenya in the August 2015 bilateral talks. However, Uganda in October 2015 expressed interest to potentially develop a pipeline with Tanzania which will reach Tanga, a port city in Tanzania. Total, which is a lead operator in Uganda, supports the pipeline to Tanzania. While on the other hand, Tullow's project is highly favourable towards the Uganda-Kenya pipeline. This is a classic example of conflict of interest arising due to geopolitics. The construction of the pipeline between Uganda and Tanzania started in 2017.

– Various Types of Players

There are three distinct categories of upstream players in Africa.

First, the government-owned companies. These companies have existed in different forms and have experienced different levels of success. Nigeria's NNPC has experienced great difficulties in financing its share of joint ventures' investment and now prefers production sharing contracts. The position is the same in the Congo where SNPC, which has replaced Hydrocongo, also favours PSCs. In Angola, Sonangol is an active partner in the joint ventures but with limited financial commitments. The youngest national company was created in Gabon (Gabon National Oil Company) a few years ago.

Second, the major international companies: ExxonMobil, has a strong presence in Nigeria, Angola and Equatorial Guinea thanks to its former Mobil interests. Shell is the operator for a major portion of production in Nigeria and Gabon, while Chevron is the leading producer in Angola, and well established in Nigeria and Congo Brazzaville. Total is active in all the countries except Equatorial Guinea, and is a leading player in Angola, Congo and even Gabon. Agip is very active in all countries. Only BP[6] seems to lack interest in the region, apart from its significant presence in Angola.

Total's position obviously owes much to Elf's investments in the past. But Elf's privatisation in 1994 and its takeover by TotalFina in 1999 had profound consequences for the company's position and role in the region. Before its privatisation Elf's activities were aligned to the way in which France's African policy had developed. After 1994, Elf and subsequently Total, largely refocused its policies in its commercial interests and assessed this in relation to the international competitive scene in which, as a non-government owned company, it is a stakeholder.

Because Total's positions are increasingly distancing themselves from the French government's strategic and diplomatic interests, the company's centres of interest in Sub-Saharan Africa are being gradually, but significantly, shifted from the francophone area (mainly Gabon and Congo) to the two flagship oil countries, Nigeria and Angola. That is in line with Total's strategy of focusing its activities where it can best compete with the other international players. In those two countries, the most powerful companies, the majors, are in competition for exploration and production contracts. In this worldwide competitive framework, each company's strength is increasingly a function of its financial capacity (which was the raison d'être for the mega-mergers in the petroleum industry at the end of the 1990s) and its technical know-how.

Third the so-called "independent" companies. Their size varies considerably but they are all much smaller than the majors. Their positioning policies are tightly targeted. The Gulf of Guinea is full of opportunities for these small independent companies seeking geographical diversification, firstly, because offshore exploration is still in a very early stage and the reserves as yet undiscovered are thought to be abundant; secondly, all the governments in the region are particularly well disposed to foreign investors, regardless of their size.

Because the capital strength of the "independents" is so much smaller than that of the majors, the former can only compete with the latter by pursuing niche policies. There are two of these. The first is to follow the example of a strategy used in the North Sea, by re-launching exploration or production in marginal fields or in a zone that has reached maturity and which the majors have abandoned. The second involves a much greater risk but also offers the potential of a greater profit: it is to pioneer exploration in untried areas. The way in which the offshore areas around the Gulf of Guinea have been developed is the best example of the independent companies' new strategies and the way in which roles are shared between the majors, who focus on the highest-growth countries (Nigeria, Angola, or even the Congo), while the independents operate in the other countries (e.g. Cameroon and Gabon), including those where, up to now, there has been virtually no production.

Heritage and Tullow have now succeeded in establishing themselves as key players in the regional oil game, without trying to compete directly with the large companies. Because companies in these two categories do not target the same markets or the same sectors of activity, they do not compete directly with each other.

The history of the oil exploitation consortium in Chad is a perfect example of how the way of dealing with the challenges of upstream oil has developed over the past 50 years. Oil was discovered at the beginning of the 1970s and a consortium that included three US companies (Conoco, Exxon and Chevron)

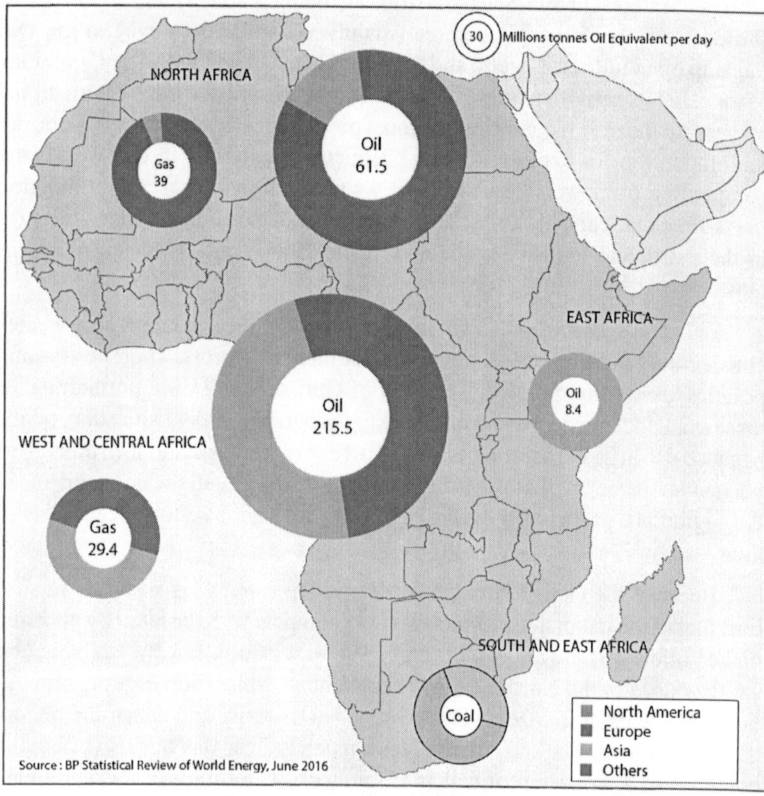

Figure 70: Destination of African Energy Exports – 2015.

and Shell was formed to develop it. War then broke out in 1979 and the project was abandoned. In 1981, Conoco, the project's operator, withdrew and Exxon took over; Chevron sold their share to Elf Aquitaine in 1993 (after Idriss Déby, who regarded France more favourably than his predecessor Hissène Habré, came to power), Shell and Elf then withdrew from the project in 1999 (officially due to its lack of profitability) and Petronas, the Malaysian state-owned company, and Chevron, bought their stakes in 2000. Recently Société des Hydrocarbures du Tchad bought the Chevron 25 per cent participation in the Doba fields (Exxon has 40 per cent and Petronas 35 per cent) thanks to a loan of one billion dollars from Glencore, one of the largest trading companies.

Petronas is also in Equatorial Guinea and Sudan, and PetroChina is also in the latter.

AFRICAN NATIONS IN OIL GLOBALISATION

In their relationships with oil companies, African nations have one substantial power: their sovereign right to control access to their oil. When prices are low or moderate, i.e. the period to the end of the 1990s, this power is reduced as liberal economic standards are imposed that give priority to the opening of borders as a means to economic development. In addition, oil producing African nations have very high levels of debt. Access to international capital markets is vital to finance the development of oil resources but, in many cases, is only open to oil companies whose credit in these markets is beyond question.

• Africa: A Very Attractive Zone that Gives Rise to Strong Rivalry between Consuming Nations[7]

African reserves are among the most accessible for Western oil companies. The other main producing regions (the Middle East, Venezuela, Mexico, Russia, etc.) are either closed to foreign investors, or open but under conditions that are often far less advantageous than in Sub-Saharan Africa. For these reasons, the Gulf of Guinea, together with the Caspian, has become a key region in the geopolitical oil game in the twenty-first century, and a central pillar in the development strategies of every major multinational oil company. That is why the Gulf of Guinea accounts for some 15 per cent of Shell's upstream activities (mainly in Nigeria), 30 per cent of Total's (in Angola, Nigeria and the francophone countries) and 35 per cent of Chevron's (in Angola and Nigeria). Although, historically ExxonMobil have been less involved in this region that others regarded as an "exclusive preserve", they have now invested substantially. They already have a strong presence in Nigeria and have seen a substantial increase in their African production.

The Chinese government and Chinese companies are also very active. Beijing's leaders visited nearly half of the countries in Africa, including Egypt, Nigeria, Angola, etc. The Chinese presence is especially strong in Sudan. CNPC is the main actor in the country. However, the political situation has reduced the amount of oil available. Chinese companies are also trying to increase their production in Nigeria and Angola.

- **The Increasing Power of Civic Society: the Shell Nigeria Case**

With the end of the period of "exclusive preserves", increasingly open competition and the rapid growth of offshore production, the economic environment of African oil has changed profoundly in recent years. Another major trend since the mid-1990s has posed a challenge to the balance of power between governments and oil companies: the growth in the power and influence of civil society at both a local and trans-national level. In parallel with the process of globalisation, an increasing number of NGOs are mobilising to raise ethical issues concerning the oil industry and forcing companies to engage in dialogue on them. The case of Shell in Nigeria is an excellent example that illustrates this new balance of power between oil companies and representatives of civil society.

In Nigeria, Shell is older than the state itself. Shell's presence in the country goes back to 1937, when the company (in association with BP) was granted exclusive exploration rights by the colonial government. Today, Shell is no longer in a hegemonic position, but nonetheless still accounts for nearly 50 per cent of national production. Its long history in the country and the concentration of its activities in one of the most densely populated regions of Africa helped to develop a very close relationship between Shell and the local communities. For the inhabitants of the delta, the company symbolises the entire oil industry.

At the end of the 1980s, ethnic separatist organisations were flourishing in Nigeria, particularly in the Niger delta. They claimed to be political and ecological movements; fighting for regional autonomy and the protection of local cultures; denouncing the injustice of the way in which oil revenues were distributed on the grounds that local inhabitants did not receive their fair share, and the environmental damage caused by oil production. Among these movements, MOSOP (Movement for Survival of Ogoni People)[8] was the first to articulate these aims, no longer confining them to the issue of redistributing revenue from the centre to the producing region but also raising the environmental impact of oil production and, in that context, demanding significant financial compensation not only from the Federal government but also from the oil companies (Shell, Chevron and NNPC). Under the impetus of the writer Ken Saro-Wiwa, MOSOP became a mass movement, like the American civil rights movement. It quickly became well-established locally and went on to form close relationships with other "oil-related" ethnic groups in the region, with opposition parties at the federal level and, particularly importantly, with intellectual, political and media circles abroad.

This gave the political and ecological campaign waged by MOSOP against Shell an international voice involving large trans-national NGOs such as Greenpeace and Human Rights Watch. In the field, acts of violence against Shell (sabotaged pipelines, machine-gunned vehicles, physical attacks against expatriate or Nigerian personnel, etc.) became so commonplace that, in January 1993, the company decided to withdraw from the Ogoni region and close its facilities there. They have not been re-opened since. This decision, unprecedented in its scope, hardened the position of the Nigerian authorities, who sent the army to surround the Ogoni territory and increased repression against MOSOP leaders. Ken Saro-Wiwa was arrested and sentenced to death in 1995. That provoked intense international concern, both diplomatic and in the media, aimed not only at the government of General Abacha that was in power at the time, but also at Shell who were accused of, at least passive, complicity.[9]

The conviction and execution of Ken Saro-Wiwa took place at a very bad time for Shell who was already targeted by environmental activists in Europe regarding the Brent Spar platform[10]. The combination of the two events (Nigeria and Brent Spar) had a devastating effect on the oil company's image in the eyes of the public, including its customers and its own employees. It was also the determining factor in making Shell's management aware of the difficulty of resisting international NGOs organised into networks and having greater credibility in the public's eyes than the company. Having to fight such well coordinated and skillfully managed campaigns at two levels, locally in Nigeria and globally when civic society mobilised internationally around the themes of the protection of human rights and the environment which are by their nature global, was a traumatic shock for Shell. In fact it was a major turning point for them, as in consequence, they adopted a strategy based on the company's ethical commitment. The company also radically changed its communication policy, making the principle of transparency the central pillar of its new corporate culture from then on. However, in 2004, the CEO of Shell had to resign when it was found that the hydrocarbon reserves published in Shell's annual report did not fulfil the criteria required by SEC and the figures had to be reduced.

After the MOSOP, came the Movement for the Emancipation of the Niger Delta (MEND), created in 2006, which succeeded in reducing oil production in Rivers State by several hundred thousand barrels per day. This movement was seeking "total" control of oil money, since the government does not take into consideration the legitimate demands of the people for fair distribution of revenues as well as greater respect for environmental standards.

MEND also took action against the Nigerian Army, which protects foreign oil companies (particularly Chevron and Shell). Several soldiers, and several oil company employees, were killed. MEND had significant resources that enabled it to purchase speedboats and weapons, so it could attack off-shore oil platforms. In September 2008, MEND declared war on oil companies, damaging facilities and kidnapping many company employees on site.

The situation improved after the death of President Umaru Yar'Adua who was replaced by President Goodluck Jonathan, born in this region, who devoted considerable energy to resolve this problem.

In 2015, Goodluck Jonathan was replaced by Mohamed Buhari, a man from the North of Nigeria and the situation deteriorated again. It is estimated that up to 15 per cent of the Nigerian oil production is simply stolen and the militants' actions reduce production at times by 30 or 40 per cent.

Recently a new group, "Nigeria Delta Avengers", attacked and destroyed a number of oil installations. This new movement does not have any support from the MEND which disagrees with these actions.

Niger Delta Militants

Militant groups in the oil-rich Niger Delta region took hold in the early 2000s following the deterioration of the living conditions of people due to the increase of oil-related activities by foreign exploration corporations. Tensions flared up in the local communities as some ethnic groups felt they were being exploited and did not benefit from the presence of crude oil on their land.

The repeated oil spills that considerably damaged the environment and affected people's health further deepened the communities' frustration. After being elected in 2015, Buhari extended a 2009 amnesty granted to some 30,000 former militants in the area.

- **Oil – the Problem of Financial Transparency**

In Angola, oil's second flagship West African country, petroleum is an essential means of integrating the country into the world's economic system, and it is also the key to an understanding of Angola's political system. It was oil that determined the regime's military and political survival in the civil war against UNITA, but oil also gives the government the ability to disconnect itself from the population. Oil revenues free the government from the need to impose taxes on economic activity to raise finance; they also provide the regime with resources they can use for financial redistribution based on political patronage. In Angola, because all production is offshore and so not near populated areas, companies do not have the problems of cohabitation with local people or the ecological difficulties that have arisen in the Niger Delta. However, although the civil war did not stop production growing rapidly, information disclosed through the financial transparency imposed on international oil companies attracted the attention of militant international civic organisations.

In the second half of the 1990s, certain NGOs took an interest in the armed conflict in Angola and publically criticised those who were economic partners of the warring sides, i.e. the rebels and the government. A human rights group called Global Witness[11] published a report, *A Crude Awakening*, in 1999 on the role of the oil revenues paid by international companies in financing the government's war effort. The irony is that before making itself extremely disagreeable to the Angolan government with the accusations in this report, the same NGO had published another report denouncing the impact of diamond trafficking by UNITA on their ability to sustain the armed conflict. At the time, Luanda did not hide its pleasure at seeing its adversary placed in the dock and did all it could to translate this report into action, pushing the international community to declare an embargo on UNITA diamonds.

However, the importance of the publication of the British NGO's report had more to do with its media impact than the investigation's revelations. The rigor of the information, the gravity of the facts denounced and the identity of the incriminated parties (the major oil companies), meant that, *A Crude Awakening,* was distributed far beyond the traditional networks of militant groups. Its wide distribution not only resulted in a series of articles on the issue in the international press[12], but also to it becoming the de facto reference for anything written on Angola, whether published by the IMF, an NGO like Amnesty International, research theses or even articles in the press including specialist oil journals.

Immediately afterwards, Global Witness launched an international campaign called *Publish What You Pay*. Its objective was that the revenues paid to governments by oil companies, i.e. taxes or royalties, delivery of the governments' share of the oil produced should be made transparent by companies publically disclosing this information in their accounts. BP announced its intention to begin meeting this public disclosure requirement in its future annual reports.[13] Recently BP published a report to disclose payments made to the government globally in the year 2015 which was nearly $15 billion.

Finally, the Extractive Industries Transparency Initiative (EITI) also seeks to increase the transparency of revenues paid to producing governments.

CONCLUSION: THE NEW OIL STAKES IN AFRICA

Today, a consensus has been reached on the fact that, although it is not a new Middle East, Africa is already a significant player on the world oil stage and its importance will increase over the medium term. Although it is a much newer oil producer than other major zones such as the US, Russia, the Middle East and South America, Africa has several advantages that should favour its development, particularly in the Sub-Saharan region.

First, technical progress, particularly offshore E&P technology, now makes it easy and economically viable to develop oil fields located off the coast of West Africa, in the Gulf of Guinea or in the territorial waters of Angola. The oil produced is of high quality and the region is also well-positioned to supply the European and US markets.

North Africa (principally Algeria and Libya), mainly because of its location, remains important as a supplier to Europe but, as discussed previously, has many characteristics similar to those of Middle East countries.

The laws applied in most Sub-Saharan African countries, particularly relating to access to oil deposits, and the taxes levied on oil production, are more favourable to foreign investors while, in relative terms, other producing countries remain closed. Oil field development and production is largely undertaken by joint ventures (95 per cent of the production of Nigeria, which is the principal African producer) or through production sharing contracts between a state-owned company and one of the leading majors.

However, these major international companies must now take account of both local and international NGOs acting in areas as diverse as the environment, humanitarian problems, financial transparency and human rights. While action taken by these NGOs does not always lead them to oppose company projects, they have succeeded in making companies work extensively to redefine their relationship with the African political and economic environment.

The cozy relationship between oil companies and governments that marked the colonial period has been replaced by a new one defined by contractual obligations. The balance of power has been changed.

References

1. Biomass is mainly used for cooking. The quantities required could be substantially reduced by the use of improved kilns.
2. African crude oils are typically light, giving good yields of gasoline and diesel fuel, and have low sulfur contents. They are therefore very attractive to refiners, particularly in Europe.
3. However, the high coal consumption of South Africa masks the fact that, in the rest of Africa, oil accounts for nearly 60 per cent of energy consumption (excluding firewood).

4. See Oil Revenues and their Use, in chapter 2.

5. As its name suggests, "Dutch Syndrome" was first observed in the Netherlands in the 1950s and 60s when production from the huge Groningen gas deposit began. Gas exports led to a sudden influx of currency that increased Dutch purchasing power and encouraged imports, yet also increased the cost of labour and decreased the competitiveness of Dutch products. The economic results are similar in many countries where oil revenue is "easy money" that encourages imports to the detriment of local production. Also see Chapter 2.

6. BP has been historically absent from the region since its holdings were nationalised in Nigeria in 1979. This is the only case in history of the nationalisation of a foreign company's oil assets by a government in Sub-Saharan Africa. BP's holdings in Nigeria were nationalised for reasons of foreign policy, in reaction to the British government's support (while the government was a majority shareholder in BP) of the white regime in Rhodesia.

7. Also see Philippe Copinschi, "Stratégie des acteurs sur la scène pétrolière africaine (Golfe de Guinée)" (in French), *Revue de l'Energie*, n°523, January 2001, pp. 33-42.

8. Movement for Survival of Ogoni People founded in October 1990 by a handful of intellectuals to state the claims of the "Ogoni people" regarding the control of oil revenue.

9. As a response to all who denounced its neutral attitude regarding the fate of Ken Saro-Wiwa, in December 1995 the company took out a full page ad in the New York Times explaining: "Some campaigning groups say we should intervene in the political process in Nigeria. But even if we could, we must never do so. Politics is the business of governments and politicians. The world where companies use their economic influence to prop up or bring down governments would be a frightening and bleak one indeed."

10. At the start of 1995, Shell publicly announced its intention to sink the abandoned Brent Spar platform in the deep Atlantic Ocean. Immediately following the announcement, Greenpeace launched an intense media campaign to denounce the project saying, incorrectly, that Shell intended to sink the platform in the North Sea. This was generally believed and Greenpeace's call for a boycott of Shell products was widely followed in Northern Europe, particularly in Germany where sales of fuel in the company's service stations fell by 50 per cent during the period of the crisis covered by the media. Despite Shell's attempts to argue the soundness of its project, after two months of battling Greenpeace, the company had to resign itself to abandoning its project, capitulating against the environmental conservation NGO.

11. Global Witness is an NGO based in London, whose mission is to study the links between the exploitation of natural resources and the infringement of human rights. Its objective is to inform the international public regarding these problems, but also to produce elements (information, proof, etc.) that can be used for lobbying governments and international organisations. The copyright notice in its publications states that the prohibition on reproduction does not apply to "anyone wishing to use them to promote the environment and human rights".

12. Le Monde, the Financial Times, the Economist, etc., who generally see their role as printing a faithful summary of such report's conclusions, effectively acted as loudspeakers for the denouncements it contained.
13. Speaking in February 2005 BP's then CEO said: "We believe that transparency is the best way in which to conduct business, because it is the only possible basis for the development of long-term mutual advantage. That's why we publish what we pay. It's why we have strict rules against bribery and facilitation payments. We have every interest in eradicating corruption because corruption is a business cost. We will continue to publish what we pay and, wherever possible, we will do so on a disaggregated basis. But transparency on one side isn't enough. We need to ensure that "publish what you pay" is matched with the publication of what is spent."

Chapter - 10

Asia Pacific

Asia Pacific can be considered in four major sub-regions:

- The Indian subcontinent comprises Afghanistan, Pakistan, India, Nepal, Bhutan, Bangladesh, Sri Lanka and the Maldives. It has a population of 1.7 billion, or more than 22 per cent of that of the world. The population of India alone is more than 1.3 billion. The background is one of unequal economic development which, coupled with ethnic and religious disputes, is the cause of the high level of tension in the region. The rivalry between India and Pakistan over Kashmir, between India and China for the control of Nepal and Aksai Chin (lost in 1962 by India), and religious conflicts (between Hindus and Muslims in India, and between Christians and Muslims in Sri Lanka) destabilise the region and impede its development.
- Northeast Asia includes China, South Korea, Japan, Mongolia, and Taiwan. It is now Asia's most dynamic region, with 1.5 billion inhabitants, or 20 per cent of the world's population. China, having pursued a liberal and open economic policy since 1978, has become a key player in international trade and in the market for hydrocarbons. The other countries, e.g. Japan and South Korea, are developed market economy countries but are totally dependent on foreign countries for their energy supplies. Finally, this region includes Mongolia, whose energy significance remains very limited, North Korea (Democratic People's Republic of Korea) for which no reliable official statistics are published, and Taiwan, in latent conflict with the People's Republic of China.
- Southeast Asia includes Thailand, Laos, Cambodia, Vietnam, Myanmar (Burma), Malaysia, the Philippines, Brunei, Singapore and Indonesia. These are emerging countries which, at the start of

the 1990s, experienced rapid growth but, since the 1997–1998 financial crisis, have seen that growth slow. Indonesia, Malaysia, and to a lesser extent Vietnam and Brunei, are significant oil producers. Indonesia, the region's most important player, suspended its OPEC membership in the year 2009 since 2003, Indonesian demand has exceeded its crude oil production.

– The final sub-region, Oceania, is made up of Australia, New Zealand and New Guinea. Only Australia is important in energy geopolitics because of its coal and gas reserves.

The Asian continent alone has 55 per cent of the world's population, or slightly less than 4.5 billion inhabitants. The size of the Chinese and Indian populations means that these two countries dominate the region (Fig. 71).

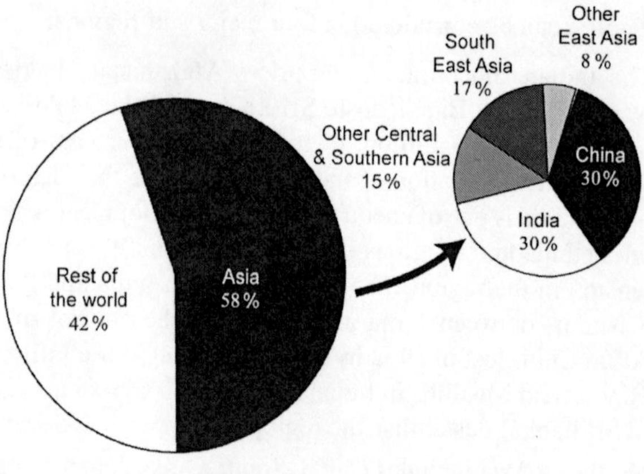

Figure 71: Breakdown of World Population.

An important characteristic of the region is the very strong economic growth that its countries (China, India, Taiwan, Indonesia, etc.) have achieved. As a result, there has been a large and sustained increase in energy demand. Asia has substantial coal reserves but few other energy resources, i.e. hardly 2.4 per cent of world oil reserves and 8.3 per cent of gas reserves (Fig. 72).

OIL

• Reserves and Production

Asia only has small reserves of oil, amounting to 2.4 per cent of the world total and mainly located in Northeast Asia. China is the only country with significant reserves, which are estimated at 18.5 billion barrels or 43 per cent of total Asia Pacific reserves. The two largest Chinese oil fields, *Daqing* and *Liaohe*, in the northeast of the country, yield a large proportion of Chinese production but they are now in decline. Daqing which currently accounts for 16 per cent of the total production of China once accounted for 35 per cent of the domestic production at its peak in the year 1999 but due to the recent slump in the oil price the field is barely economic.

Promising new fields have been discovered in the autonomous region of Xinjiang, in the west of China, which should increase that region's share of

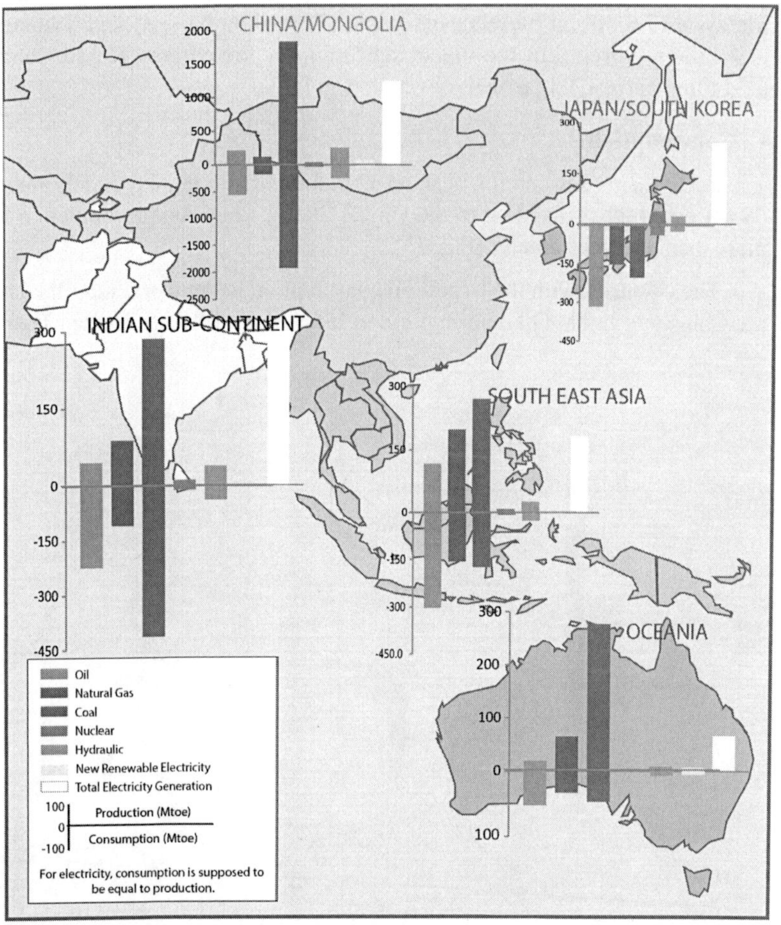

Source: BP Statistical Review, 2016 and doe/eia.

Figure 72: Asian 2015 Energy Balance.

China's proved oil and gas reserves to about a third. However, at present only some of these fields are in production, firstly, because Xinjiang is remote from the eastern coastal provinces which are the main areas of oil consumption, and secondly, because an Uighur separatist movement has been confronting the Chinese government with a demand for an independent state, "East Turkestan", since 1979. The vigour with which this movement is being repressed by China is at least partially due to the geostrategic interest given to this territory by the discovery of the oil. Additionally, China discovered over 100 million tonnes of tight oil in the Changqing field in 2015 which is the largest tight oil discovery in China till date.

Southeast Asian reserves total about 16 billion barrels, mainly located in Malaysia (3.6 billion barrels), Indonesia (3.6 billion barrels) and Vietnam (4.4 billion barrels). In the Indian subcontinent proved reserves are some 6.2 billion barrels, 93 per cent of which is in India.

- **Consumption**

Total Asian consumption of about 32 million barrels per day is only about 68 per cent higher than that of the United States, while Asia's population is more than ten times greater (Fig. 73).

The countries with the largest oil consumption in the world after the US are China and India. Oil consumption in India at 4.2 Mb/d surpassed Japan

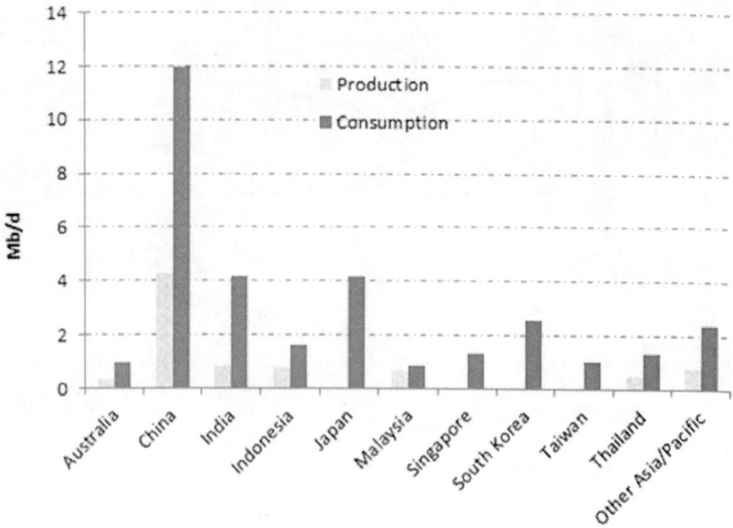

Source: BP Statistical Review, 2016.

Figure 73: Oil production and consumption in Asia Pacific in 2015.

for the first time in the year 2015. Chinese demand, currently over 12 million barrels per day, is growing quickly despite the economic slowdown.

Japanese consumption, on the other hand, has fallen from 5.3 million barrels per day in the year 2005 to 4.1 million barrels per day while India's consumption increased from 2.6 to 4.2 million barrels per day during the same period. All Japan's oil requirements are imported, mainly from the Middle East and Russia while India imports mainly from Middle East, West Africa and Latin America.

India's position is similar to China's in that it has experienced strong and stable economic growth for several years, making for a significant increase in oil demand in the years to come (Fig. 74). However India's energy consumption remains far below that of China.

South Korea is the region's other major oil consuming country with nearly 2.5 million barrels per day consumption.

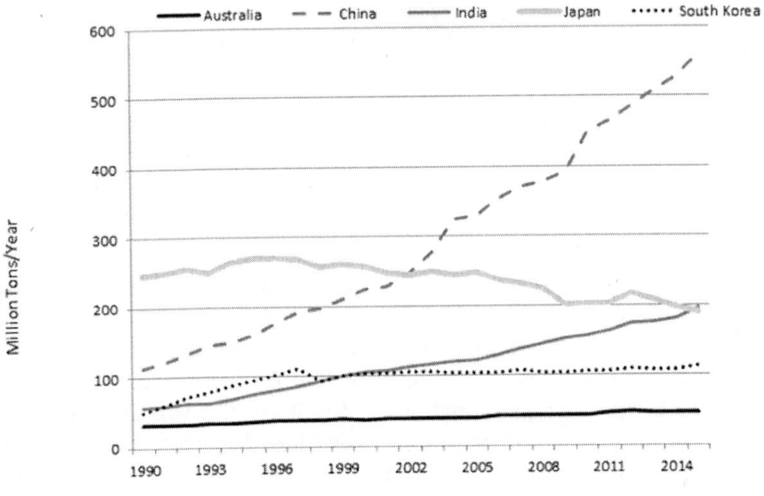

Source: BP Statistical Review, 2016.

Figure 74: Oil Consumption in Certain Asian Countries.

- **Oil Imports Constantly Increasing**

Compared with this demand, Asia's oil production is limited. It is currently some 8.3 million barrels per day. Only Brunei (a small emirate) is a net exporter. Japan and South Korea have virtually no hydrocarbon resources. China and India's production covers an increasingly small proportion of their consumption and their import requirements will grow substantially over the next few years.

In total, Asia currently imports some 24 million barrels per day, 60 per cent of which comes from the Middle East. Imports from West Africa and Russia are increasing, which provides for some diversification of supplies and so increases supply security. In the recent years, the US has drastically reduced its imports from West Africa and therefore a major part of the Nigerian exports left after exporting to Europe is supplied to Asian countries.

Different countries in Asia that have sought to limit the risk of supply disruptions as much as possible, have adopted a wide range of differing solutions. Japan, which has been the leading oil importer in Asia for many years, relies on international companies for its supplies, but has also developed close relationships with several individual countries (Saudi Arabia, Kuwait, Iran, etc.). China's policy is to diversify widely, so they have established a strong presence in Sudan, and there have been visits by the Chinese President to a number of producing countries in North and West Africa. India has strong diplomatic hold in the Middle East especially with Iran which is a major oil supplier to India. Nigeria in West Africa and Venezuela in Latin America have become major suppliers in the recent years.

The Middle East was China's top oil supplier in 2015 with 50 per cent of their imports, against West Africa's 16 per cent and Russia's and Latin America's 13 per cent. In Latin America, China has secured oil supplies from Venezuela and Ecuador in exchange of loans. China has lent $ 65 billion to Venezuela.

NATURAL GAS

Asian gas reserves are only eight per cent of the world's total. Historically, Japan was the first country in Asia to use fair amounts of gas, with other nations insufficiently developed to be able to construct the costly distribution infrastructure needed for gas. But, more recently, natural gas consumption in China has grown rapidly from about 40 Mtoe in the year 2005 to nearly 180 Mtoe in the year 2015, which has made China the largest consumer in the region. Natural gas consumption is also developing quickly in other Asian countries, particularly India, Bangladesh and Indonesia, principally for electricity generation. Total demand in Asia has increased seven-fold since 1980 and will continue to increase (Fig. 75 and 76).

While China is importing fair amount of gas by pipeline from Central Asia, most other gas-consuming Asian countries import liquefied natural gas (LNG); and these imports amount to 70 per cent of worldwide LNG trade. China produces 70 per cent of its demand, and the biggest importers are Japan, and South Korea. All their imports are made as LNG, 30 per cent of them are from the Middle East, where Qatar is their largest exporter, but Malaysia, Indonesia and Australia are also important suppliers.

China has the potential to produce and consume much more in the future. The role of natural gas in the country's energy mix remains low due to the availability of cheap coal locally. China has already announced plans for the development of the natural gas industry but with the recent slowdown in the economic growth of the country, it will be difficult to invest in the exploration, production and development of the infrastructure required for gas import and distribution.

For the supply side, the domestic production has increased from 51 bcm to 138 bcm from 2005 to 2015 which is a 170 per cent increase and the natural gas imports which were nil till 2006 increased from one bcm to nearly 60 bcm in 2015 with pipeline accounting for 56 per cent of the imports and the rest by LNG.

Turkmenistan is the major gas exporter to China through pipeline with exports of 28 bcm in 2015. Central Asian natural gas from Turkmenistan is transported to China through three pipelines. Another one is expected to come onstream by 2020 which will boost the combined transportation capacity of the lines to 65 bcm per year. Also, in 2014, China signed a 30 year, deal with Russia to secure a supply of 38 bcm annually through a new pipeline deal valued at $400 billion which is due for completion in 2018 but the recent slump in the oil price and slowdown in China may result in the reduction of the size of the project as the gas contracts are linked to the oil prices.

China has 13 operational LNG terminals with a combined capacity of 54.5 bcm, the largest being the Guangdong Dapeng LNG terminal in the Guangdong. However, the LNG terminals operate significantly below their capacity mainly because the internal pipeline network in China is controlled by the state companies and no third party access is allowed. China currently imports 27 per cent of LNG from Australia, 25 per cent from Qatar, 17 per cent from Indonesia and around 15 per cent from Malaysia. Australia has surpassed Qatar as a major LNG supplier to China.

Australia: An emerging regional LNG supplier

Australia has 123 Tcf of natural gas reserves. The domestic consumption is about half of the production and Australia has developed LNG terminals to export the gas. There are three LNG facilities which are currently operational and seven are under development. Australia is expected to be the world's largest LNG exporter by 2018 with an aggregate capacity of 86 mtpa. A majority of these exports will be to the Asian importers under long-term contracts with their price linked to the oil price.

However, huge cost overruns on the projects under development and the low crude prices to which LNG prices are linked have posed a big question on the economics of the projects under development. Additionally, a number of other factors can affect the Asia Pacific LNG market in the next few years because the US is on track to export potentially 60 million tonnes of LNG by year 2020 with the rapid development of their LNG export terminals. Many Asian importers have already started negotiations with the US LNG exporters. In fact, with the development of the US LNG export market, spot LNG cargoes are expected to be available because of the global competition among the LNG suppliers and many Asian importers might avoid signing long-term contracts with the Australian exporters since they could get better prices through other deals.

Therefore, the Asia Pacific LNG market will be more competitive than ever in the near future with very low marginal cost producers like the US entering the market.

Although no deal has been signed with the US, China has expressed interest in importing LNG from US in the future.[1]

India's natural gas consumption has increased from 36 bcm in 2005 to nearly 51 bcm now which is a 42 per cent increase while the production has remained flat at 29 bcm despite a major gas discovery offshore the southeast coast of India. Nearly 75 per cent domestic natural production comes from the national oil companies because the gas prices are regulated and the government has indexed the gas prices to the gas prices in the international market which are already quite low. So the gas regime is unattractive for the domestic and foreign investors and this is a challenge even for the development of the new discoveries in the eastern and western offshore.

The current gas deficit is fulfilled by LNG imports and therefore LNG has a critical role in the Indian natural gas market. There are four active and operational terminals Dahej (10 Mtpa), Hazira (5 Mtpa), Dabhol (5 Mtpa) and Kochi (5 Mtpa) with a combined capacity of 25 Mtpa in India. During 2010–2015, the LNG imports increased at an average rate of 11.1 per cent to 21.7 bcm and the market share of LNG in the domestic gas supply increased from 20 per cent to nearly 40 per cent during the same period. There are two additional LNG terminals which are proposed and four under planning stage. The development of these terminals will depend on the policy framework, transportation infrastructure and a growing gas market in India. The government has no control over the prices for LNG import and the prices are fixed based on the contract between the importer and supplier. For instance, Petronet LNG imports 7.5 Mtpa on a long-term contract with price linked to the price of oil.

Coal is the key driver of energy in India but with focus on low carbon emissions, the gas sector is expected to get a push from the government and the demand is likely to double in the next 10 to 15 years, thereby making India the top importer of LNG after Japan alongside of China.

Bangladesh, one of India's neighbours, also has substantial gas reserves.

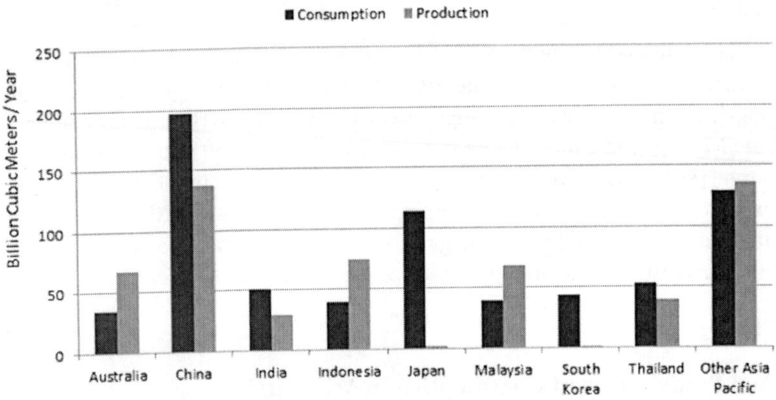

Source: BP Statistical Review, 2016.

Figure 75: Natural Gas Production and Consumption in Asia.

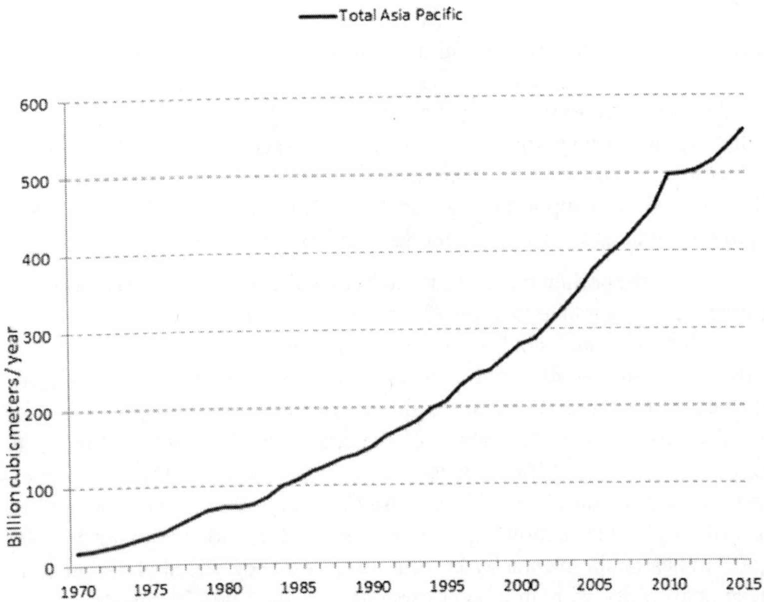

Source: BP Statistical Review, 2016.

Figure 76: Natural Gas Consumption in Asia.

Private companies estimate that these resources are even greater than the official figures. An agreement between the two countries for the export of natural gas from Bangladesh to India could be beneficial to both of them but their mutual relations are poor.

Natural gas transport by pipeline between Asian countries is currently limited to 31 billion cubic meters p.a., from Indonesia to Malaysia and Singapore, from Malaysia to Singapore, from Myanmar (Burma) to Thailand, from Myanmar to China. There is also a 4,000 km (2,500 miles) gas pipeline to transport the gas from the Xianjiang autonomous Western China region to the regions in the east where demand is high, commissioned at the end of 2004. An additional line bringing gas to China from central Asia (Turkmenistan and Kazakhstan) came into operation at the end of 2009.

COAL

Coal Production and Consumption in Asia Pacific

Asia Pacific reserves total 288 billion tons of coal (138 billion toe), or nearly one-third of total world reserves. They are concentrated in three countries: China with 115 billion tons, Australia with 76 billion tons and India with 61 billion (Fig. 77).

Its low production cost means that coal is still the basic energy source for many countries in this region and that, on an average, it accounts for a large fraction of total primary energy consumption. China is both the largest producer and the largest consumer of coal in the world, ahead of the United States. Chinese coal consumption is 1.9 billion toe, 50 per cent of total world demand and 64 per cent of China's primary energy consumption. In the past 10 years, Chinese coal consumption has grown by 134 per cent, to fuel the country's rapid economic growth and continuously increasing demand for electricity.

Despite the pollution that is caused by coal use, Chinese internal demand is expected to continue to grow. Technological process will probably limit coal pollution. China's coal consumption will continue to grow through 2025 before a decline is witnessed as a result of implementation of the climate change policies[2]. By 2040, the share of coal in the global energy mix is expected to fall to 46 per cent. As a result of the economic slowdown and reduced demand, China closed 1000 mines in 2016 out of the 10,760. This is part of the new policy by the National Energy Administration to eradicate 500 million tons of surplus production capacity in the next three to five years. In fact, 5,600 mines could eventually be shut under a policy which is designed to close coal mines with an annual capacity less than 90,000 tonnes but the timeline for implementation is unclear.[3]

India's consumption is more than 407 million toe of coal per year, which is more than half of its primary energy demand. As in most neighbouring countries, coal is mainly used for electricity generation. India is the world's third leading coal consumer, behind China and the US, and fourth largest producer (also behind Australia). As per IEA forecast, India will account for nearly one-half of the increase in coal consumption in the world from 2012–2040. India surpassed US as the second largest consumer of coal in the world after China in 2015. The coal industry in India is mainly dominated by Coal India Limited a public sector company and India plans to increase its production capacity to 1500 million tons annually by 2020 for which CIL alone will have to increase its capacity by 400 million tons in five years. Private mining in India was permitted from 1993 with certain regulations for the trade in place and 200 blocks were offered to private players. Most of the private licenses were cancelled in the year 2014 because of non-transparent allocation of coal blocks. In March 2015, the government passed a special provision bill for coal mines which allows the private and foreign investors to enter the commercial mining with resale permission. Additionally, the cancelled blocks were reallocated through electronic auction, which is considered a fair and transparent way to allocate licenses.

Japan is the world's fourth-largest coal consumer (roughly 119 million toe in 2015) but has only very small reserves. Its domestic production is not competitive and its last mine closed in January 2002. That made Japan the world's largest coal importer, its supplies make up a quarter of the world's internationally traded coal. Australia is the principal supplier, furnishing about 70 per cent of the total, other traditional suppliers are the US, Canada, and South Africa, but recently coal imports have started from China.

Australia's coal reserves are substantial. It has been the world's leading coal exporter since 1986 and is one of its top producers, behind the US and China. It is the only OECD country that is a net energy exporter (Fig. 77). Most of the coal mines are located along country's east coast. Ninety five per cent of production comes from Queensland and New South Wales; the Bowen basin, containing the country's largest deposit with an estimated 34 billion tons of coal, is in Queensland.

Other Asian coal producers have been faced with a number of problems, e.g. mines have been closed in China for safety reasons and facilities have been damaged by rains in Indonesia; so these factors as well as the increase in coal demand have contributed to the growth in Australian exports.

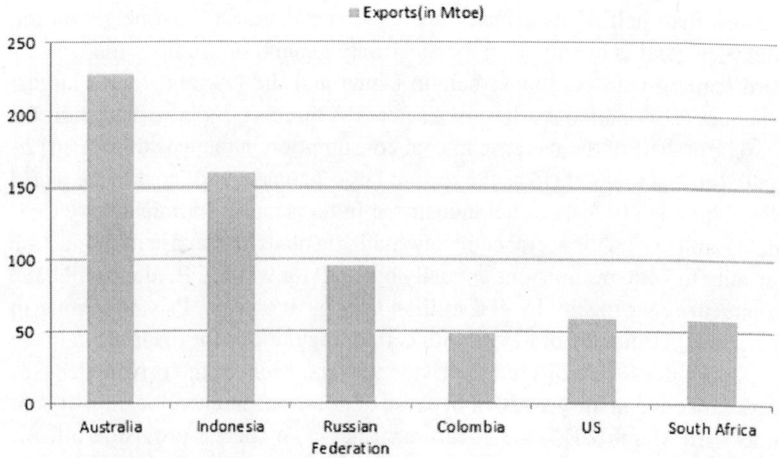

Source: BP Statistical Review, 2016.

Figure 77: Principal World Coal Exporters in 2015.

- **Coal and the Environment**

In China, as in neighboring countries, the advantages of coal in terms of cost and abundance of resources are counterbalanced by the hazards of the pollution resulting from its use, particularly the sulfur dioxide and particulate contamination. According to a report by the World Health Organisation (WHO), seven of the ten most polluted cities in the world are in China. A large proportion of the population suffers from respiratory illnesses caused by these coal combustion emissions. China is now the largest CO_2 emitter in the world.

The threat from this massive use of fossil fuel is clear. The high level of industrial pollution creates a vast brown cloud that covers South Asia from April to October. In Japan, forests on the east coast are withering because of the acid rain caused by the sulfur dioxide emitted by Chinese coal-fired power plants. Depletion of the tropical forests and of arable land in South and Southeast Asia is clearly a major cause of concern. The development of renewable energies will allow a reduction of pollution but due to the size of the demand and the cost of renewable energy, coal will remain an important source of energy.

ELECTRICITY

Electricity demand in Asia is expected to grow at nearly 4 per cent per year until 2020; in China growth will be even higher. In 2013, total electricity generation in Asia was about 10000 TWh, with 75 per cent of it in just three countries: China (5486 TWh—the leading producer in Asia and second in the world), India (1,193 TWh) and Japan (1045 TWh).

Electricity generation in China is mainly in coal-fired thermal plants. However an increasing number of new plants are planned to use nuclear energy, hydroelectricity or natural gas. Coal's share is therefore expected to fall to roughly 70 per cent over the next two decades.

China's hydroelectric potential is enormous and it has been realizing this since the 1990s by the construction of massive projects. The Three Gorges Dam, with a power capacity of 22.5 GW, was completed on May 20, 2006. Other hydroelectric projects are also being developed on Chinese rivers and they could provide more than 40 GW of additional capacity. Once all these projects have commissioned, they could supply more than 10 per cent of Chinese electricity demand.

The Three Gorges Dam

This is a colossal project whose completion was delayed for more than a century. Sun Yat-Sen, the father of the Chinese Republic, first had the idea for a hydroelectric dam on the country's longest river, the Yangtze in 1919. The project was abandoned several times, re-launched in 1980, ratified in 1992 by only two-thirds of the National People's Congress, i.e. nearly one-third of the members abstained or even voted against it, which is a very rare occurrence.

This project is a one that relates to the key geopolitical issues concerning the country. The construction is so enormous (its length is 2300 meters, its height 100 meters, the reservoir covers an area of 650 square kilometers) that it affects not only the region but the whole of China. 1.2 million people have been displaced, more than 100 towns and villages as well as some historic sites flooded. However, it has had real benefits. The dam has decreased the risks of the river flooding, which has caused the deaths of more than 1 million people over the last 100 years, 35,000 in 1954 alone. Next, the river has been improved to make it navigable by vessels of up to 10,000 tons, given them access to the country's interior and so permitting the transport of commercial goods in both directions. The dam also allows China to rebalance its water resources between the south, where there is abundant water, and the north which is much drier. Finally, the 26 generators, with a combined capacity of 22.5 million kilowatts can produce up to 5 per cent of China's electricity demand.

Electricity production from the Three Gorges dam is now close to 100 Twh per year. To generate that electricity thermally would take close to 40 million tons of coal per year.

China has thirty four nuclear reactors with a capacity of nearly 29 GW and there are 20 reactors which are under construction, which on completion will add an additional capacity of 22 GW. China aims to increase the share of nuclear in the electricity generation to six per cent from the present three per cent by 2020. The Chinese nuclear market uses Russian, French and Canadian technology. Lately, China has become self-sufficient in reactor design and construction and also in other aspects of the fuel cycle, but it is using Western technology to improve their domestic nuclear programmes. China aims to go global to export their nuclear technology.

Finally, new renewable energies can be an efficient source of electricity for rural areas. Renewable is one of the fastest growing sectors among the fossil fuel and nuclear sector. China also became the largest producer of photovoltaic power in 2015 with installed capacity of 43 GW and is the leading exporter of photovoltaic panels. China aims to have 100 GW of wind power capacity by 2020. China also has the world's largest wind farm i.e. the Gansu wind farm in the Gansu province of China with a current installed capacity of 6,000 MW in 2012 with a target of 20,000 MW in 2020.

India is the third largest electricity producer globally after China and US with a installed capacity of 304.7 GW in 2016 and the gross electricity generation is 1193 TWh of which 28 per cent is renewable and 72 per cent non-renewable. Coal is the principal source of electricity, accounting for 73 per cent, with hydroelectricity providing 16 per cent. There are 21 nuclear reactors with a total capacity of 6.78 GW and production of 30.3 TWh of electricity.

The Indian electricity market is similar to that of its Chinese neighbour in that its growth is strong and there is a deficit in generation capacity. India aims to build energy security by diversifying the supply from coal, hydro, nuclear and gas to significantly expand levels of wind, solar and biomass and therefore the government targets 175 GW of renewables by 2022 and development of micro grids. The key to this transformation is the reduction of the aggregate, technical and commercial losses by 26 per cent and restructuring of the state based distribution companies which have accumulated large debts. Additionally, for the country's ambitious renewable projects plan, access to international finance will be a key. It is important for India to secure sufficient energy by considering the economic growth rate expected to be close to seven percent over the next years.

Electricity generation in Japan is 1,045 TWh, making Japan the world's fourth-ranking producer.

– *A New Indian Nuclear Policy*

The use of nuclear power is currently being expanded in India which has ambitious programmes. India aims to add 14.6 GW capacity by 2024 and 63 GW capacity by 2032 and the country also aims to supply 25 per cent of the electricity from nuclear power by 2050 which currently is just 1.2 per cent. The nuclear development in India has been a result of the cooperation agreement with the United States, signed in 2005 between the Indian Prime Minister Manmohan Singh and President George W. Bush. The agreement authorised India to acquire civil nuclear power technology and uranium as nuclear fuel from international sources. In return India agreed to open its civil nuclear generating sites to the International Atomic Energy Agency (IAEA). The final obstacle was the need for approval from the Nuclear Suppliers Group (group of 45 countries whose goal is to reduce nuclear proliferation), which was achieved as well. India, despite possessing nuclear arms, is therefore exempt from the rules of the world's non-proliferation treaty and can benefit from civil nuclear technology transfer. This decision represented a diplomatic victory for the Bush administration and provides significant opportunities for the sale of nuclear power plants for a number of countries. During the 34 years sanction on civil nuclear trade, India has uniquely been developing a thorium nuclear cycle to exploit its reserves of thorium and the commercial application is in the very nascent stage. India has a vision to become the world leader in nuclear technology because of its expertise in fast reactors and thorium fuel cycle.

– *The Mekong River: Rivalries for a Substantial Regional Energy Source*

The Mekong River (4,200 km or 2,600 miles long) ranks eighth in the world and third in Asia in terms of its flow (475 million m^3 p.a.). However, despite the bountiful potential of nature's gift, the river and its many tributaries remain little exploited.

One of the main advantages the region could gain from development of the Mekong is energy supply. The river's hydroelectric potential is enormous and electricity could be provided to many countries, while others, such as Laos, could gain substantial revenues.

But there are several obstacles that prevent the realisation of this potential. Firstly, the river is shared between six countries. Its source is in China, it is the frontier between Laos and Burma, then between Laos and Thailand. Next it crosses Cambodia, and finally reaches the South China Sea via the Mekong Delta in Vietnam. It is not easy to find an agreement that will satisfy so many countries, especially since there are still tensions between some of them. There were border conflict between Laos and Thailand in July 2000 over the islands of the upper Mekong. Before the problem was resolved by an agreement in 2001, China had increased the number of dams in the Yunnan region to twenty four, with nine under construction, on the Mekong itself; and was considering a project to use the water over its entire territory. Unilateral initiatives of that nature militate against the optimal exploitation of the river system, which can only be achieved by close cooperation between all the governments concerned.

NGOs, concerned for the environment and the protection of human rights, often oppose the construction of dams and hydroelectric plant. They believe that such projects can damage the environment and harm the living conditions of millions of people.

However, the Nam Thuen II dam built in Laos on the Thuen tributary with a capacity of 1,070 MW was inaugurated in April 2010. This dam is highly controversial but the sale of hydroelectric power to Thailand is already Laos' leading source of revenue (with Thailand re-exporting electricity to Laotian cities which are remote from the Vientiane valley) and it is anticipated that 90 per cent of the dam's production would be sold to Bangkok. In 2005, the World Bank reversed its previous decision and agreed to finance part of the construction costs of this dam. A new cooperation called the The Lancang-Mekong River cooperation was established which is a new sub-regional cooperation platform discussed, constructed and shared by the six countries. All countries are equal and uphold principles of consensus, equality, mutual benefit and others. The countries jointly plan cooperation according to the actual situation and need.

The Lancang-Mekong River cooperation sticks to the pragmatic cooperation orientation, adopting government guidance, multi-participation and project-based models to fully mobilise all resources of governments, industries and people and jointly promote the implementation.[4]

AGRO-FUELS AND GEOTHERMAL ENERGY IN ASIA

Although the use of ethanol and biodiesel is still marginal in Asia, its rate of growth is accelerating. China is making up for lost time and is now the world's third largest ethanol producer. Malaysia and Indonesia, as leaders in palm oil production (with all the environmental consequences that are so widely discussed) are concentrating more on biodiesel; their objective is the substitution of 10 per cent of demand for conventional fuel over the medium term.

Indonesia and the Philippines: Development of Geothermal Energy

The Philippines, the world's second producer of geothermal energy, has a target of increasing geothermal electricity capacity to 2.5 MW by 2020 from the current capacity of 1.87 GW. Indonesia, via the state oil company Pertamina, already has a geothermal capacity of 1.34 GW, which gives them a leading position in that industry. The new plan to invest some $20 billion over 10 years should increase geothermal capacity to about 7 GW which will make Indonesia the second largest geothermal energy producer after US.

ASIA – THE CHALLENGE OF SUPPLY DIVERSIFICATION

- **Asia's Geographical Dependence**

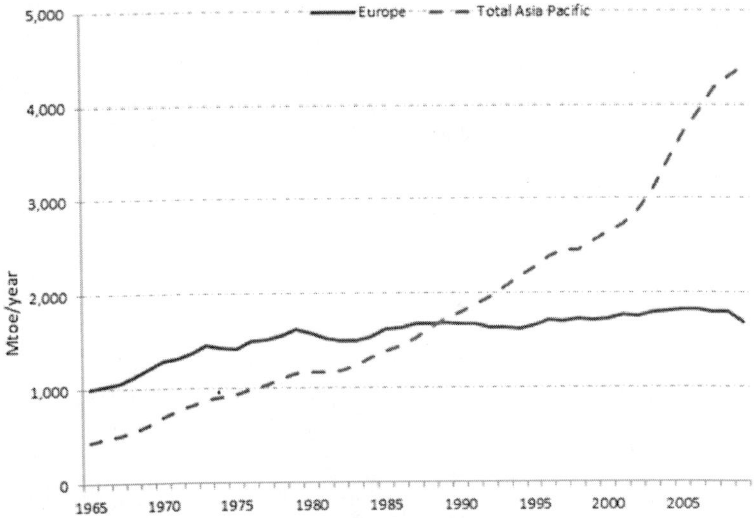

Source: BP Statistical Review of World Energy, June 2016.

Figure 78: Primary Energy Consumption in Asia and in Europe.

The position of the Asia Pacific region is similar to that of Europe in that energy demand in both regions is substantial and their resources are insufficient to meet it. However, there are two major differences which mean that Asia has a higher risk of problems in meeting its requirements. The first is that, while growth in the European Union's energy demand has been moderate since the mid-1970s, with the vast majority of countries having attained a high stage of development and demographic growth being low, Asia, with China and India in the lead, has strong energy consumption growth because of both the demographic and economic growth. The second is that Europe's geographical position gives it the benefit of easy access to a variety of the world's hydrocarbon resources (Gulf of Guinea, Russia, the Middle East via the Suez Canal, etc.), whereas most hydrocarbon supplies for the Asia Pacific region are sourced from the Middle East (Fig. 78).

In overall energy terms, the Asia Pacific's strength is its coal production. China, India, Australia and Indonesia are the world's first, third, fourth

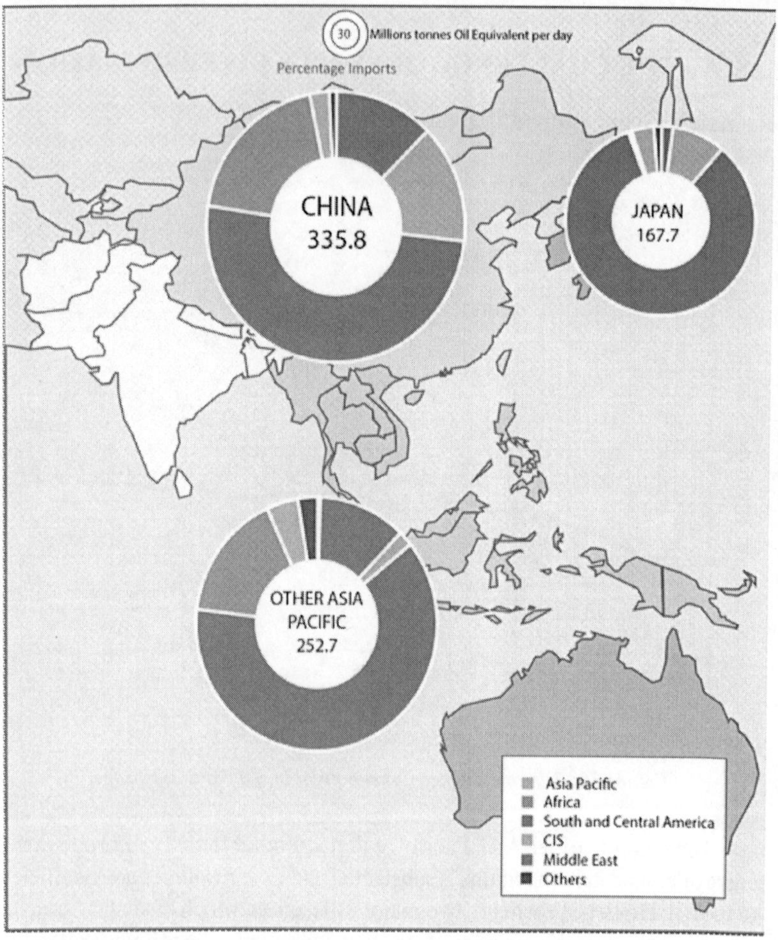

Source: BP Statistical Review, 2016.

Figure 79: Origin of Asian Oil Imports in 2015 (millions of oil equivalent).

and fifth largest producers. So the region's gross imports only represent 3.4 per cent of its demand; for China that figure is five per cent but for Japan it is 99 per cent. However, for hydrocarbons the position is different. The region's gross imports are 58 per cent of its demand, China imports are 30 per cent of total demand for hydrocarbon but for Japan it is 97 per cent. Sixty-six per cent of the region's oil imports come from the Middle East; this proportion is expected to increase with the growth in OPEC's importance of the world's oil supply source (Fig. 79). Qatar and Australia are the biggest natural gas suppliers but Indonesia and Malaysia are also important.

So the Middle East remains Asia's principal hydrocarbon supplier. During the Cold War, the USSR could not finance construction of pipelines to export hydrocarbons to Asia; and the area between the Caspian Sea/West Russia and the Eurasian eastern coast was then, difficult for the development of export facilities (political problems in Central Asia, Sino-Indian tensions, severity of Siberian geographical conditions, etc.). Today, the share of the CIS in the Asia Pacific market is increasing.

West Africa has become an important supplier to China along with the Middle East which is the main supplier for Asian countries, simply because it is the nearest source.

But Asia's dependence on energy and dependence on the Middle East for energy supplies is worrying. There could be increasing competition between different countries for Middle East supplies and for access to new resources. There is the risk of friction developing between them, and such friction exacerbating the conflicts that already exist (China-Japan, China-India, China-Taiwan, North Korea, etc.) (Fig. 80).

- **Asian Supply Security Policies**

  – *China's Policy: Widespread Investment*

China had to diversify both the energies it uses and their supply sources. The government relies on state owned corporations to implement this policy.

Two companies have been created to manage the entire hydrocarbon sector, from exploration to marketing: the China National Petroleum Corporation (CNPC), and the China Petrochemical Corporation (Sinopec). Other companies are the China National Offshore Oil Corporation (CNOOC) specialised in offshore exploration and production; and China National Star Petroleum, created in 1997. Finally, in 1999, CNPC created PetroChina, which was the largest oil company in the world in terms of market capitalisation.

These large companies have to compete on equal terms with the major oil and gas multinationals. So these companies have laid off a considerable number of their staff to become profitable; they have directly invested to acquire hydrocarbon reserves on an international scale. The Chinese government has supported this through the development of bilateral relationships with as many producing countries as possible.

Africa has been one of the regions where this policy has been developed. Over a number of years a series of diplomatic visits have been made by the Chinese at the highest level. These have included an official visit of the Chinese Prime Minister to Nigeria in 1997, a meeting with the government of Chad in 1998, a visit by the Chinese Foreign Minister to Nigeria in 2000, a further

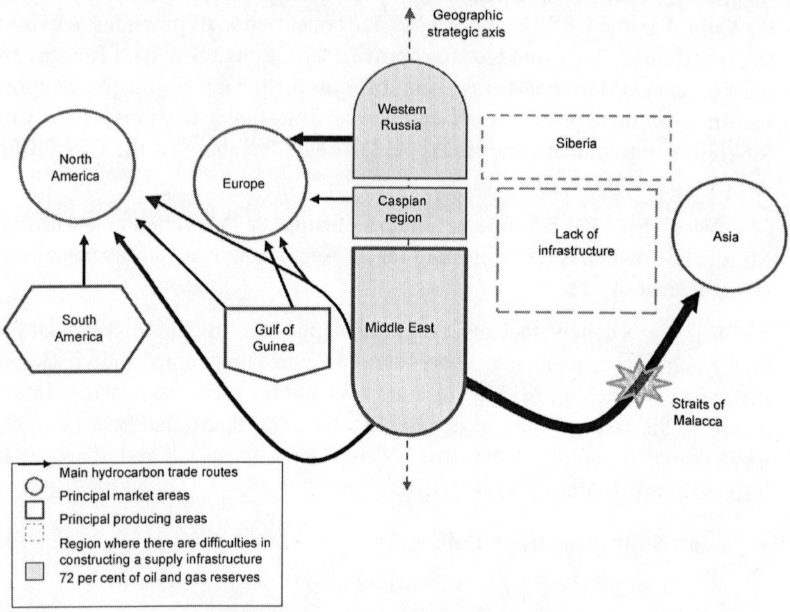

Figure 80: Oil and Gas Export Routes from the Russia/Caspian/Middle East Region.

visit by President Jiang Zemin to Nigeria's capital Abuja in 2002, with a follow-up by his successor, Hu Jintao, (who also went to Egypt, Gabon and Algeria) in 2004. Hu Jintao made another visit to four African countries (plus Saudi Arabia) in 2009, etc. All this diplomatic activity shows how important Africa is in China's strategy for diversifying hydrocarbon supplies. It has resulted in the Chinese state companies directly acquiring exploitation concessions, as they did in Sudan from 1997. In 2013, the trade value between China and SSA (Sub-Saharan Africa) was $170 billion out of which 62 per cent of the Chinese imports from SSA were oil imports. Today, 19 per cent of Chinese oil imports come from Africa.

The Chinese state-owned companies' policy of acquiring exploration-production blocks extends to all corners of the world (Mexico, Venezuela, the Middle East, Canada, Indonesia, Kazakhstan, etc.). They are even interested in buying major foreign companies. However, although China did succeed in buying a Kazakh company in 2005, their attempts to buy the Russian company Yuganskneftegaz and the US company Unocal failed, in the latter case because of the opposition of the US government and the House of Representatives in Washington. China is also trying to develop overland transport routes from neighbouring hydrocarbon producing countries (Russia, Kazakhstan and Turkmenistan). Several pipelines have been constructed (all discussed in Chapter 8 on the Commonwealth of Independent States) to transport oil and gas to China's economic centre on the east coast.

The Chinese government has also established strategic oil reserves as protection against temporary disruptions in supplies. The initial stock building was in 2005 and a three phase expansion was announced in 2007. In a recent move National Energy Administration of China drafted rules to allow private investors to build and operate some strategic petroleum reserves in order to expand the storage capacity rapidly. China stockpiled nearly 190.5 million barrels of oil under the Strategic Petroleum Reserves (SPR) programme which is nearly 30 days net import. The plan is that, by 2020, government controlled reserves together with mandatory commercial reserves will amount to 90 days consumption.

– *Japan: Reduce Oil Dependence*

Japan, which together with South Korea and Taiwan is the most advanced Asian country, is largely dependent on crude oil imports for its energy needs. Eighty-three per cent of these come from the Middle East. The Japanese government is therefore concentrating on reducing oil consumption, and demand has fallen by 40 per cent since its peak of 5.8 million b/d in 1996.

Japan's principal advantage was the capacity of its nuclear power plants, which generated 27 per cent of the country's electricity but the 2011 Fukushima disaster resulted in the shut down and suspension of nearly all the nuclear plants in Japan. The 2002 ten-year energy plan provided for nuclear energy's share of electricity generation to exceed 40 per cent by 2011. For this, ten new reactors had to be built but the situation has changed. In the past, Japan has experienced a number of technical problems in its nuclear plants. In September 1999, an explosion occurred in a uranium processing plant; in 2002, TEPCO (Tokyo Electric Power Company) nuclear reactors had to be closed for monitoring inspections after the discovery that safety reports had been falsified for several years; in August 2004, a pipe exploded in the building housing reactor number 3 of the Mihama power plant; and in July 2007 an earthquake led to the stoppage of an 8.2 GW power plant. Because of all these, and the earthquake of 2011 which led to the major Fukushima nuclear disaster (covered in detail in chapter 2), the Japanese government was faced with protests against the nuclear power industry Today only very few plants have restarted operations and some could start soon.

The move away from nuclear power for Japan has made Japan turn to natural gas, particularly LNG and therefore the natural gas consumption has gone up from 85 Mtoe in 2010 to 102 Mtoe in 2015 and it is expected to increase further as many of the planned combined gas cycled power plants come on stream. The country has no indigenous resources but does have multiple suppliers: Australia, Malaysia and Qatar supply 57 per cent of LNG imports. Russia and Indonesia are also important suppliers. Gas contracts have the advantage of being long-term (20 years), thereby offering some supply security. Like China, Japan is deploying considerable diplomatic effort in support of its needs for gas supplies and is strengthening its bilateral relations with potential suppliers among Middle East countries. The Japanese have even initiated negotiations with Iran and it recently pledged an investment of $10 bn in Iran in the oil and gas industry, which can secure oil and gas deliveries. As a further way of diversifying its geographical and energy supplies, Japan has participated in the development of gas projects on the Russian island of Sakhalin. In Sakhalin 2, Mitsui and Mitsubhisi have interest and Japan imported nearly 10 bcm of LNG from Sakhalin 2 in 2015. They are even considering construction of a 1500 km gas pipeline from Sakhalin to Japan, which would cross the country from north to south (Fig. 81).

THE RISKS FROM INCREASED COMPETITION

The race for energy resources between the countries of the Asia Pacific region has truly begun. There is a proposal for the creation of a regional organisation to handle energy problems and develop a strategic storage policy, but that does not mean that such different countries will really succeed in cooperating on a common energy policy. There is a clear risk that competition between China and India, the two countries with the strongest growth, will be particularly intense. Both countries are developing their infrastructure and encouraging their state-owned companies to invest abroad.

The main countries in the region are attempting to build close relationships with Middle East producing countries. China has done that with Riyadh. Japan has made substantial investments in Iran, seeking to ensure stable supplies of oil and gas over the long term. India is also developing close contacts with Tehran by increasing trade and investments. India recently invested $550 million for the development of the Chabahar port in Iran and there are regular discussions on projects for gas pipelines between the two countries. There is a political obstacle that is difficult to overcome, that is the need to cross Pakistan, but laying the pipeline offshore could obviate this problem.

China's strategic and territorial ambitions make the South China Sea, a vital economic area, one of the main areas of rivalry between the competing

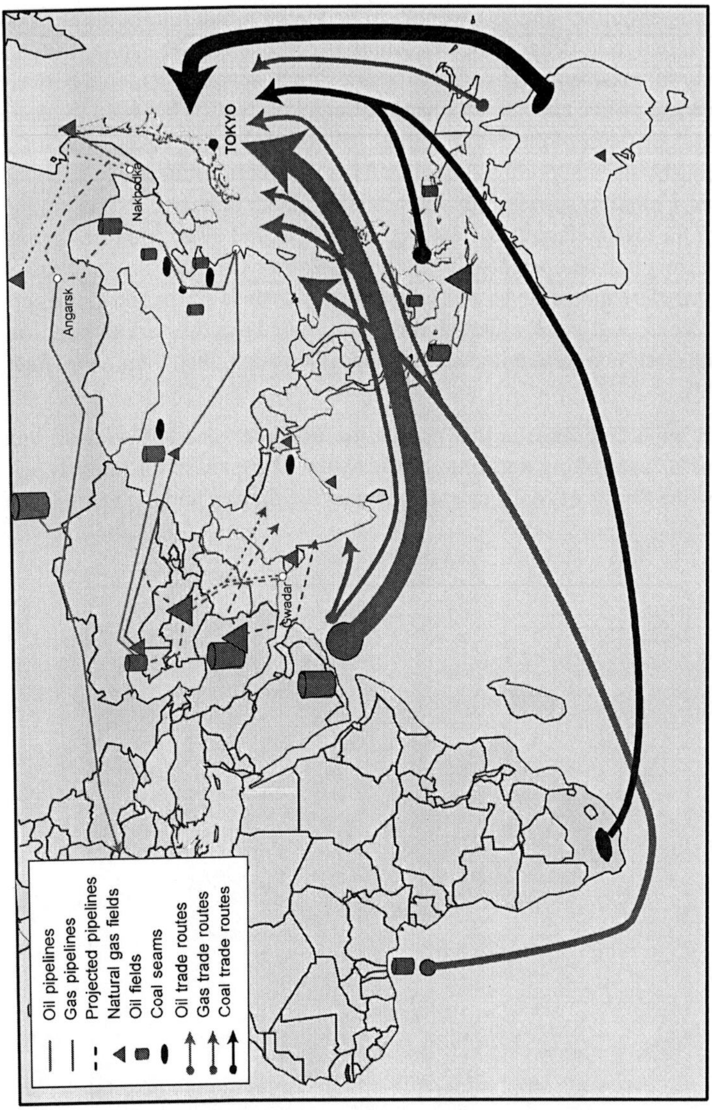

Figure 81: Principal Fossil Fuel Trade Routes and Pipelines for Asian Supplies.

countries. The People's Republic of China claims ownership over several islands and archipelagos which may hold substantial subterranean hydrocarbon resources. They include the Spratly Islands, claimed by six countries (China, Vietnam, Malaysia, Indonesia, the Philippines and Taiwan), the Paracel Islands, whose possession by Beijing is contested by Vietnam, and finally, the Senkaku Islands (Diaoyu in Chinese) which China is contesting with Japan, which is currently in possession. There have already been several incidents between the Japanese police and Chinese demonstrators, as well as between the naval and merchant fleets of the two countries. In 2004, Tokyo provoked great anger in Beijing by starting preliminary oil and gas exploration studies. In nearly all disputes, China has successfully imposed its military presence on one or more parts of the archipelago it is claiming. Of course, the other countries cannot risk entering into an open conflict with the region's strongest military power. China therefore appears to be able to impose its demands and so take possession of the resources at stake, although it has been noted that the various countries of South East Asia have initiated programmes to strengthen their naval fleets (Fig. 82).

An important issue is that possession of these islands would provide a means of controlling maritime traffic. Most of Japanese oil imports pass through the Straits of Malacca and then near the Spratly and Paracel Islands.

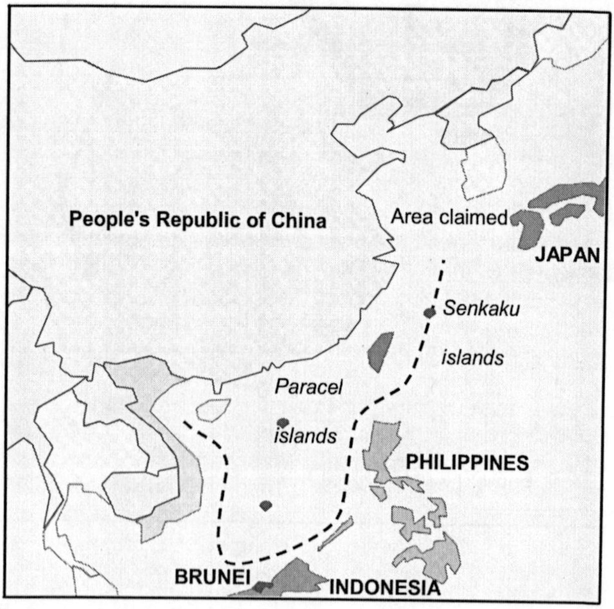

Figure 82: Territorial Claims Made by the People's Republic of China.

So control would enable China to put pressure on its Japanese neighbour and ensure the security of its own supplies by contesting the American military monopoly in the region (see Chapter 4).

In July 2016, an arbitral tribunal of the United Nations Convention on the Law of the Sea ruled against China's maritime claims in Philippines vs. China, although it is not enforceable. China does not acknowledge the tribunal nor abide by its ruling, insisting that any resolution should be through bilateral negotiations with the other claimants.

United States and China are under disagreement over the South China Sea issue and what makes it worse is that the US itself is not a member of the United Nations Convention on the Law of the Sea (UNCLOS).

Regional Tensions and Conflicts: A Destabilising Factor for Energy Policies

- *China – Japan:*

Relations between China and Japan are always very tense when past events are in question. The Chinese want Japan to apologise for the 1937 Nanking massacre, while comments from the Japanese government make the position worse. Then there is the further dispute over ownership of the Senkaku Islands.

- *China – India:*

Since Indian independence, there have been two Sino-Indian wars (1957 and 1962), and the disputes that caused them have still not been completely resolved. China still claims ownership of the territory of Arunachal Pradesh, while India wants to recover its sovereignty over Aksai Chin (Kashmir). But the Sino-Indian wars also led to an alliance between Islamabad and Beijing, with the latter providing the aid Pakistan needed to develop its nuclear arms programme. Nevertheless, more recently, China voted against India for its entry into the NSG (Nuclear Suppliers Group), despite India having the support of US, Russia and majority of the NSG members. Additionally, in 2015, China agreed to invest £35 billion in Pakistan's roads, railways, power and ports over the next 15 years. The China-Pakistan Economic Corridor (CPEC) investment is Pakistan's largest source of foreign direct investment which clearly depicts the policy of China to maintain dominance in the region and to counter India on economic and diplomatic fronts.

• *India – Pakistan:*

The armed Kashmiri conflict focuses all the tensions and resentments that have built up between countries that should be brothers but which have been enemies for over seventy years. Although the "outstretched hand policy" initiated by India and accepted by Pakistan has led to better relations, any significant incident in Kashmir could undo all the gains made. The killing of the militant Burhan Wani in July 2016 by the Indian armed forces led to protests as the militant was labeled "Hero" by some of the local population of Kashmir. Pakistan declared Burhan Wani as "Martyr" and even marked the day of his killing as a black day in Pakistan. In a twist of events, Indian Prime Minister Narendra Modi, during his speech on the Indian Independence day, openly supported the people of Balochistan in their fight against Pakistan for freedom. Through this diplomatic step, India has clearly signaled that it can intervene in Pakistan territory as well, if required. In the middle of all this conflict, it must not be forgotten that both countries possess nuclear weapons.

References

1. *China's Natural Gas: Uncertainty for Markets*, https://www.fas.org/sgp/crs/row/R44483.pdf
2. EIA Forecast.
3. http://www.bloomberg.com/news/articles/2016-07-20/china-official-says-coal-price-shouldn-t-rise-too-fast-too-much
4. http://www.fmprc.gov.cn/mfa_eng/zxxx_662805/t1349239.shtml

Chapter - 11

The Middle East

As typically accepted, the Middle East covers an area stretching from Palestine and Turkey to Iran, and includes the Arabian Peninsula. Strictly speaking it includes the Near East (Syria, Lebanon, Israel, Palestinian Autonomous Territories, and Jordan) as well as Iraq, Iran and the nations of the Arabian Peninsula: Saudi Arabia, Kuwait, Bahrain, Qatar, United Arab Emirates, Oman and Yemen. Turkey has been excluded from this chapter because of its wish to move closer to the European Union and its role as an energy importer. It is therefore included in Chapter 7 on Europe.

With a total population of 218 million, the 14 countries individually vary from several hundred thousand (Bahrain and Qatar) to 77 million (Iran) inhabitants. The region is a mosaic of different nations, ethnic groups and faiths. Its tumultuous history has given rise to a range of conflicting claims by its peoples, victims of a succession of territorial modifications often resulting from the demands of neighbouring states or major Western powers.

It encompasses Iran, the nations of the Fertile Crescent (Iraq, Israel, Jordan, Lebanon and Syria) and the desert nations of the Arabian Peninsula (Saudi Arabia, Bahrain, United Arab Emirates, Kuwait, Oman, Qatar and Yemen).

Its geographical location makes the Middle East the contact region between the Mediterranean world and Asia; it contains the major trade routes that have been travelled since antiquity. The construction of the Suez Canal in 1869 greatly benefited maritime transport between Asia and Europe.

ENERGY CONSUMPTION: "ALL HYDROCARBON"

The size of their oil reserves and, albeit to a smaller extent, gas, makes these hydrocarbons the principal energy source used in the Middle East. To show the comparison, oil accounts for 32 per cent of energy consumption worldwide but nearly 47 per cent in this region. For gas, it is nearly the same in the Middle East. Qatar, for example, has the world's third largest gas reserves and uses natural gas for 80 per cent of its energy requirements (Fig. 83).

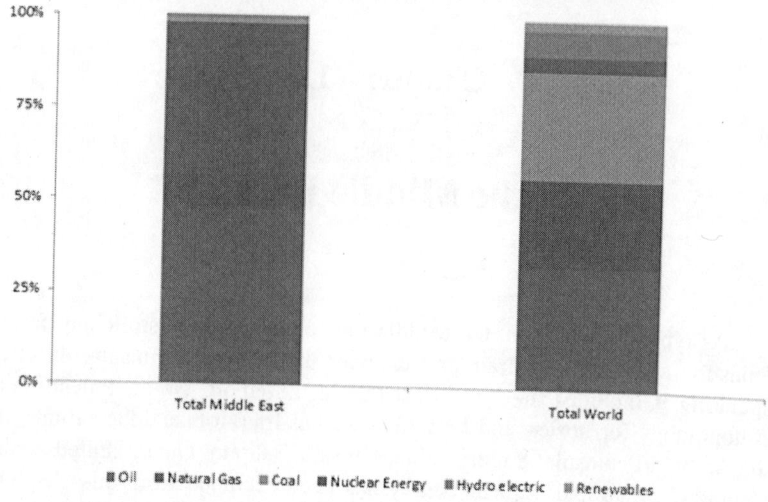

Source: BP Statistical Review, 2016.

Figure 83: Middle East Primary Energy Consumption 2015.

Oil's advantages are both the abundance of its reserves throughout the region and the fact that it is also cheap and easy to produce. The reservoirs are at shallow depths, both on and offshore. Production costs, at only a few dollars per barrel, are the lowest in the world.

People living in the region benefit from the availability of oil products at very low costs, well below world levels, because the governments' policy is to subsidise energy prices. This encourages waste: the ratio in the Middle East between wealth and energy consumption per capita is in fact one of the world's highest (see Section 1, Chapter 2), which shows the inefficient way in which energy is used. Since 2014, the fall in oil prices allows the governments to reduce subsidies and improve the efficiency of energy use.

As another example, electricity consumption in Saudi Arabia has doubled. It has not only resulted in the burning of more natural gas and fuel oil but also it has increased the consumption of crude oil especially during the summer. Crude oil burnt for electricity generation is more than 1 Mb/d at some time. Additionally, the Middle East is the only region where energy intensity has increased over the last 40 years. On the contrary, energy intensity has decreased by 70 per cent in China.

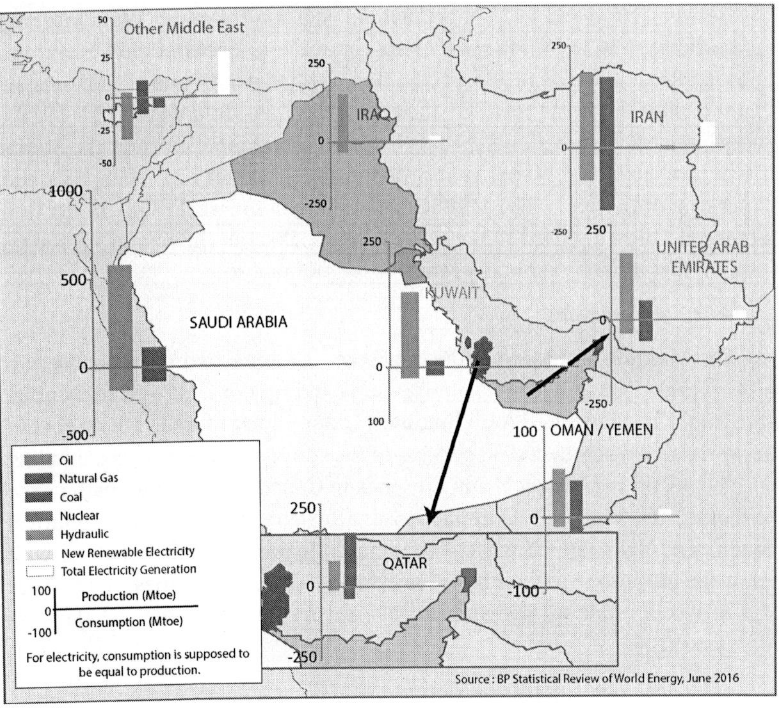

Source: BP Statistical Review, 2016 and doe, eia.

Figure 84: Middle East 2015 Energy Balance.

THE EMERGENCE OF THE MIDDLE EAST OIL GIANTS

- **Historical Summary**

  – *First Discoveries*

The first oil production was in the United States, then in Russia, in Indonesia and in Europe. The first oil discovery in the Middle East was in Iran (then Persia) in 1908. The Anglo-Persian Oil Company was formed to exploit it, the company subsequently became Anglo-Iranian, then BP after the nationalisation of oil in Iran in 1951. Later, in 1927, the Iraq Petroleum Company discovered the Kirkuk field. Then oil exploration started in the Arabian Peninsula in the 1930s.

The first discoveries were made in Bahrain, then in Kuwait (Burgan deposit in 1935) and Saudi Arabia where the initial discoveries were in 1935 and Ghawar (the world's largest conventional oil field) was discovered in 1948. By 1945 geologists were already convinced that the region contained an extraordinary concentration of oil.

Between 1945 and 1975, this potential was confirmed. In 1960, reserves were estimated at 25 billion tons, or six times the reserves of the US and the then USSR combined. In 1975, production reached nearly one billion tons, or 35 per cent of the world total. By the eve of the Iran– Iraq war (1980–1988), a very large fraction of global oil consumption was shipped through the Straits of Hormuz, including 40 per cent of US imports, 85 per cent of Japan's and 60 per cent of Europe's. The Middle East's share of the world's oil production decreased following the 1973 and 1979 oil shocks, but the region's reserves are such that it must eventually return to a dominant role.

– *Huge Reserves*

The Middle East has by far the largest conventional hydrocarbon reserves in the world. The six OPEC countries surrounding the Gulf—Saudi Arabia, Iran, Iraq, Kuwait, United Arab Emirates, Qatar—have close to 50 per cent of the world's oil reserves and 60 per cent of the conventional reserves excluding extra heavy oil in Venezuela and oil sands in Canada. In the aftermath of the oil shocks, non-Middle East production significantly increased for geopolitical reasons and the share of these six countries in world production was well below the proportion of their reserves. Even so, the Gulf supplies some 30 per cent of world crude oil demand and plays a fundamental role in balancing energy needs.

– *Inconsistent Production Levels* – Fig. 85

Production fell significantly because of the decisions by consuming countries to diversify their supply sources that resulted from the 1970s oil shocks. However, the production increased rapidly after 1985 when the oil price fell to a low level after the decision of Saudi Arabia to enforce net back contracts. The oil price fell from $28 to $10 per barrel.

In 2014, after the decrease of the price during summer, Saudi Arabia decided not to reduce its production, but wanted to keep its maket share in order to combat the production of shale oil (Light Tight Oil). Most countries in the Gulf (except Iran due to the sanctions) followed the same strategy and maximised their production resulting in a prolonged period of low oil prices up to 2017 when OPEC decided to limit its production. Price recovered.

– *Massive Exports* – Fig. 86

Over 20 million barrels per day of the region's total oil production of about 30 million, are exported. Saudi Arabia, the world's leading crude oil producer, exports on average 8 million b/d out of the 12 million it produces.

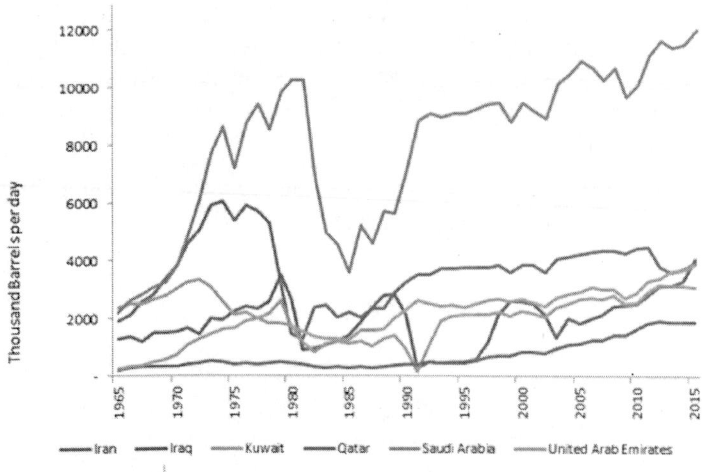

Source: BP Statistical Review, 2016.

Figure 85: Middle East Crude Oil Production.

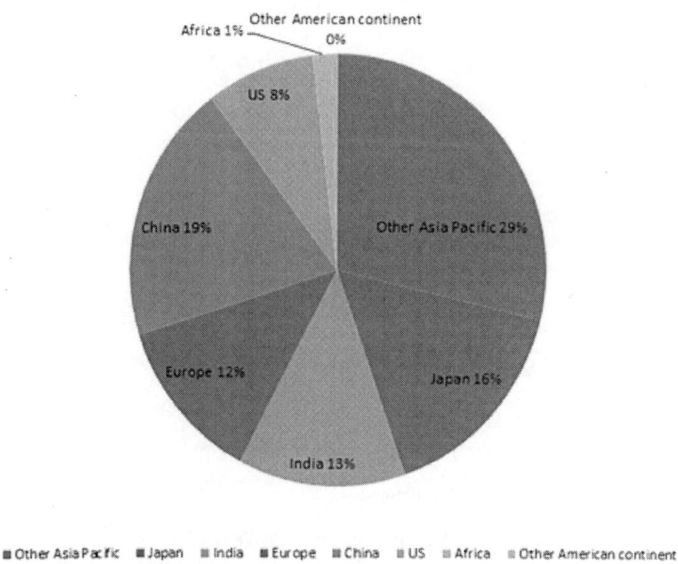

Source: BP Statistical Review, 2016.

Figure 86: Middle East Oil Exports by Destination.

75 per cent of Middle East crude oil exports go to Asia.

About 10 per cent of oil exports of the Middle East are going to the US. In turn, 20 per cent of US oil imports are coming from the Middle East, mainly from Saudi Arabia. Saudi Arabia wants to keep a market share in the US and has a joint venture, mainly with Shell for refining and distribution. Iraq is also a source of oil for the US.

Today the Middle East Covers 74 per cent of Japanese consumption and 30 per cent of China's consumption. (Fig. 86 and 87).

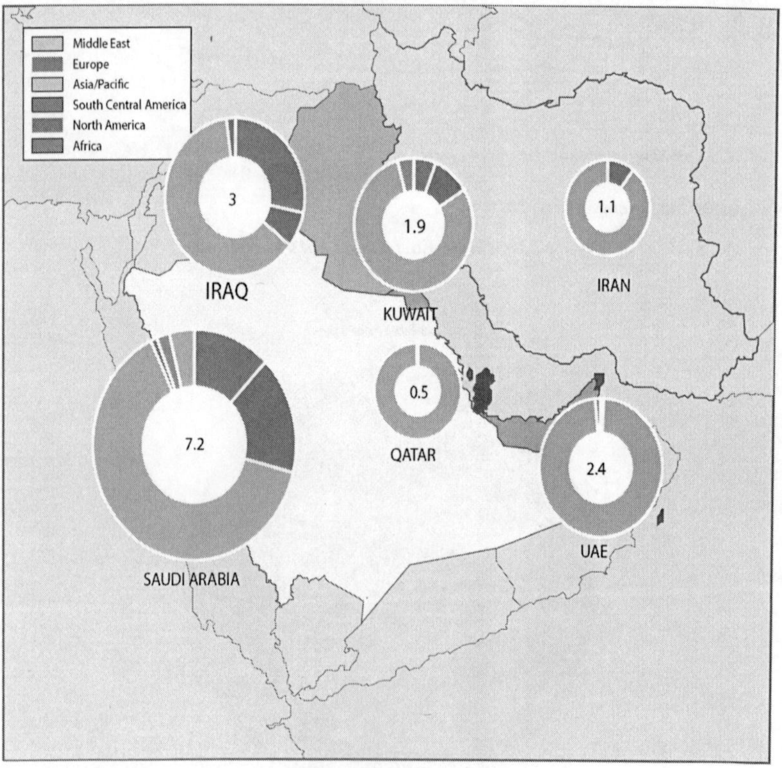

Source: OPEC Annual Statistical Bulletin, 2016.

Figure 87: Middle East 2015 Crude Oil Exports by Destination (millions of barrels per day).

- **Position by Country**

Reserves, Production and Exports of the Main Middle East Producing Countries

2015	*Production (billion barrels)*	*Reserves (million b/d)*	*Exports (million b/d)*
Saudi Arabia	12	266.6	8.2
Iran	3.9	157.8	2.0
Iraq	4.0	143.1	3.2
Kuwait	3	101.5	2.5
UAE	3.9	97.8	3.0
Qatar	1.8	25.7	1.5
Oman	0.9	5.3	0.8
Yemen	0.1	3	0

Source: BP Statistical Review of World Energy, 2016.

– Saudi Arabia

With 15 per cent of the world's reserves and 13 per cent of its production, Saudi Arabia was the largest crude oil producer in the world up to 2013. In 2014 and 2015, US surpassed Saudi Arabia because of the increase in the production of shale oil (Light Tight Oil). In 2016, Saudi Arabia was again the largest oil producer.

Hydrocarbons are by far the country's main resource and most of the budget revenue comes from oil. The revenue is substantial since the total production cost, including depreciation of capital expenditure on both exploration and production, is only a few dollars per barrel because of the size of the oil fields. Most of the income from crude oil sales goes to Saudi Aramco, the state oil company and they in turn pay much of it to the government.

Saudi Arabia is pursuing ambitious development programmes in the fields of infrastructure, education and health, launched in the 1970s when they could be paid for by the increased oil prices. Also, the Kingdom has a rapidly increasing population. Their current revenue needs are therefore substantial.

The fall in oil price since 2014 has substantially reduced the oil revenue which has resulted in a fiscal deficit of $98 billion in 2015. Since Saudi Arabia had a Sovereign Wealth Fund of $758 billion, reduced to less than $600 billion in 2016, the current situation can be sustained for some time but it is quite necessary to diversify the economy. For this, the government intends to sell part of Saudi Aramco to increase the size of the reserve fund to finance the new activities.

– Kuwait and United Arab Emirates

Kuwait and the United Arab Emirates, small countries and neighbours of Saudi Arabia, are important because of the size of their reserves and their production. Kuwait owns one of the world's largest oil fields: Burgan, discovered in 1938, which has been producing for more than 70 years. By 1990 this small country of two million inhabitants, including a large immigrant population, had accumulated very substantial financial reserves from the oil revenue it had invested abroad to enable it to prepare for "after oil". The revenue from these reserves exceeded that from oil sales. But following the invasion by Iraq, the Kuwaiti government's need to finance the military liberation of their territory meant that they had to realise a major portion of these investments. United Arab Emirates is a federation of seven small countries that has been independent since the start of the 1970s. The only significant producer is the Emirate of Abu Dhabi. Dubai's production is declining strongly. Abu Dhabi and, to a lesser extent, Kuwait, own substantial sovereign funds. ADIA (Abu Dhabi Investment Authority) is the largest sovereign fund in the Middle East, it does not disclose its total assets but estimates of them range from $800 to over 875 billion. Clearly the total value of the fund's assets has decreased because of the financial crisis.

– Iran

Oil has been produced in Iran since the very beginning of the twentieth century. A key event in country's oil history was the nationalisation of the industry in 1951. It happened when the Iranian government wanted to subject Anglo-Iranian to the tax regimes applied in other major producing countries, particularly in Venezuela, based on the principle that profits should be shared 50/50.

Anglo-Iranian refused. A conflict started. Nationalisation was envisaged. The Iranian Prime Minister made a broadcast rejecting nationalisation. He was then assassinated. Doctor Mosaddeq, chairman of the committee that had proposed nationalisation, became Prime Minister and that policy was enacted[1]. Either way, a long conflict began. Anglo-Iranian closed its Iranian operations, withdrew its staff and took legal proceedings against buyers of Iranian oil anywhere in the world. Oil production fell from 32 million to one million tpa. Eventually relations deteriorated between the Shah and Mosaddeq and the latter was toppled by a coup organised by Western interests and replaced by a more "moderate" government.

Even then American diplomacy was needed to help end the conflict. Under the settlement agreed, the principle of nationalisation was accepted by the West, NIOC (*National Iranian Oil Company*) became the owner of the oil fields and a consortium was created to operate them. British Petroleum, which Anglo Iranian had become, had its share reduced to a 40 per cent stake and had to accept the entry of American and French companies into the consortium.

Full production was resumed and, by the time of the first oil shock, had reached six million barrels per day, more than that of all other countries in the region except Saudi Arabia. The workers' strikes of 1978 that preceded the Shah's departure in January 1979 and his replacement by Ayatollah Khomeini, sharply reduced production to a very low level. Production fell to nil because of the effects of the Iraq–Iran war; the oil fields were near combat zones and production facilities suffered serious damage. Production never returned to the 1970s levels.

Iran was subject to sanctions from the US for long. Sanctions were taken by the Clinton administration as a response to the Iranian nuclear programme and to the Iranian support for Hezbollah, Hamas, and Palestine Islamic Jihad, which were considered as terrorist organisations by the US. In 1996, the Iran–Libya Sanctions Act was introduced as a new version of the sanctions. In 2006, sanctions on Libya were lifted and ILSA became ISA.

Long discussions took place around the Iranian nuclear proramme between Iran and the 5+1 group (Five permanent members of the Security Council of the United Nations: China, France, Russia, UK, US plus Germany). The fear was that the programme would lead to the development of nuclear weapons.

Eventually an agreement was reached on July 14, 2015 and the sanctions were progressively lifted. Iran expects to increase its oil production to the previous level. One of the difficult point is to set up a new IPC (Iranian Petroleum Contract) attractive enough for the foreign oil companies but acceptable by the parliament (Majis).

The Iran produced 4.6 Mb/d in 2016. The Iranian constitution prohibits foreign companies in principle from equity participation in Iranian oil projects (this is a consequence of the nationalisation of the industry in 1951) and this is why implementing the new IPC is a challenge.

– Iraq

Iraq was founded in 1932 as a kingdom in part of the former Ottoman Empire. It has substantial oil reserves. There has been very considerable damage to its oil production facilities caused by the three wars the country has experienced since the beginning of the 1980s. These were the Iran–Iraq war from 1980–1988; then the first Gulf War in 1991 when, after the invasion of Kuwait by Iraq, a large coalition liberated Kuwait and defeated Iraq; finally, in 2003, the US, again in a coalition with several other countries, once more attacked Iraq on the grounds that it was aiding international terrorism and that it possessed weapons of mass destruction[3]. Production was reduced to very low levels in 1981, 1991 and 2003.

After 2003, the US expected to quickly develop already discovered but not developed fields and increase the production from 3 to 6 Mb/d. However, the situation deteriorated quickly (one of the reason being that the US made a major mistake by firing most of the army when it would have been more adapted to keep the soldiers while reshaping the army). Many army commanders joined what would soon become the Islamic State.

Terrorist attacks against oil facilities reduced for many years the level of production that could be achieved. There were repeated bomb attacks that damaged the pipelines between Kirkuk and Ceyhan (in Turkey) and between Roumaila and Fao which are essential for the exports of Iraqi crude.

The situation has now improved.

At the end of 2009, the very large fields identified but not already in production have been allocated to different oil companies. Their total theoretical potential capacity is huge and could permit Iraq to produce more than 10 million b/d. But is this theoretical potential really possible, especially in the present context? Would it be acceptable to Iran and, more importantly, Saudi Arabia whose production would be close to, or even less than, Iraq's? In 2016, the oil production in Iraq was 4.5 Mb/d.

It is clear that all of the various parties involved, i.e. the US, Europe, the UN, and the different Iraqi factions (the Kurds, the Shiites and the Sunni minority) share a common interest which is that, somehow, the situation should be stabilised. Then the country's oil revenues will be available for the vital needs of funding the country's reconstruction.

– Other Countries

The other Gulf countries (Qatar, Oman and Yemen) are also significant producers. Qatar has substantial natural gas reserves and is the largest LNG exporter in the world. Oman plays an important role amongst non-OPEC countries.

- **Oil Revenue and Wealth**

In 1980 the oil revenues of the six Middle East OPEC Countries amounted to $ 360 million. These revenues decreased after 1986.

Since that date, the financial situation of these countries has obviously improved and the high oil prices of recent years have restored the Gulf producers' financial health. In 2008 OPEC revenues reached $1000 billion, but fell to $ 400 million in 2015.

As an example, Kuwait's revenues were $104 billion in 2014 and $55 billion in 2015, the fall in revenue is mainly due to the drop in oil price. Their public expenditure is about $28 billion, leaving them a surplus even in a low-price environment. The country's financial reserves are estimated at nearly $600 billion. In accordance with the Kuwait's prevailing law, 10 per cent of the annual revenue is paid into the Future Generations Fund, managed by the Kuwait Investment Authority. This applies whether the budget is in surplus or deficit (Fig. 88).

In the past, OPEC countries invested their surpluses in the US banking system. Now, however, contrary to the position during the 1970s oil shocks, a significant portion of these petrodollars is immediately recycled into the world economy. The foreign assets of OPEC producing countries currently amount to more than $1 trillion.

Despite the above, rapid population growth in OPEC countries has meant that their per capita income has fallen, particularly in the Middle East. Those countries are among the last in the world to have maintained very high birth rates. The population of the Gulf countries has quintupled in the last 50 years.

The distribution of the Middle East's oil wealth makes for profound inequalities between the different countries, and in the Arabian Peninsula where average per capita income varies by as much as 1 to 25. For example, it is $94,000 in the Qatar with its population of 2.6 million but only $1500 in Yemen with 28.3 million.

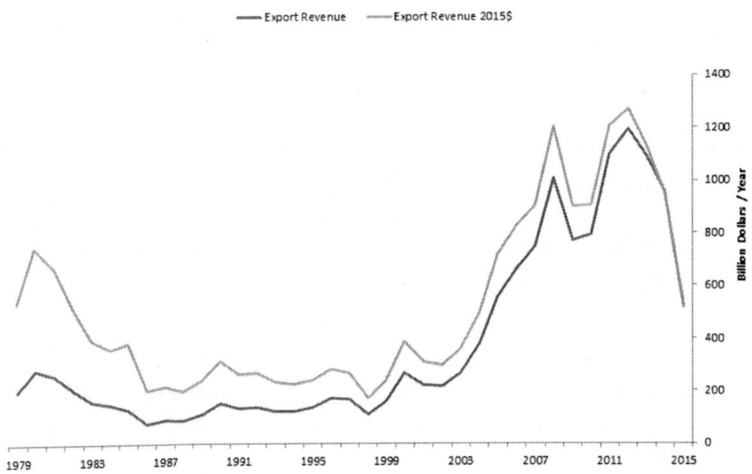

Source: eia/OPEC.

Figure 88: OPEC Countries' Oil Revenues, 1972-2015.

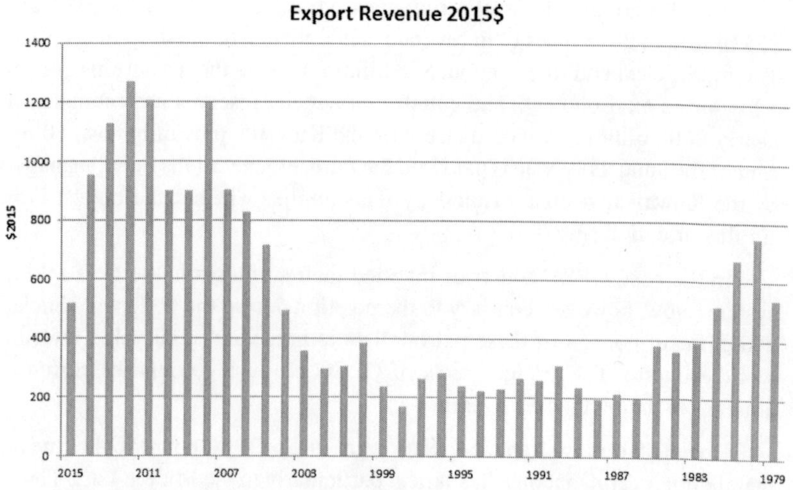

Figure 89: OPEC Oil Export Revenue Per Capita 1971-2015.

NATURAL GAS

As well as its oil reserves, the Middle East has very large natural gas reserves, estimated at 80,000 Gm³ (2,826 Tcf). The region's role in the global gas market is therefore a central one, despite its production being only 17 per cent of the world total.

Iran and Qatar are ranked first and third in the world respectively in terms of reserves, Russia being the second; together accounting for almost 30 per cent of the world total. The principal gas fields are off-shore Qatar, including North Field which, with 12,000 Gm³, is the largest in the world. The major Iranian field is the off-shore South Pars which accounts for 40 per cent of total Iranian reserves and is thought to contain 9,000 Gm³ although the most optimistic estimates put that at 17,000 Gm³ (Fig. 90). It should be noted that North Field and South Pars are the two parts of the same huge gas field which extends from Qatar to Iran.

Because of the regional nature of the natural gas market, the economic potential of these reserves is, at present, not fully exploited. Iranian production is used almost exclusively for domestic consumption, mainly for electricity generation but also for reinjection in mature oil fields to increase production.

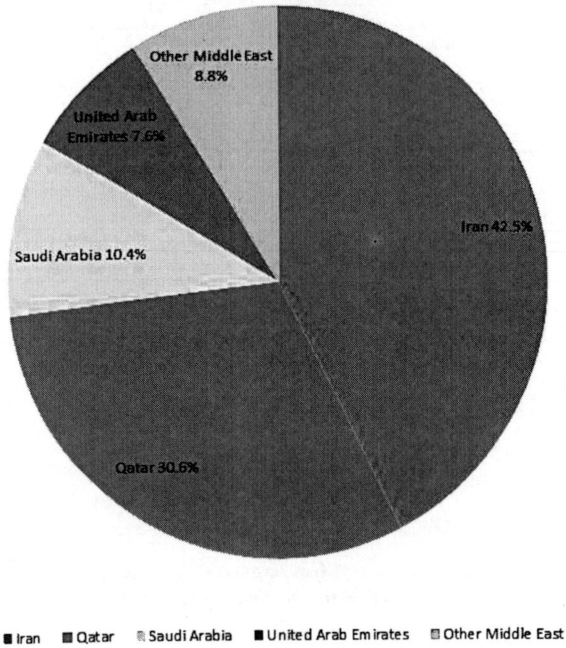

Source: BP Statistical Review, 2016.

Figure 90: Middle East Natural Gas Reserves 2015.

Despite the size of these gas reserves, exports remain limited except in Qatar. Iran and Saudi Arabia consume most of the gas they produce. Iran produced 192 bcm of gas in 2015 which is the highest the country has produced ever mainly because of the new developments in South Pars. South Pars is expected to be fully developed after 2020. At this date, the surplus naural gas production could be exported to neighbouring countries through proposed pipelines Iran–Iraq, Iran–Oman and Iran–Pakistan which are under different phases of development.

Qatar is—and will continue to be by far—the region's largest exporter. In addition to its exports to Asia and Europe, gas is sold to neighbouring countries thanks to the Dolphin gas project pipeline which supplies to United Arab Emirates and Oman (Fig. 91).

Most of the gas produced in Qatar is exported in the form of LNG. A fraction of the gas is transformed into petroleum products (gasoline, diesel etc) in two GTL (Gas to Liquids– conversion of natural gas into liquid fuels) plants which are the ORYX GTL plant commissioned in 2008[4] with Qatar

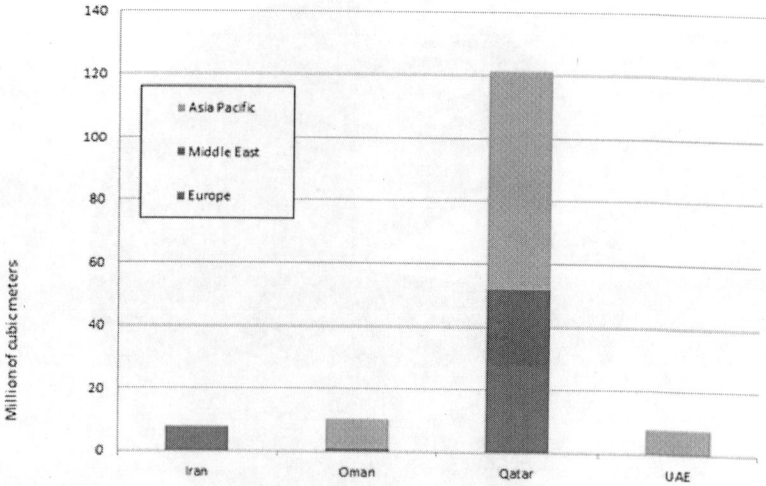

Source: BP Statistical Review, 2016.

Figure 91: Natural Gas Exports (LNG and by Pipeline) and Main Destinations in 2015.

Petroleum and Sasol as shareholders and Pearl GTL, commissioned in 2012 and operated by Shell which produces 120,000 b/d of liquid fuels (gasoline, diesel) and ethane. The combined production capacity of both the plants is 154,000 b/d.

OTHER ENERGY SOURCES

- **Coal**

The Middle East has only 0.1 per cent of worldwide coal reserves, coal is not an important energy there, and in fact there is no real potential for it given the dominance of oil and natural gas. Coal production is insignificant; only Iran and a few small countries use coal industrially, and total regional consumption is only 0.3 per cent of world demand.

- **Electricity**

The combination of rapid demographic growth and subsidised electricity sales prices in some countries have resulted in an average growth rate of nearly six per cent per year for Middle East electricity demand. Electricity generation in the region has increased by a factor of 2.5 over the last 15 years.

Nearly all the Saudi Arabia's generating plants, which supplied 284 TWh in 2015, currently operate on oil and gas but natural gas will be the preferred fuel in future as its use will free more oil for exports. In 2012,

32 per cent of electricity generation was by gas, 35 per cent by crude oil, 20 per cent by diesel and 6 per cent by fuel oil. Saudi Arabia plans to more than double its available generating capacity from 58 gigawatts (GW) to 120 GW through the development of solar and nuclear power generation by 2032. The country is looking for additional reserves of gas. A good example is the Under Wasit Gas Program, an initiative to develop two offshore natural gas fields.

Iran is the region's second-largest electricity producer, generating some 270 TWh in 2015. The country's current capacity is 74 GW, most of which is powered by natural gas, but there is also oil, hydroelectric, wind and nuclear based plants which fulfill the power demand of the country.

Iran is planning a nuclear energy development program; its target is to have 7 GW nuclear capacity by 2020. This programme was a source of major disputes with other countries, particularly with the US, because they believed that Iran also has the objective of developing nuclear weapons. There was considerable tension at the beginning of 2008, with threats to bomb Iranian nuclear facilities being met with Iranian threats to close the Straits of Hormuz. The agreement of July 14, 2015 between Iran and the 5+1 group (China, France, Germany, UK, US, Russia) has reduced the tension.

Two nuclear plants in Abu Dhabi are under construction by Korean companies.

THE ROLE OF MIDDLE EAST OIL PRODUCTION CAPACITY IN WORLDWIDE SUPPLY SECURITY

Following the second oil shock (1980), the oil demand fell because of the high price. This reduced the outlets available for OPEC crude and their production fell from 32 Mb/d in 1979 to 17 Mb/d in 1985. Of course, there was considerable destruction of production capacity in the Iran–Iraq war, but even so very large amount of the capacity remained unused, particularly in the Middle East. This spare capacity was used to replace the oil exported from Iraq and Kuwait when these supplies were stopped in 1990. There was still significant surplus capacity in 2003. In March that year it was clear that the US would intervene in Iraq and that Iraqi exports (more than 2 Mb/d) would be stopped for at least several weeks. At the same time production in Nigeria was badly disrupted by popular revolts and Venezuelan production was still struggling to return to its pre-strike levels. Production of more than five million barrels per day was threatened. Yet the American intervention on March 20 was followed by a fall in prices. The players remained convinced that the market would continue to be well-supplied. In fact, Saudi Arabia and the neighbouring countries were able to compensate for most of the exports that had been lost from Iraq.

The Gulf countries, particularly Saudi Arabia, were virtually the only countries in the world to have the surplus production capacity available that is essential if supply disruptions are to be managed. Everywhere else, the rule was to produce at full capacity.

It should be stressed that this overcapacity had not been brought about deliberately, it was the unintended consequence of the oil shocks. Only Saudi Arabia used its surplus capacity as a market management tool, threatening its OPEC (and non-OPEC) partners to throw open its valves if they did not respect their quotas.

Debate about Reserves: Matt Simmons vs. Aramco

There has been controversy raging on the subject of the size of oil reserves since oil prices started to rise in 1973. As shown in Chapter 2, quoted oil reserves of most Middle East OPEC countries have increased by a factor of two or three because these higher figures result in higher production quotas. The arguments concentrate on the Middle East and Saudi Arabia simply because they contain the largest reserves.

Pessimists, who believe that the estimate of Middle East reserves is considerably exagerated, argue that the estimates were massively increased in the 1980s without any new major discovery to justify. The late Matt Simmons, a US banker, published a book Twilight in the Desert in 2005 questioning Saudi Arabia's claimed proved reserves of 261 billion barrels and stressing the fact that these reserves are concentrated in only a few fields in the northeastern part of the country, and that few new fields seem to have been discovered recently.

In response, Saudi Aramco declares that it is able to produce 15 million barrels per day for 40 years if the market so demands. The Saudi Oil Minister regularly announces that the Kingdom's oil reserves could be revised upward.

THE DOMINANCE OF THE MIDDLE EAST AND WORLD ENERGY SUPPLY SECURITY

- **Geopolitical Consequences of the First Oil Shock**

In 1970, oil from the Middle East was a very important part of western countries' supplies, particularly so for the US and Europe. Coupled with the fact that the transport sector is completely dependent on oil products, the switch from coal to heavy fuel oil made by heavy industry and the electricity generating sector increased the industrialised countries' dependence on this politically sensitive zone. As an example, in 1973, 70 per cent of France's energy requirements were met by oil, mainly supplied from the Middle East. The position was similar for other European countries and for Japan.

Because the first oil shock (1973) occurred at a time when both oil consumption and Middle Eastern production were growing quickly, it caused grave concern, and in some areas even panic, among western countries. Shortly after the start of the Yom Kippur (or Ramadan) War, the fourth war between Israel and the Arab countries, OAPEC[5] (Organisation of Arab Petroleum Exporting Countries) decided to use oil as a weapon. They increased prices and declared a selective embargo against the countries they saw as supporting Israel. Consuming countries realised that supplies of the oil that had become essential for their day to day economic life (and also for undertaking armed conflicts) were in the hands of the few countries that controlled oil production. A further cause for concern was that the programme of oil industry nationalisation, started in a number of countries in the 1960s, was accelerated in the 1970s: Aramco (Arabian American Oil Company), which until 1973 was fully owned by the four major US oil companies[6] and symbolised how Western companies operated concessions, became 100 per cent Saudi-owned Saudi Aramco in 1980.

The reactions of the consuming countries to the embargo was rapid. In 1974, consuming countries created the IEA[7] (International Energy Agency), whose objective was to draw up plans for sharing supplies in case of shortages. Beyond the technical aspect, the message was political. To confront OPEC, consuming countries wanted to show that they constituted a united front. Another reaction was the implementation of energy conservation and diversification policies (e.g. in France, tackling "waste" and accelerating its nuclear programme).

Finally, consuming countries sought to diversify their supplies. Their oil companies developed new fields in the North Sea, Alaska and many other non-OPEC countries. These trends (decreased oil demand and development of non-OPEC production) became significantly stronger as a result of the second oil shock.

- **The Second Oil Shock and the Events of the 1980s**

Only a few years after the Yom Kippur war, the change in the government of Iran[8] led to the second oil shock. 1978 in Iran was marked by strikes that affected the oil sector and led to a near halt in Iranian oil exports. The world's supplies were reduced by six million barrels per day, i.e. 10 per cent. Panic buying drove up the price to over $30/barrel on the "free" markets that were starting to develop[9]. OPEC were happy to accept this, indeed the official Arabian light crude price (Arabian light was then the benchmark crude) rose above $35/bbl in the next few months.

In October 1980, the war between Iraq and Iran initially increased pressure on prices, but from 1981, the market moved into surplus. The fall in demand was accentuated by the second oil shock, and non-OPEC oil production grew rapidly, encouraged by the very high price of crude. These two factors led to a collapse in production in OPEC generally and in the Middle East in particular. In 1985, Middle East production was only 10.6 million barrels per day, or 18 per cent of the worldwide level, whereas it had been twice that, both as a percentage and in absolute terms, in 1979. The worst affected country was Saudi Arabia whose production fell from 10 million barrels per day in 1979 to 3.6 in 1985. The quotas instituted by OPEC in 1982[10] to control production levels and prevent prices collapsing because of excess oil supplies were inadequate to achieve that. OPEC, which had been created to stabilise prices, was no longer able to do so without reducing its production to an intolerable extent. In 1986, Saudi Arabia decided to start a price war to regain market share.

During the 1980s, there was a series of events which contributed to the general level of insecurity and uncertainty regarding supplies.

- The Iranian revolution of 1979 led to the second oil shock and the tripling of the price of oil. It also altered the political balance in the region. The Shah's imperial regime was supported by America, the Islamist regime considered the US to be the Great Satan. In 1981, the aborted attempt to free the hostages from the US Embassy in Iran only made their relations worse.
- The Iraq–Iran war started in October 1980 and lasted eight years. There was considerable damage to oil facilities. This damage had no impact on Middle East oil exports since OPEC's production was falling significantly in any case, so other countries could easily compensate for the production lost by the combatants.
- Tensions had been increased by the USSR's invasion of Afghanistan in 1979. Tsarist Russia, and subsequently the Soviet Union, had long had a policy of attempting to play a controlling role in Iran and the region to its north. The USSR had supported the Shah of Iran's opponents before 1979, and also supported the Ba'athist regimes in Syria and Iraq. For Western powers, the presence of the USSR in Afghanistan constituted a permanent threat to the Gulf region and to their oil supplies. Groups opposing the government of Afghanistan, which was supported by the Russians, were themselves supported by Islamist countries, the most important of which was Saudi Arabia. Finally, when the pro-Soviet regime fell, this led to the establishment of the Taliban government in Kabul. The Taliban had been indirectly supported by the United States since both were hostile to the communist regime. However, the September 11, 2001 attacks in the

US were organised by Osama bin Laden, of Saudi origin but stripped of his citizenship in 1994, who had taken refuge in Afghanistan and was protected by the Taliban. So, the Taliban and America became enemies.

- In 1989, the Russians withdrew from Afghanistan. But just as it seemed that calm in the region might return, Iraq's invasion of Kuwait provoked a major crisis.

Finally, there is the Israeli–Palestinian conflict, which remains an important problem in the region. It is impossible for the Gulf countries to dissociate themselves from the Palestinians. Indeed in 1973, the oil producing Arab nations had used an embargo on oil deliveries to the US as a weapon of in order to put pressure on America who supported and supplied weapons to Israel during the Yom Kippur war.

- **The First Gulf War**

Although Western countries, and particularly the United States, try in every way to reduce their dependence on a zone they see as troubled and insecure, the size of the region's hydrocarbon reserves are such that they can never break their links with it. The First Gulf War was proof of that.

On August 2, 1990, Iraqi forces invaded Kuwait. For several months, oil prices had been low and Saddam Hussein, after his war with Iran, was in desperate need of oil revenue to rebuild a country devastated by a war that had lasted eight years (1980–1988). He accused Kuwait of producing above their quota and therefore of being responsible for the low price of oil. In addition, Iraq had never accepted the "independence of Kuwait", a region or state considered by Bagdad to be part of Iraq.

The United Nations placed an embargo on exports of oil from both Iraq and Kuwait oil immediately following the invasion. Apart from limited quantities of oil exported by Iraq to and via Jordan, exports from both countries ceased. More than three million barrels per day were taken off the world market.

This abrupt reduction in oil supply resulted in a sharp increase in the oil price, by autumn that year it was over $40 per barrel. However, the shortfall could be made up by other producers, particularly by Saudi Arabia which increased its production by nearly two million barrels per day. The United Arab Emirates and Venezuela supplied most of the balance.

The United States formed a coalition and assembled an army of over 600,000 men, including 500,000 US soldiers stationed in Saudi Arabia, to take action under a UN mandate. 60,000 British soldiers, 15,000 French soldiers and troops from several tens of other countries also took part in "Operation Desert Storm". Saddam Hussein's seizure of Kuwait had given him control of over 20 per cent of the world's oil reserves and was a direct threat to Saudi Arabia (25 per cent of reserves) and United Arab Emirates (10 per cent of reserves). This threat was unacceptable.

This intervention may well have been necessary to ensure that international law was respected, but it was more necessary still to ensure western countries' access to oil supplies. On the night of January 17, 1991, the first American bombs fell on Bagdad. Ground operations started at the end of February and Kuwait was liberated very quickly. The war resulted in the death of several tens of thousands of Iraqi soldiers and considerable destruction of oil facilities. Before withdrawing, the Iraqis set fire to more than 700 Kuwaiti oil wells, covering the country with a thick black cloud that changed the weather pattern and lasted for several months. It could have taken several years to put out the fires, in fact, thanks to the efficiency and ingenuity of the service companies that were called in, it was much quicker. Even so, the losses of oil were substantial: some analysts estimate that nearly 10 per cent of Kuwaiti reserves were destroyed or damaged.

The leaders of the coalition, and in particular Presidents Bush[11] (United States) and Mitterrand (France), refused to continue the offensive into Bagdad and halted the troops near the Iraq–Kuwait border. They stated that their objective was not to overthrow Saddam Hussein, but rather to liberate Kuwait. This decision had dramatic consequences for Iraqi movements that had earlier been hostile to Saddam Hussein and that revolted against him when the coalition crushed the Iraqi forces occupying Kuwait. These movements, comprised of Kurds in the north and of Shiites in the south, were violently repressed and thousands of people were massacred by Saddam Hussein's Republican Guard.

After the war, the "Oil for Food" agreement was set up by UN Resolution 986, approved by the Security Council in 1995 and accepted by Iraq in 1996. Its purpose was to ensure the survival of an Iraqi population deprived of necessities but to avoid strengthening Saddam Hussein's power. Under the terms of this agreement, Iraq was permitted to export a given volume of oil every six months so that the country had a constant source of revenue. However, the money was held in a New York escrow account and used, under UN monitoring, to buy food and also spare parts for the maintenance of production facilities in Iraq.

THE MIDDLE EAST AND THE UNITED STATES: THE DETERIORATION OF A VITAL RELATIONSHIP – THE SECOND GULF WAR

The relationship between the United States, consuming 20 per cent of world energy and 22 per cent of world oil demand, and Saudi Arabia, the main exporter with 20 per cent of the world's reserves, remains central to the international energy scene. But the relationship has been significantly changed by the attacks of September 11 and recently by the development of oil shale production in the US.

- **An old and close Partnership**

In 1933, Abdulaziz bin Abdelrahman Al-Saud, who one year earlier had founded the Kingdom that would be named after him, granted the first oil concession to Standard Oil of California (Socal). Numerous discoveries were made, both before and after World War II. Among them was the Ghawar field, discovered in 1948, which is the largest oil field ever found. The quantities of oil that had to be produced and put onto the market, and the capital investment required, were such that Socal formed a partnership, initially with Texaco and subsequently also with Exxon and Mobil, to ensure that the means needed were available to exploit these vast resources. The company formed by this partnership was called Aramco (American Arabian Oil Company); its shareholders were four of the five American majors and so the exploitation of Saudi oil was reserved for American interests.

In 1944, a famous meeting was held onboard the USS Quincy between King Saud and President Roosevelt who was returning from Yalta (and who died several weeks later). This meeting resulted in a new fundamental agreement between the two countries. The United States agreed to ensure the security of Saudi Arabia and the perpetuity of the Saudi regime. In exchange[12], Saudi Arabia would supply oil to the West and would be a loyal ally of the US in their fight against communism. It was under the provisions of this agreement that Saudi Arabia supported Islamist opponents of the Russian backed government in Afghanistan between 1979 and 1988.

The First Gulf War demonstrated the solidity of this agreement: the US intervened to liberate Kuwait, as well as to protect Saudi Arabia. Between the end of that war and the successful invasion of Iraq in 2003, 4,500 American soldiers were stationed on three bases on Saudi soil.

- **Convergence of Interests**

The alliance between the two countries is reinforced by their complementary interests relating to oil. The US remains—despite the development of LTO (Shale oil) production—an oil importer. America will remain, directly or indirectly, dependent on the Middle East. The oil market is a global one and every cargo can, at any time, be diverted to another of the major consuming markets.

- **High Tensions**

But the alliance between Washington and Riyadh is also a cause of considerable discontent. In Arabia, the presence of US troops contravened one of the first fatwas of the Umayyad caliphs: leave the "Land of the Prophet" free from all non-Muslims. This incited anger among some factions in Saudi Arabia; in 1996 an attack against American forces resulted in 19 deaths in Dharan. Other attacks also resulted in a number of deaths.

In the United States, there were increasingly distinct criticism from some elements of US public opinion against the Riyadh regime, and this in turn offends a major segment of the Saudi Arabians. Not only is the Saudi monarchy in the hands of the royal family, it is also an absolute monarchy and virtually theocratic. The royal family has maintained power since the Kingdom was founded in 1932 by prohibiting any political opposition; there are no political parties, no right to vote and no unions.

Only divine law—the Koran and prophetic tradition (Sunna)—may contest the King's power. The King's power is justified by its religious standing based on Sunni tradition and Wahhabism. The King is supported by the Supreme Council of Ulemas, the educated class of the Koranic faith, and compliance with the principles of Sharia, the Muttaween, is enforced by the religious police.

Convergence of Interest between the United States and Saudi Arabia on Prices

Until 2002 there was a consensus between the two countries. The US did not want high oil prices as they would inhibit its economic growth. But too low an oil price would also be disastrous because part of American oil production comprises a multitude of marginal fields (stripper wells, producing no more than 10 b/d) belonging to small owners. The US is the only country where the subsoil mineral rights belong to private individuals. An oil price that is too low, as in 1986, drives thousands of Texan producers into ruin.

Similarly, Saudi Arabia did not want:

– Too high a price, since this leads to the substitution of oil by alternative energy sources, as happened at the beginning of the 1980s (replacement of heavy fuel oil by nuclear energy or coal for electricity generation, or replacement of home heating oil with gas for home heating). A moderate price ensures a large market share for oil.

– A price that is too low, since budget needs are large. Most of the Kingdom's resources come from oil sales.

The increase in the price of a barrel to nearly $150 in July 2008 clearly ran counter to the long-term interests of the Saudi Kingdom. The recent decrease to $40, while sustainable over the short-term because of the Kingdom's financial reserves, is difficult to tolerate over the medium-term. At the end of 2008, King Abdullah declared that the "right price for oil" was $75 per barrel.

As already stated, relations between the two countries deteriorated after September 11, 2001. Fifteen of the twenty terrorists that hijacked the planes and flew them into the World Trade Center towers and the Pentagon carried Saudi identity cards. Osama bin Laden himself is of Saudi origin. This has led to the American press taking a very critical attitude towards the Wahhabite kingdom.

The Middle East remains necessary to the US. Saudi Arabia (and some neighbours) continues to supply oil to the US, and the US has a strong interest in the entire region. That raises the question as to whether the war against Iraq, started on March 20, 2003 by the coalition led by the US and Great Britain, was a war for oil? The answer is probably not, although oil played an important role, as it did during the First Gulf War in 1991. The Americans, as major consumers and importers of oil, cannot but be interested in the leading region for the production and export of black gold.[13]

Europe, economically strong but militarily weak[14], must rely on US power to guarantee the world order, particularly with regard to energy.[15]

CONCLUSION

The prominent role of the Middle East in the oil sector is clear. Rarely has such a small number of countries dominated the production of a natural resource to such an extent. Unless there is a major transformation, the world will depend on the Gulf for many years to meet a large proportion of its energy requirements, particularly for transport fuel.

Increasingly, the Middle East will be "the world's oil—and undoubtedly gas—supply source". The proved reserves of oil there are sufficient to maintain current production rates for 85 years. Outside OPEC, that figure is less than 15 years. All forecasts assume significantly increased production from the Middle East.

There have been times in recent years, for example in 2010, when it has been possible to think that a period of price stability in the oil business might have returned but the fall of oil price in late 2014 has completely changed the scenario. Prices in the short-term and in the long-term are uncertain. But that is typical of the oil industry.

References

1. http://www.forbes.com/sites/drillinginfo/2016/02/29/iran-post-sanctions-oil-gas-opportunities-and-challenges/#3425a99a456a
2. From Our Industry Petroleum, published by BP in 1977.
3. The suspicions turned out to be unfounded. The American objective was to overthrow Saddam Hussein and re-establish democracy. Their hypothesis was that this example would spread to neighbouring countries. This reverse "domino theory" (the domino theory was seen by the US government in 1970 as justifying

the Vietnam War; it held that should one country fall into the hands of a communist regime, the influence of that would make neighbouring countries fall the same way just like a stack of dominos) proved to be no more valid than the first one.

4. This plant also uses the Fischer-Tropsch synthesis employed by Sasol in their plant producing automotive fuels from coal, see Chapter 9.
5. Besides the OPEC Arab member countries (Algeria, Saudi Arabia, United Arab Emirates, Iraq, Kuwait, Libya and Qatar), OAPEC includes Egypt, Syria and Tunisia.
6. Standard Oil of California, Texaco, Exxon and Mobil.
7. France, because of its concern to maintain close relationships with third-world countries, and in the Gaullist tradition, refused to participate. Eventually they joined IEA in 1992.
8. The Shah of Iran left power, driven out by popular discontent. The Iranian monarchy was replaced by a theocracy with Ayatollah Khomeini, who arrived in Tehran on January 30, 1979, becoming Supreme Leader.
9. From 1859 to about 1960, the price of oil was controlled by the majors. Between 1960 and 1973, prices were "negotiated" between the majors and OPEC. From 1974 until the beginning of the 1980s, OPEC set the oil price. Until 1980, most sales were made at fixed process under long-term contracts. The free, or spot price markets that operate today, in which prices are negotiated on an individual basis, developed with the second oil shock.
10. Quotas are production limits allocated by OPEC to each member state. When they were first instituted in 1982, they totalled nearly 20 million barrels per day. They were then regularly decreased in an attempt to avoid the market being flooded; by 1985 the total was only 15 million barrels per day. Nevertheless, as history has shown, these decreases were insufficient.
11. The father of George W. Bush, President from 2001 to 2009.
12. See "Divorce entre Maison Blanche et maison des Saoud" (in French), Alexandre Adler in *Le Monde*, March 2002.
13. Recall once again the Carter Doctrine (President of the United States from 1976 to 1980): the US will do everything possible to ensure that it receives the energy supplies it needs, that oil flows unhindered from Middle Eastern deposits and to American consumers (see Chapter 5).
14. Supply security also relies on markets functioning correctly. It should also be noted that, if the US managed to become totally independent of the Middle East (or simply Saudi Arabia) for their oil supplies, the production that had become available as a result would go to Europe or Asia, who would still, at least in theory, have the same concerns for supply security.
15. Again, it should be noted that the quality of the statistical information published on the production, consumption, and storage of oil and other energy sources is a key factor in the correct functioning of the market. Some erratic price movements are more likely to have been the result of statistical errors than real supply shortages or surpluses.

Index

D

E

W

X

Y

Z